ELFQUEST:
THE **GRAND**
QUEST
VOLUME FIVE

ELFQUEST CREATED BY
**WENDY &
RICHARD PINI**

ELFQUEST:
THE GRAND
QUEST
VOLUME FIVE

WRITTEN BY
WENDY & RICHARD PINI

ART AND LETTERING BY
WENDY PINI

ELFQUEST: THE GRAND QUEST VOLUME FIVE
Published by DC Comics. Cover, timeline, character bios, and compilation copyright © 2004 Warp Graphics. All Rights Reserved.

Originally published in single magazine form in ELFQUEST 15-18. Copyright © 1982-1983 Warp Graphics, Inc. All Rights Reserved. All characters, their distinctive likenesses and related elements featured in this publication are trademarks of Warp Graphics, Inc. The stories, characters and incidents featured in this publication are entirely fictional. DC Comics does not read or accept unsolicited submissions of ideas, stories or artwork.

DC Comics, 1700 Broadway, New York, NY 10019
A Warner Bros. Entertainment Company
Printed in Canada. First Printing.
ISBN: 1-4012-0142-3
Art assists by Jane Fancher and Joe Barruso.

Cover illustration by Wendy Pini
Publication design by John J. Hill

The ElfQuest Saga is an ever-unfolding story spanning countless millennia that follows the adventures of humans, trolls and various elfin tribes. Some of the events that occur prior to the time of this volume are outlined below using the very first published ElfQuest story as a benchmark.

OUR STORY BEGINS HERE...

7 YEARS LATER

Recognition has given Cutter and Leetah twin children, Ember and Suntop, and the two tribes at last live in peace. The arrival of nomadic humans, though, alerts the elves to the continuing threat. Cutter and Skywise, seeking strength in numbers, set out to find other elfin tribes. Their journey leads them through the mysterious Forbidden Grove where they encounter fairylike Petalwing, one of the Preservers.

After a harrowing series of adventures, Cutter and Skywise are reunited with Leetah, the twin cubs and the Wolfriders. Together, they enter the fabled Blue Mountain where they meet the Glider elves – including bizarre, winged Tyldak and the beautiful, enigmatic Winnowill, who shocks everyone when she claims to be a High One.

Though Winnowill tries her best to force the Wolfriders to leave, she cannot stop Cutter and Leetah from awakening a long-forgotten dream in Lord Voll — to find the actual Palace of the High Ones. Voll's own desire is so overwhelming that he kidnaps the Wolfrider chief and his children to force the tribe to follow him to the frozen north.

2,000 - 3000 YEARS BEFORE

Goodtree, eighth chief of the Wolfriders, founds a new Holt deep in the woods and creates the Father Tree where the Wolfriders can all live. Her son, Mantricker, is the first in several generations to have to deal with nomadic humans again.

Mantricker's son, Bearclaw, discovers Greymung's trolls who live in the caverns and tunnels beneath the Holt. Bearclaw becomes the Wolfriders' tenth chief.

In the distant Forbidden Grove near Blue Mountain, Petalwing and the preservers tirelessly protect their mysterious wrapstuff bundles.

Among the Wolfriders, Treestump, Clearbrook, Moonshade, Strongbow, One-Eye, Redlance, Pike, Rainsong and Woodlock are born.

4,000 YEARS BEFORE

Freefoot leads the Wolfriders during a prosperous time. Game is plentiful, and life is easy.

Freefoot's son, Oakroot, subsequently becomes chief and later takes the name Tanner.

9,000 YEARS BEFORE

Wolfrider chief Timmorn feels the conflict between his elf and wolf sides, and leaves the tribe to find his own destiny. Rahnee the She-Wolf takes over as leader, followed by her son Prey-Pacer.

10,000 YEARS BEFORE

Over time, the early High Ones become too many for their faraway planet to support. Timmain's group discovers the World of Two Moons, but as the crystalline ship approaches, the trolls revolt. The High Ones lose control and crash-land far in the new world's past. Ape-like primitive humans greet them with brutality, and the elfin High Ones scatter into the surrounding forest.

In order to survive, Timmain magically takes on a wolf's form and hunts for the other elves. In time, the High Ones adapt, making a spartan life for themselves. Timmorn, first chief of the Wolfriders, is born to Timmain and a true wolf.

0

1,000

2,000

3,000

4,000

5,000

6,000

7,000

8,000

9,000

10,000

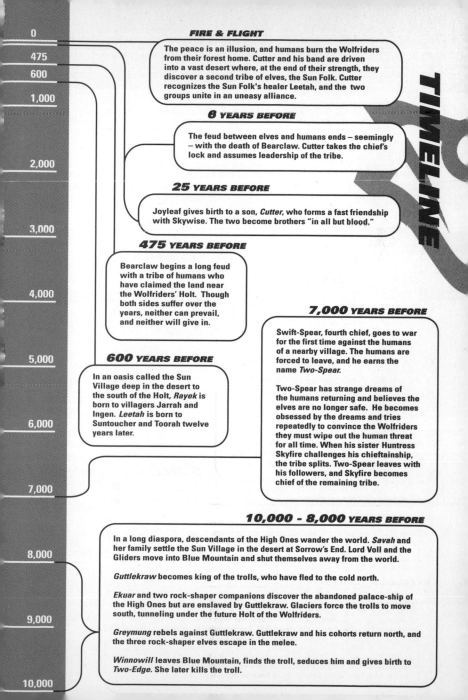

TIMELINE

0

FIRE & FLIGHT

The peace is an illusion, and humans burn the Wolfriders from their forest home. Cutter and his band are driven into a vast desert where, at the end of their strength, they discover a second tribe of elves, the Sun Folk. Cutter recognizes the Sun Folk's healer Leetah, and the two groups unite in an uneasy alliance.

475

600

1,000

8 YEARS BEFORE

The feud between elves and humans ends — seemingly — with the death of Bearclaw. Cutter takes the chief's lock and assumes leadership of the tribe.

2,000

25 YEARS BEFORE

Joyleaf gives birth to a son, *Cutter*, who forms a fast friendship with Skywise. The two become brothers "in all but blood."

3,000

475 YEARS BEFORE

Bearclaw begins a long feud with a tribe of humans who have claimed the land near the Wolfriders' Holt. Though both sides suffer over the years, neither can prevail, and neither will give in.

4,000

7,000 YEARS BEFORE

Swift-Spear, fourth chief, goes to war for the first time against the humans of a nearby village. The humans are forced to leave, and he earns the name *Two-Spear*.

Two-Spear has strange dreams of the humans returning and believes the elves are no longer safe. He becomes obsessed by the dreams and tries repeatedly to convince the Wolfriders they must wipe out the human threat for all time. When his sister Huntress Skyfire challenges his chieftainship, the tribe splits. Two-Spear leaves with his followers, and Skyfire becomes chief of the remaining tribe.

5,000

600 YEARS BEFORE

In an oasis called the Sun Village deep in the desert to the south of the Holt, *Rayek* is born to villagers Jarrah and Ingen. *Leetah* is born to Suntoucher and Toorah twelve years later.

6,000

7,000

10,000 – 8,000 YEARS BEFORE

In a long diaspora, descendants of the High Ones wander the world. *Savah* and her family settle the Sun Village in the desert at Sorrow's End. Lord Voll and the Gliders move into Blue Mountain and shut themselves away from the world.

Guttlekraw becomes king of the trolls, who have fled to the cold north.

Ekuar and two rock-shaper companions discover the abandoned palace-ship of the High Ones but are enslaved by Guttlekraw. Glaciers force the trolls to move south, tunneling under the future Holt of the Wolfriders.

Greymung rebels against Guttlekraw. Guttlekraw and his cohorts return north, and the three rock-shaper elves escape in the melee.

Winnowill leaves Blue Mountain, finds the troll, seduces him and gives birth to *Two-Edge*. She later kills the troll.

8,000

9,000

10,000

The ElfQuest saga spans thousands of years and to date has introduced readers to hundreds of characters. At the time of the stories in this volume, these are the major characters you will meet and get to know.

THE ELVES

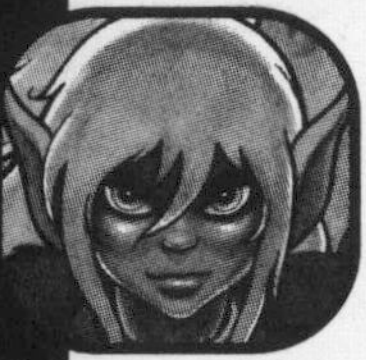

CUTTER

While his name denotes his skill with a sword, Cutter is not a cold and merciless death-dealer. Strong in his beliefs, he will nevertheless bend even the most fundamental of them if the well-being of his tribe is at stake. Skywise believes that what sets Cutter apart from all past Wolfrider chieftains is his imagination and ability to not only accept change, but take advantage of it.

LEETAH

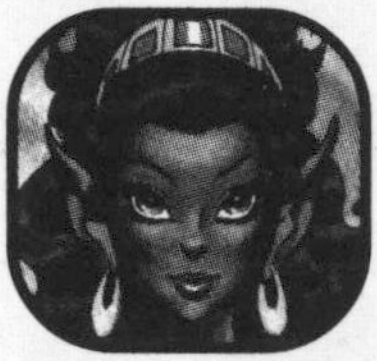

Her name means "healing light" and – as the Sun Folk's healer – she is the village's most precious resource. For over 600 years she has lived a sheltered life, surrounded by love and admiration, knowing little of the world beyond her desert oasis. Though delicate-seeming, beneath her beauty lies a wellspring of strength that has yet to be tested.

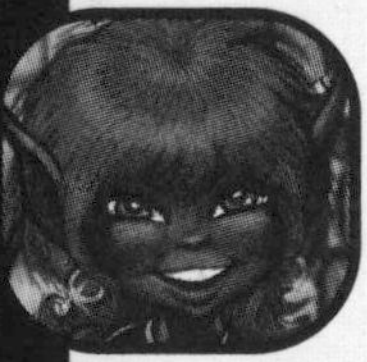

EMBER

Named for her fire-red hair, Ember is destined to be the next chief of the Wolfriders. As such, she constantly watches and learns from her father's actions; she also learns gentler skills from Leetah. As Cutter was a unique blend of his own parents' qualities, so too is Ember. She shares a close bond with her twin brother Suntop, giving her strength.

SUNTOP

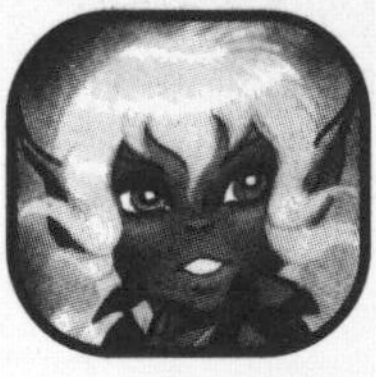

Suntop is the gentle, enigmatic son of Cutter and Leetah. Although a true Wolfrider, Suntop was born in the Sun Village and considers it home. Content that Ember will become chief of the Wolfriders, he says of himself, "I'll be what I'll be." Suntop has powerful mental abilities; his "magic feeling," as he calls it, alerts him when magic is being used by other elves.

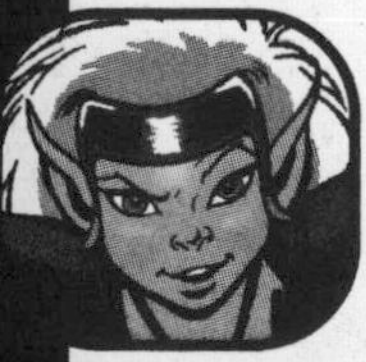

SKYWISE

Orphaned at birth, Skywise is the resident stargazer of the Wolfriders, and only his interest in elf maidens rivals his passion for understanding the mysteries of the universe. Skywise is Cutter's counselor, confidant, and closest friend. While he is capable of deep seriousness, nothing can diminish Skywise's jovial and rakish manner.

TREESTUMP

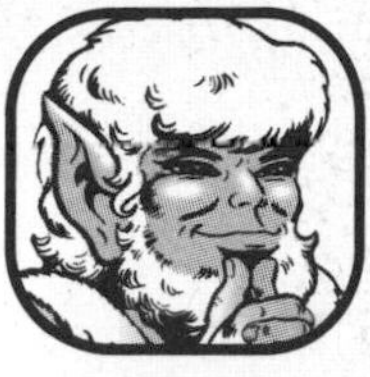

Seemingly gruff and no-nonsense, Treestump also has a vulnerable side, especially when it comes to protecting the well-being of his tribemates. More than a thousand years of living with "the Way" has given Treestump a wellspring of wisdom, allowing him to find calm even in the face of great danger. He is something of a father figure to the entire tribe.

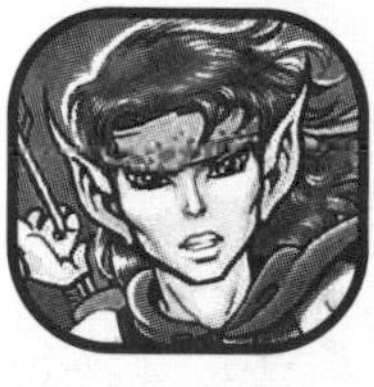

STRONGBOW

Strongbow is the reserved, silent master archer of the Wolfriders. Ever the devil's advocate, he is often proved right but finds no value in saying "I told you so." Strongbow is extremely serious, rarely smiles, and prefers sending to audible speech. He is completely devoted to his lifemate, Moonshade, and intensely proud of their son Dart, who has remained in the Sun Village to train its people in the art of combat.

NIGHTFALL

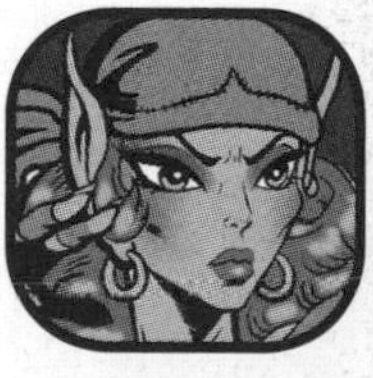

Nightfall is the beautiful counterpoint to her lifemate, Redlance, and one of the most skilled hunters in the tribe. She is cool and calculated, neither vengeful nor violent unless absolutely necessary. The relationship between Nightfall and Redlance is very much one of yin and yang. Nightfall grew up with Cutter and is strongly loyal to the young chief.

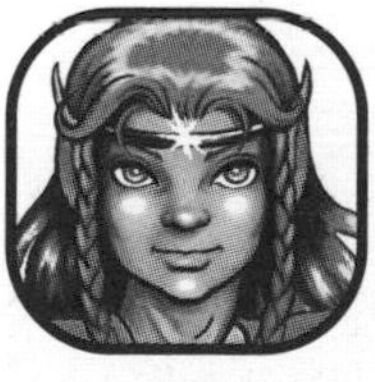

REDLANCE

Redlance is the sweet-natured plantshaper of the Wolfriders. Indeed, he will only use his talents defensively to protect the tribe. Redlance is too much a pacifist at heart to do willful harm, and this gentleness makes him a natural to care for the cubs of the tribe. Redlance is a master of the soft counsel, gently prodding other, more headstrong elves in the right direction.

MOONSHADE

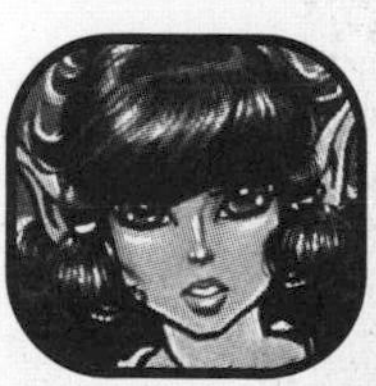

Moonshade is the Wolfriders' tanner. Though the process can be lengthy and tedious, she enjoys the quiet hours spent bringing the beauty out of a supple hide. Moonshade, like her lifemate Strongbow, is very much a traditionalist, strong-minded and with unshakable beliefs. Completely devoted to her mate, Moonshade will defend him even when she knows he's wrong.

SCOUTER

Scouter has the sharpest eyes of all the Wolfriders. He is steadfast, loyal, and often overprotective. He is also extremely intolerant of anyone, tribemates included, whom he perceives as putting his loved ones in jeopardy. Dewshine and Scouter have been lovemates for most of their lives, yet are not Recognized.

ONE-EYE

Woodhue gained his new sobriquet after his right eye was put out by humans. Needless to say, this seeded a lifelong hatred and distrust of the "five-fingers." Although he still considers Cutter a cub, One-Eye never questions Cutter's judgments; Cutter is chief and that is that. One-Eye is fierce in battle, especially when his cub, Scouter, or his lifemate, Clearbrook, is endangered.

PIKE

Pike is the Wolfriders' resident storyteller, taking his name from his preferred weapon. The most ordinary and happy-go-lucky of the Wolfriders, Pike has no grand ideals or desires for quests – he is a follower and rarely questions his chief's orders. Fully immersed in "the now of wolf thought," he clings through thick and thin to his two greatest loves: dreamberries and taking the easy path.

SAVAH

By far the eldest elf known to either the Wolfriders or Sun Folk, Savah – the "Mother of Memory" for the village – is a child of the original High Ones who first came to the World of Two Moons. Infinitely wise and compassionate, she is the keeper of both history and ritual for the desert elves, yet all her years have not dimmed the twinkle of humor in her eyes.

OTHERS

PETALWING

Petalwing is a Preserver – a carefree, fairylike creature that arrived on the World of Two Moons with the original High Ones. Petalwing lives under the grand illusion that "highthings" (elves) cannot live without it, and must be watched over and protected. Petalwing is the closest thing that the Preservers have to a leader. Cutter considers Petalwing to be a major annoyance; the sprite is unperturbed by this.

LORD VOLL

Lord Voll is a firstborn of the High Ones and the leader of the Glider elves who live within Blue Mountain. By the time the Wolfriders arrived, Voll had suffered the effects of centuries of apathy and has an air of melancholy about him. Though he still sees himself as lord, Winnowill effectively ruled in his name.

WINNOWILL

Beautiful, seductive, manipulative, enigmatic, black-hearted... Winnowill is all these, but she was not always thus. Countless centuries of boredom and uselessness have caused her healing powers to fester and turn in on themselves, taking her down into a subtle madness. Her only known child is the half-elf/half-troll Two-Edge, and she is not above lying, abduction, or even murder in order to realize her ends.

TYLDAK

Tyldak is a Glider elf who wished desperately to fly, rather than merely glide or levitate as the rest of his folk do. He begged Winnowill to use her flesh-shaping powers to give him true wings that he might ride on air currents and soar with the birds.

TWO-EDGE

Two-Edge is the half-troll, half-elf son of Winnowill and a troll named Smelt. He is an ingenious mastersmith and inventor. Immortal, he has already lived for many thousands of years. Two-Edge is unique on the World of Two Moons — a half-elf, half-troll hybrid. Emotionally abused as a child by Winnowill, Two-Edge was devastated when she killed his father and ever since has played a bizarre cat-and-mouse mind game with his mother...

KAHVI

Kahvi is the devil-may-care leader of the northern elf tribe called the Go-Backs (so named because they hope someday to "go back" to the Palace of the High Ones). She is a superb fighter, even to the point of recklessness, who believes that life is to be lived to the fullest every day, for one never knows when death is just around the corner.

EKUAR

Ekuar is one of the most ancient elves on the World of Two Moons. He is a rock-shaper, who long ago was abducted by trolls who forced him to use his powers to search for precious metals and gems. To keep him in line, the trolls tortured and maimed the gentle elf, but rather than becoming bitter, Ekuar has turned his misfortune into an outlook that is amazingly life-affirming!

IN THE PREVIOUS VOLUME

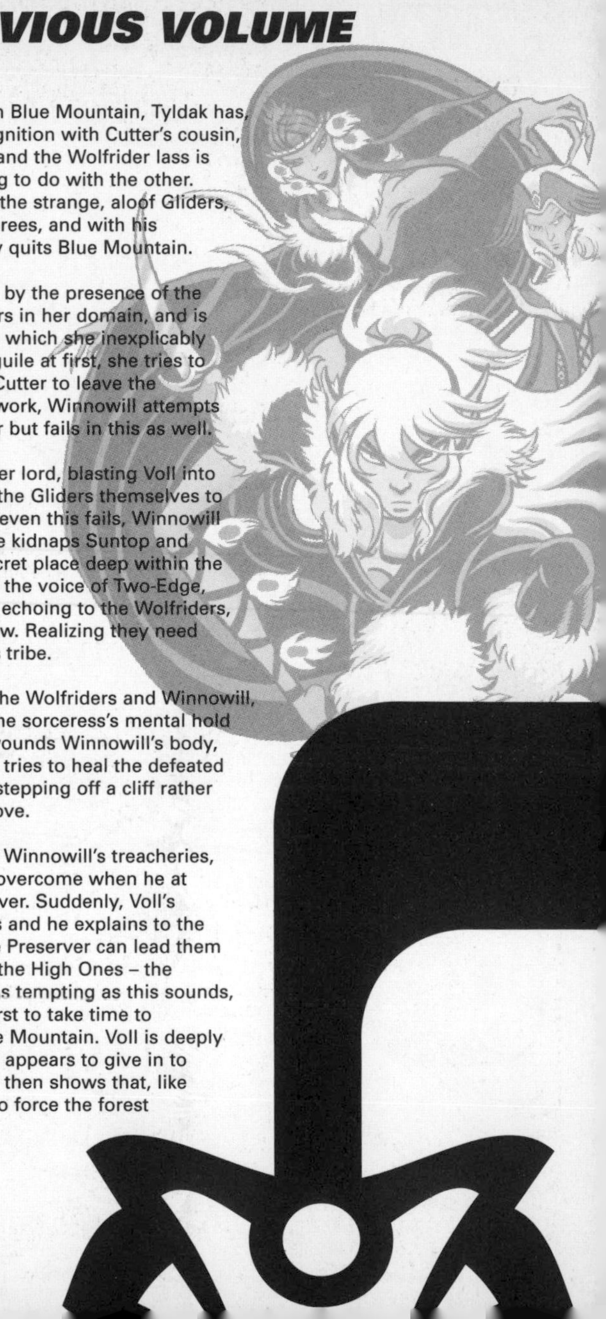

As Winnowill schemes deep in Blue Mountain, Tyldak has, shockingly, experienced Recognition with Cutter's cousin, Dewshine. Tyldak is repulsed and the Wolfrider lass is defiant; neither wants anything to do with the other. Cutter wants to learn more of the strange, aloof Gliders, but Strongbow violently disagrees, and with his lifemate Moonshade forcefully quits Blue Mountain.

Winnowill is greatly disturbed by the presence of the "young and savage" Wolfriders in her domain, and is especially upset by Petalwing, which she inexplicably sees as a great threat. Using guile at first, she tries to enlist Leetah into convincing Cutter to leave the mountain; when that doesn't work, Winnowill attempts threat and force against Cutter but fails in this as well.

Desperate, Winnowill defies her lord, blasting Voll into unconsciousness, and enlists the Gliders themselves to destroy the Wolfriders. When even this fails, Winnowill resorts to the unthinkable: She kidnaps Suntop and flees with Cutter's son to a secret place deep within the mountain. All seems lost until the voice of Two-Edge, ever the game-master, comes echoing to the Wolfriders, telling the elves a way to follow. Realizing they need him, Strongbow returns to his tribe.

In a climactic battle between the Wolfriders and Winnowill, Suntop finds a way to break the sorceress's mental hold on Savah, while Strongbow wounds Winnowill's body, further weakening her. Leetah tries to heal the defeated Glider, but Winnowill resists, stepping off a cliff rather than submit to the power of love.

Awakened, Lord Voll learns of Winnowill's treacheries, but his sadness is more than overcome when he at last sees Petalwing the Preserver. Suddenly, Voll's long-dimmed memory returns and he explains to the astonished Wolfriders that the Preserver can lead them all to the legendary Palace of the High Ones – the fulfillment of Cutter's quest! As tempting as this sounds, Cutter nevertheless decides first to take time to establish a new Holt near Blue Mountain. Voll is deeply disappointed. The Glider lord appears to give in to the Wolfrider chief's wish, but then shows that, like Winnowill, he too has a way to force the forest elves to cooperate...

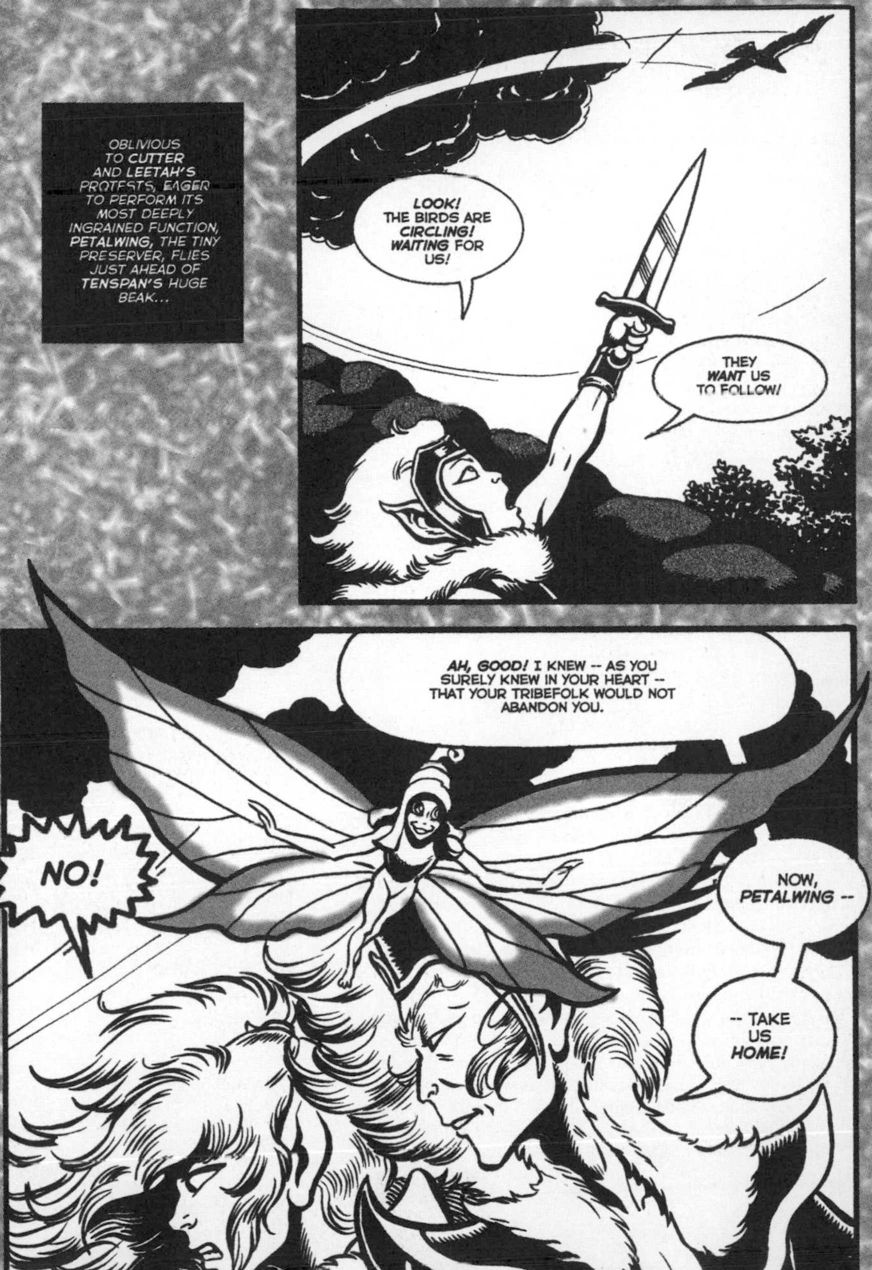
OBLIVIOUS TO CUTTER AND LEETAH'S PROTESTS, EAGER TO PERFORM ITS MOST DEEPLY INGRAINED FUNCTION, PETALWING, THE TINY PRESERVER, FLIES JUST AHEAD OF TENSPAN'S HUGE BEAK...
LOOK! THE BIRDS ARE CIRCLING! WAITING FOR US!
THEY WANT US TO FOLLOW!
AH, GOOD! I KNEW -- AS YOU SURELY KNEW IN YOUR HEART -- THAT YOUR TRIBEFOLK WOULD NOT ABANDON YOU.
NO!
NOW, PETALWING --
-- TAKE US HOME!

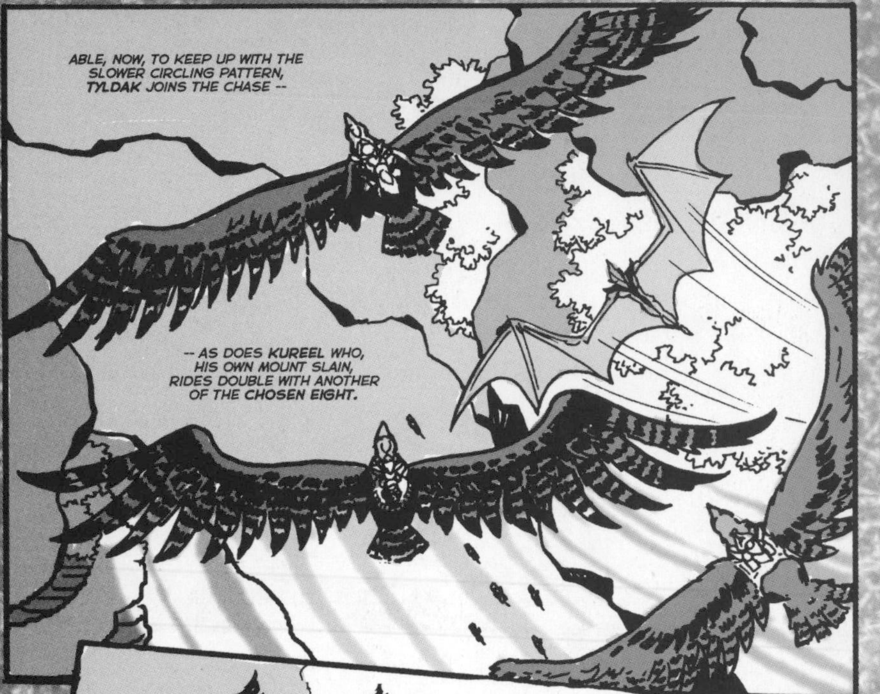
ABLE, NOW, TO KEEP UP WITH THE SLOWER CIRCLING PATTERN, TYLDAK JOINS THE CHASE --
-- AS DOES KUREEL WHO, HIS OWN MOUNT SLAIN, RIDES DOUBLE WITH ANOTHER OF THE CHOSEN EIGHT.

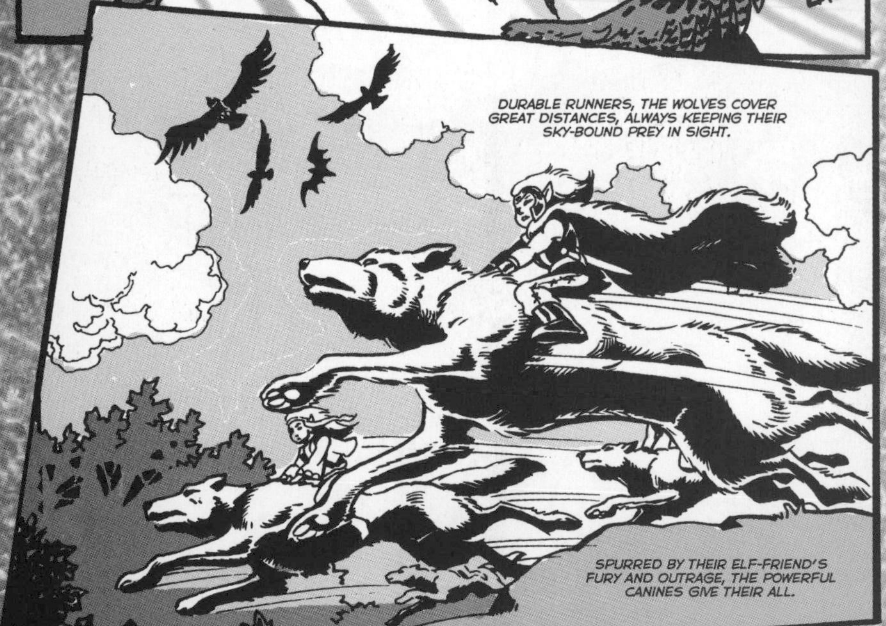
DURABLE RUNNERS, THE WOLVES COVER GREAT DISTANCES, ALWAYS KEEPING THEIR SKY-BOUND PREY IN SIGHT.
SPURRED BY THEIR ELF-FRIEND'S FURY AND OUTRAGE, THE POWERFUL CANINES GIVE THEIR ALL.

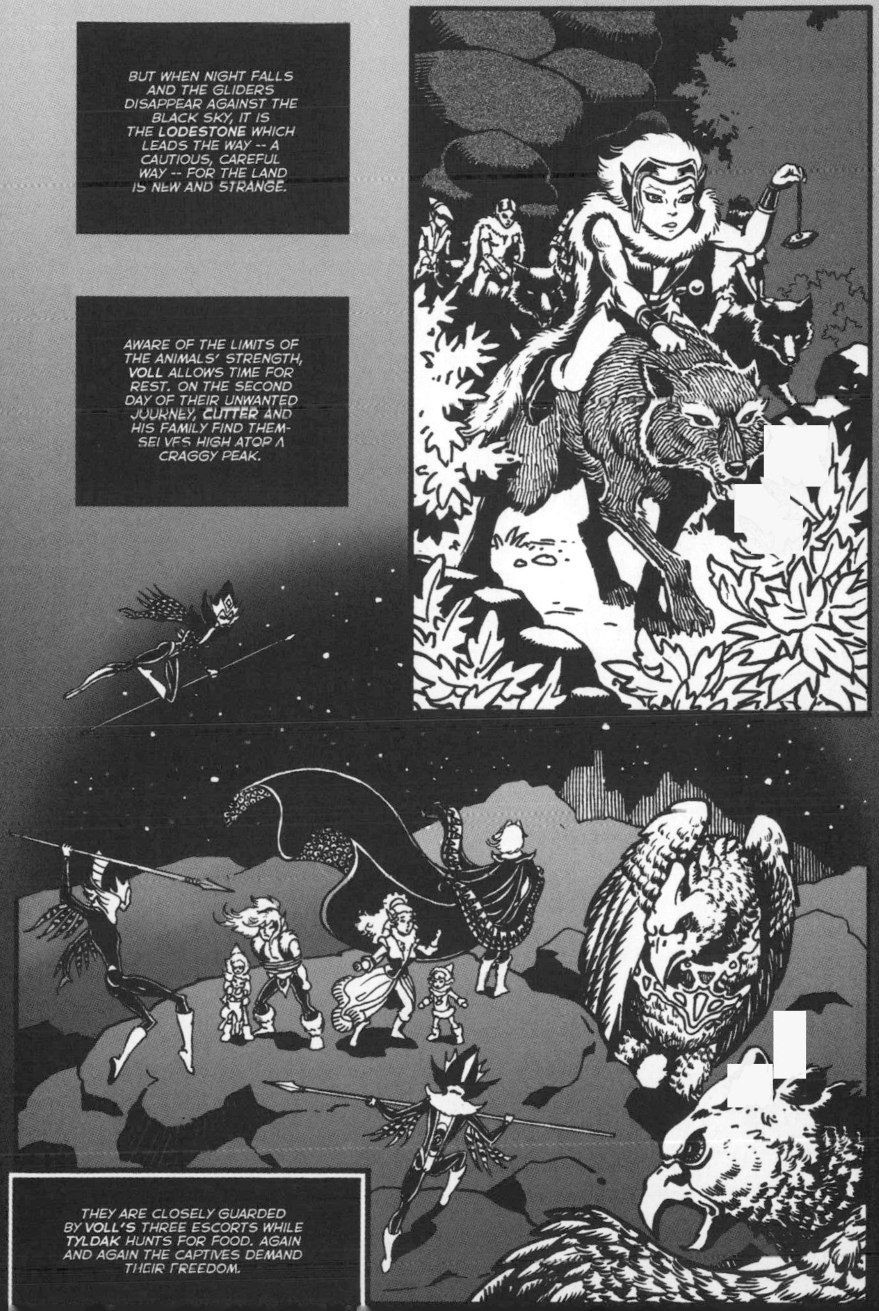
BUT WHEN NIGHT FALLS AND THE GLIDERS DISAPPEAR AGAINST THE BLACK SKY, IT IS THE LODESTONE WHICH LEADS THE WAY -- A CAUTIOUS, CAREFUL WAY -- FOR THE LAND IS NEW AND STRANGE.
AWARE OF THE LIMITS OF THE ANIMALS' STRENGTH, VOLL ALLOWS TIME FOR REST. ON THE SECOND DAY OF THEIR UNWANTED JOURNEY, CUTTER AND HIS FAMILY FIND THEMSELVES HIGH ATOP A CRAGGY PEAK.
THEY ARE CLOSELY GUARDED BY VOLL'S THREE ESCORTS WHILE TYLDAK HUNTS FOR FOOD. AGAIN AND AGAIN THE CAPTIVES DEMAND THEIR FREEDOM.

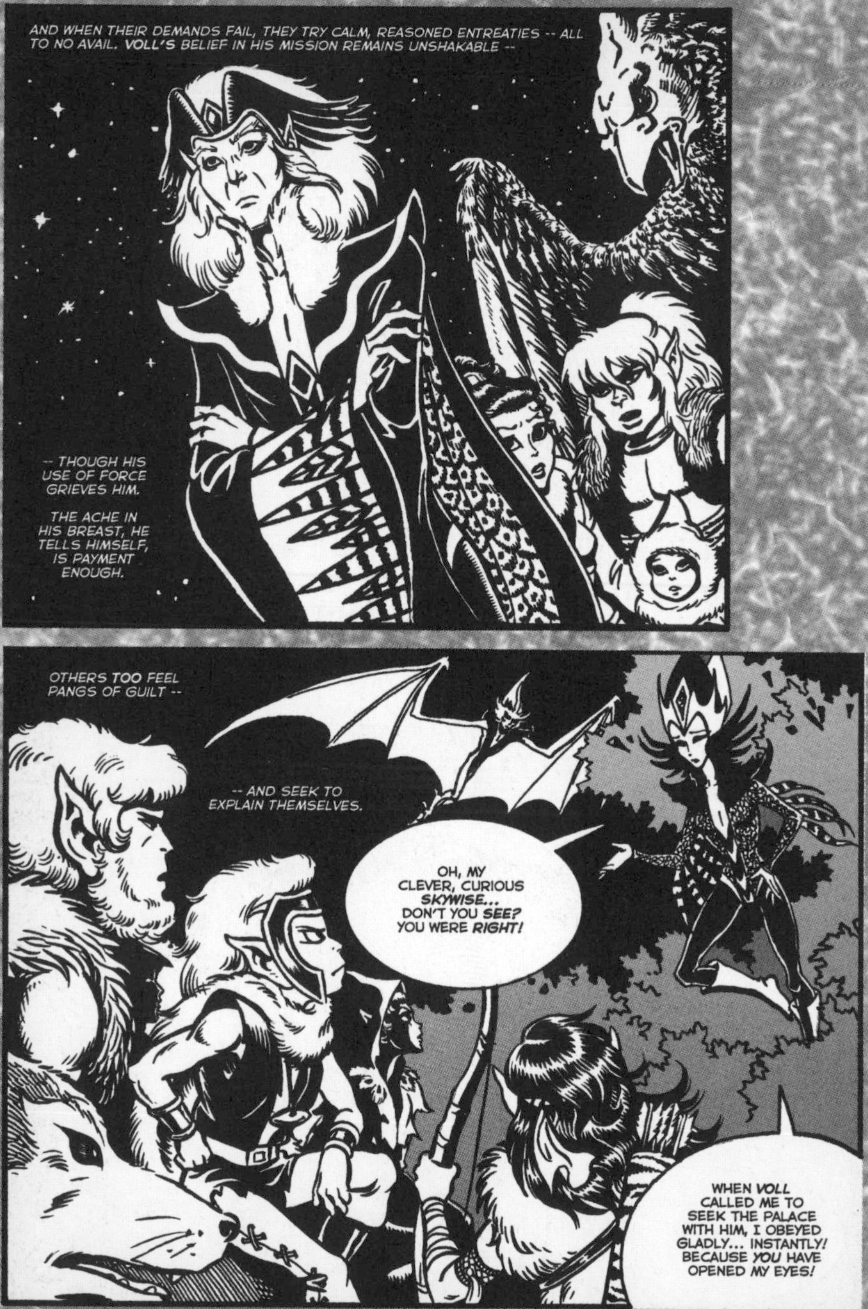

AND WHEN THEIR DEMANDS FAIL, THEY TRY CALM, REASONED ENTREATIES -- ALL TO NO AVAIL. VOLL'S BELIEF IN HIS MISSION REMAINS UNSHAKABLE --
-- THOUGH HIS USE OF FORCE GRIEVES HIM.
THE ACHE IN HIS BREAST, HE TELLS HIMSELF, IS PAYMENT ENOUGH.
OTHERS TOO FEEL PANGS OF GUILT --
-- AND SEEK TO EXPLAIN THEMSELVES.
OH, MY CLEVER, CURIOUS SKYWISE... DON'T YOU SEE? YOU WERE RIGHT!
WHEN VOLL CALLED ME TO SEEK THE PALACE WITH HIM, I OBEYED GLADLY... INSTANTLY! BECAUSE YOU HAVE OPENED MY EYES!

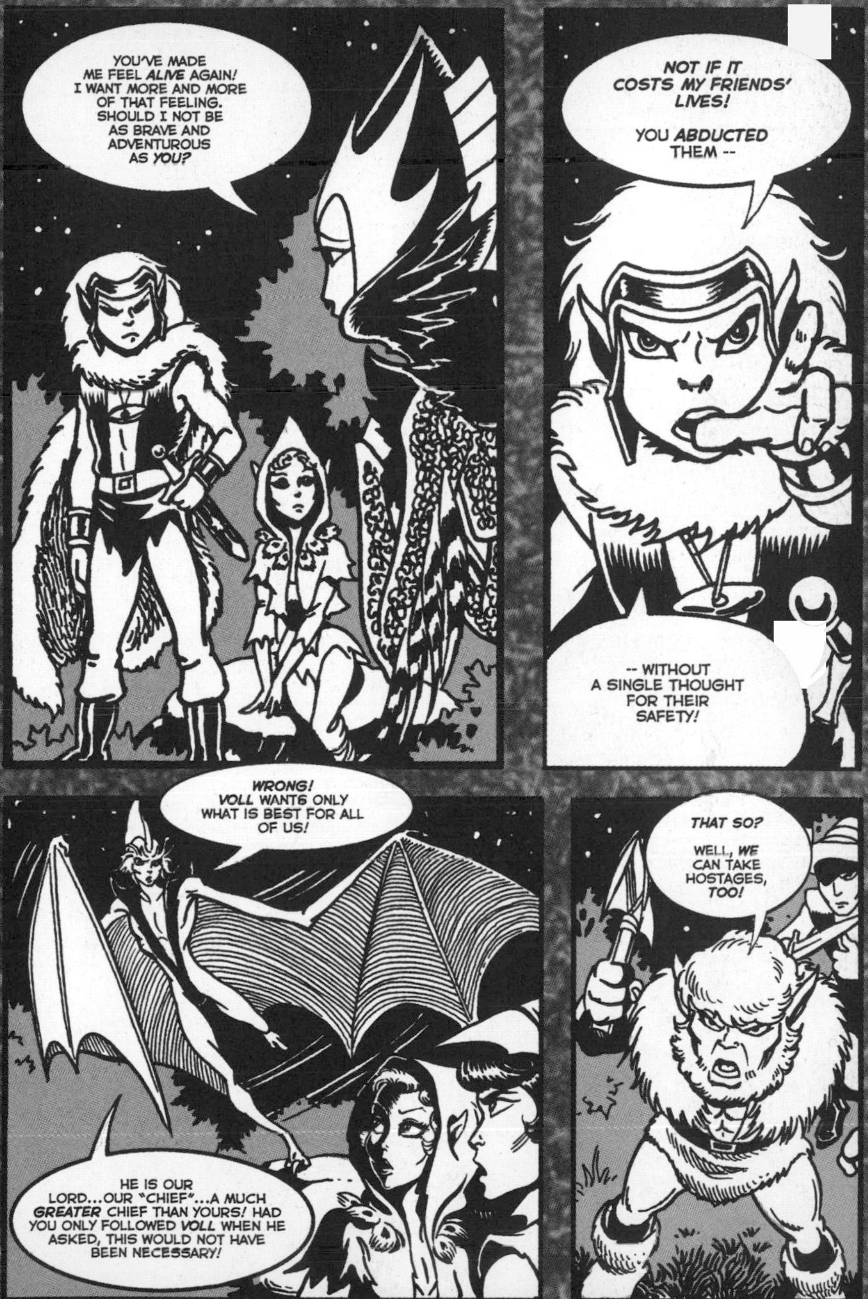
YOU'VE MADE ME FEEL ALIVE AGAIN! I WANT MORE AND MORE OF THAT FEELING. SHOULD I NOT BE AS BRAVE AND ADVENTUROUS AS YOU?
NOT IF IT COSTS MY FRIENDS' LIVES!
YOU ABDUCTED THEM --
-- WITHOUT A SINGLE THOUGHT FOR THEIR SAFETY!
WRONG! VOLL WANTS ONLY WHAT IS BEST FOR ALL OF US!
HE IS OUR LORD...OUR "CHIEF"...A MUCH GREATER CHIEF THAN YOURS! HAD YOU ONLY FOLLOWED VOLL WHEN HE ASKED, THIS WOULD NOT HAVE BEEN NECESSARY!
THAT SO?
WELL, WE CAN TAKE HOSTAGES, TOO!

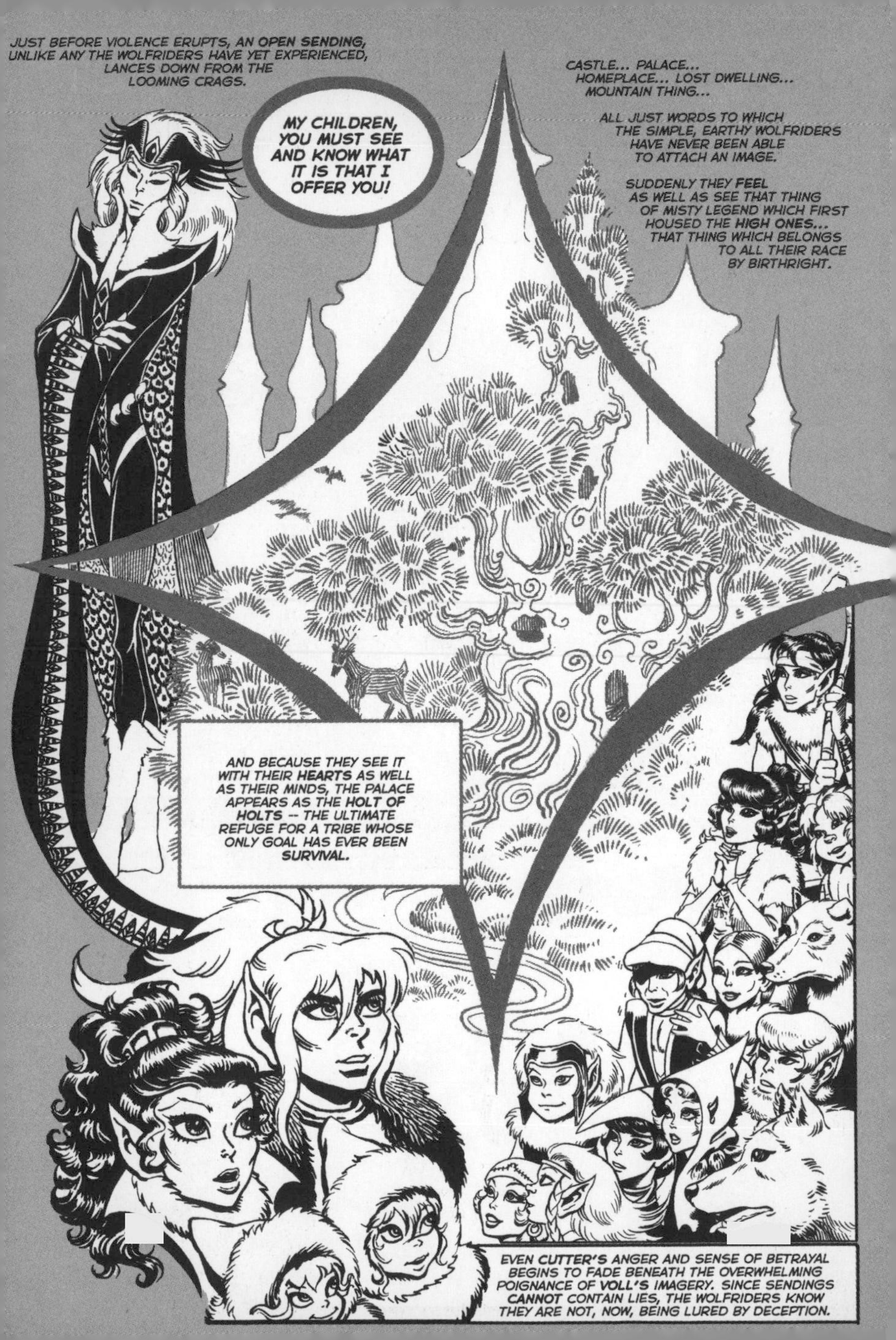

JUST BEFORE VIOLENCE ERUPTS, AN OPEN SENDING, UNLIKE ANY THE WOLFRIDERS HAVE YET EXPERIENCED, LANCES DOWN FROM THE LOOMING CRAGS.
MY CHILDREN, YOU MUST SEE AND KNOW WHAT IT IS THAT I OFFER YOU!
CASTLE... PALACE... HOMEPLACE... LOST DWELLING... MOUNTAIN THING...
ALL JUST WORDS TO WHICH THE SIMPLE, EARTHY WOLFRIDERS HAVE NEVER BEEN ABLE TO ATTACH AN IMAGE.
SUDDENLY THEY FEEL AS WELL AS SEE THAT THING OF MISTY LEGEND WHICH FIRST HOUSED THE HIGH ONES... THAT THING WHICH BELONGS TO ALL THEIR RACE BY BIRTHRIGHT.
AND BECAUSE THEY SEE IT WITH THEIR HEARTS AS WELL AS THEIR MINDS, THE PALACE APPEARS AS THE HOLT OF HOLTS -- THE ULTIMATE REFUGE FOR A TRIBE WHOSE ONLY GOAL HAS EVER BEEN SURVIVAL.
EVEN CUTTER'S ANGER AND SENSE OF BETRAYAL BEGINS TO FADE BENEATH THE OVERWHELMING POIGNANCE OF VOLL'S IMAGERY. SINCE SENDINGS CANNOT CONTAIN LIES, THE WOLFRIDERS KNOW THEY ARE NOT, NOW, BEING LURED BY DECEPTION.

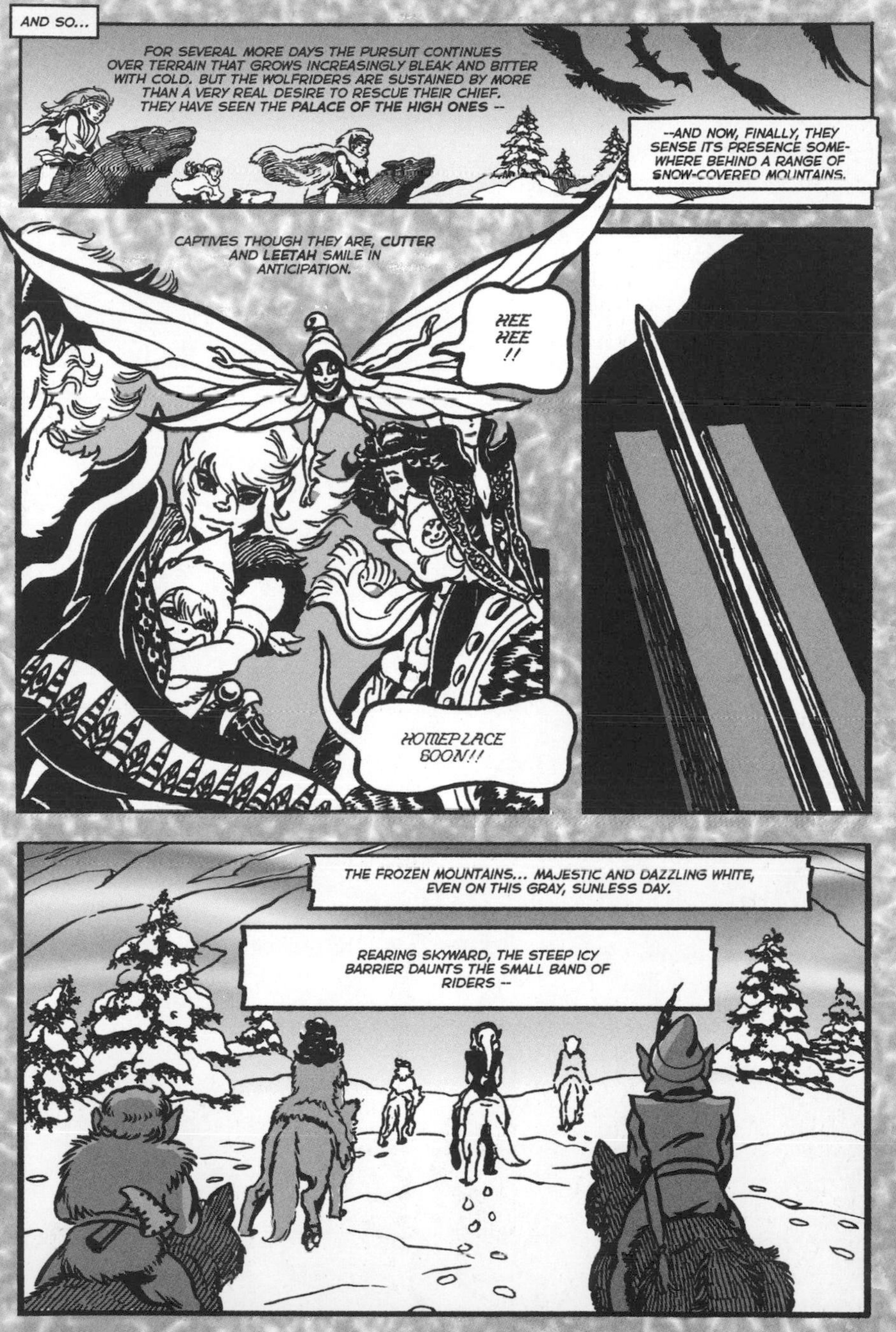
AND SO...
FOR SEVERAL MORE DAYS THE PURSUIT CONTINUES OVER TERRAIN THAT GROWS INCREASINGLY BLEAK AND BITTER WITH COLD. BUT THE WOLFRIDERS ARE SUSTAINED BY MORE THAN A VERY REAL DESIRE TO RESCUE THEIR CHIEF. THEY HAVE SEEN THE PALACE OF THE HIGH ONES --
--AND NOW, FINALLY, THEY SENSE ITS PRESENCE SOMEWHERE BEHIND A RANGE OF SNOW-COVERED MOUNTAINS.
CAPTIVES THOUGH THEY ARE, CUTTER AND LEETAH SMILE IN ANTICIPATION.
HEE HEE !!
HOMEPLACE SOON!!
THE FROZEN MOUNTAINS... MAJESTIC AND DAZZLING WHITE, EVEN ON THIS GRAY, SUNLESS DAY.
REARING SKYWARD, THE STEEP ICY BARRIER DAUNTS THE SMALL BAND OF RIDERS --

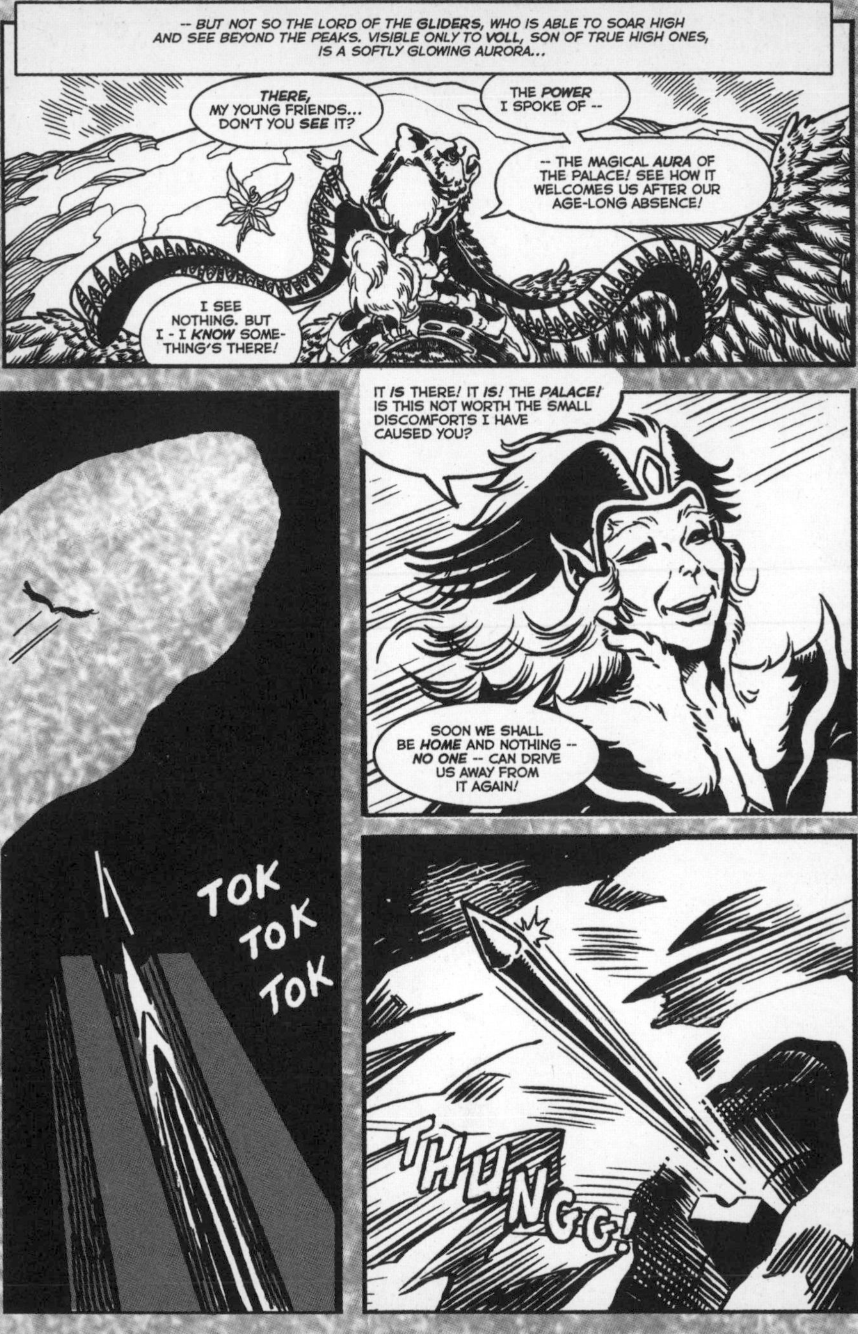
-- BUT NOT SO THE LORD OF THE GLIDERS, WHO IS ABLE TO SOAR HIGH AND SEE BEYOND THE PEAKS. VISIBLE ONLY TO VOLL, SON OF TRUE HIGH ONES, IS A SOFTLY GLOWING AURORA...
THERE, MY YOUNG FRIENDS... DON'T YOU SEE IT?
THE POWER I SPOKE OF --
-- THE MAGICAL AURA OF THE PALACE! SEE HOW IT WELCOMES US AFTER OUR AGE-LONG ABSENCE!
I SEE NOTHING. BUT I - I KNOW SOMETHING'S THERE!
IT IS THERE! IT IS! THE PALACE! IS THIS NOT WORTH THE SMALL DISCOMFORTS I HAVE CAUSED YOU?
SOON WE SHALL BE HOME AND NOTHING -- NO ONE -- CAN DRIVE US AWAY FROM IT AGAIN!
TOK TOK TOK
THUNGG!

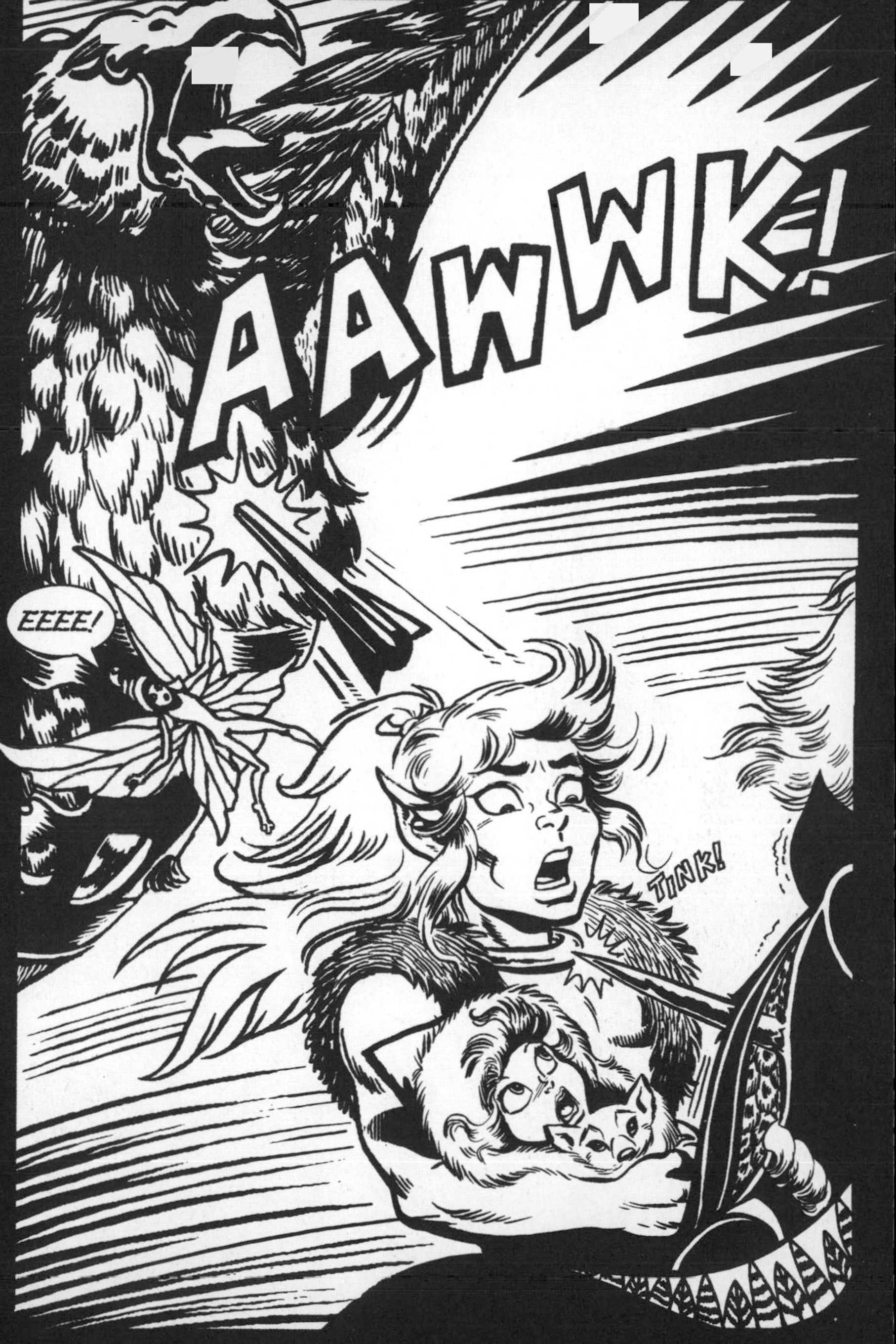
AAWWK!
EEEE!
TINK!

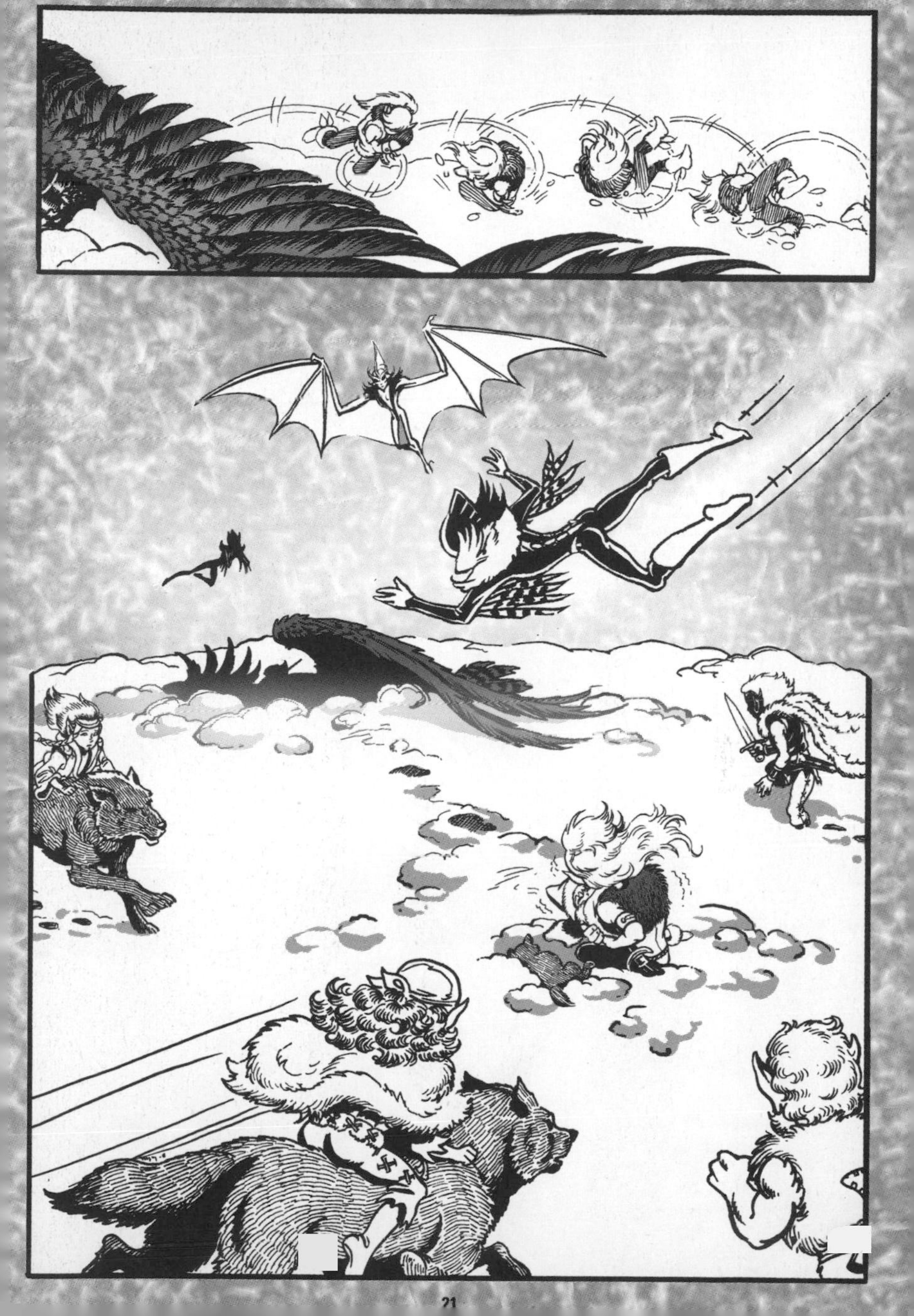

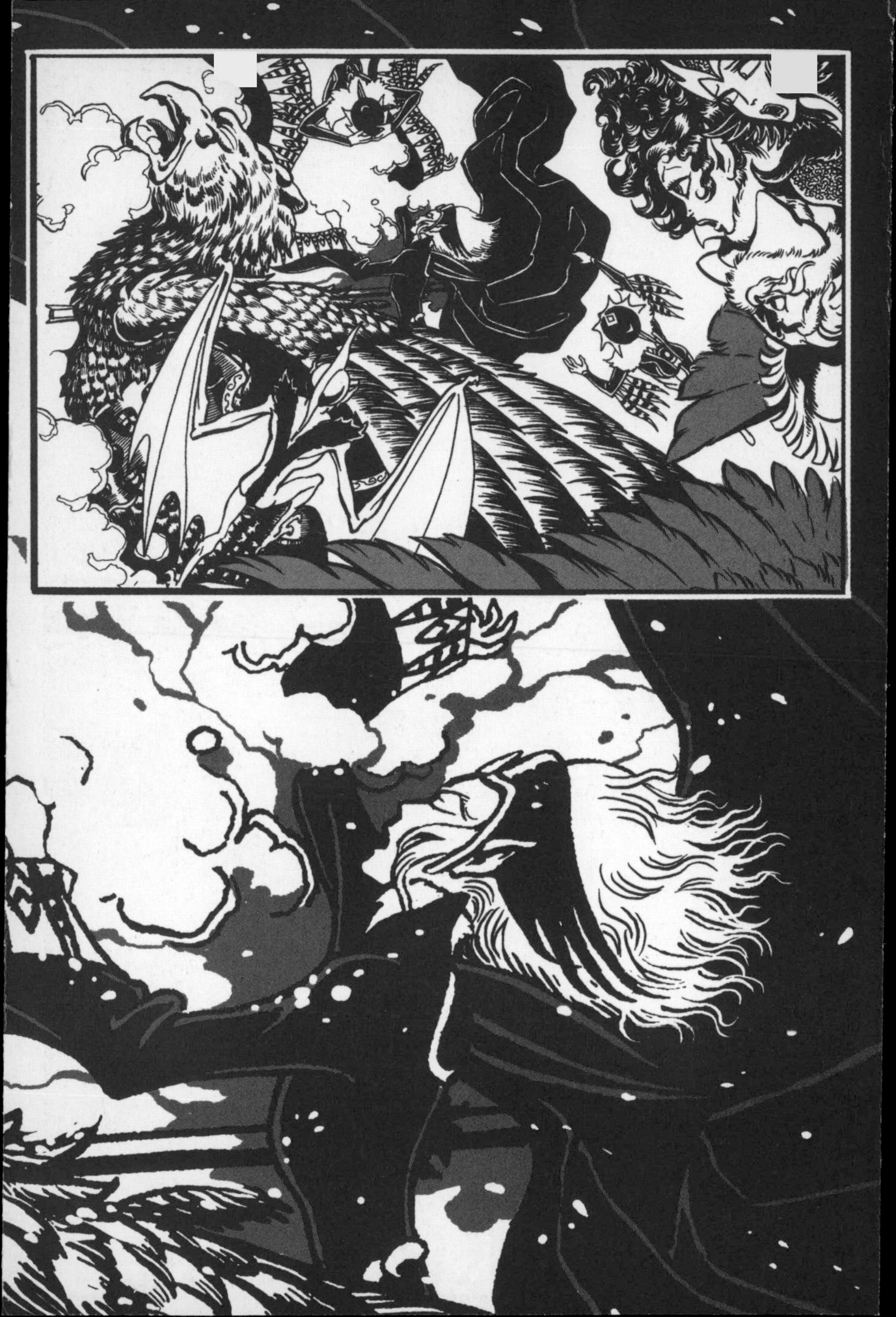

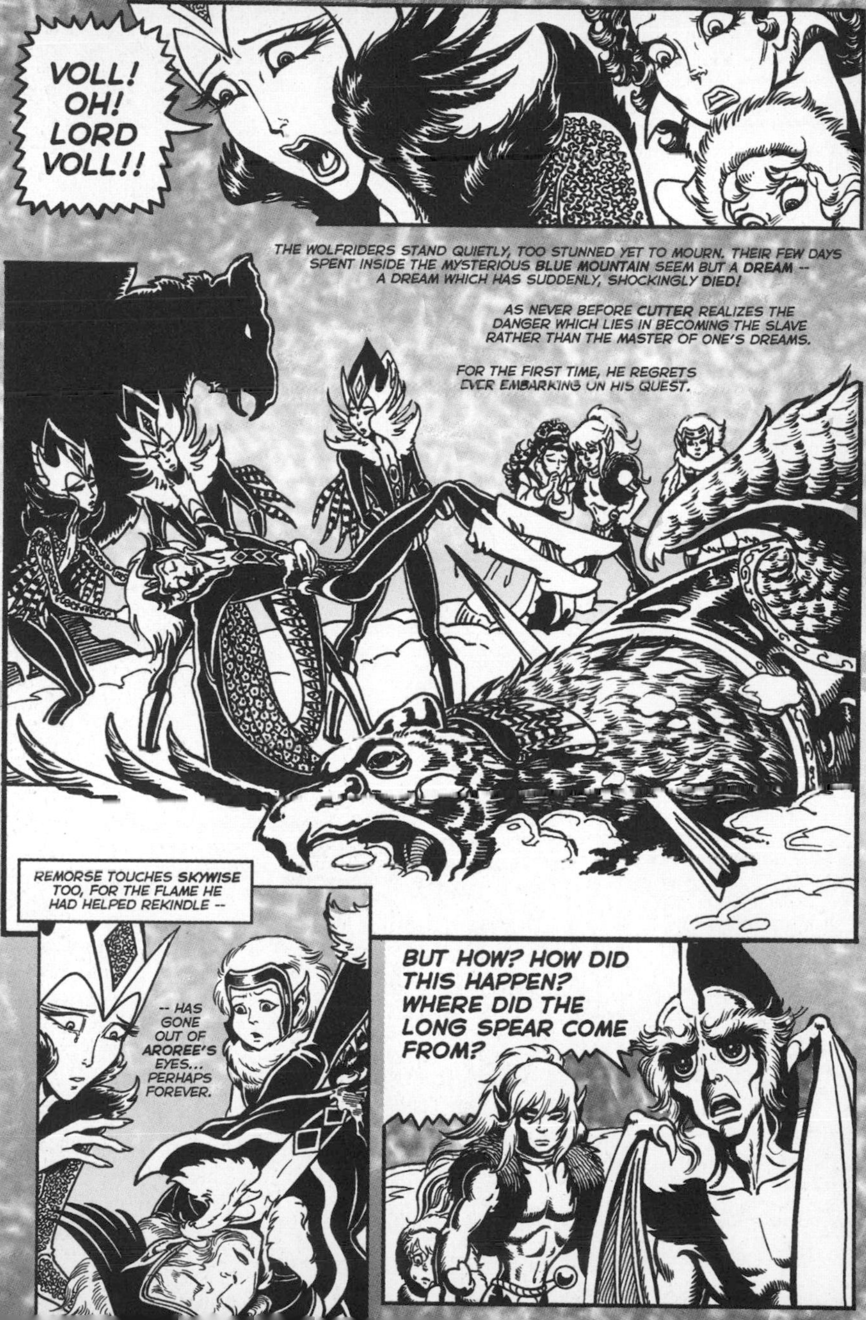
VOLL! OH! LORD VOLL!!
THE WOLFRIDERS STAND QUIETLY, TOO STUNNED YET TO MOURN. THEIR FEW DAYS SPENT INSIDE THE MYSTERIOUS BLUE MOUNTAIN SEEM BUT A DREAM -- A DREAM WHICH HAS SUDDENLY, SHOCKINGLY DIED!
AS NEVER BEFORE CUTTER REALIZES THE DANGER WHICH LIES IN BECOMING THE SLAVE RATHER THAN THE MASTER OF ONE'S DREAMS.
FOR THE FIRST TIME, HE REGRETS EVER EMBARKING ON HIS QUEST.
REMORSE TOUCHES SKYWISE TOO, FOR THE FLAME HE HAD HELPED REKINDLE --
-- HAS GONE OUT OF AROREE'S EYES... PERHAPS FOREVER.
BUT HOW? HOW DID THIS HAPPEN? WHERE DID THE LONG SPEAR COME FROM?

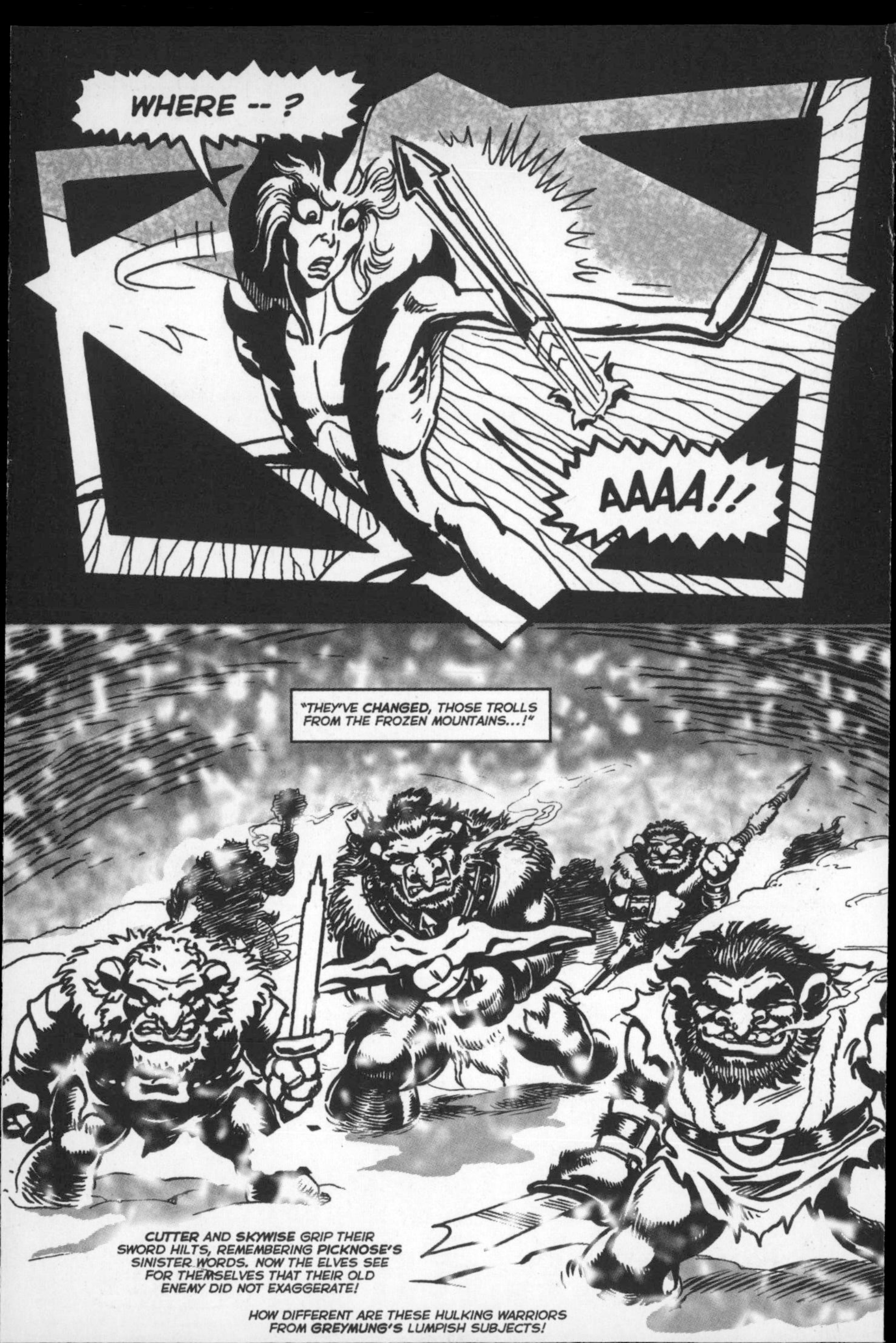
WHERE -- ?
AAAA!!
"THEY'VE CHANGED, THOSE TROLLS FROM THE FROZEN MOUNTAINS...!"
CUTTER AND SKYWISE GRIP THEIR SWORD HILTS, REMEMBERING PICKNOSE'S SINISTER WORDS. NOW THE ELVES SEE FOR THEMSELVES THAT THEIR OLD ENEMY DID NOT EXAGGERATE!
HOW DIFFERENT ARE THESE HULKING WARRIORS FROM GREYMUNG'S LUMPISH SUBJECTS!

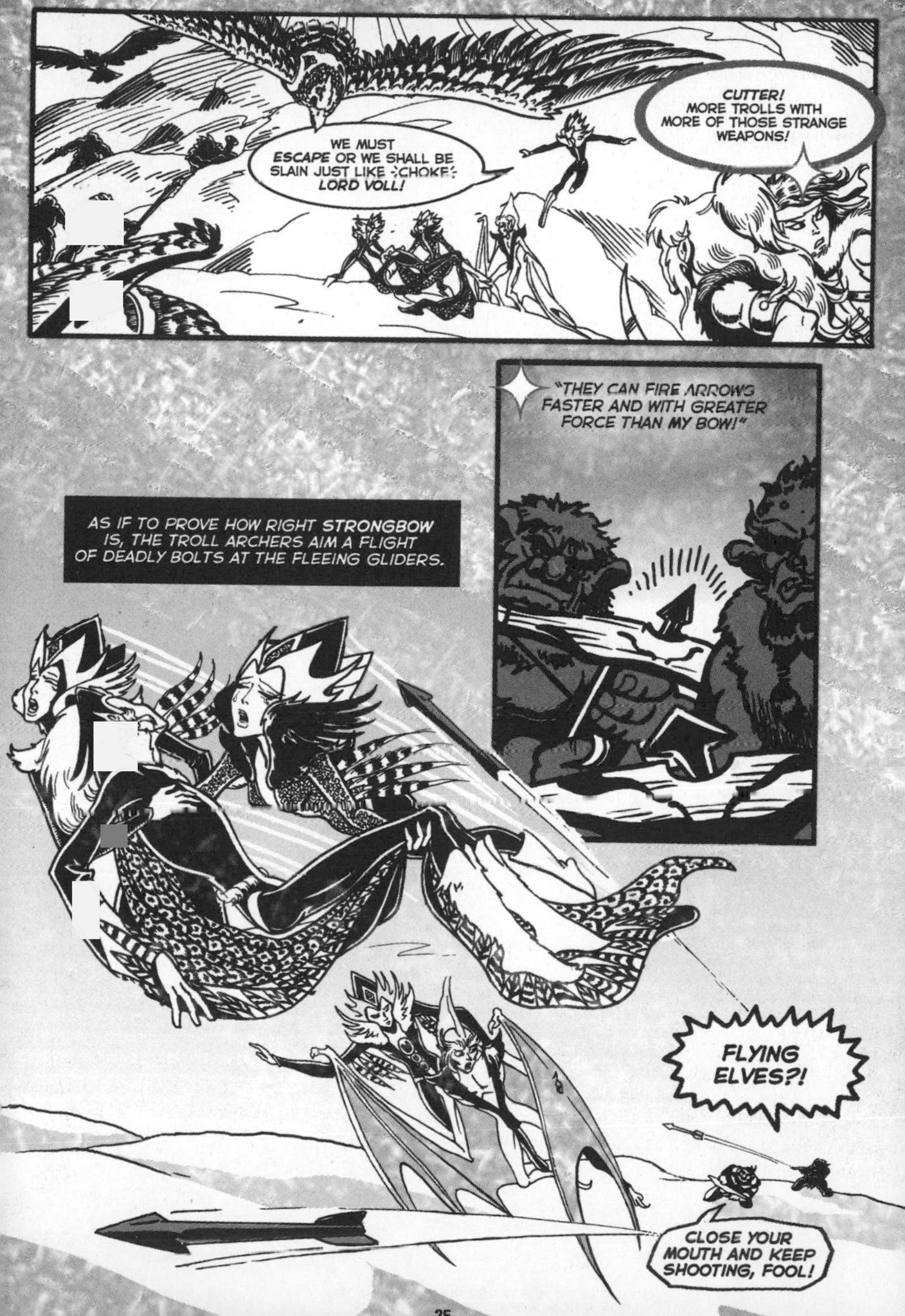
WE MUST ESCAPE OR WE SHALL BE SLAIN JUST LIKE -CHOKE- LORD VOLL!
CUTTER! MORE TROLLS WITH MORE OF THOSE STRANGE WEAPONS!
"THEY CAN FIRE ARROWS FASTER AND WITH GREATER FORCE THAN MY BOW!"
AS IF TO PROVE HOW RIGHT STRONGBOW IS, THE TROLL ARCHERS AIM A FLIGHT OF DEADLY BOLTS AT THE FLEEING GLIDERS.
FLYING ELVES?!
CLOSE YOUR MOUTH AND KEEP SHOOTING, FOOL!

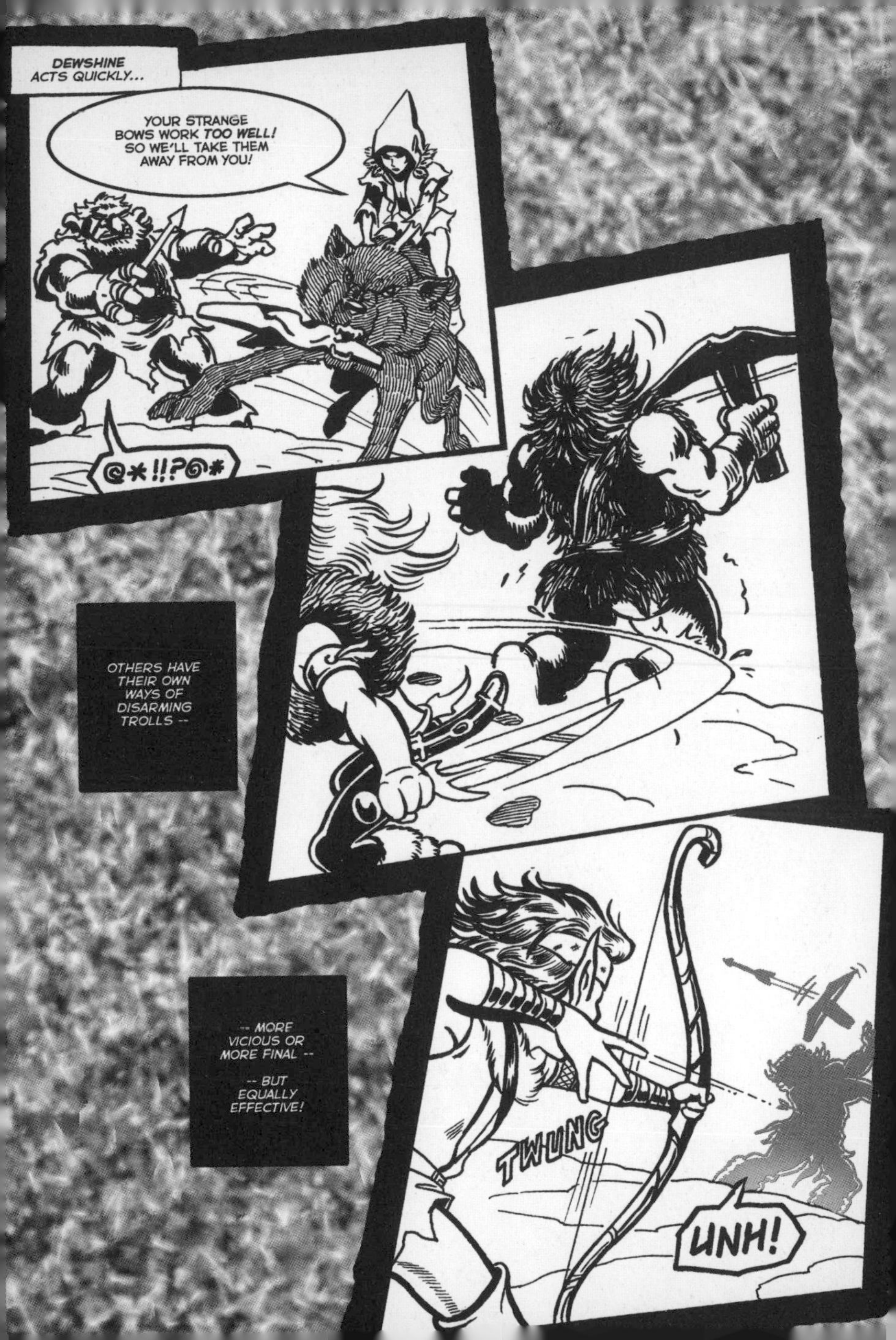
DEWSHINE ACTS QUICKLY...
YOUR STRANGE BOWS WORK TOO WELL! SO WE'LL TAKE THEM AWAY FROM YOU!
@*!!?@*
OTHERS HAVE THEIR OWN WAYS OF DISARMING TROLLS --
-- MORE VICIOUS OR MORE FINAL --
-- BUT EQUALLY EFFECTIVE!
TWUNG
UNH!

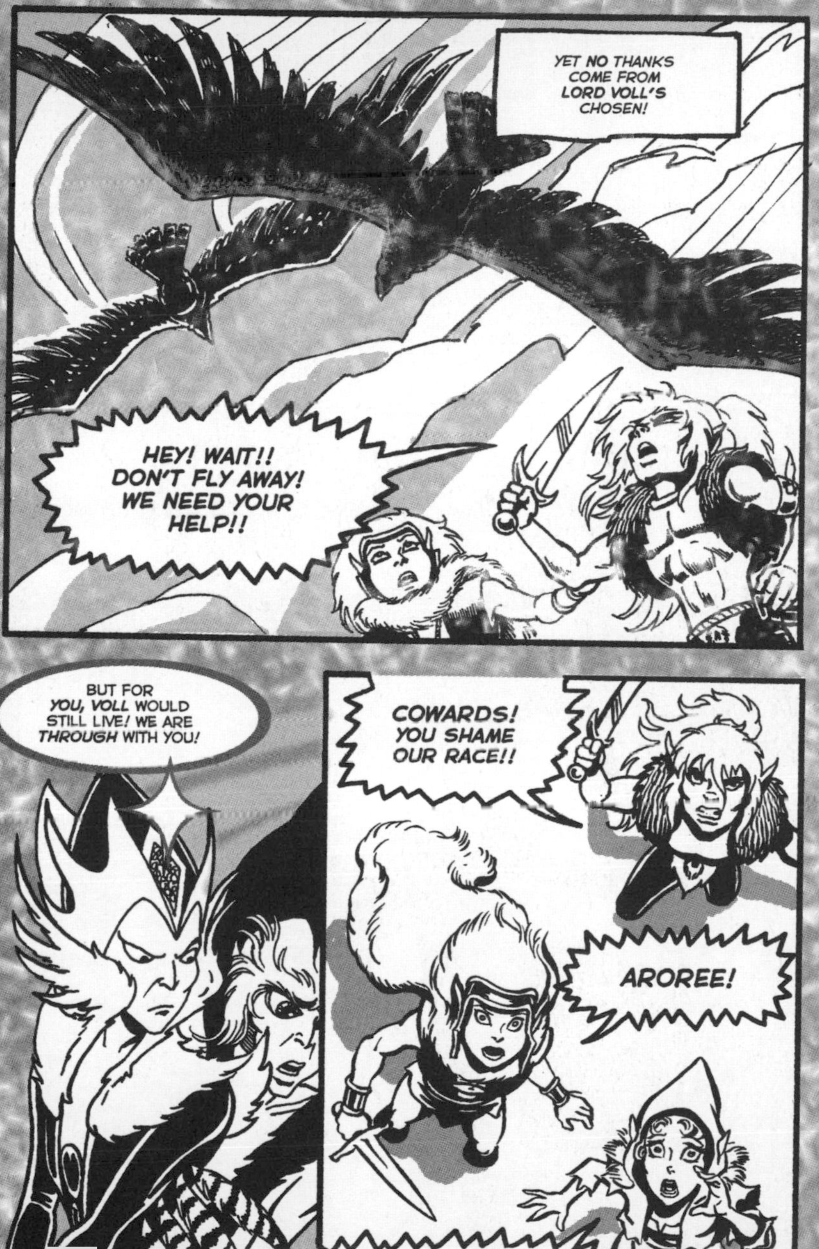
YET NO THANKS COME FROM LORD VOLL'S CHOSEN!
HEY! WAIT!! DON'T FLY AWAY! WE NEED YOUR HELP!!
BUT FOR YOU, VOLL WOULD STILL LIVE! WE ARE THROUGH WITH YOU!
COWARDS! YOU SHAME OUR RACE!!
AROREE!
TYLDAAAAAK!

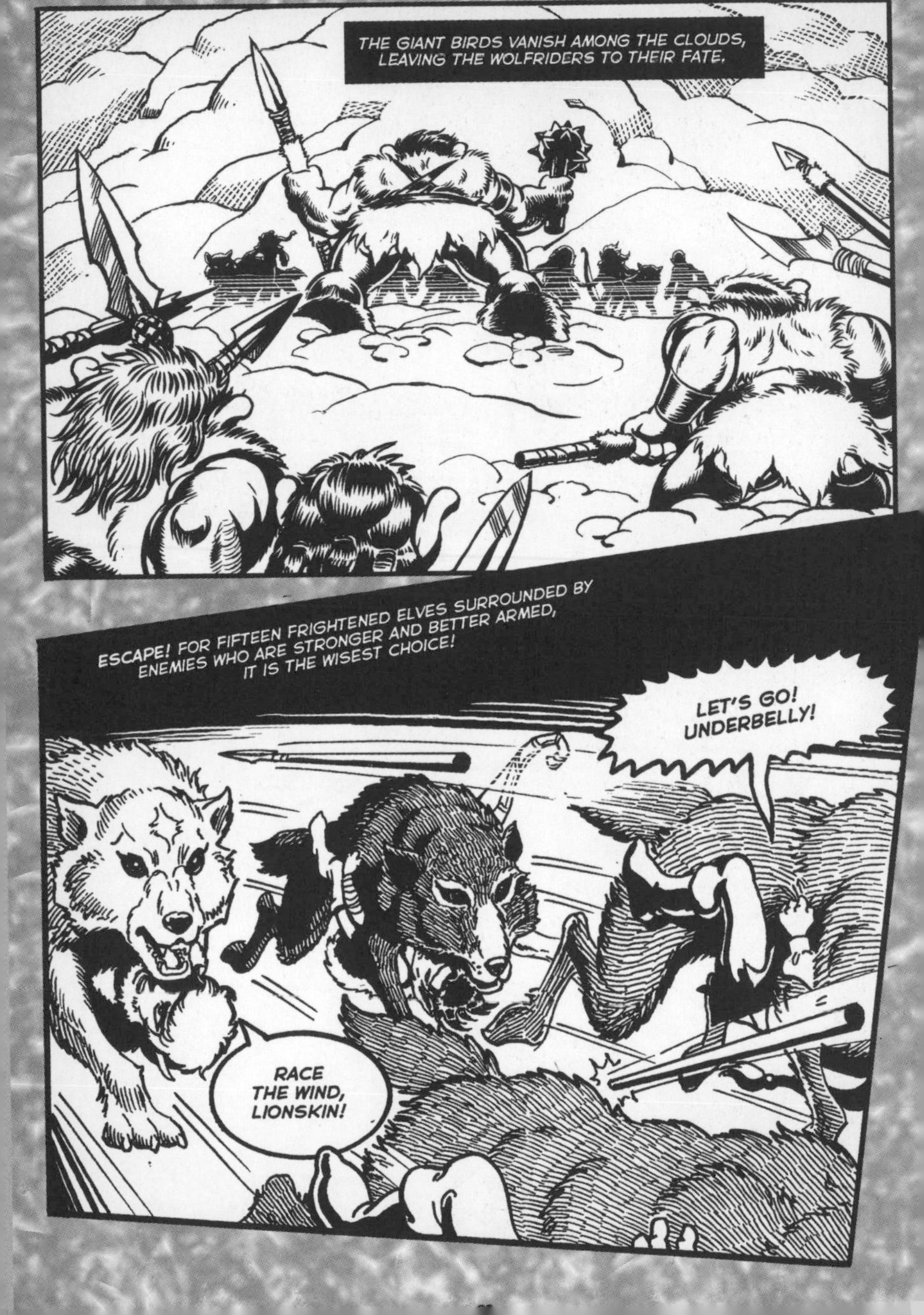

THE GIANT BIRDS VANISH AMONG THE CLOUDS, LEAVING THE WOLFRIDERS TO THEIR FATE.
ESCAPE! FOR FIFTEEN FRIGHTENED ELVES SURROUNDED BY ENEMIES WHO ARE STRONGER AND BETTER ARMED, IT IS THE WISEST CHOICE!
LET'S GO! UNDERBELLY!
RACE THE WIND, LIONSKIN!

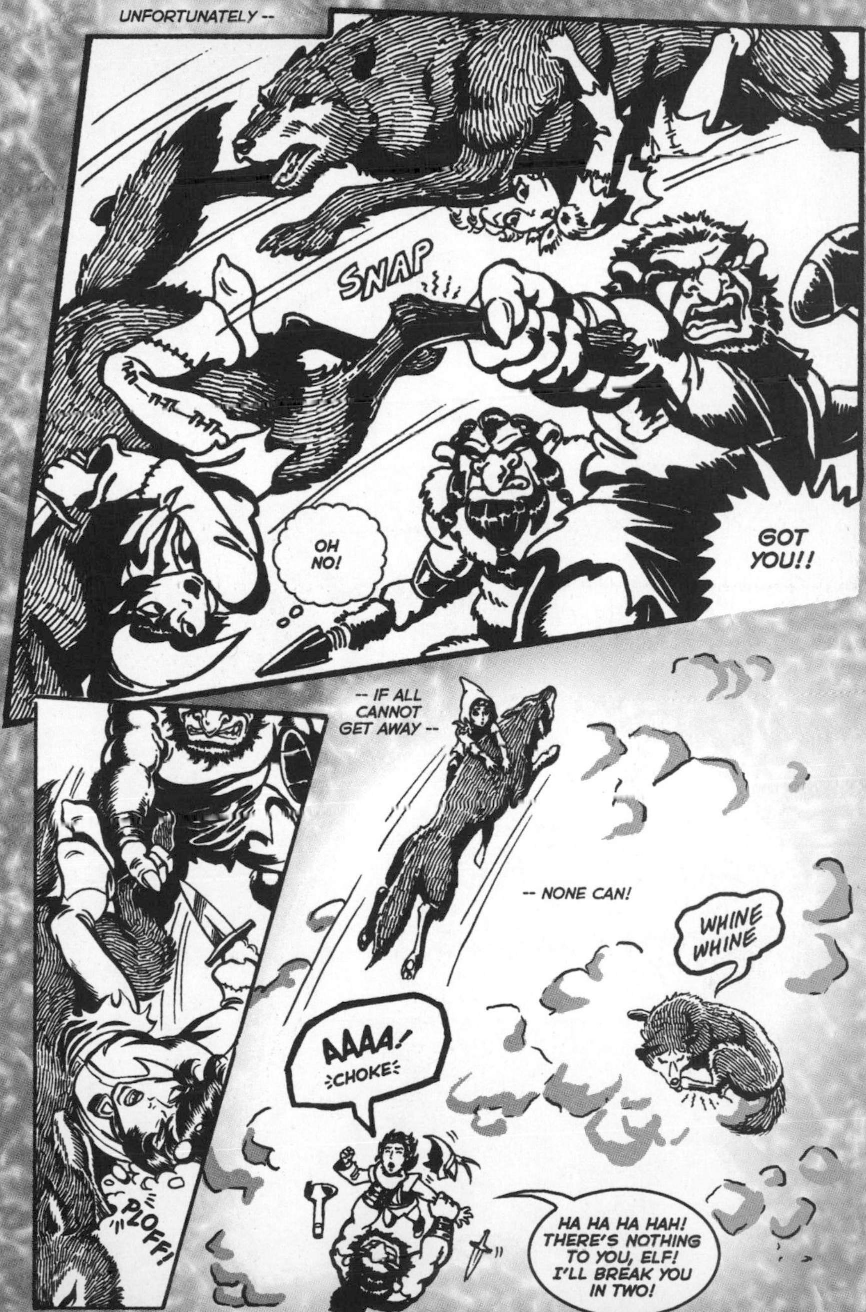
UNFORTUNATELY --
SNAP
OH NO!
GOT YOU!!
-- IF ALL CANNOT GET AWAY --
-- NONE CAN!
WHINE WHINE
AAAA! CHOKE
PLOFF!
HA HA HA HAH! THERE'S NOTHING TO YOU, ELF! I'LL BREAK YOU IN TWO!

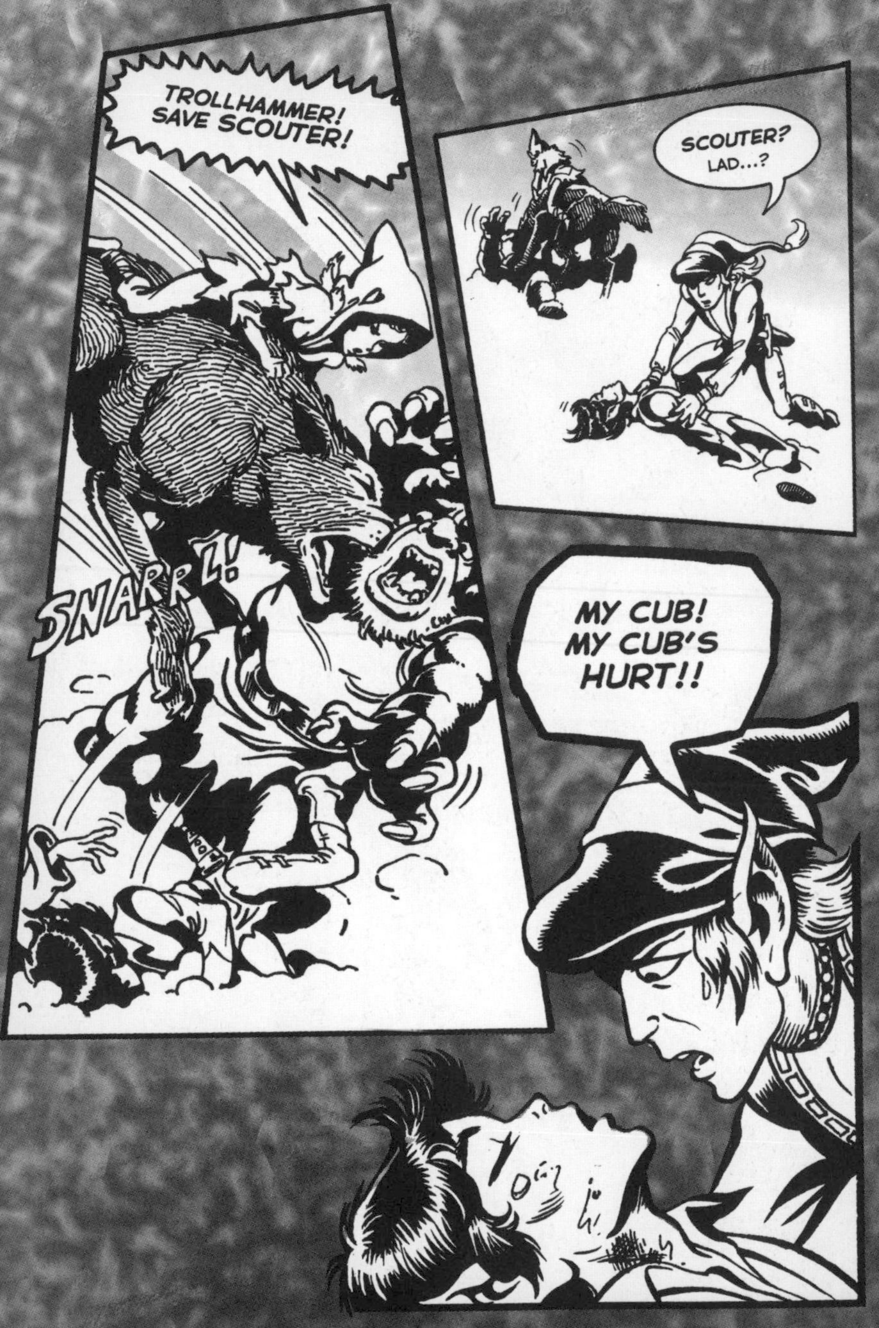
TROLLHAMMER! SAVE SCOUTER!
SNARRL!
SCOUTER? LAD...?
MY CUB! MY CUB'S HURT!!

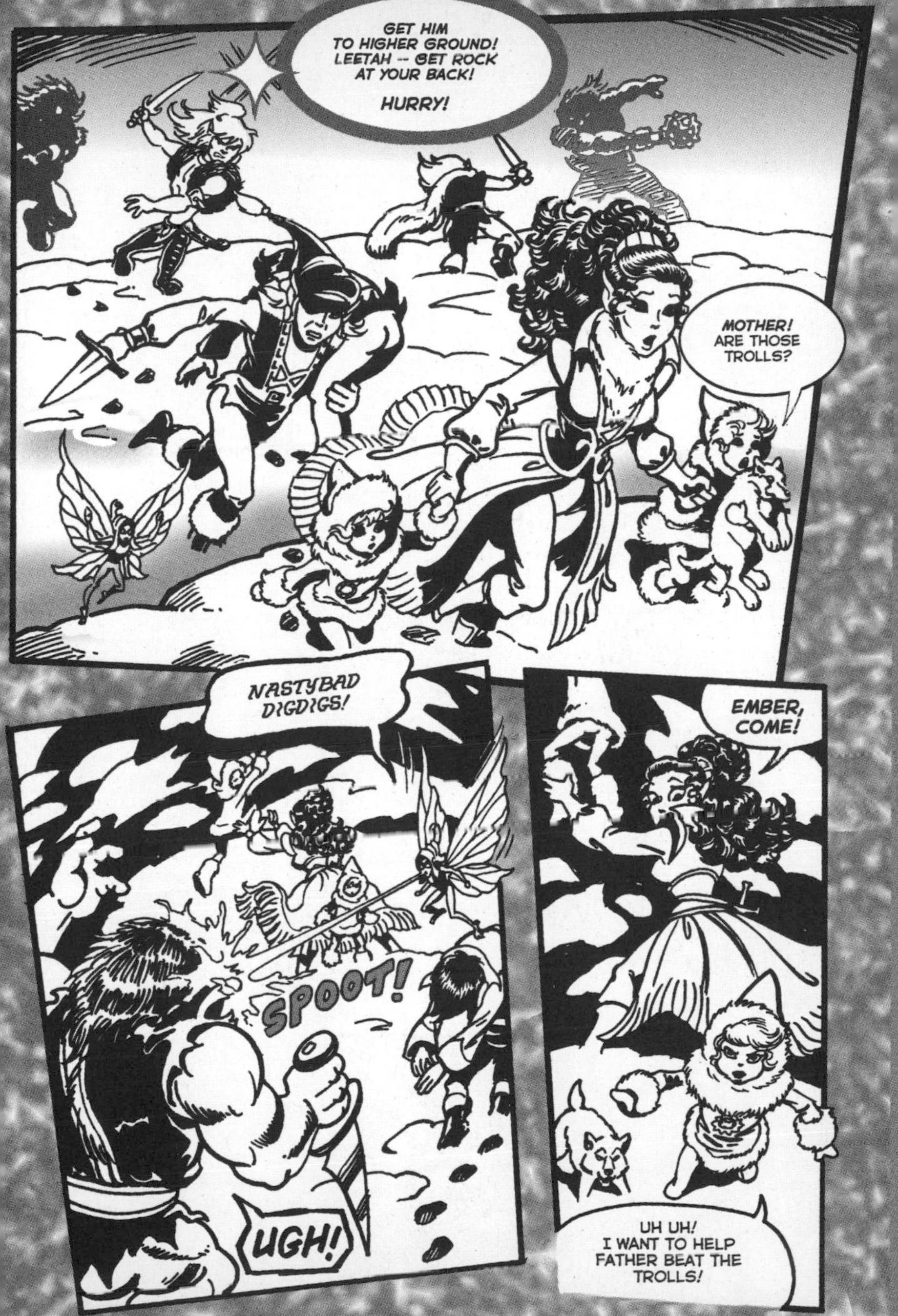
GET HIM TO HIGHER GROUND! LEETAH -- GET ROCK AT YOUR BACK!
HURRY!
MOTHER! ARE THOSE TROLLS?
NASTYBAD DIGDIGS!
SPOOT!
UGH!
EMBER, COME!
UH UH! I WANT TO HELP FATHER BEAT THE TROLLS!

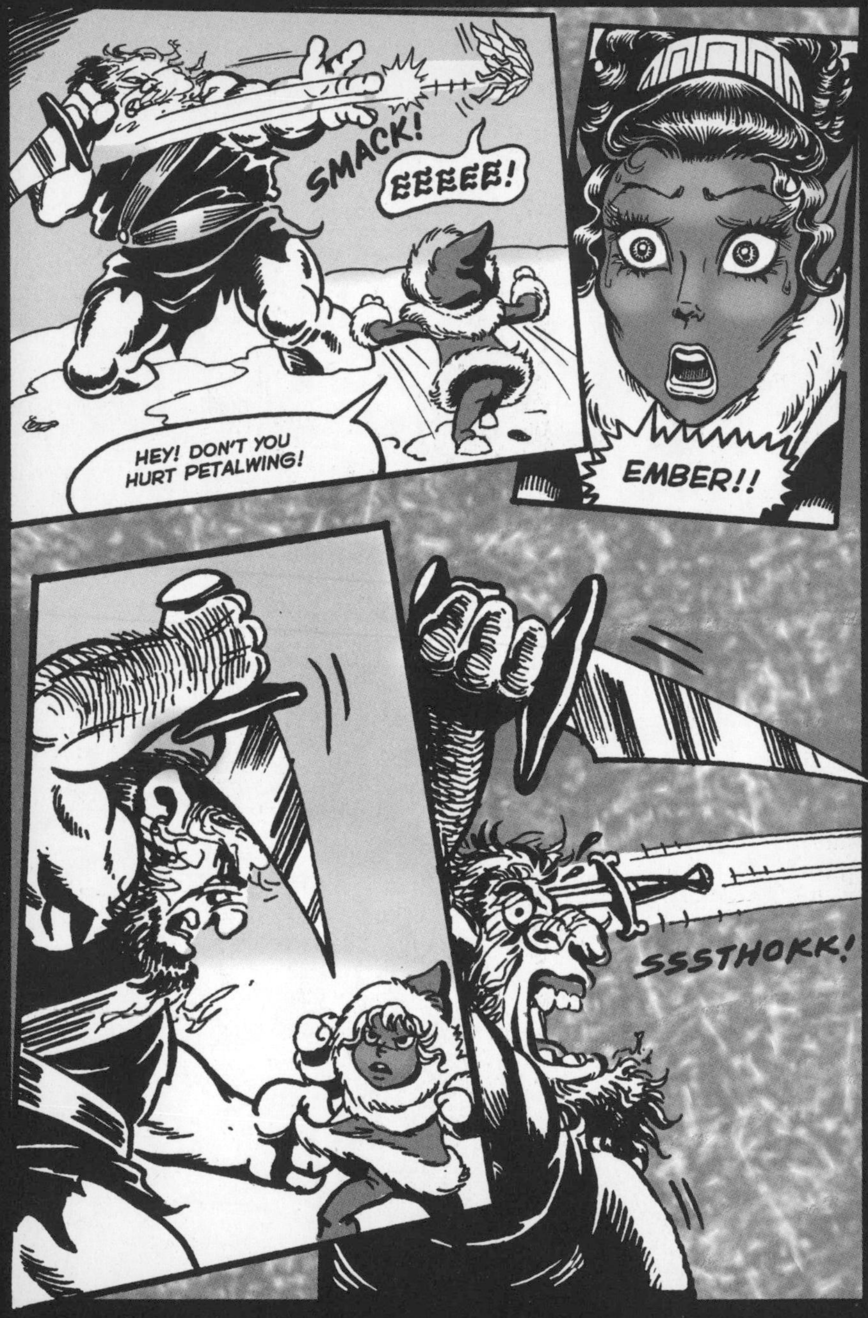
SMACK!
EEEEE!
HEY! DON'T YOU HURT PETALWING!
EMBER!!
SSSTHOKK!

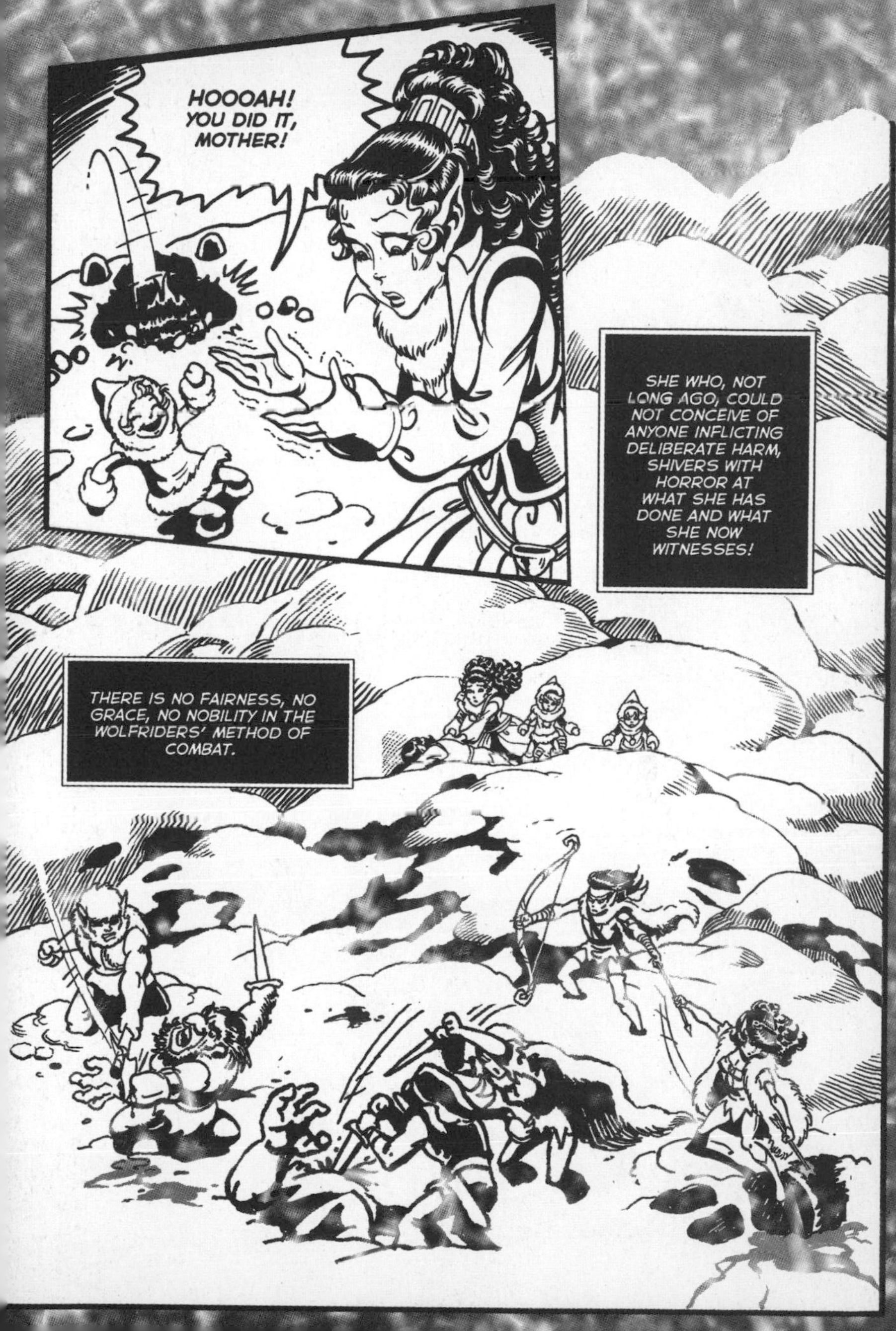
HOOOAH! YOU DID IT, MOTHER!
SHE WHO, NOT LONG AGO, COULD NOT CONCEIVE OF ANYONE INFLICTING DELIBERATE HARM, SHIVERS WITH HORROR AT WHAT SHE HAS DONE AND WHAT SHE NOW WITNESSES!
THERE IS NO FAIRNESS, NO GRACE, NO NOBILITY IN THE WOLFRIDERS' METHOD OF COMBAT.

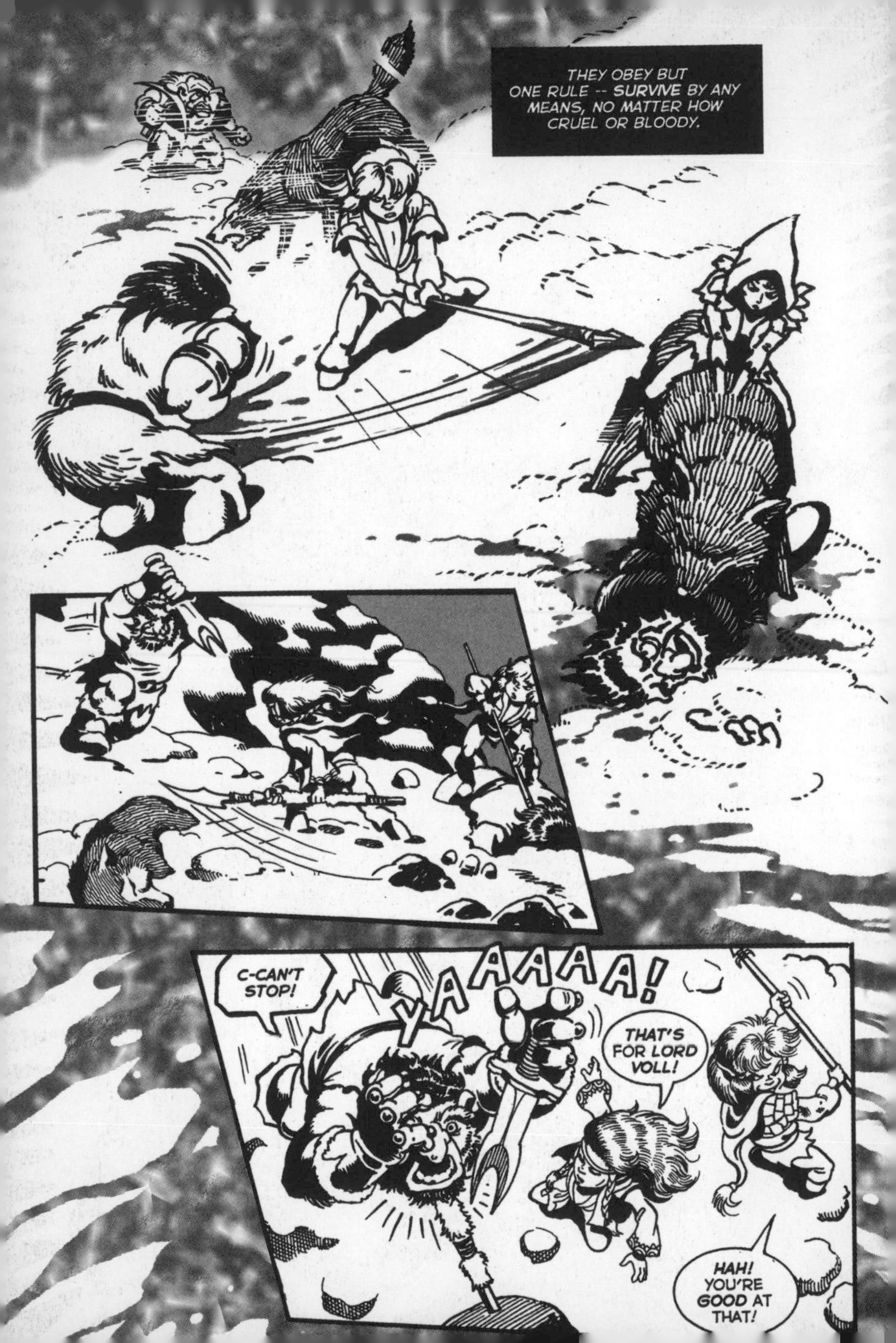
THEY OBEY BUT ONE RULE -- SURVIVE BY ANY MEANS, NO MATTER HOW CRUEL OR BLOODY.
C-CAN'T STOP!
YAAAAAA!
THAT'S FOR LORD VOLL!
HAH! YOU'RE GOOD AT THAT!

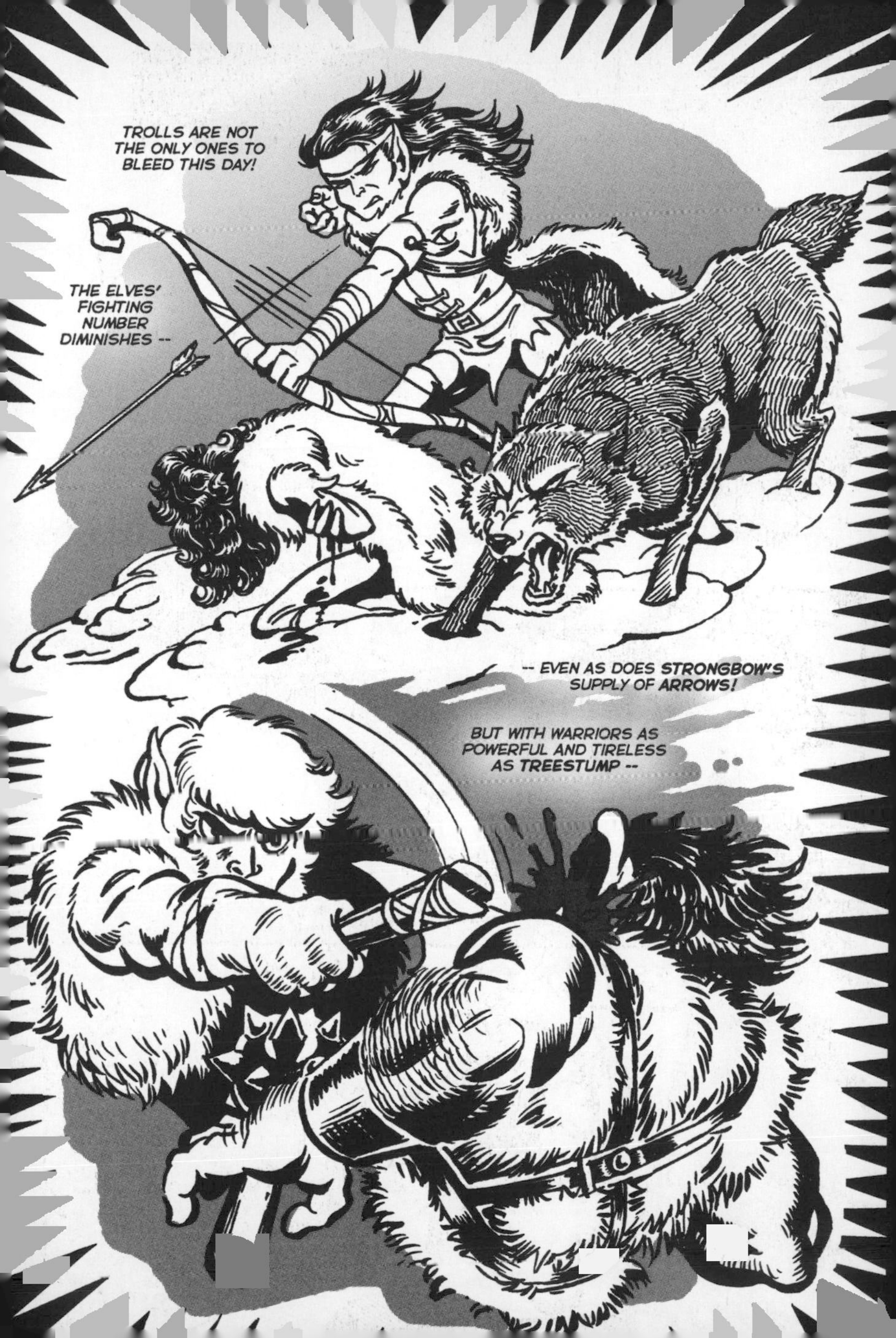
TROLLS ARE NOT THE ONLY ONES TO BLEED THIS DAY!
THE ELVES' FIGHTING NUMBER DIMINISHES --
-- EVEN AS DOES STRONGBOW'S SUPPLY OF ARROWS!
BUT WITH WARRIORS AS POWERFUL AND TIRELESS AS TREESTUMP --

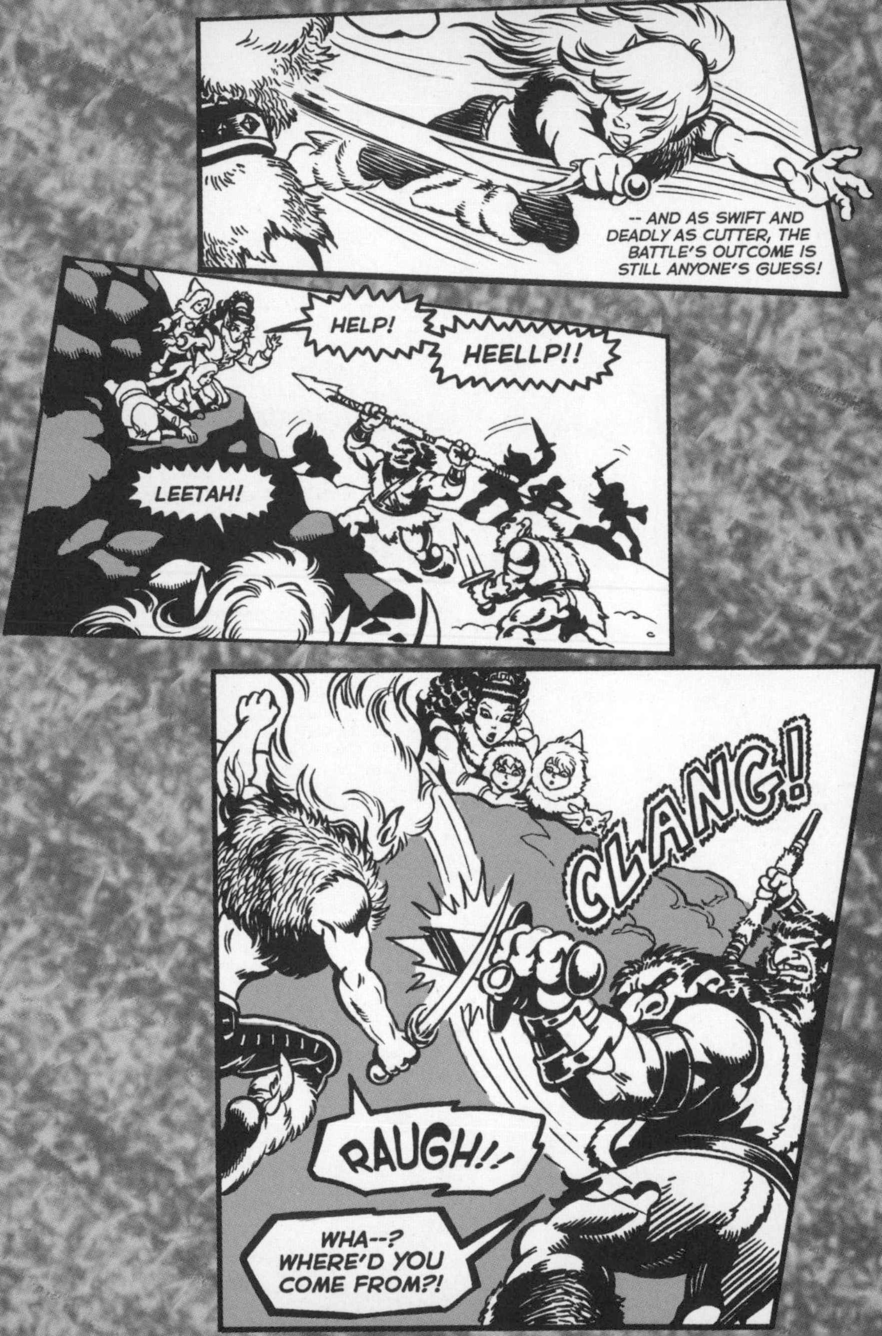
-- AND AS SWIFT AND DEADLY AS CUTTER, THE BATTLE'S OUTCOME IS STILL ANYONE'S GUESS!
HELP!
HEELLP!!
LEETAH!
CLANG!
RAUGH!!
WHA--? WHERE'D YOU COME FROM?!

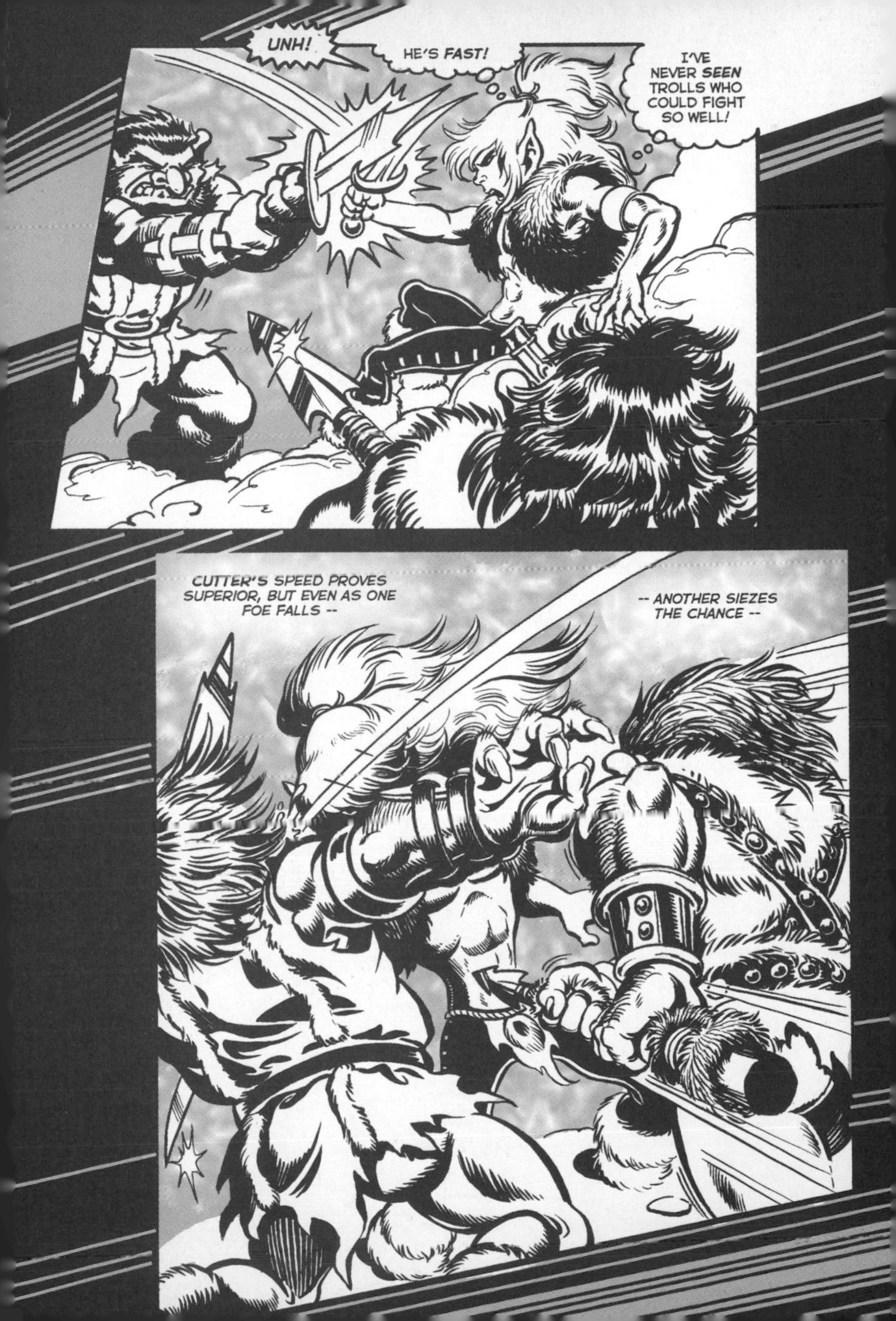
UNH!
HE'S FAST!
I'VE NEVER SEEN TROLLS WHO COULD FIGHT SO WELL!
CUTTER'S SPEED PROVES SUPERIOR, BUT EVEN AS ONE FOE FALLS --
-- ANOTHER SIEZES THE CHANCE --

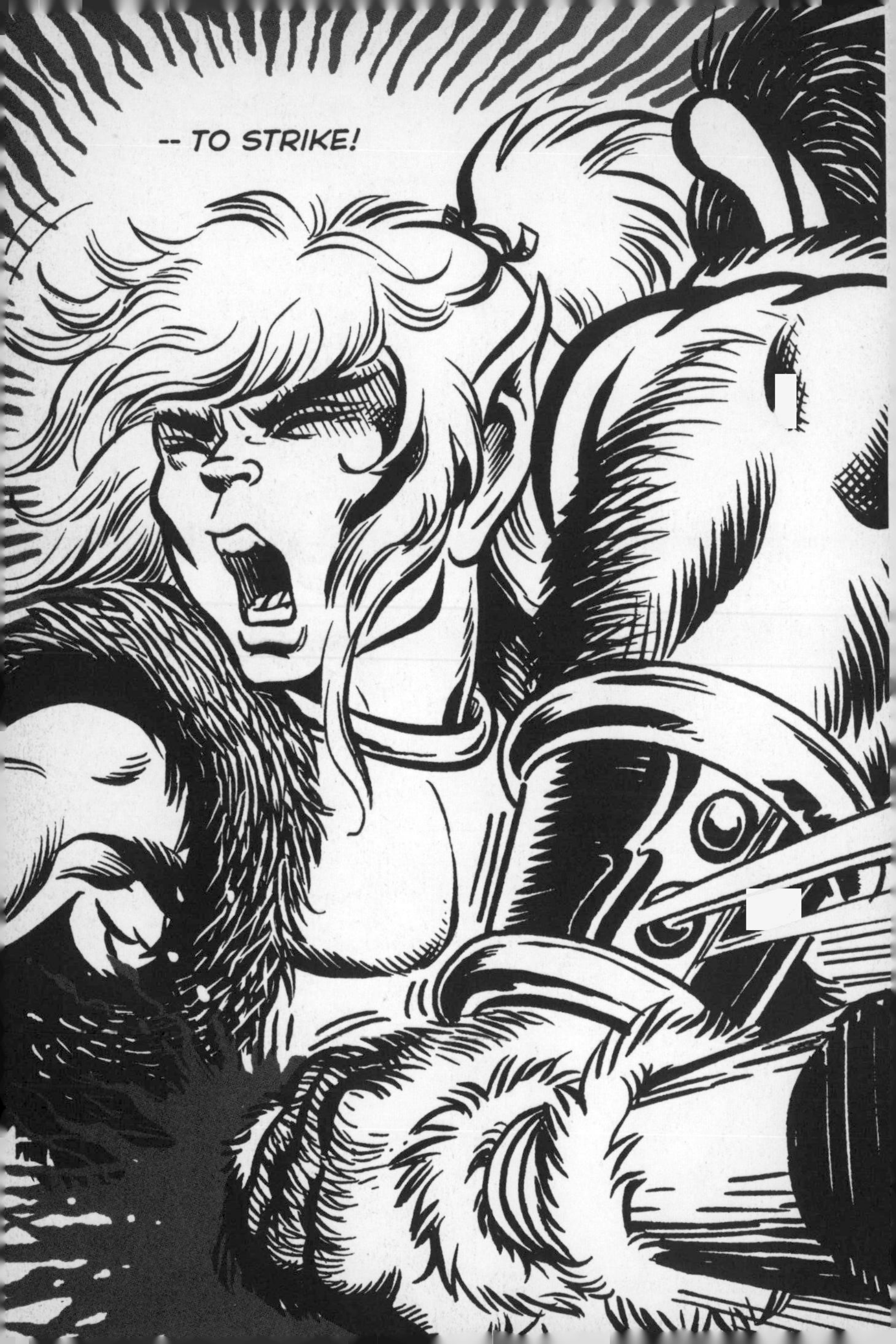
-- TO STRIKE!

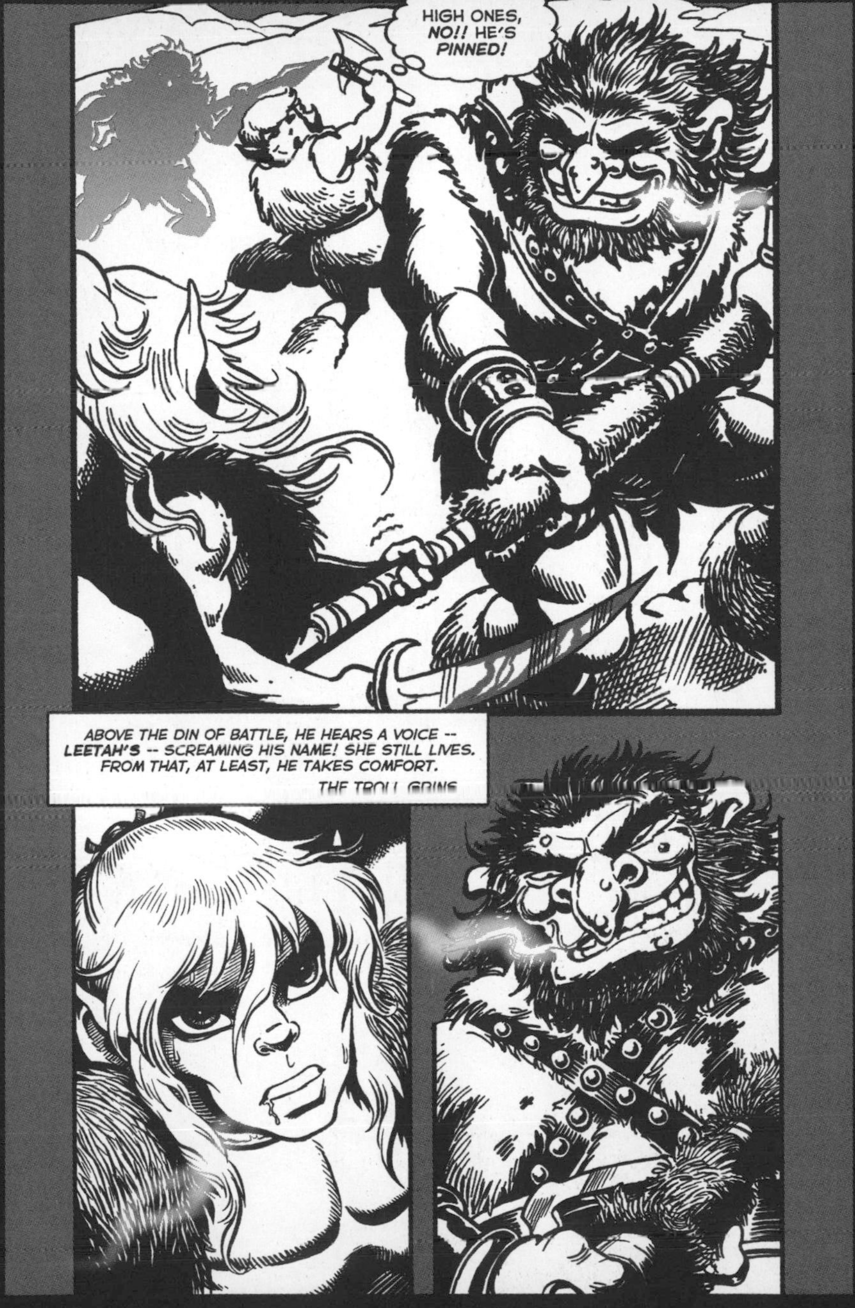
HIGH ONES, NO!! HE'S PINNED!
ABOVE THE DIN OF BATTLE, HE HEARS A VOICE -- LEETAH'S -- SCREAMING HIS NAME! SHE STILL LIVES. FROM THAT, AT LEAST, HE TAKES COMFORT.
THE TROLL GRINS

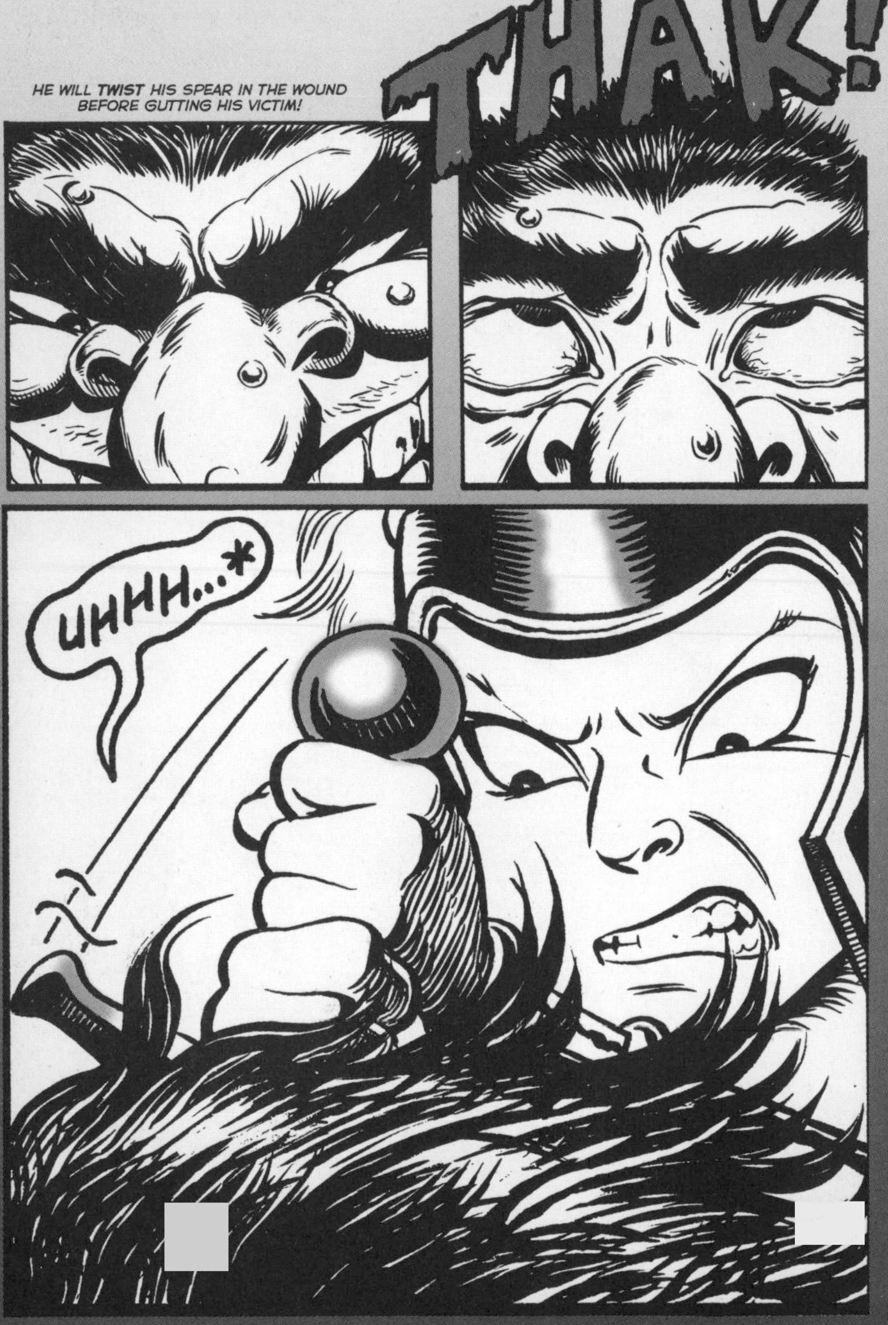
HE WILL TWIST HIS SPEAR IN THE WOUND BEFORE GUTTING HIS VICTIM!
THAK!
UHHH...*

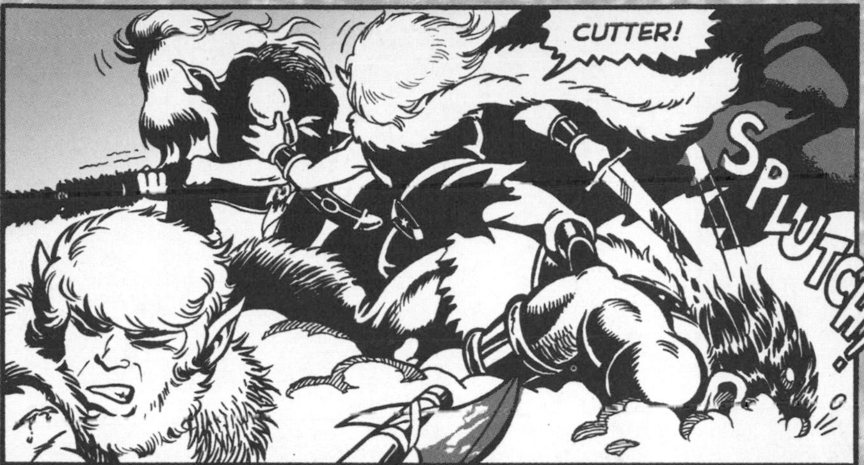
CUTTER!
SPLUTCH!

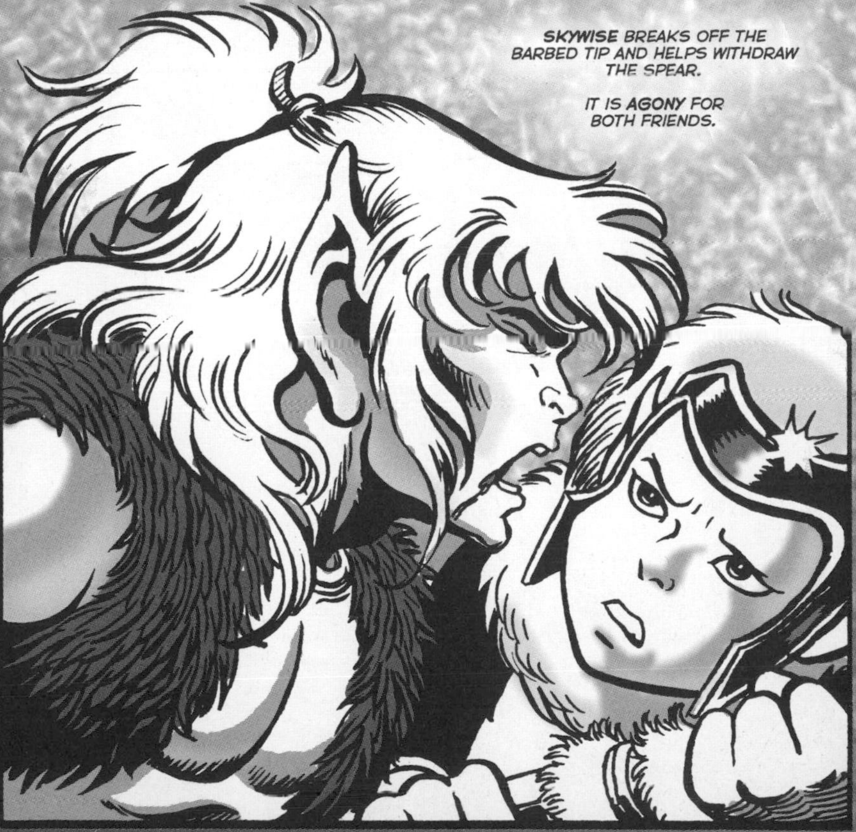
SKYWISE BREAKS OFF THE BARBED TIP AND HELPS WITHDRAW THE SPEAR.
IT IS AGONY FOR BOTH FRIENDS.

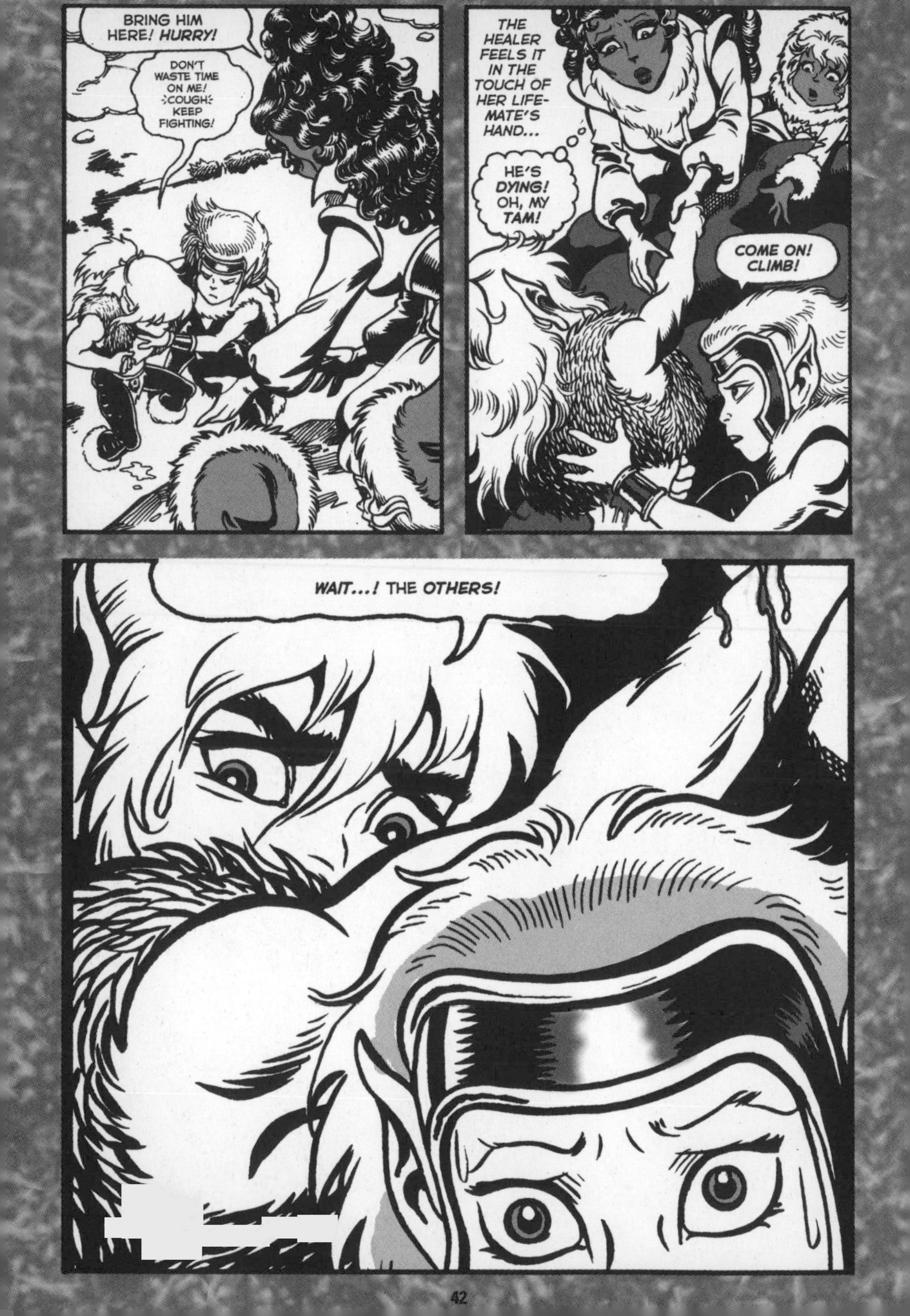
BRING HIM HERE! *HURRY!*
DON'T WASTE TIME ON ME! ·COUGH· KEEP FIGHTING!
THE HEALER FEELS IT IN THE TOUCH OF HER LIFE-MATE'S HAND...
HE'S *DYING!* OH, MY *TAM!*
COME ON! CLIMB!
WAIT...! THE *OTHERS!*

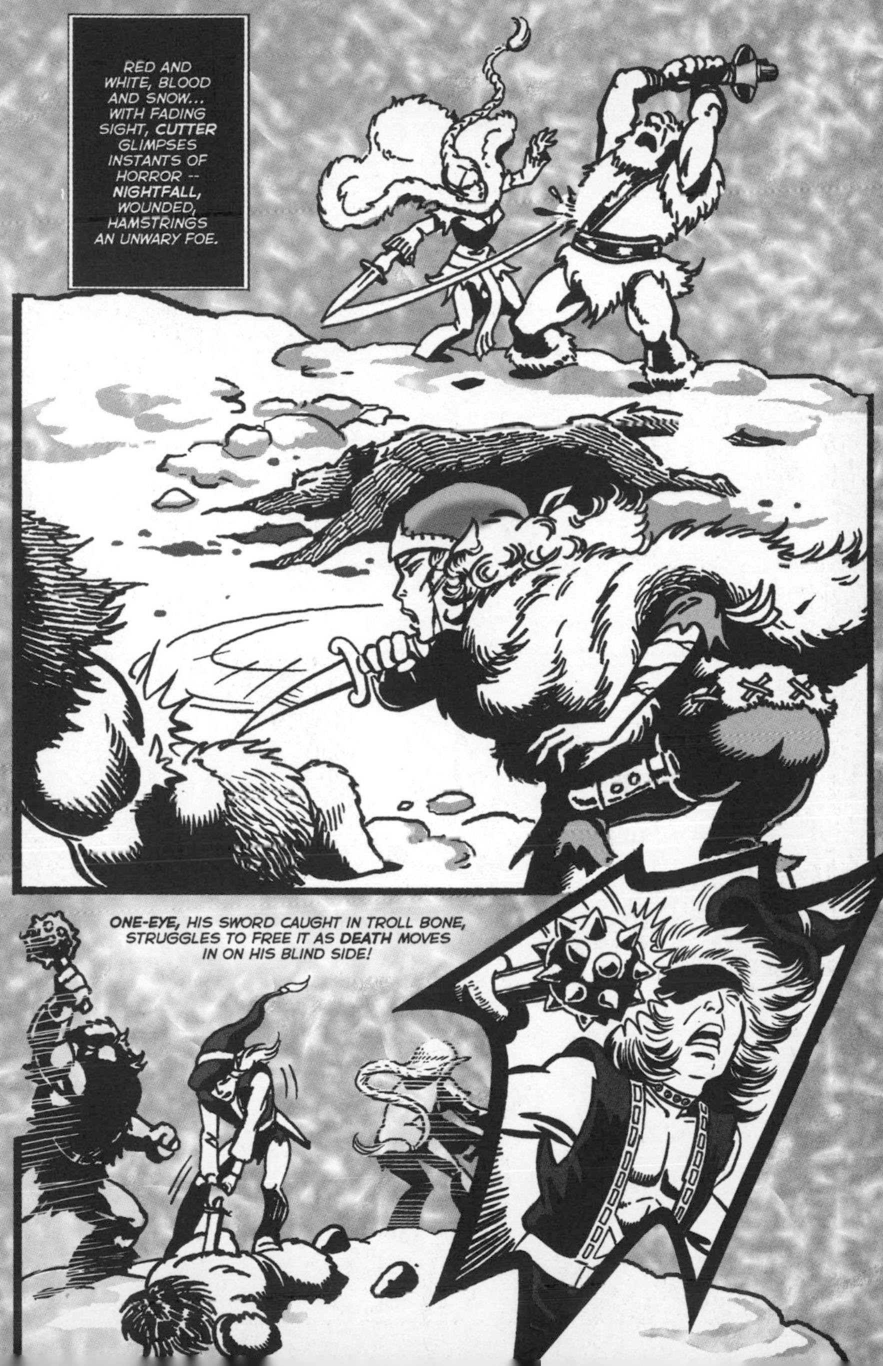
RED AND WHITE, BLOOD AND SNOW... WITH FADING SIGHT, CUTTER GLIMPSES INSTANTS OF HORROR -- NIGHTFALL, WOUNDED, HAMSTRINGS AN UNWARY FOE.
ONE-EYE, HIS SWORD CAUGHT IN TROLL BONE, STRUGGLES TO FREE IT AS DEATH MOVES IN ON HIS BLIND SIDE!

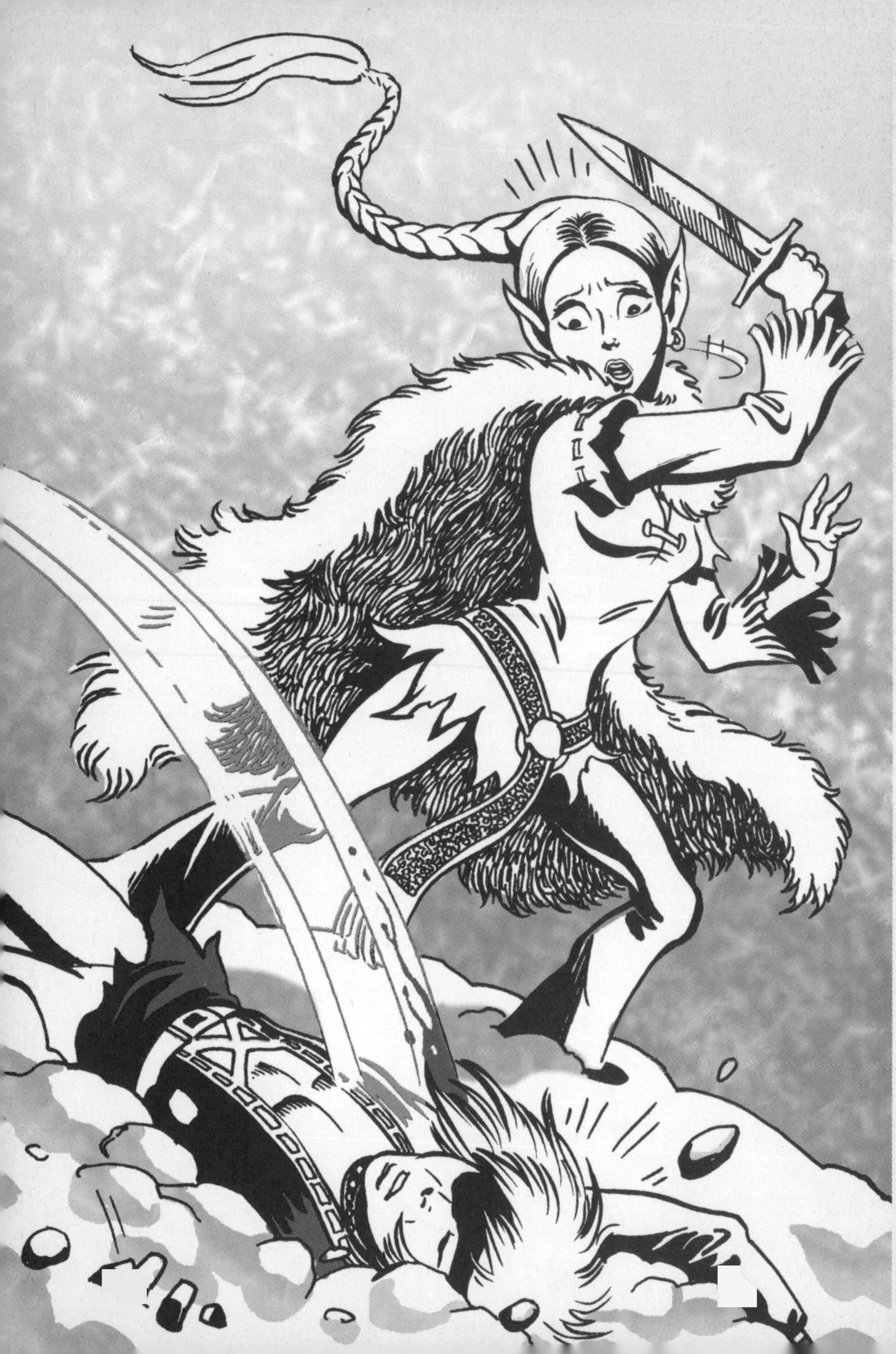

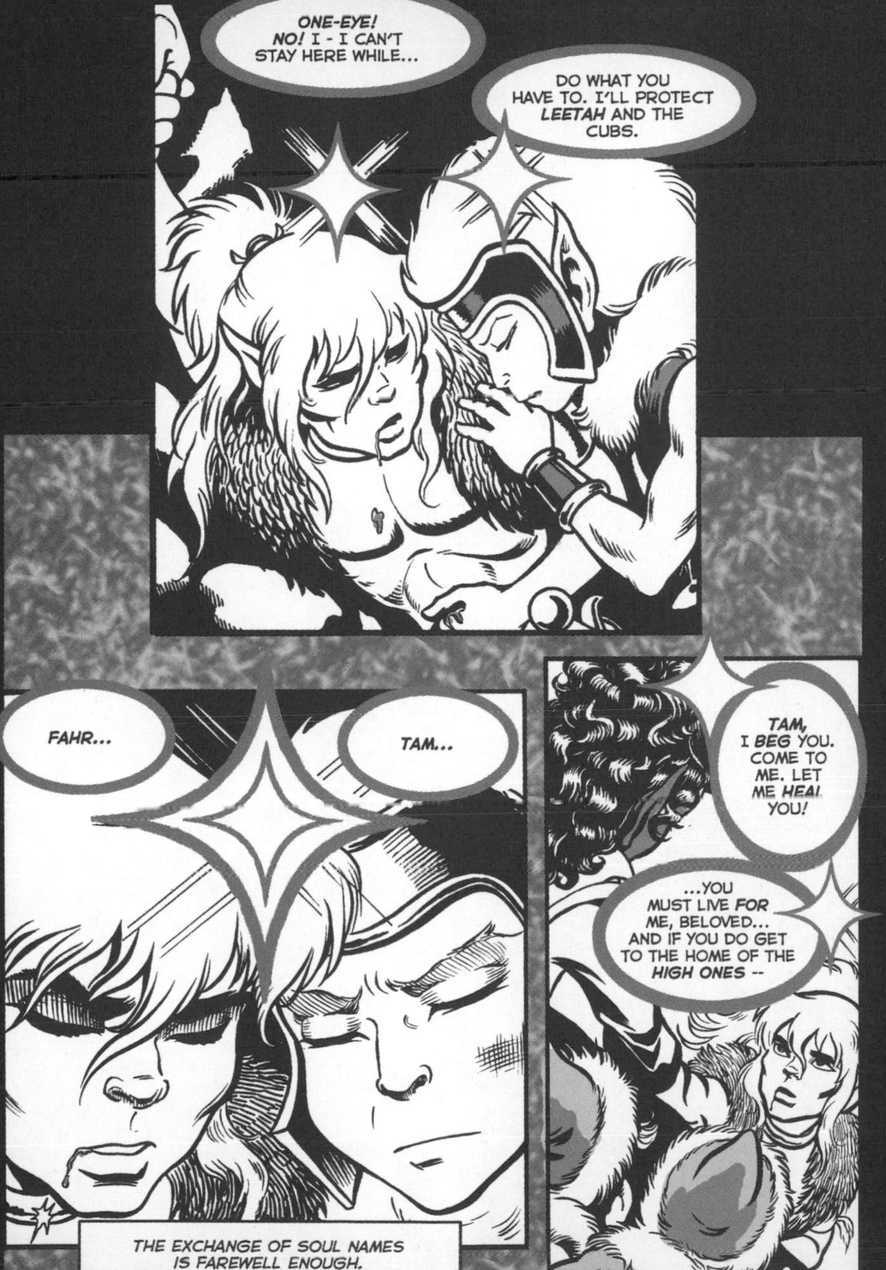
ONE-EYE! NO! I - I CAN'T STAY HERE WHILE...
DO WHAT YOU HAVE TO. I'LL PROTECT LEETAH AND THE CUBS.
FAHR...
TAM...
THE EXCHANGE OF SOUL NAMES IS FAREWELL ENOUGH. THERE IS NO TIME FOR MORE.
TAM, I BEG YOU. COME TO ME. LET ME HEAL YOU!
...YOU MUST LIVE FOR ME, BELOVED... AND IF YOU DO GET TO THE HOME OF THE HIGH ONES --

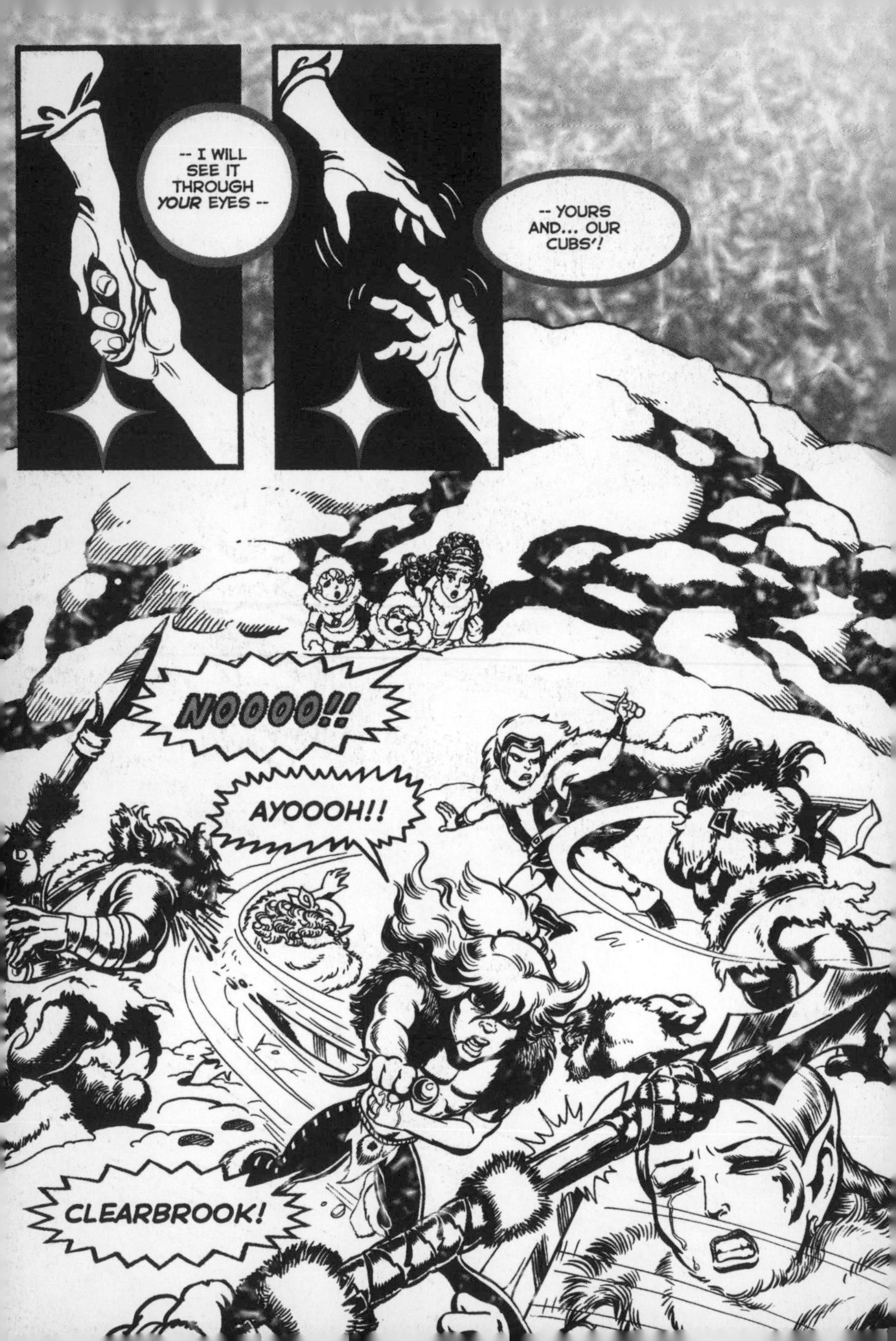
-- I WILL SEE IT THROUGH *YOUR* EYES --
-- YOURS AND... OUR CUBS'!
NOOOO!!
AYOOOH!!
CLEARBROOK!

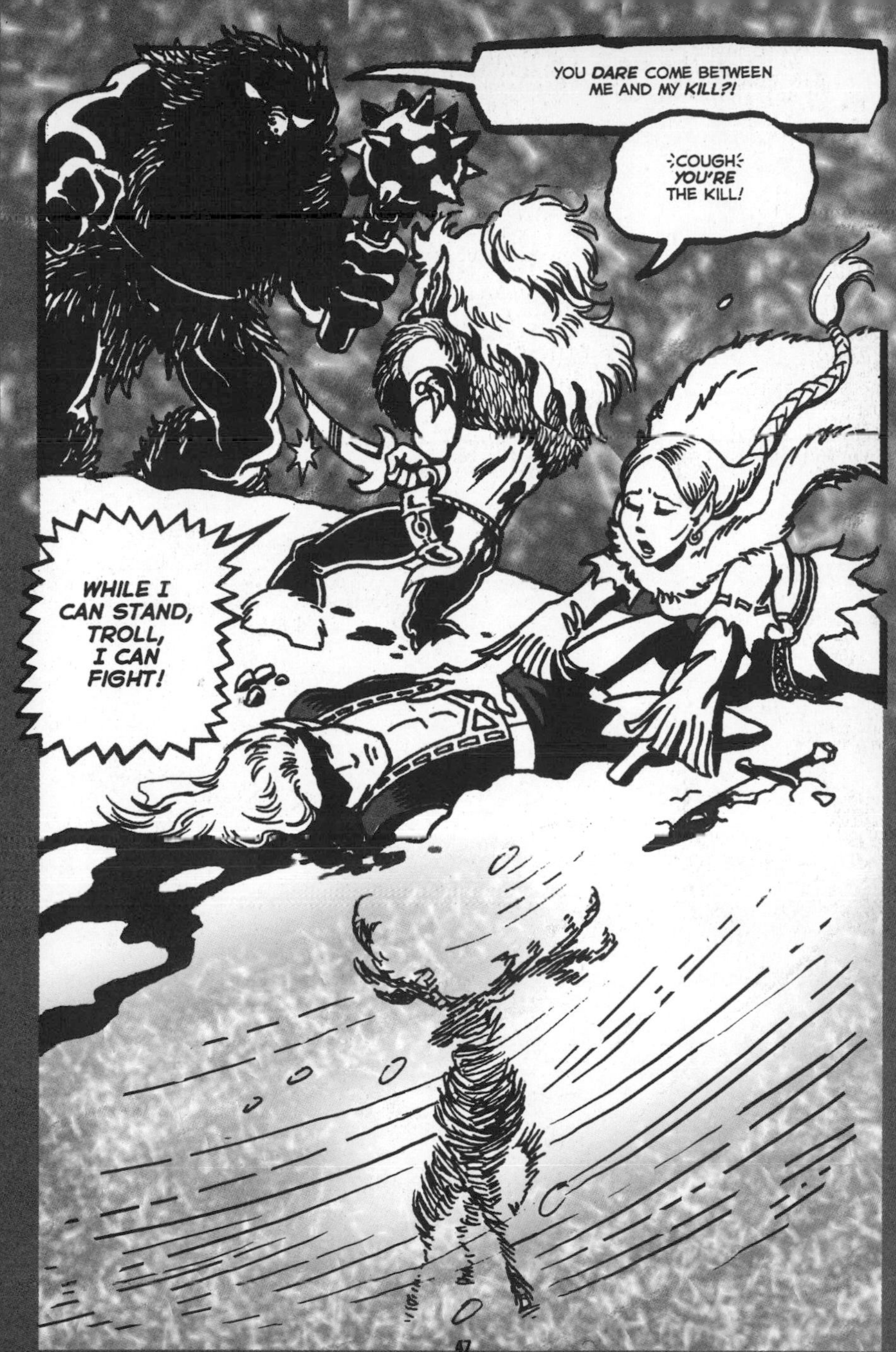
YOU DARE COME BETWEEN ME AND MY KILL?!
COUGH YOU'RE THE KILL!
WHILE I CAN STAND, TROLL, I CAN FIGHT!

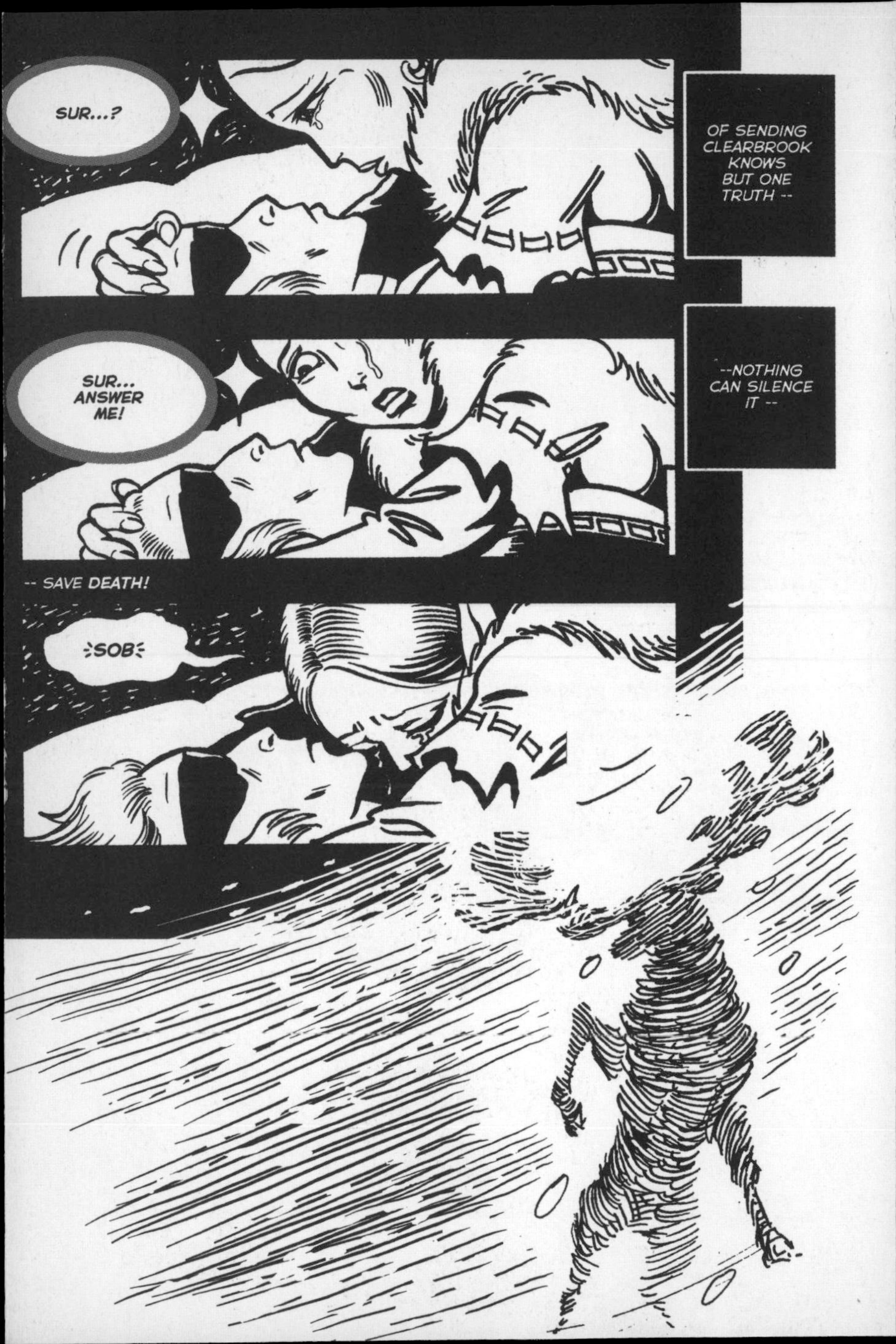
OF SENDING CLEARBROOK KNOWS BUT ONE TRUTH --
SUR...?
--NOTHING CAN SILENCE IT --
SUR... ANSWER ME!
-- SAVE DEATH!
SOB

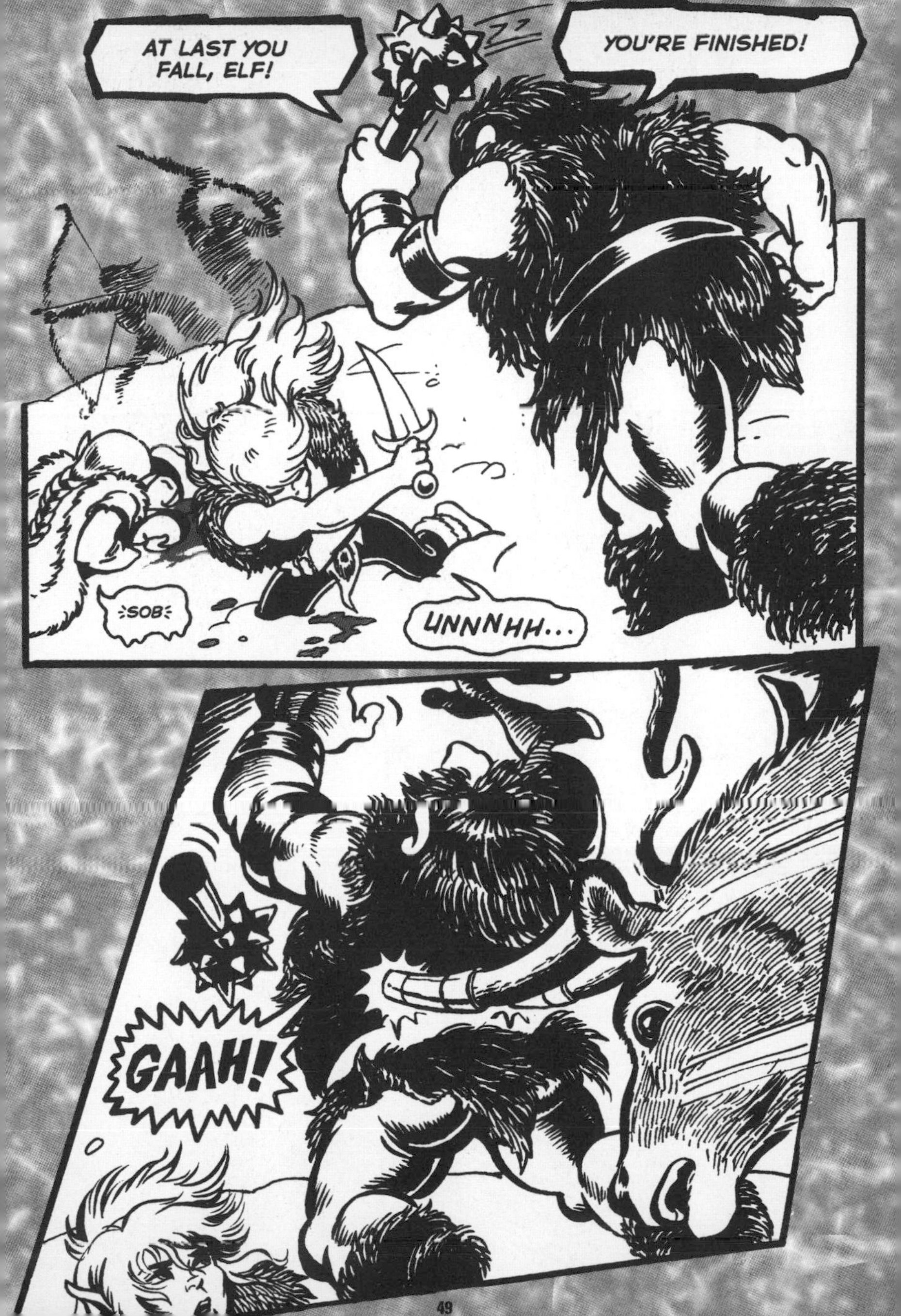
AT LAST YOU FALL, ELF!
YOU'RE FINISHED!
SOB
UNNNHH...
GAAH!

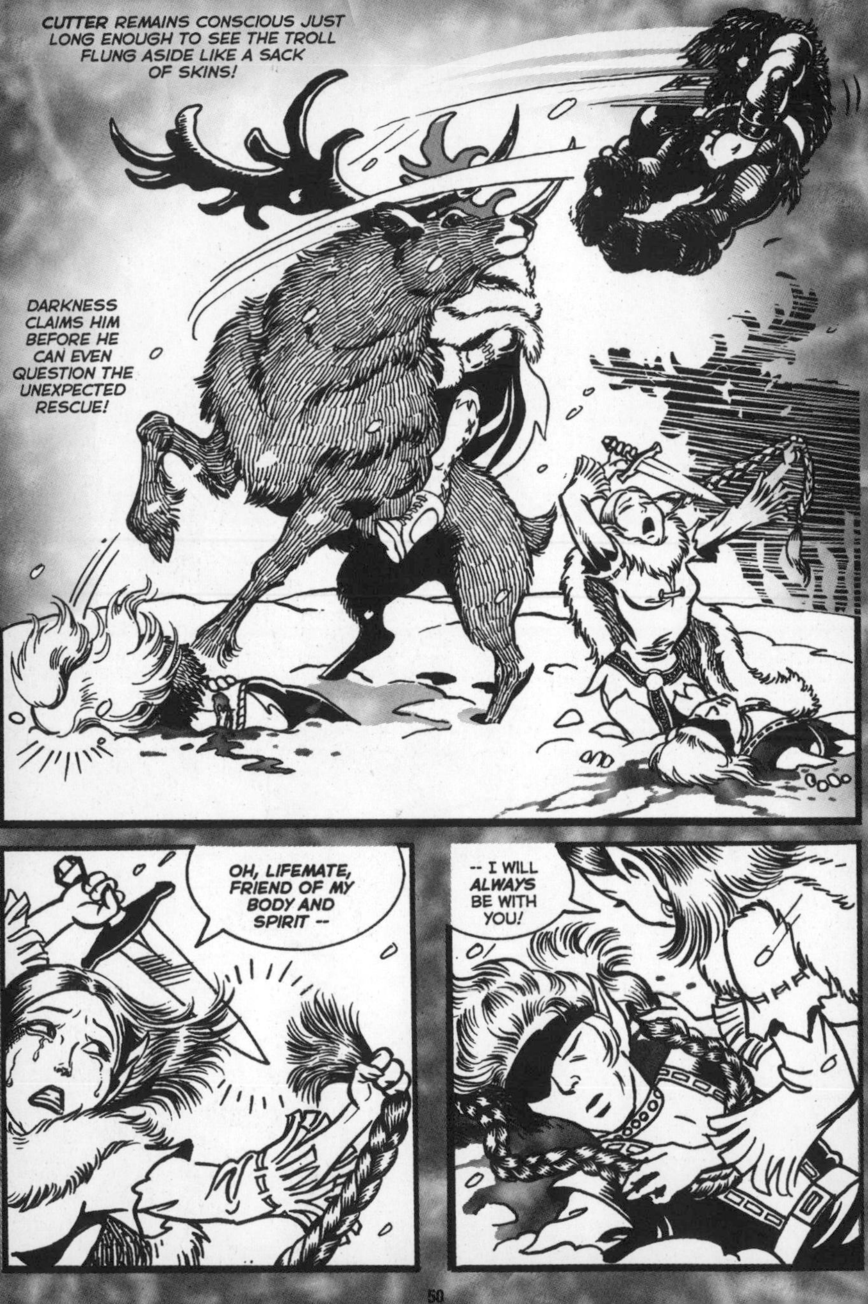
CUTTER REMAINS CONSCIOUS JUST LONG ENOUGH TO SEE THE TROLL FLUNG ASIDE LIKE A SACK OF SKINS!
DARKNESS CLAIMS HIM BEFORE HE CAN EVEN QUESTION THE UNEXPECTED RESCUE!
OH, LIFEMATE, FRIEND OF MY BODY AND SPIRIT --
-- I WILL ALWAYS BE WITH YOU!

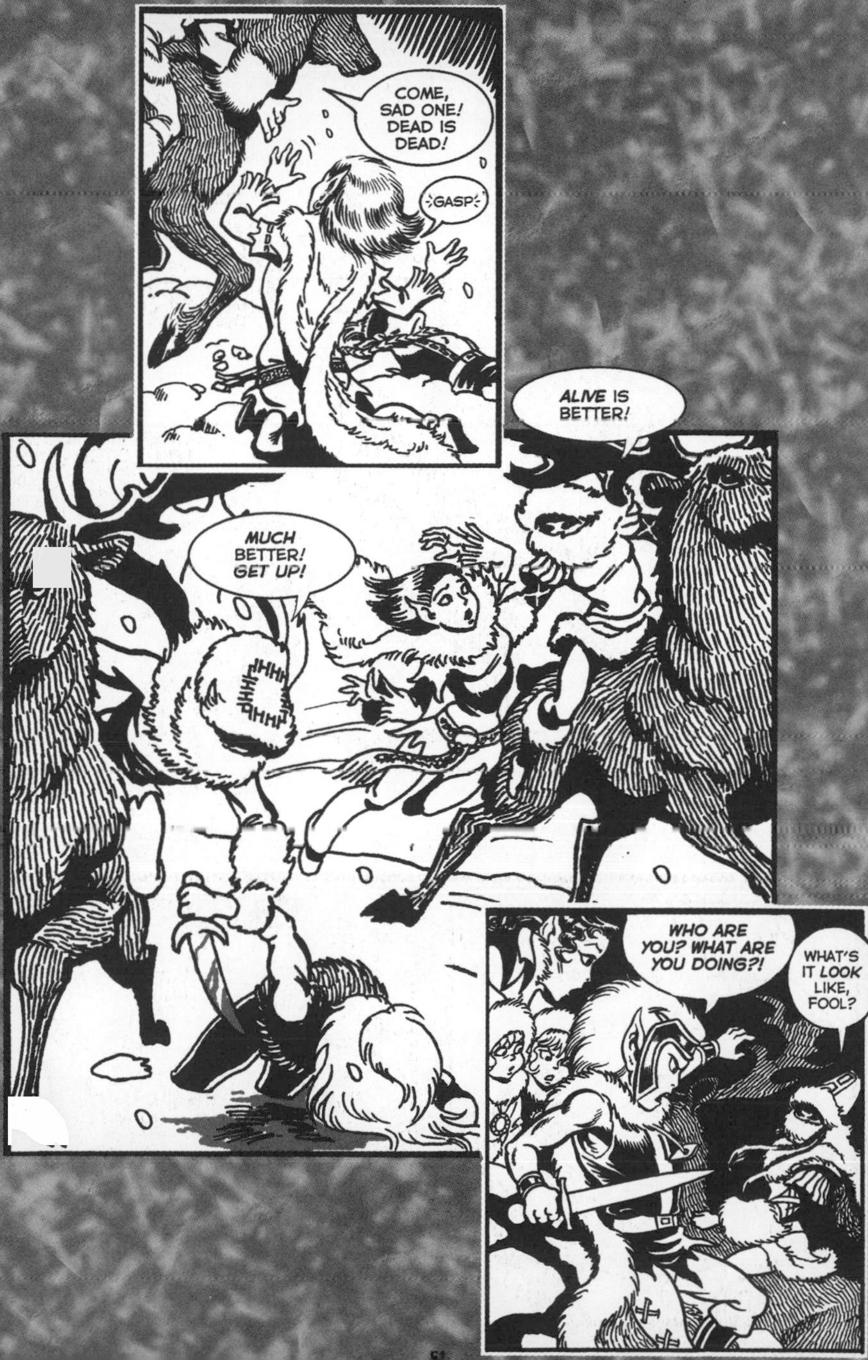
COME, SAD ONE! DEAD IS DEAD!
GASP
ALIVE IS BETTER!
MUCH BETTER! GET UP!
WHO ARE YOU? WHAT ARE YOU DOING?!
WHAT'S IT LOOK LIKE, FOOL?

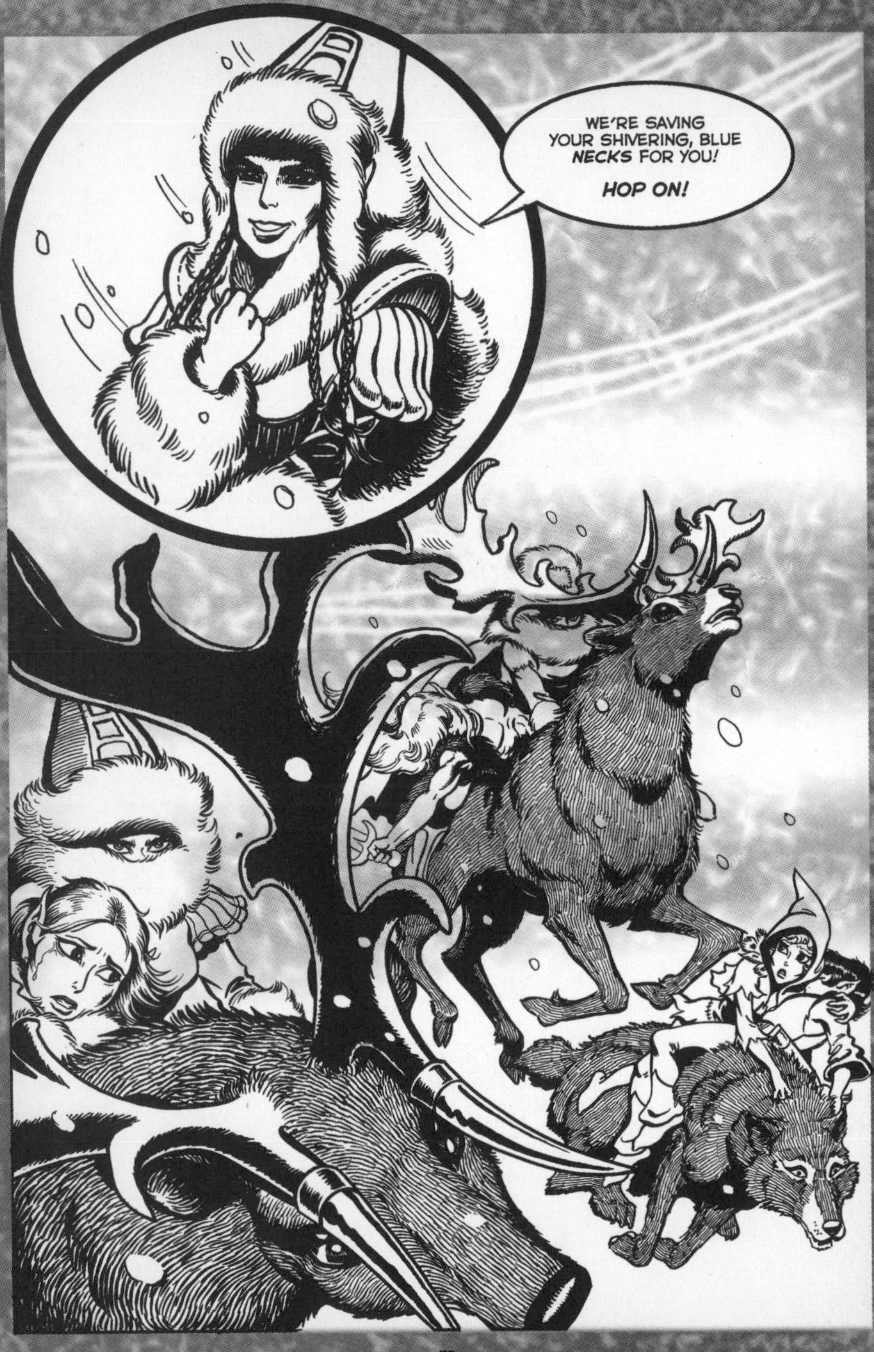
WE'RE SAVING YOUR SHIVERING, BLUE NECKS FOR YOU!
HOP ON!

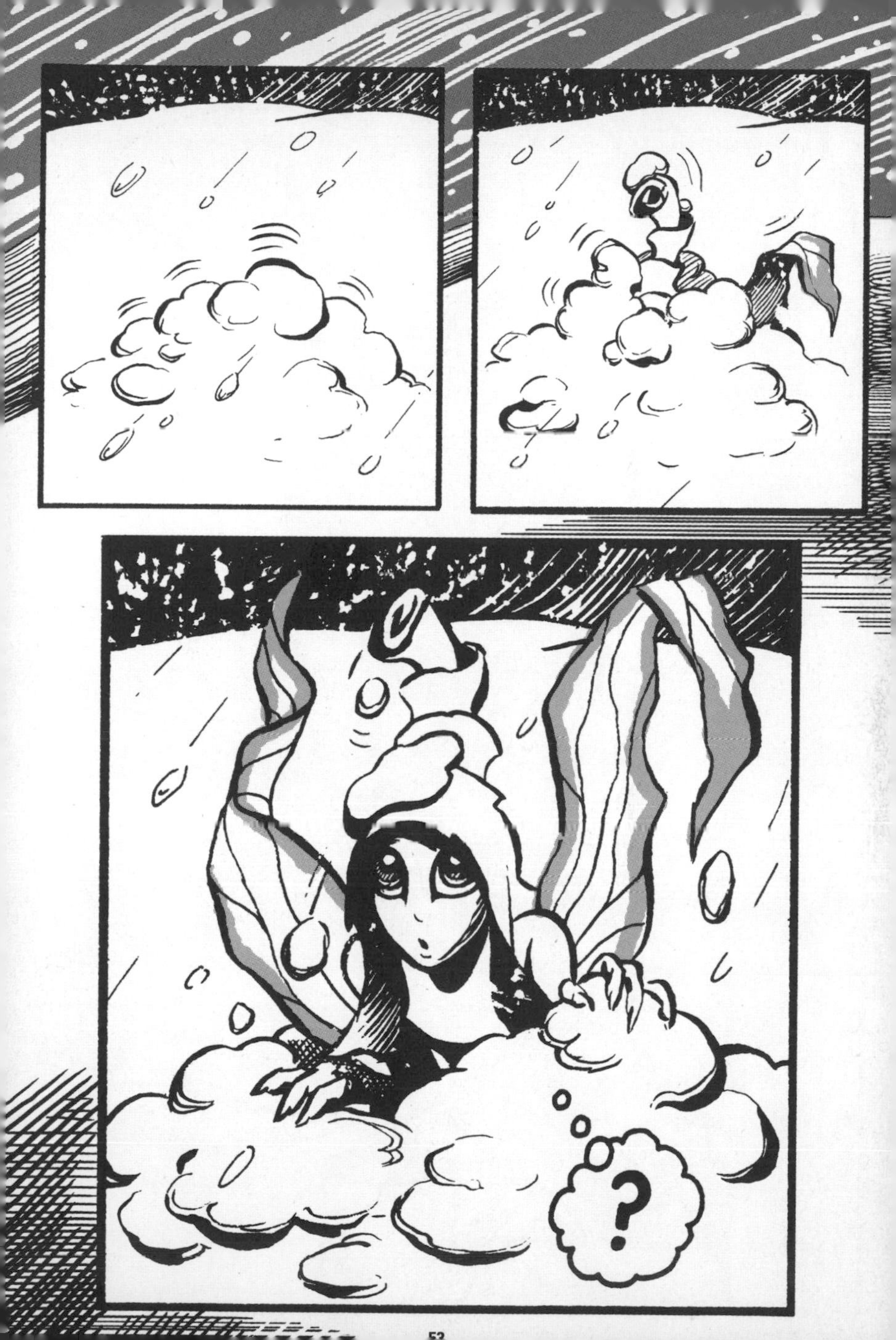
?

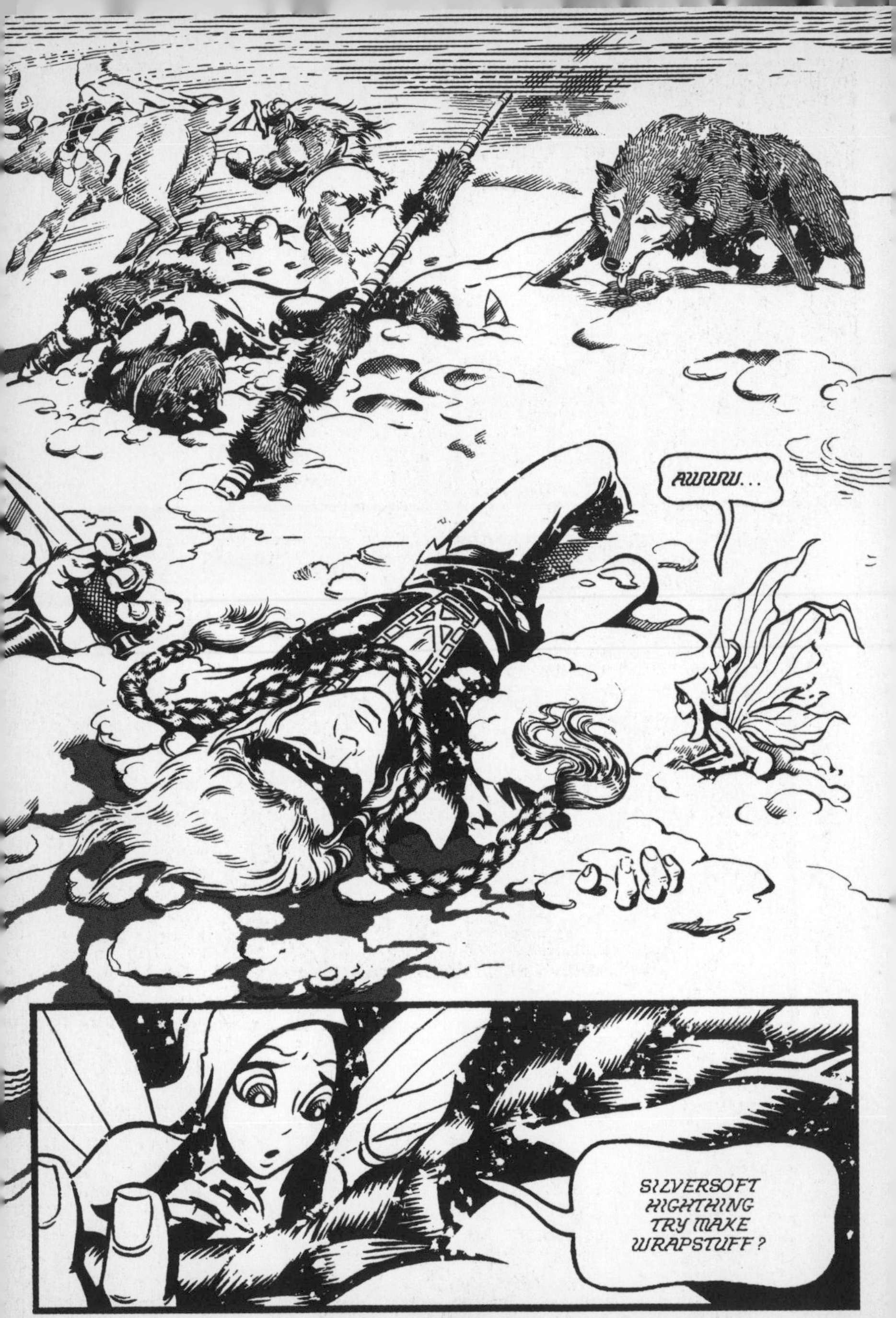
AUUUU...
SILVERSOFT HIGHTHING TRY MAKE WRAPSTUFF?

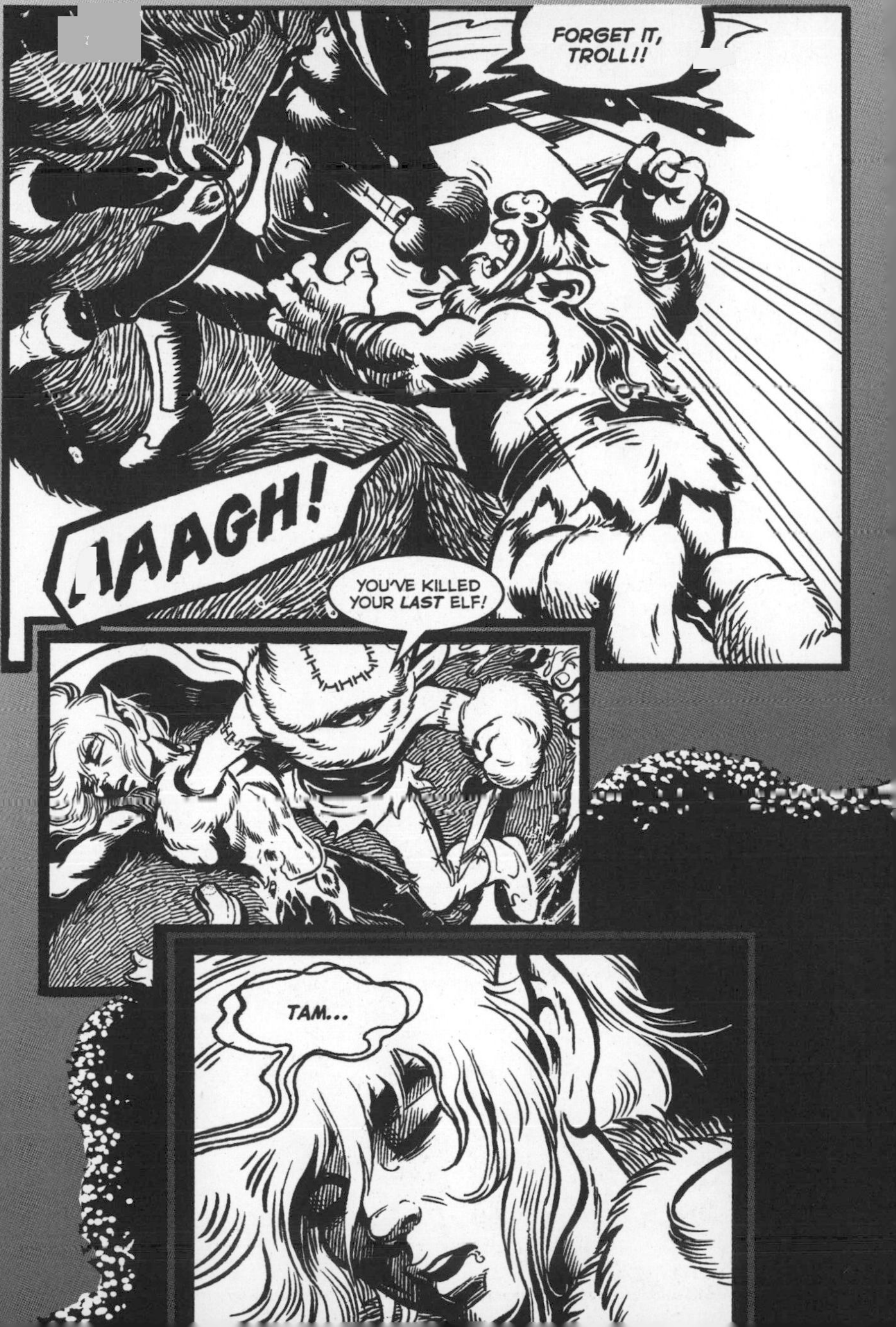
FORGET IT, TROLL!!
AAAGH!
YOU'VE KILLED YOUR LAST ELF!
TAM...

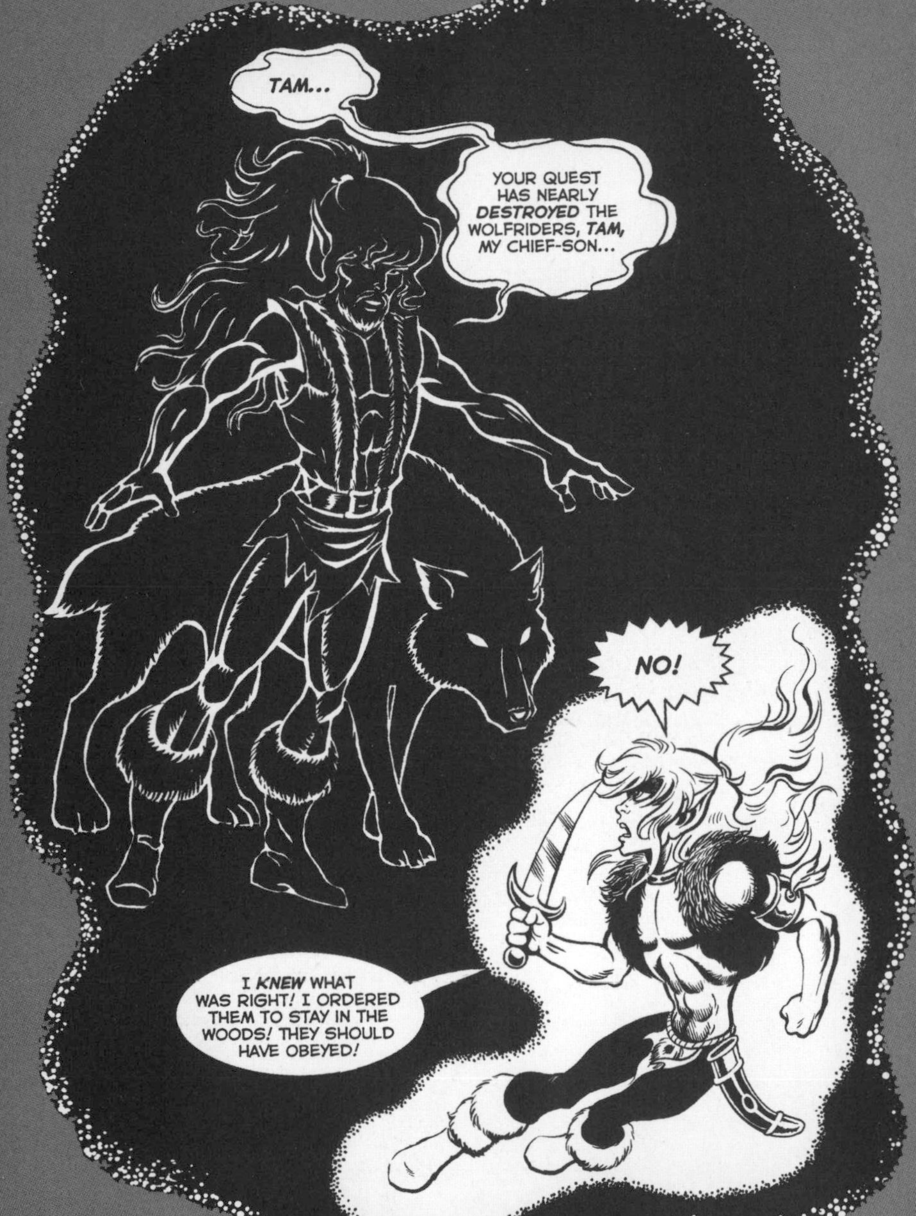
TAM...
YOUR QUEST HAS NEARLY DESTROYED THE WOLFRIDERS, TAM, MY CHIEF-SON...
NO!
I KNEW WHAT WAS RIGHT! I ORDERED THEM TO STAY IN THE WOODS! THEY SHOULD HAVE OBEYED!

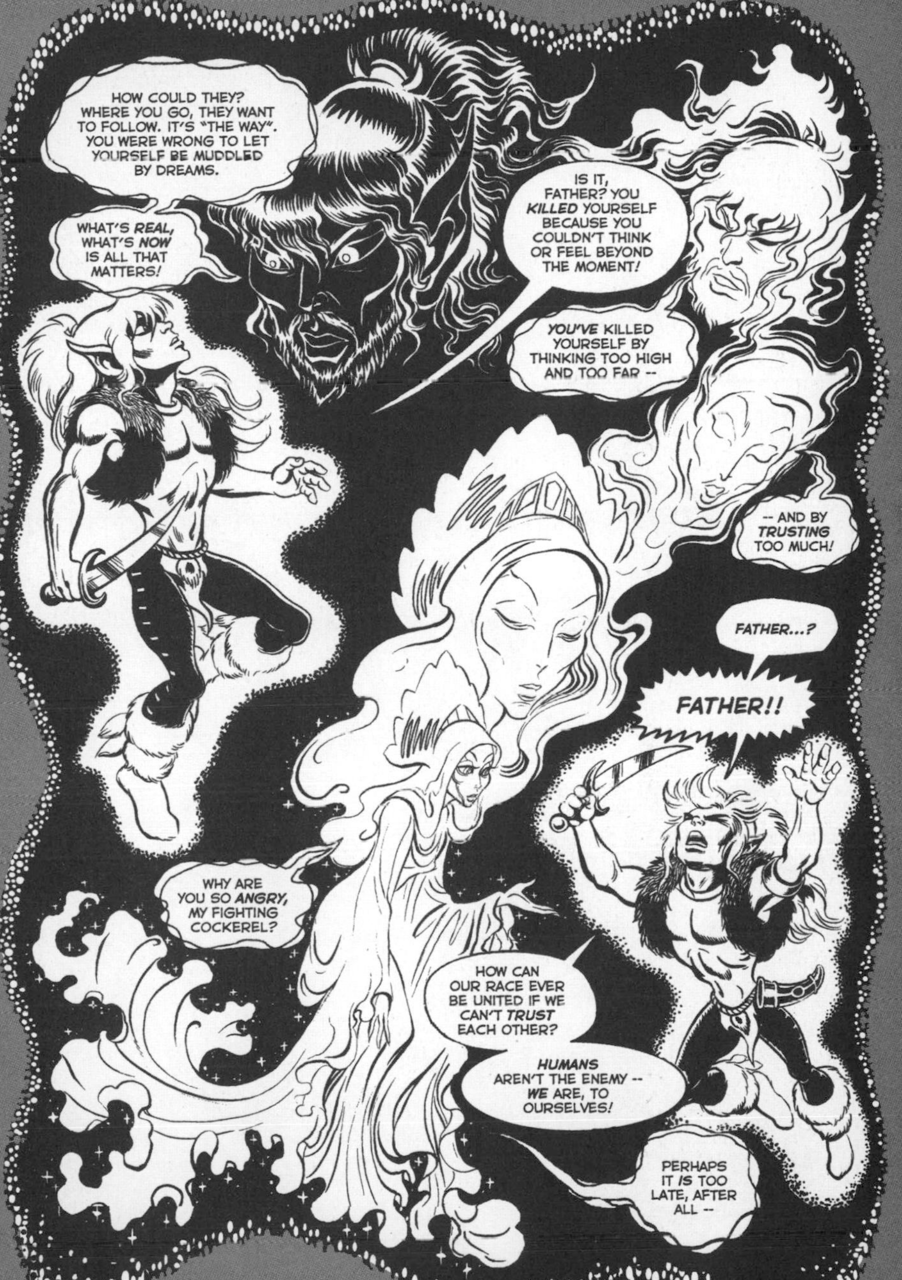
HOW COULD THEY? WHERE YOU GO, THEY WANT TO FOLLOW. IT'S "THE WAY". YOU WERE WRONG TO LET YOURSELF BE MUDDLED BY DREAMS.
WHAT'S *REAL,* WHAT'S *NOW* IS ALL THAT MATTERS!
IS IT, FATHER? YOU *KILLED* YOURSELF BECAUSE YOU COULDN'T THINK OR FEEL BEYOND THE MOMENT!
YOU'VE KILLED YOURSELF BY THINKING TOO HIGH AND TOO FAR --
-- AND BY *TRUSTING* TOO MUCH!
FATHER...?
FATHER!!
WHY ARE YOU SO *ANGRY,* MY FIGHTING COCKEREL?
HOW CAN OUR RACE EVER BE UNITED IF WE *CAN'T TRUST* EACH OTHER?
HUMANS AREN'T THE ENEMY -- *WE* ARE, TO OURSELVES!
PERHAPS IT *IS* TOO LATE, AFTER ALL --

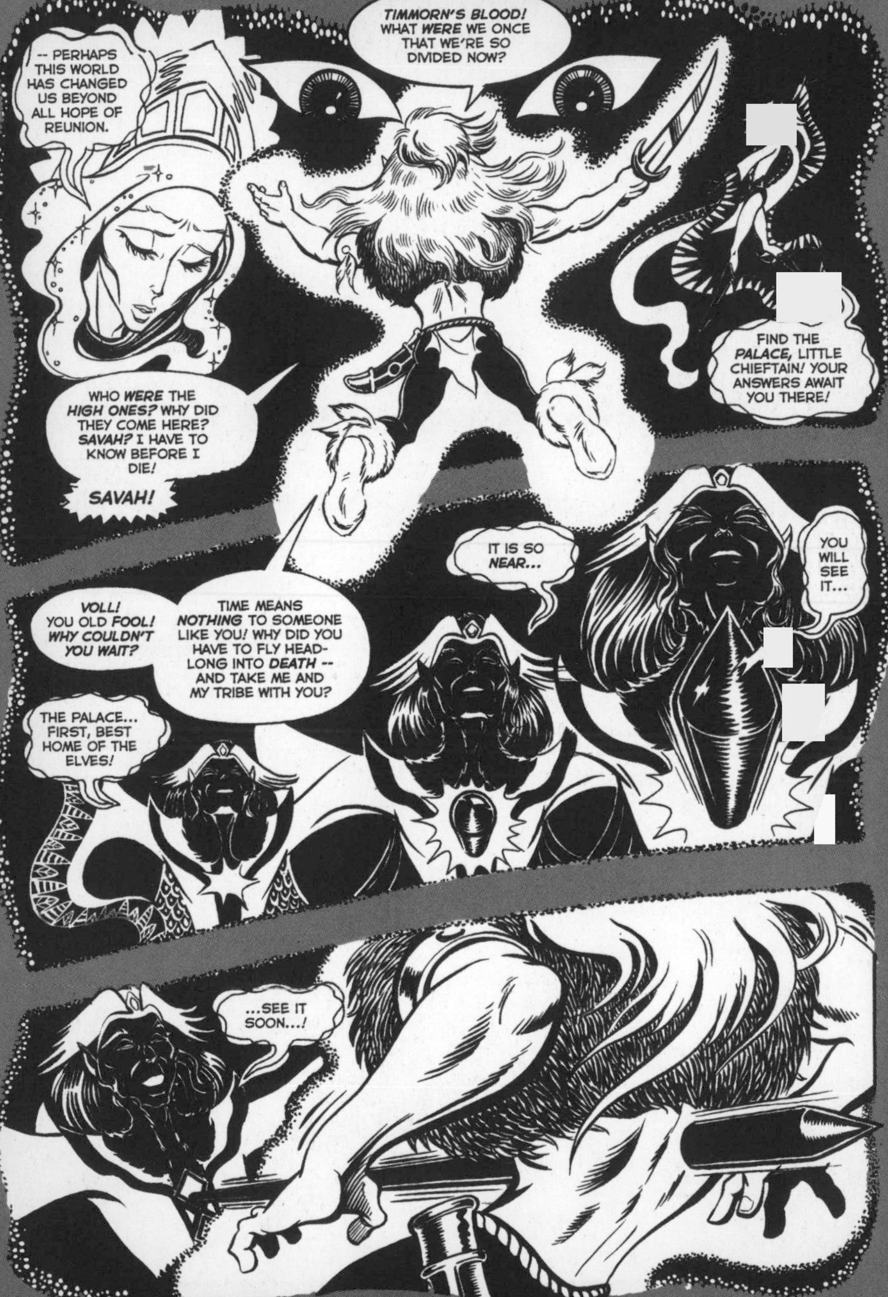
-- PERHAPS THIS WORLD HAS CHANGED US BEYOND ALL HOPE OF REUNION.
TIMMORN'S BLOOD! WHAT WERE WE ONCE THAT WE'RE SO DIVIDED NOW?
WHO WERE THE HIGH ONES? WHY DID THEY COME HERE? SAVAH? I HAVE TO KNOW BEFORE I DIE!
SAVAH!
FIND THE PALACE, LITTLE CHIEFTAIN! YOUR ANSWERS AWAIT YOU THERE!
VOLL! YOU OLD FOOL! WHY COULDN'T YOU WAIT?
TIME MEANS NOTHING TO SOMEONE LIKE YOU! WHY DID YOU HAVE TO FLY HEAD-LONG INTO DEATH -- AND TAKE ME AND MY TRIBE WITH YOU?
THE PALACE... FIRST, BEST HOME OF THE ELVES!
IT IS SO NEAR...
YOU WILL SEE IT...
...SEE IT SOON...!

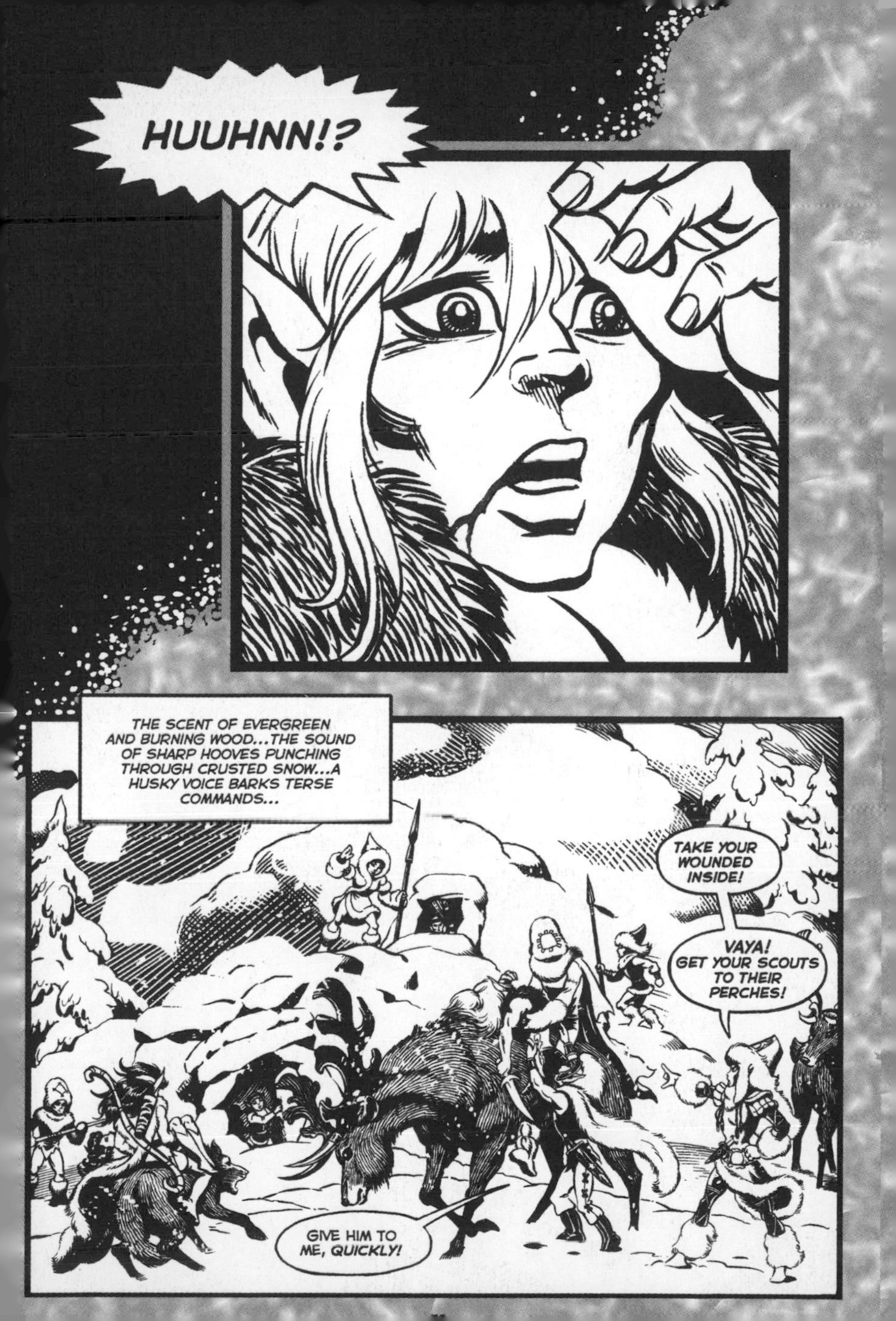
HUUHNN!?
THE SCENT OF EVERGREEN AND BURNING WOOD...THE SOUND OF SHARP HOOVES PUNCHING THROUGH CRUSTED SNOW...A HUSKY VOICE BARKS TERSE COMMANDS...
TAKE YOUR WOUNDED INSIDE!
VAYA! GET YOUR SCOUTS TO THEIR PERCHES!
GIVE HIM TO ME, QUICKLY!

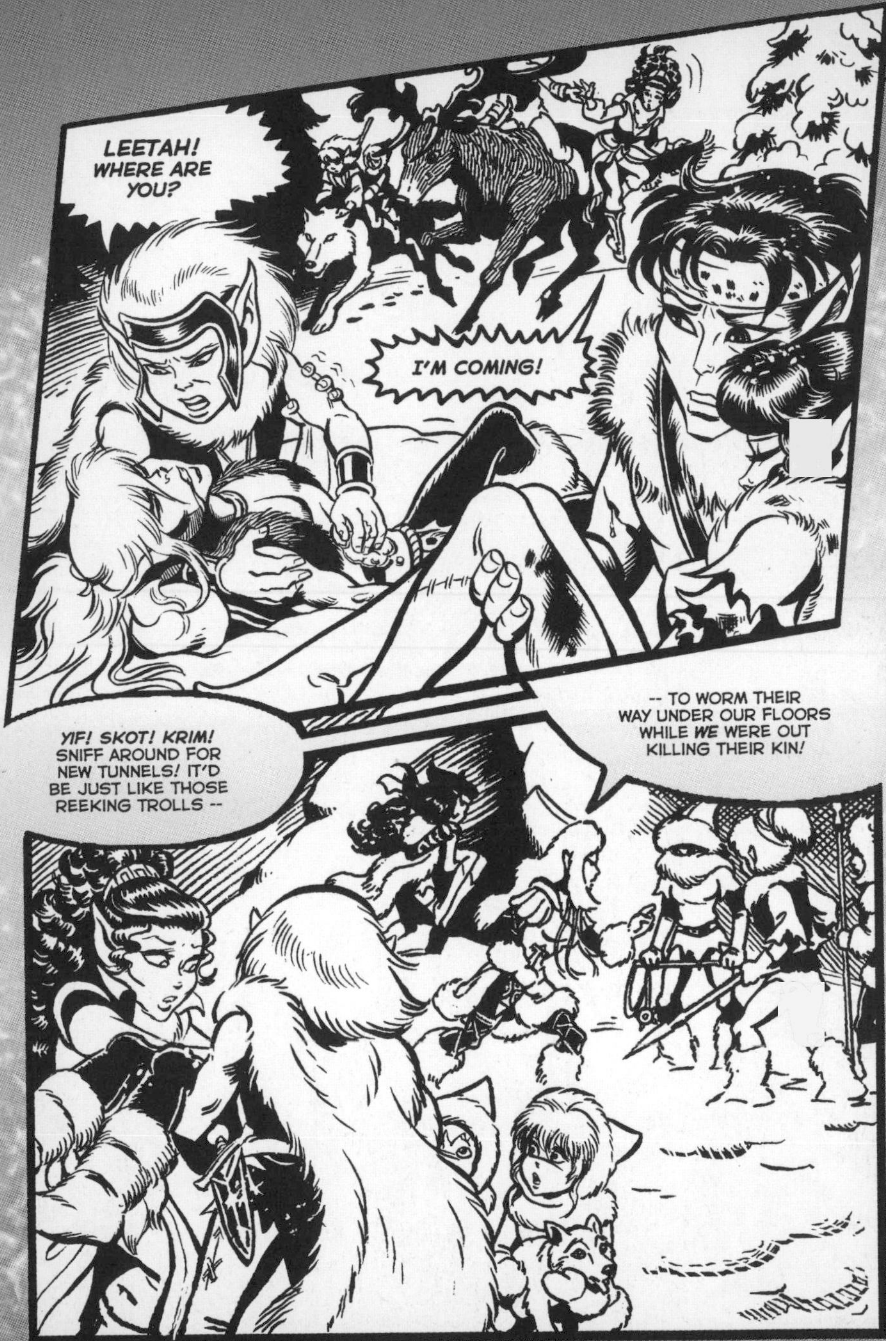
LEETAH! WHERE ARE YOU?
I'M COMING!
YIF! SKOT! KRIM! SNIFF AROUND FOR NEW TUNNELS! IT'D BE JUST LIKE THOSE REEKING TROLLS --
-- TO WORM THEIR WAY UNDER OUR FLOORS WHILE WE WERE OUT KILLING THEIR KIN!

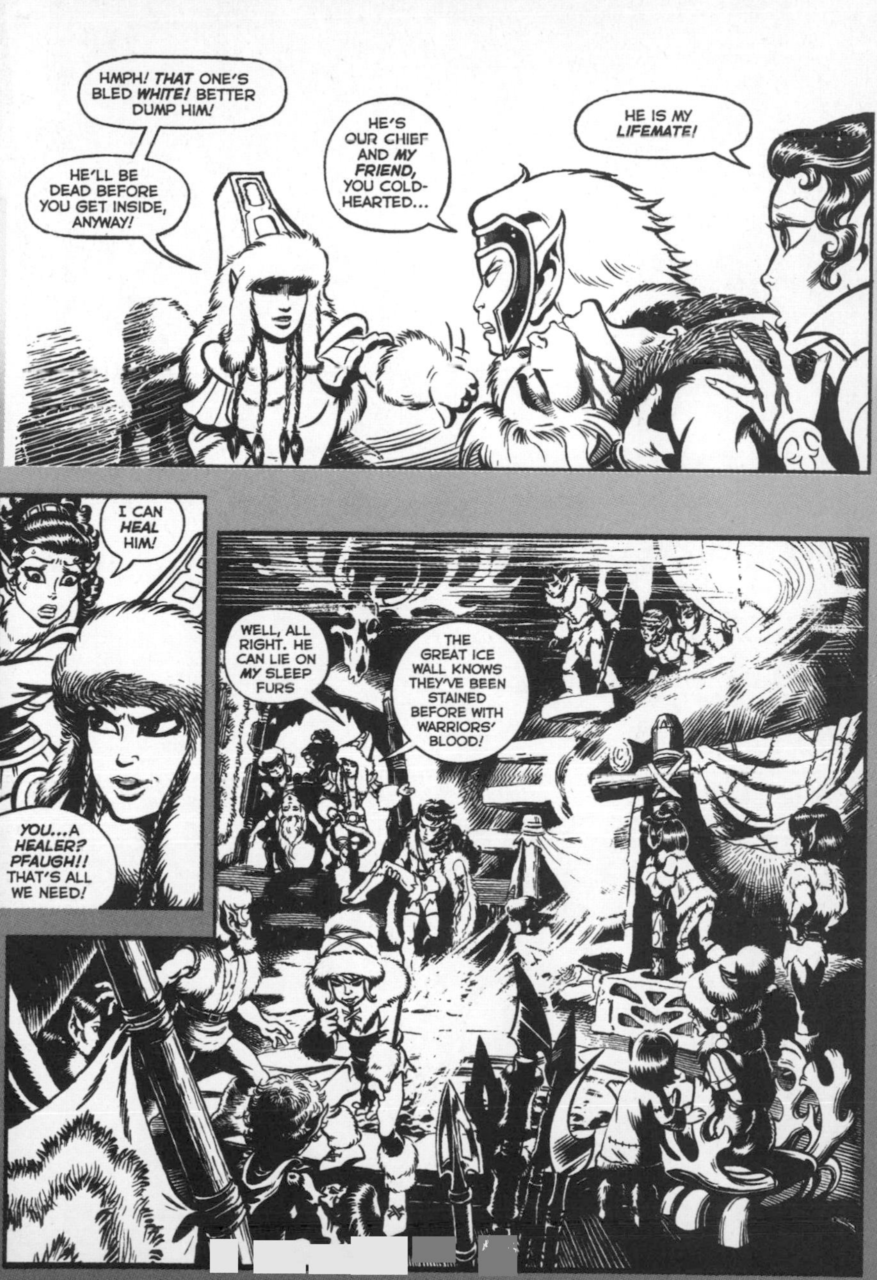
HMPH! THAT ONE'S BLED WHITE! BETTER DUMP HIM!
HE'LL BE DEAD BEFORE YOU GET INSIDE, ANYWAY!
HE'S OUR CHIEF AND MY FRIEND, YOU COLD-HEARTED...
HE IS MY LIFEMATE!
I CAN HEAL HIM!
YOU...A HEALER? PFAUGH!! THAT'S ALL WE NEED!
WELL, ALL RIGHT. HE CAN LIE ON MY SLEEP FURS
THE GREAT ICE WALL KNOWS THEY'VE BEEN STAINED BEFORE WITH WARRIORS' BLOOD!

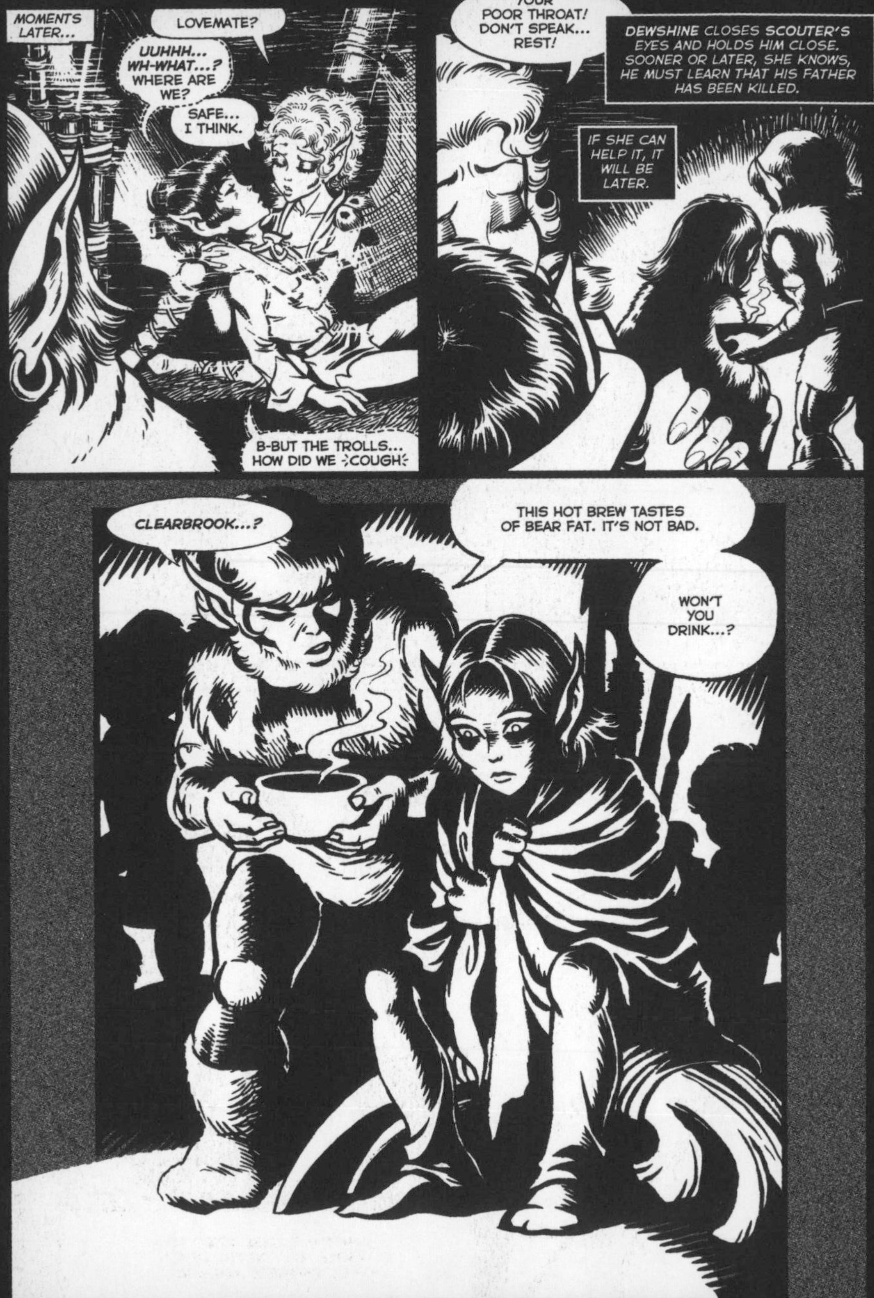
MOMENTS LATER...
LOVEMATE?
UUHHH... WH-WHAT...? WHERE ARE WE?
SAFE... I THINK.
B-BUT THE TROLLS... HOW DID WE ⁝COUGH⁝
YOUR POOR THROAT! DON'T SPEAK... REST!
DEWSHINE CLOSES SCOUTER'S EYES AND HOLDS HIM CLOSE. SOONER OR LATER, SHE KNOWS, HE MUST LEARN THAT HIS FATHER HAS BEEN KILLED.
IF SHE CAN HELP IT, IT WILL BE LATER.
CLEARBROOK...?
THIS HOT BREW TASTES OF BEAR FAT. IT'S NOT BAD.
WON'T YOU DRINK...?

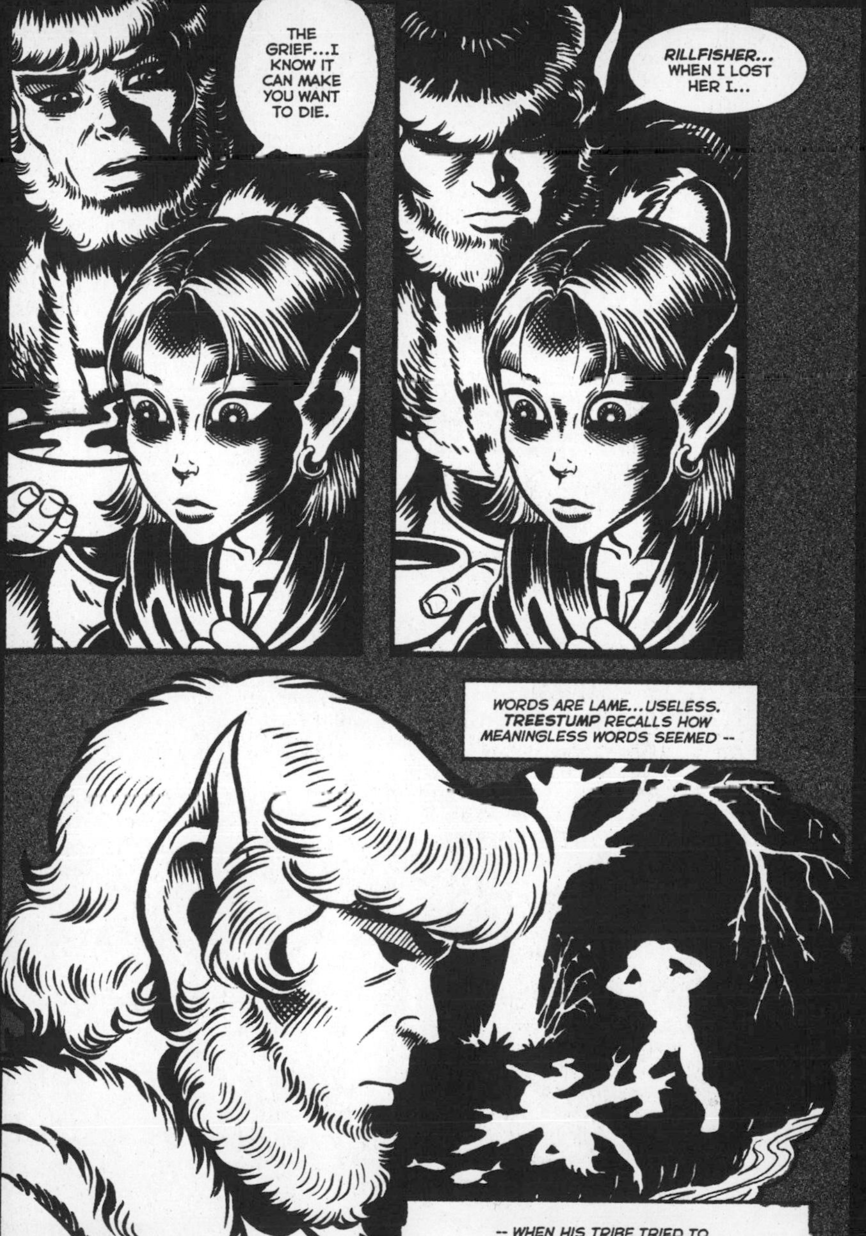
THE GRIEF...I KNOW IT CAN MAKE YOU WANT TO DIE.
RILLFISHER... WHEN I LOST HER I...
WORDS ARE LAME...USELESS. TREESTUMP RECALLS HOW MEANINGLESS WORDS SEEMED --
-- WHEN HIS TRIBE TRIED TO CONSOLE HIM FOR THE DEATH OF DEWSHINE'S MOTHER.

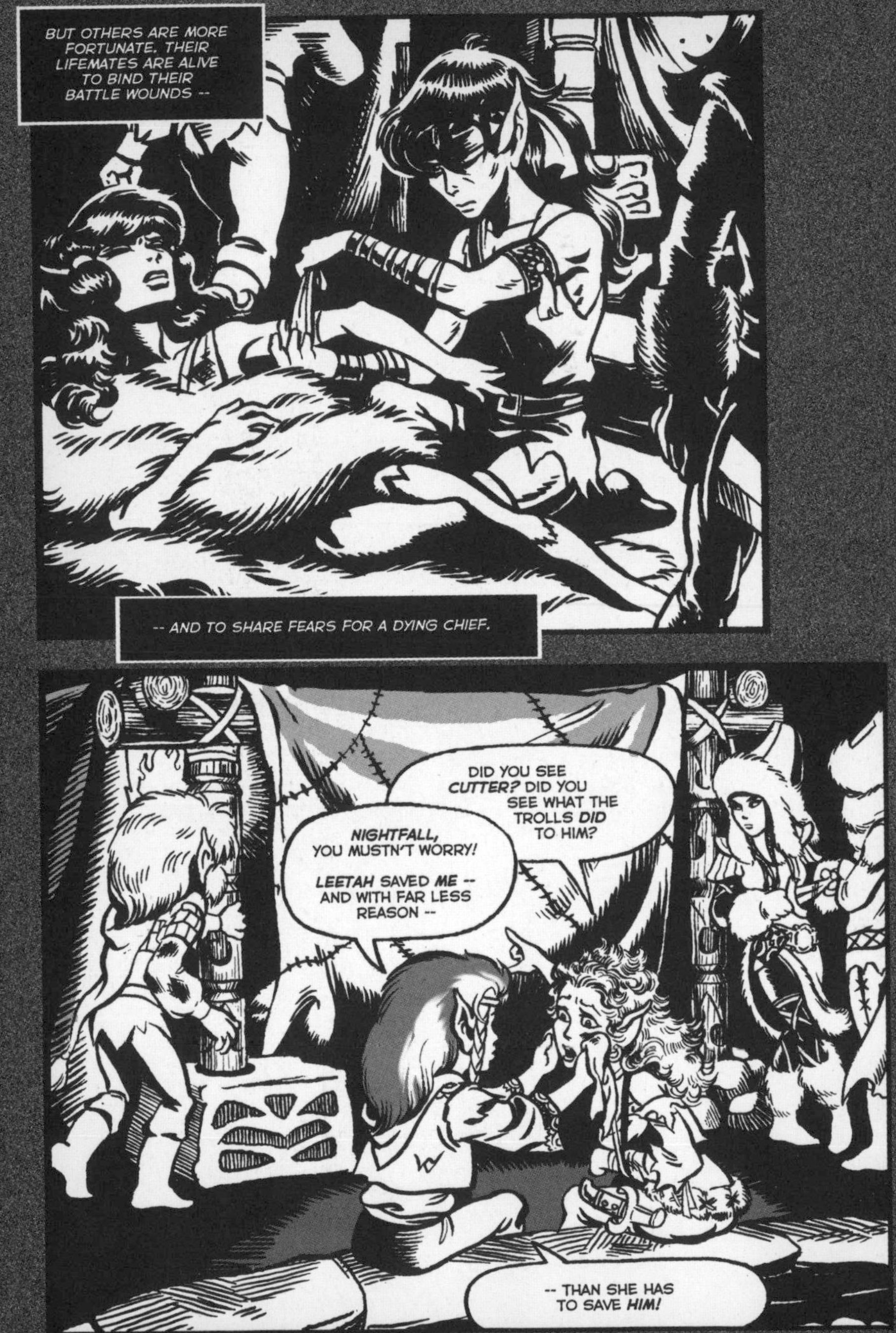
BUT OTHERS ARE MORE FORTUNATE. THEIR LIFEMATES ARE ALIVE TO BIND THEIR BATTLE WOUNDS --
-- AND TO SHARE FEARS FOR A DYING CHIEF.
DID YOU SEE *CUTTER?* DID YOU SEE WHAT THE TROLLS *DID* TO HIM?
NIGHTFALL, YOU MUSTN'T WORRY!
LEETAH SAVED ***ME*** -- AND WITH FAR LESS REASON --
-- THAN SHE HAS TO SAVE ***HIM!***

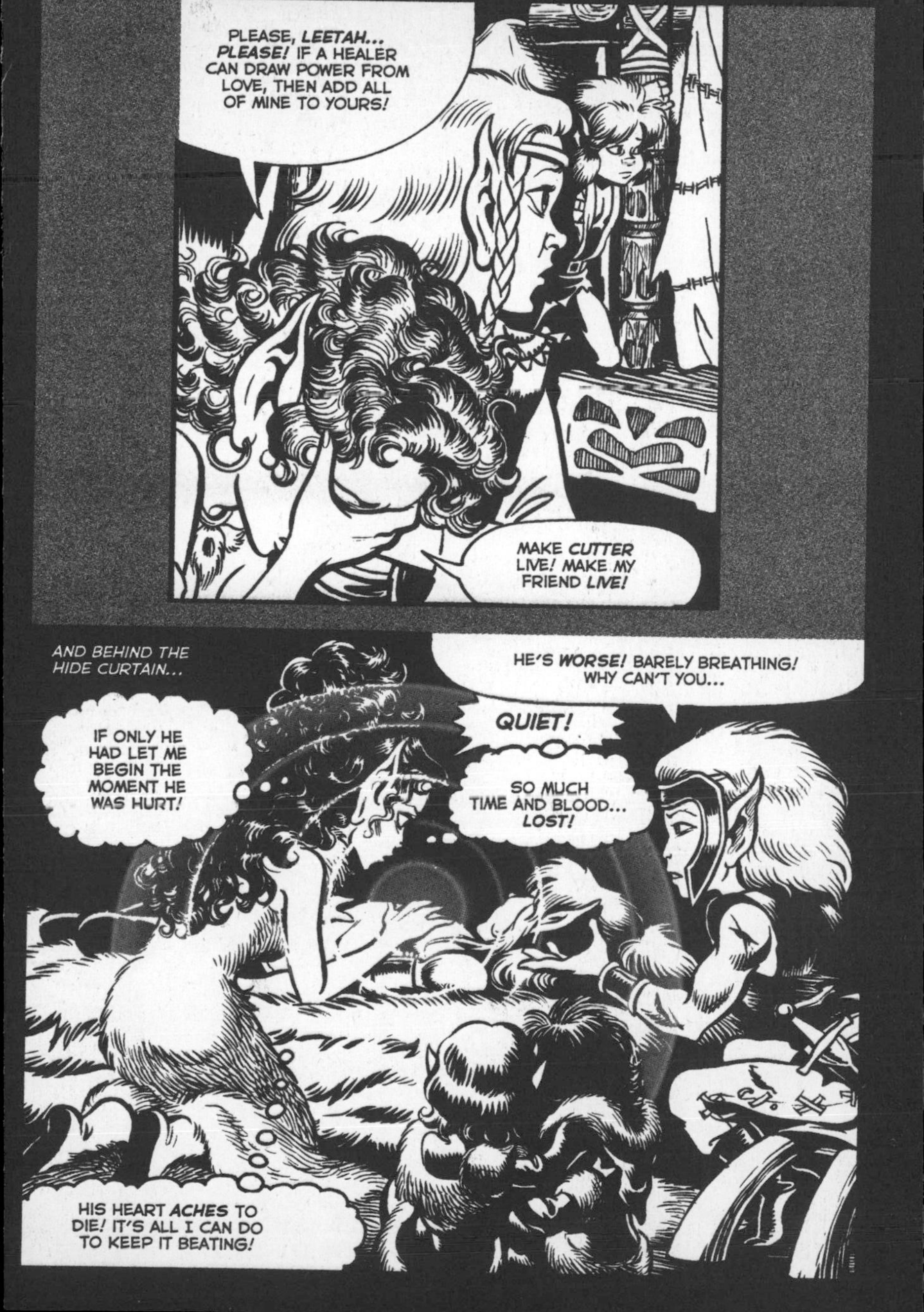
PLEASE, LEETAH... PLEASE! IF A HEALER CAN DRAW POWER FROM LOVE, THEN ADD ALL OF MINE TO YOURS!
MAKE CUTTER LIVE! MAKE MY FRIEND LIVE!
AND BEHIND THE HIDE CURTAIN...
HE'S WORSE! BARELY BREATHING! WHY CAN'T YOU...
QUIET!
IF ONLY HE HAD LET ME BEGIN THE MOMENT HE WAS HURT!
SO MUCH TIME AND BLOOD... LOST!
HIS HEART ACHES TO DIE! IT'S ALL I CAN DO TO KEEP IT BEATING!

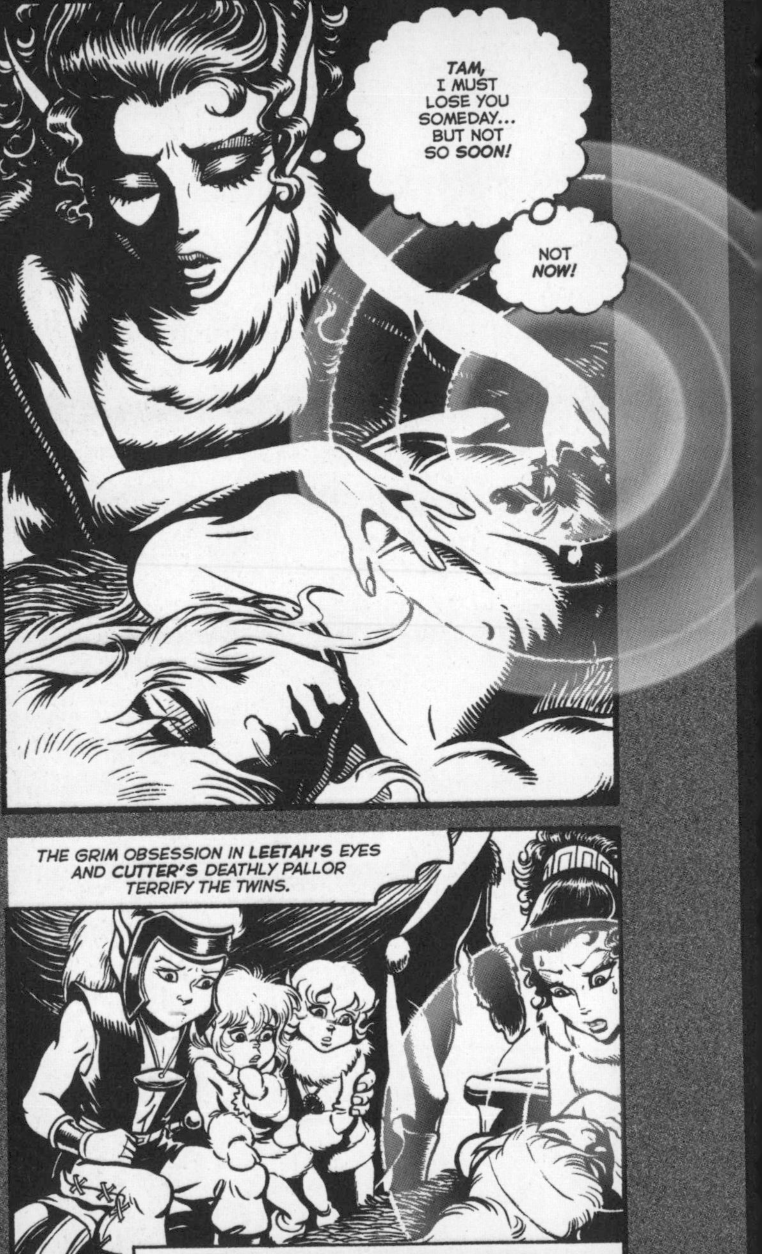
TAM, I MUST LOSE YOU SOMEDAY... BUT NOT SO SOON!
NOT NOW!
THE GRIM OBSESSION IN LEETAH'S EYES AND CUTTER'S DEATHLY PALLOR TERRIFY THE TWINS.
WHICH WILL WIN -- HEALER OR HURT?

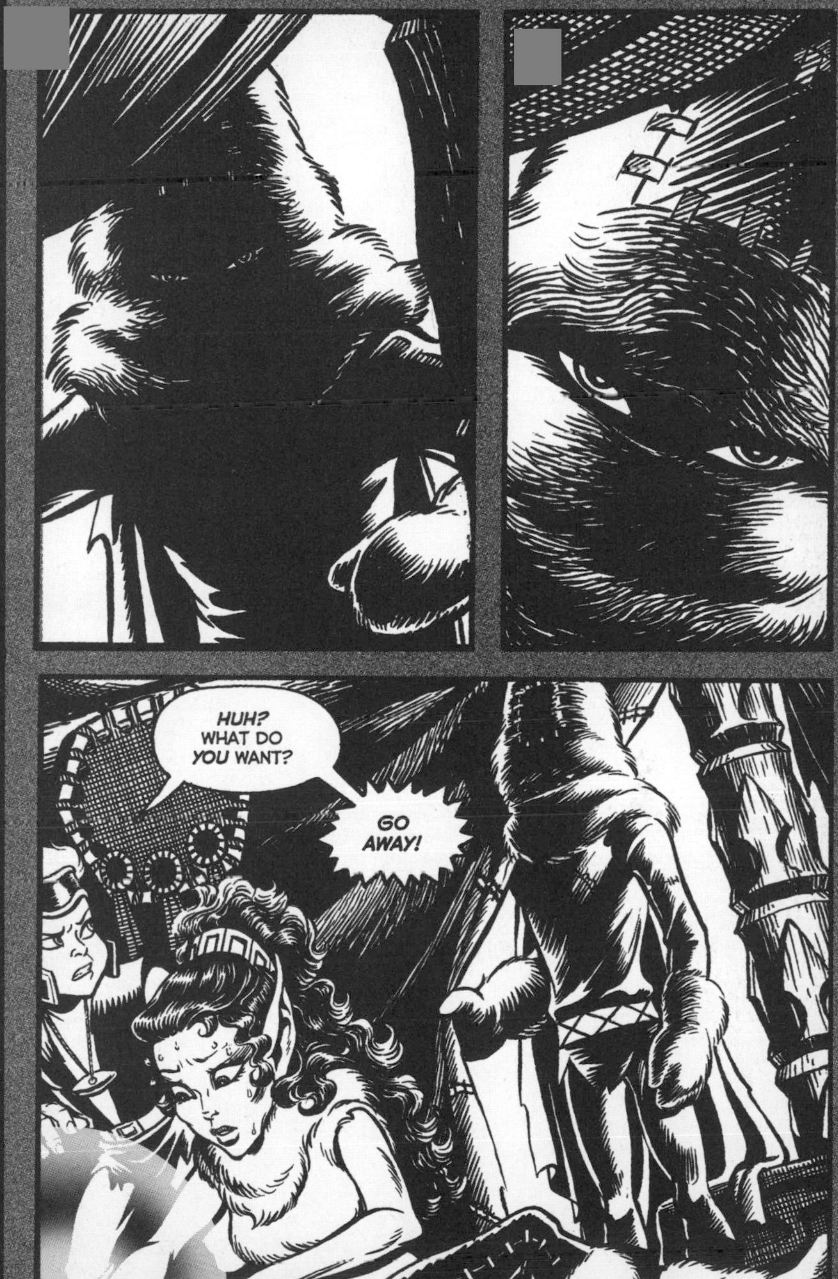
HUH? WHAT DO YOU WANT?
GO AWAY!

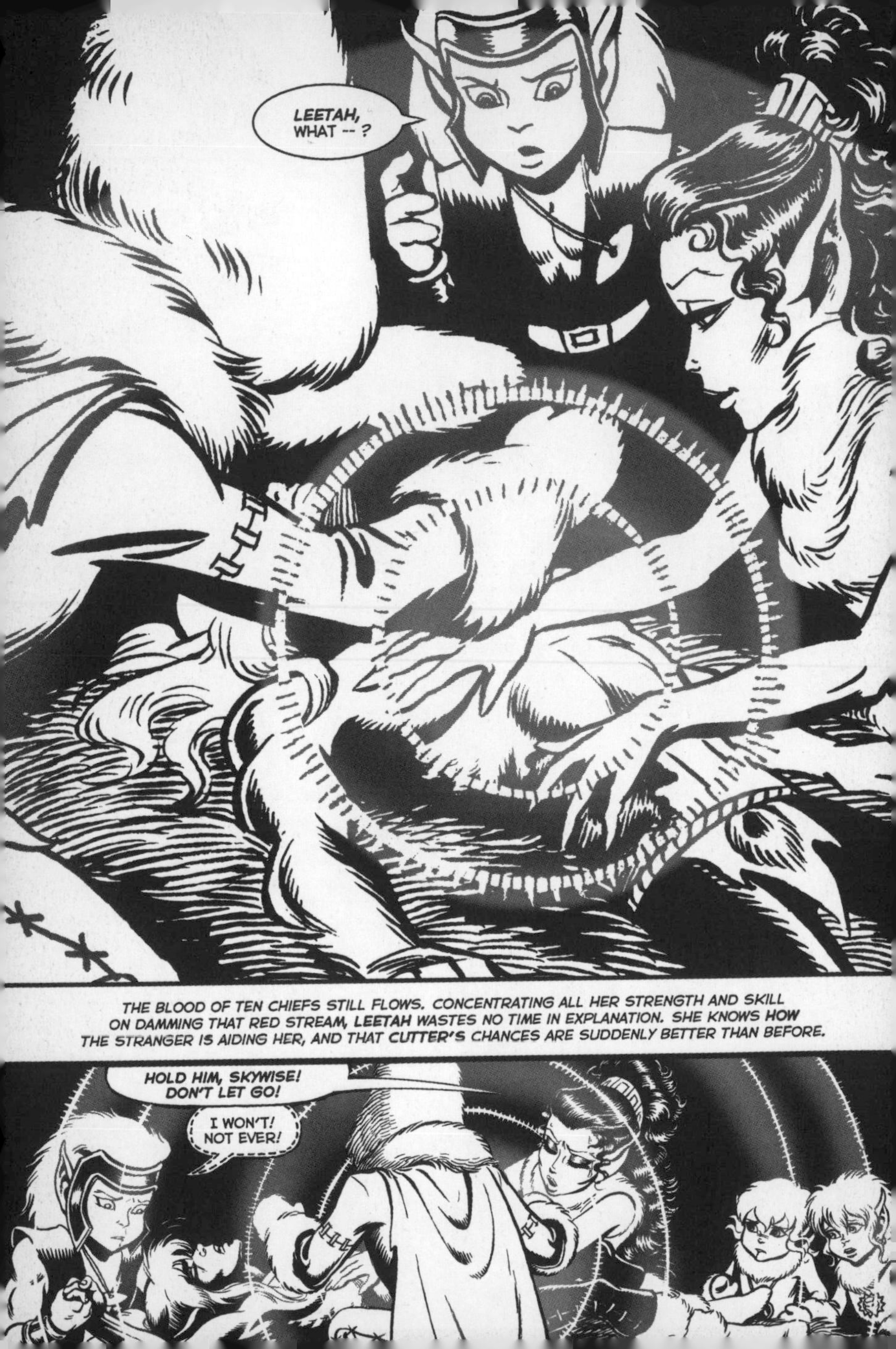
LEETAH, WHAT -- ?
THE BLOOD OF TEN CHIEFS STILL FLOWS. CONCENTRATING ALL HER STRENGTH AND SKILL ON DAMMING THAT RED STREAM, LEETAH WASTES NO TIME IN EXPLANATION. SHE KNOWS HOW THE STRANGER IS AIDING HER, AND THAT CUTTER'S CHANCES ARE SUDDENLY BETTER THAN BEFORE.
HOLD HIM, SKYWISE! DON'T LET GO!
I WON'T! NOT EVER!

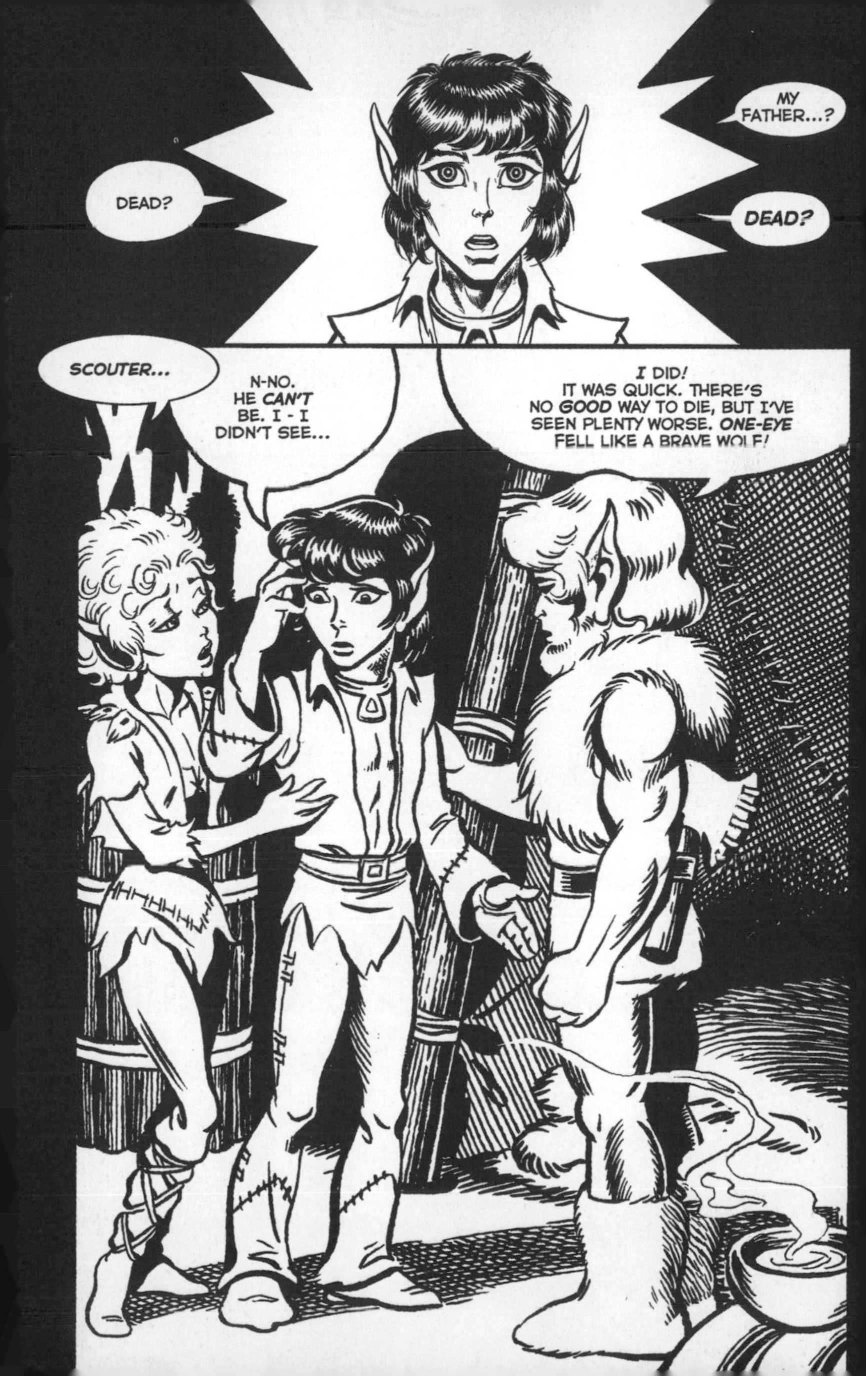
DEAD?
MY FATHER...?
DEAD?
SCOUTER...
N-NO. HE CAN'T BE. I - I DIDN'T SEE...
I DID! IT WAS QUICK. THERE'S NO GOOD WAY TO DIE, BUT I'VE SEEN PLENTY WORSE. ONE-EYE FELL LIKE A BRAVE WOLF!

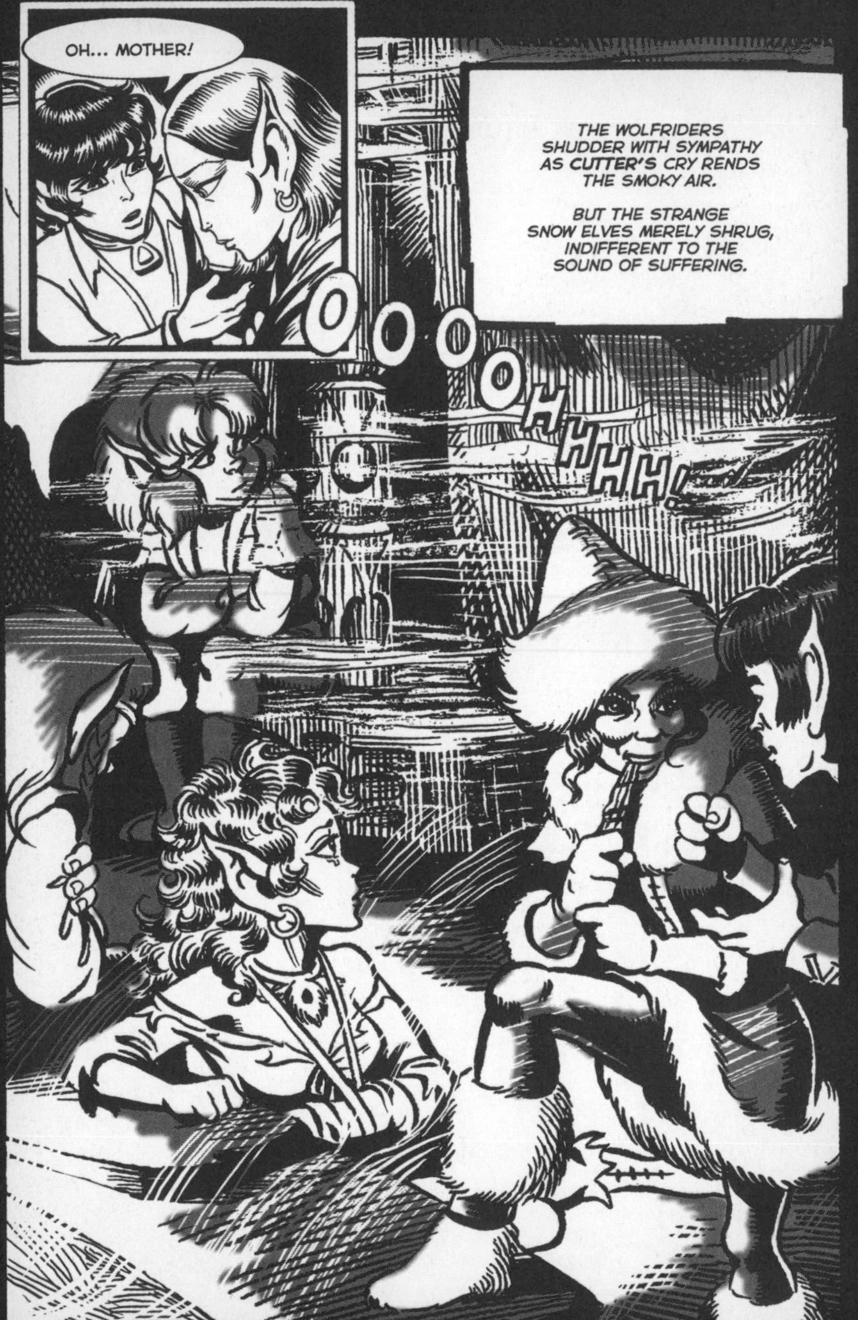
OH... MOTHER!
THE WOLFRIDERS SHUDDER WITH SYMPATHY AS CUTTER'S CRY RENDS THE SMOKY AIR.
BUT THE STRANGE SNOW ELVES MERELY SHRUG, INDIFFERENT TO THE SOUND OF SUFFERING.
OOOOOHHHHH!

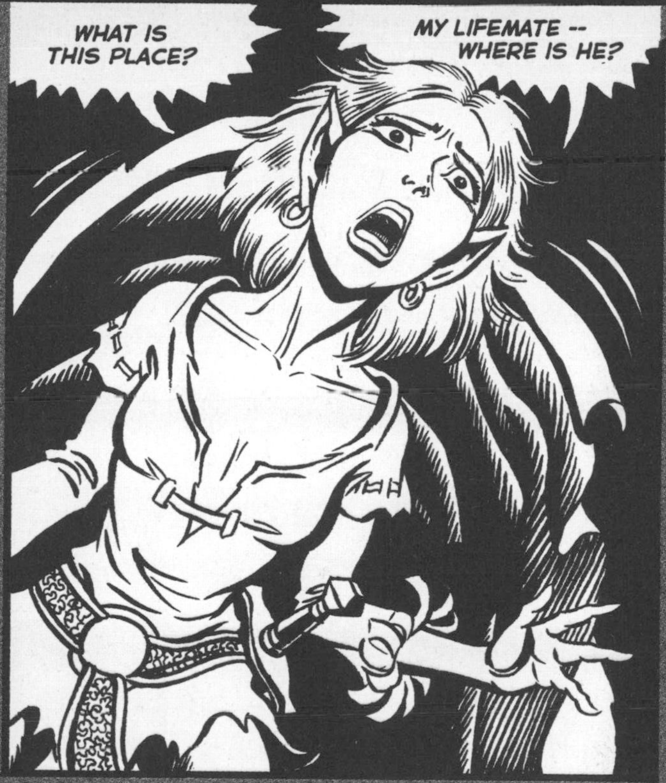
WHAT IS THIS PLACE?
MY LIFEMATE -- WHERE IS HE?

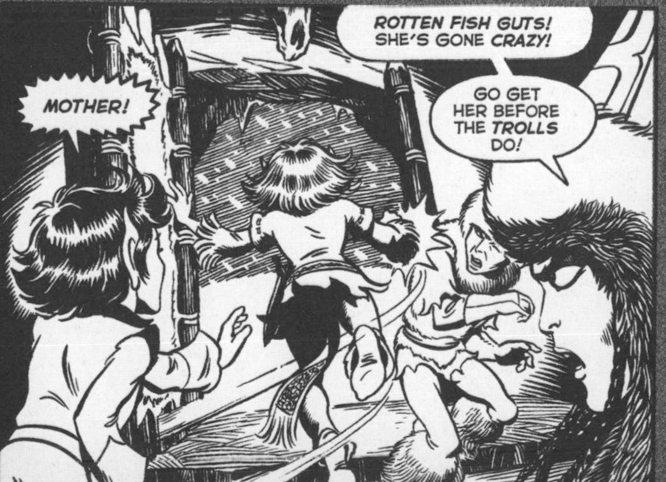
MOTHER!
ROTTEN FISH GUTS! SHE'S GONE CRAZY!
GO GET HER BEFORE THE TROLLS DO!

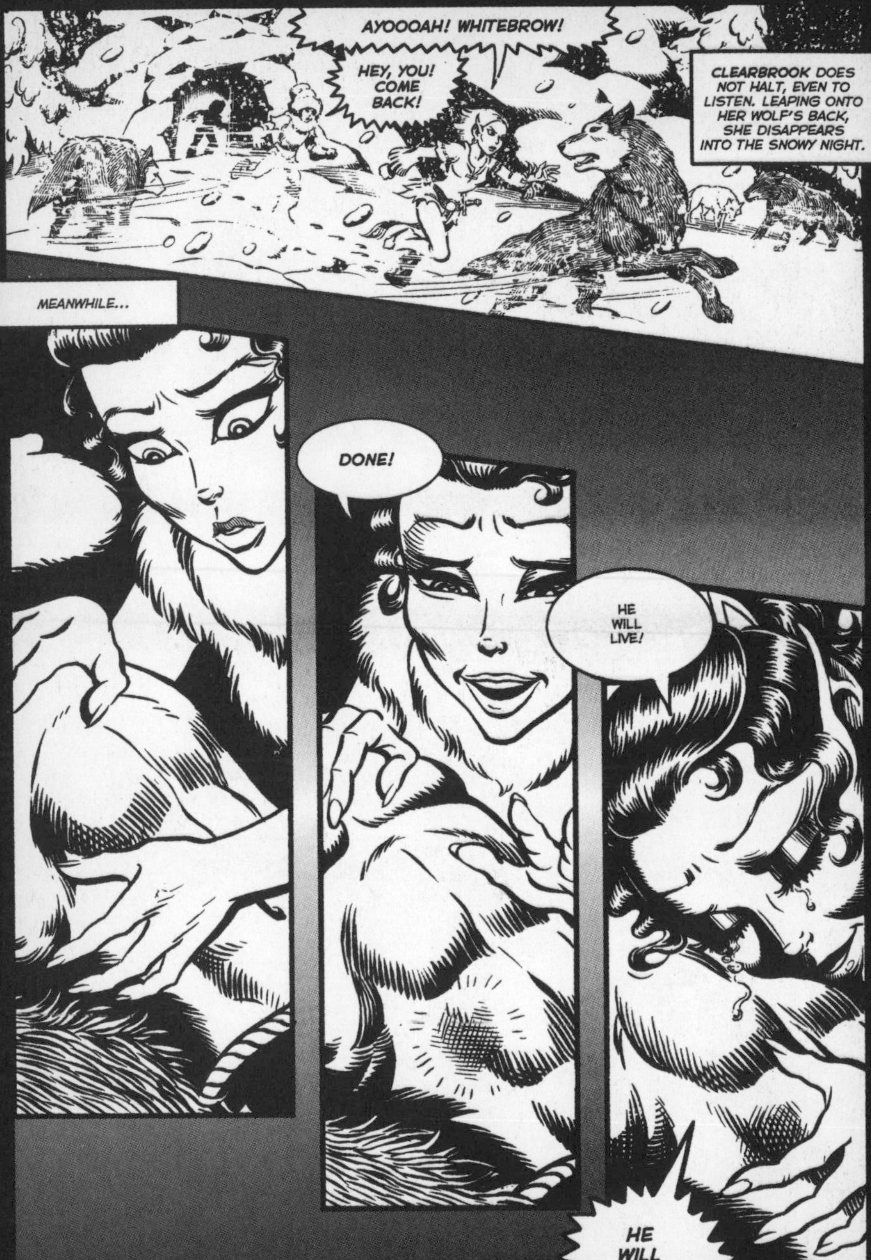
AYOOOAH! WHITEBROW!
HEY, YOU! COME BACK!
CLEARBROOK DOES NOT HALT, EVEN TO LISTEN. LEAPING ONTO HER WOLF'S BACK, SHE DISAPPEARS INTO THE SNOWY NIGHT.
MEANWHILE...
DONE!
HE WILL LIVE!
HE WILL LIVE!

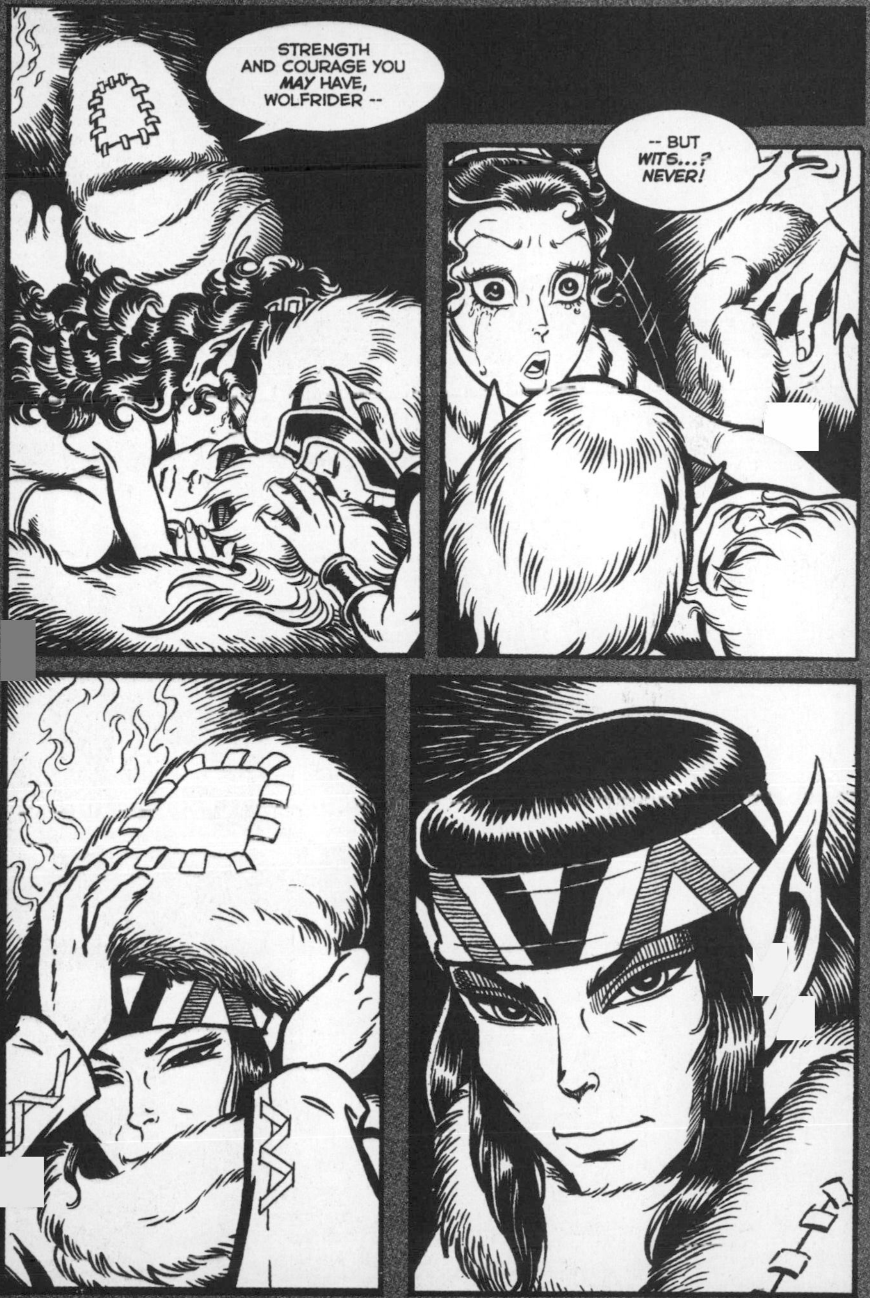
STRENGTH AND COURAGE YOU MAY HAVE, WOLFRIDER --
-- BUT WITS...? NEVER!

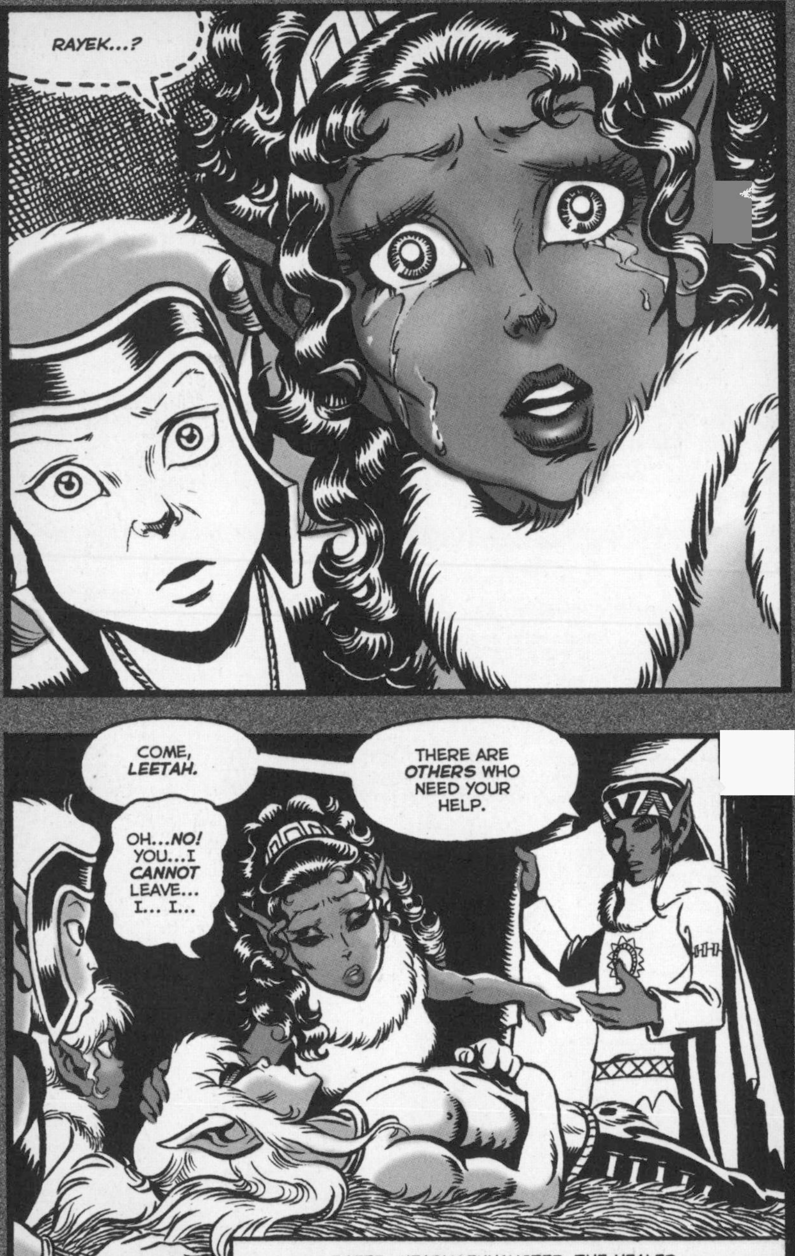
RAYEK...?
COME, LEETAH.
THERE ARE OTHERS WHO NEED YOUR HELP.
OH...NO! YOU...I CANNOT LEAVE... I... I...
DAZED. NEARLY EXHAUSTED, THE HEALER HESITATES ONE MOMENT MORE...

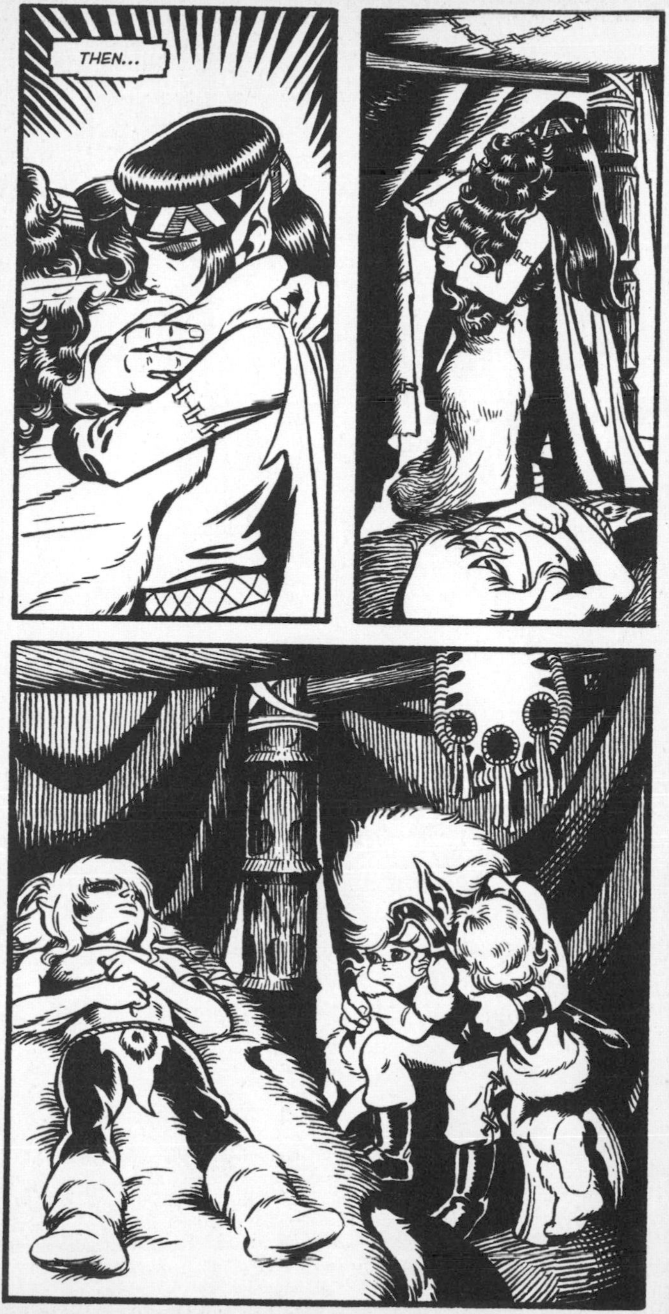
THEN...

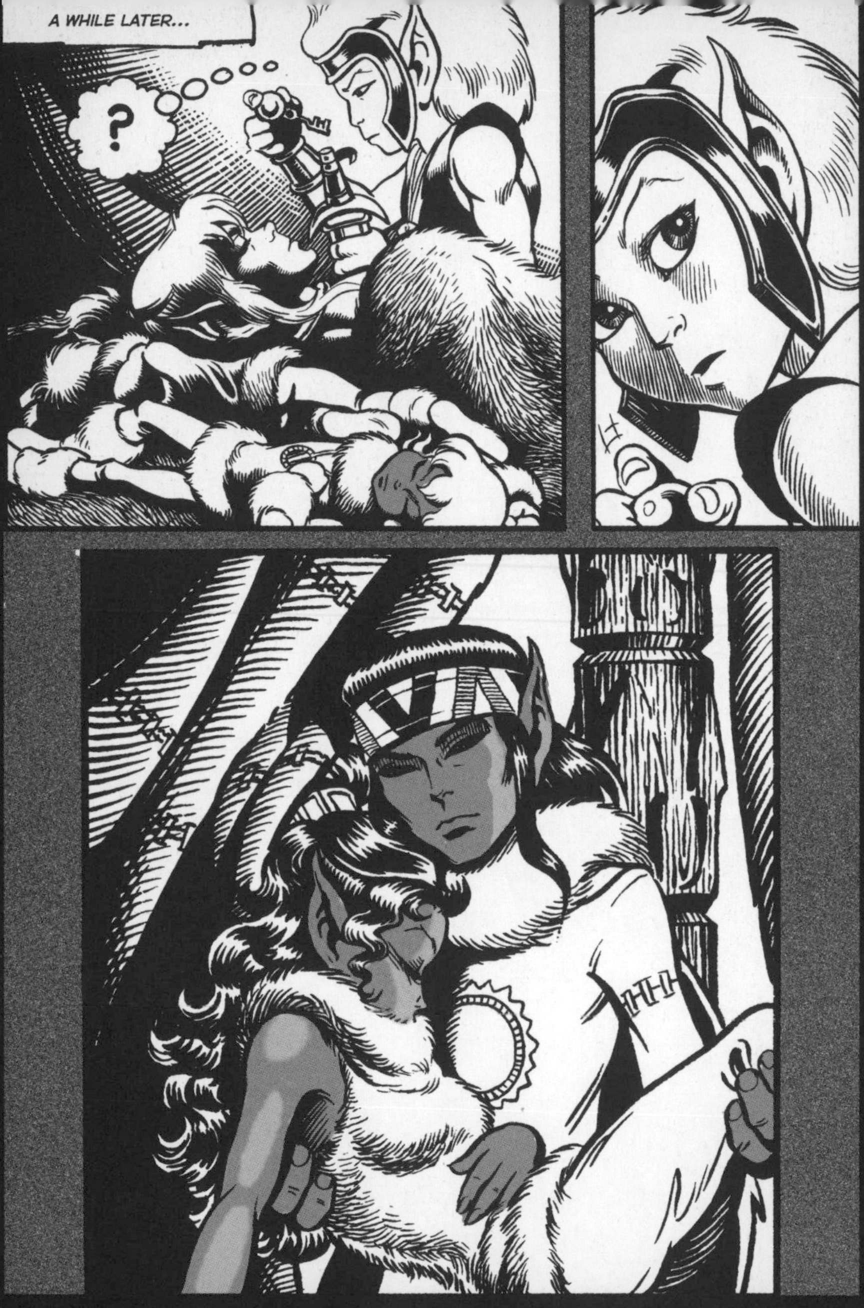
A WHILE LATER...
?

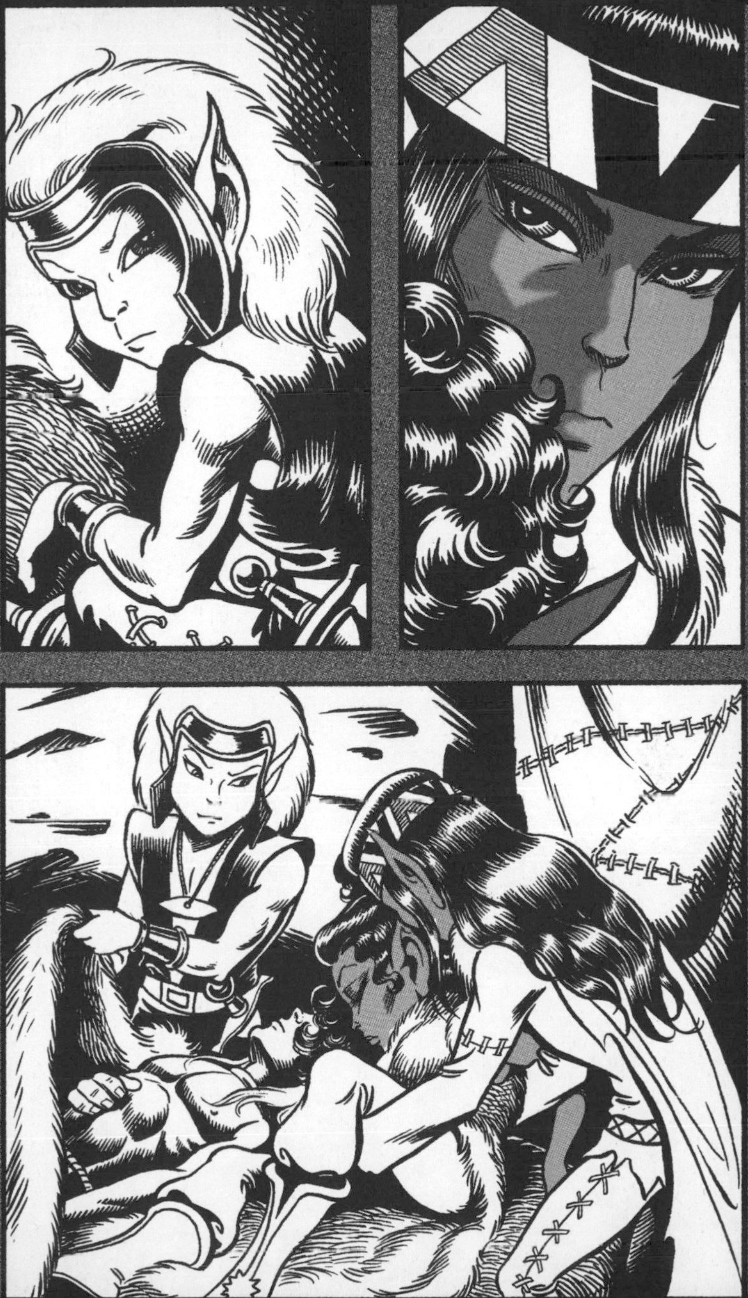

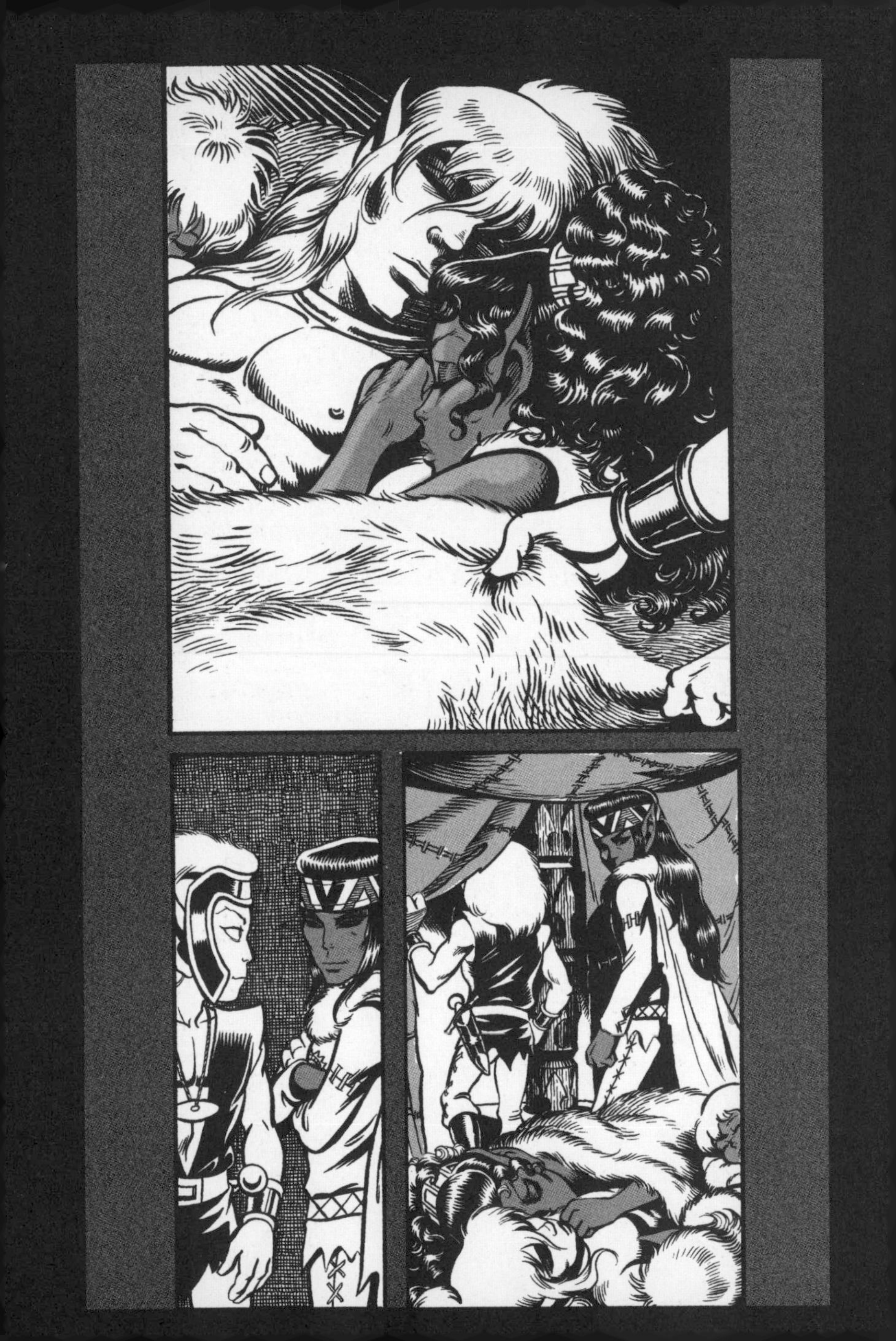

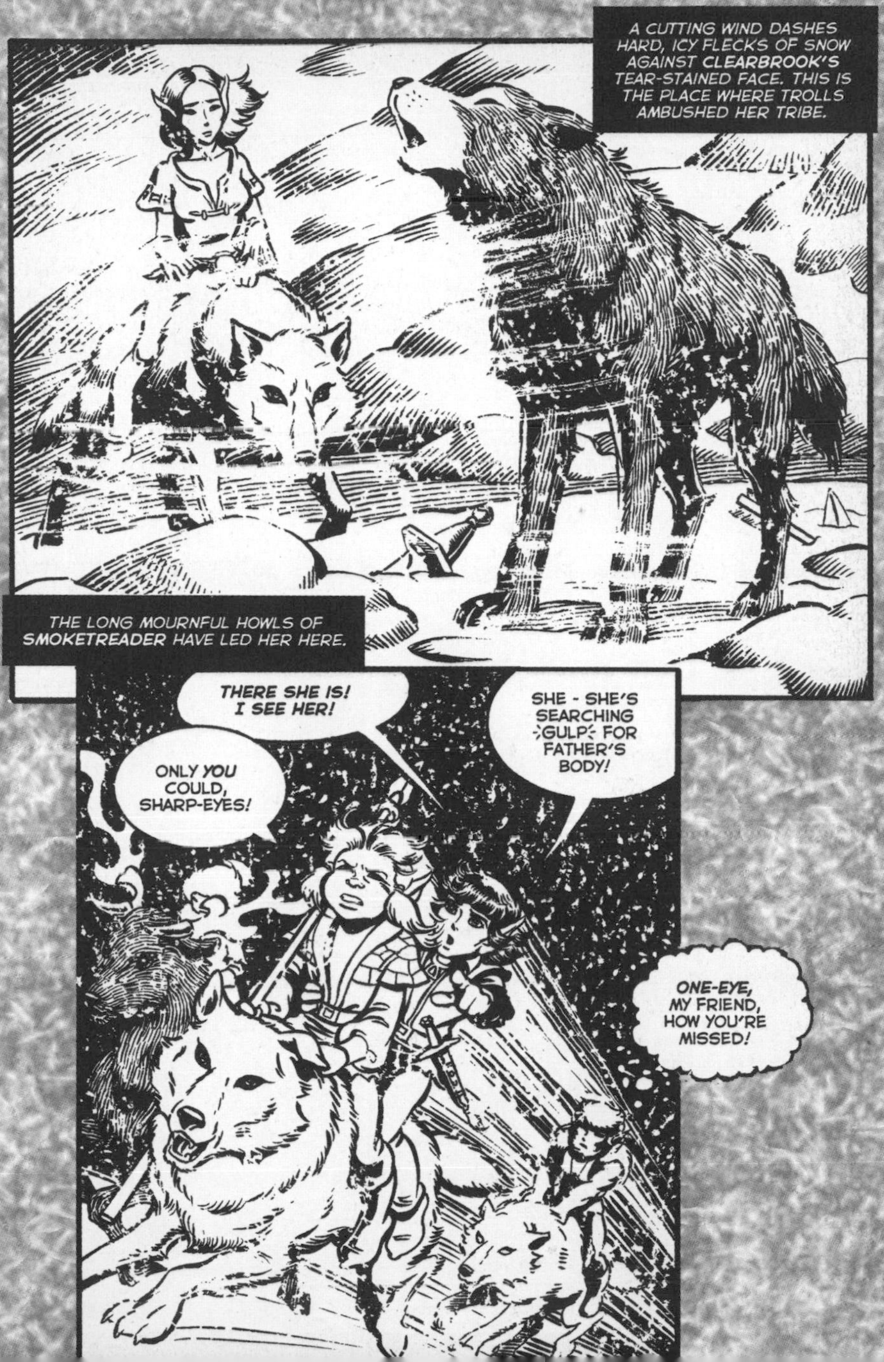
A CUTTING WIND DASHES HARD, ICY FLECKS OF SNOW AGAINST CLEARBROOK'S TEAR-STAINED FACE. THIS IS THE PLACE WHERE TROLLS AMBUSHED HER TRIBE.
THE LONG MOURNFUL HOWLS OF SMOKETREADER HAVE LED HER HERE.
THERE SHE IS! I SEE HER!
ONLY YOU COULD, SHARP-EYES!
SHE - SHE'S SEARCHING -GULP- FOR FATHER'S BODY!
ONE-EYE, MY FRIEND, HOW YOU'RE MISSED!

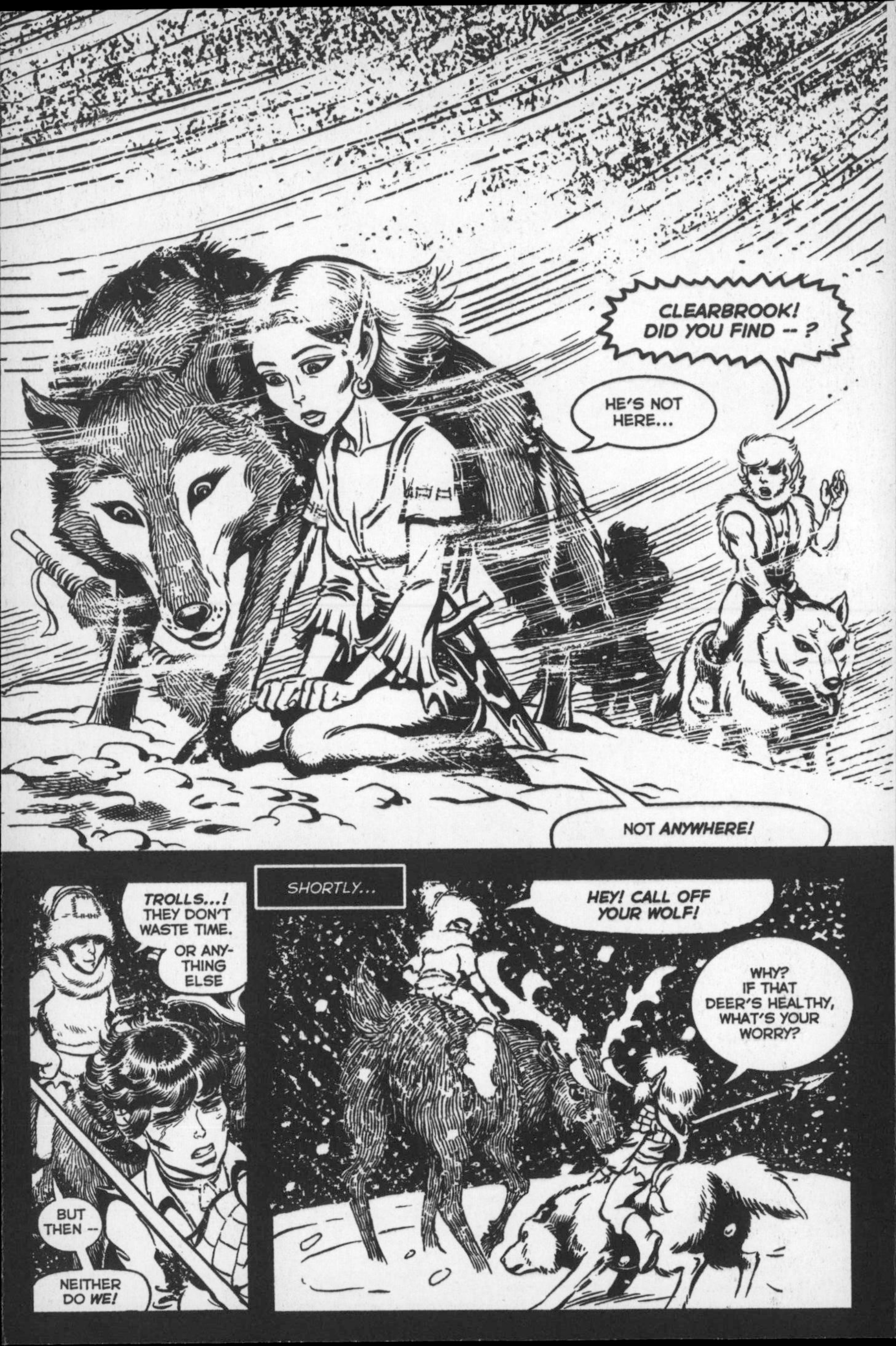
CLEARBROOK! DID YOU FIND -- ?
HE'S NOT HERE...
NOT *ANYWHERE!*
TROLLS...! THEY DON'T WASTE TIME.
OR ANYTHING ELSE
BUT THEN --
NEITHER DO *WE!*
SHORTLY...
HEY! CALL OFF YOUR WOLF!
WHY? IF THAT DEER'S HEALTHY, WHAT'S YOUR WORRY?

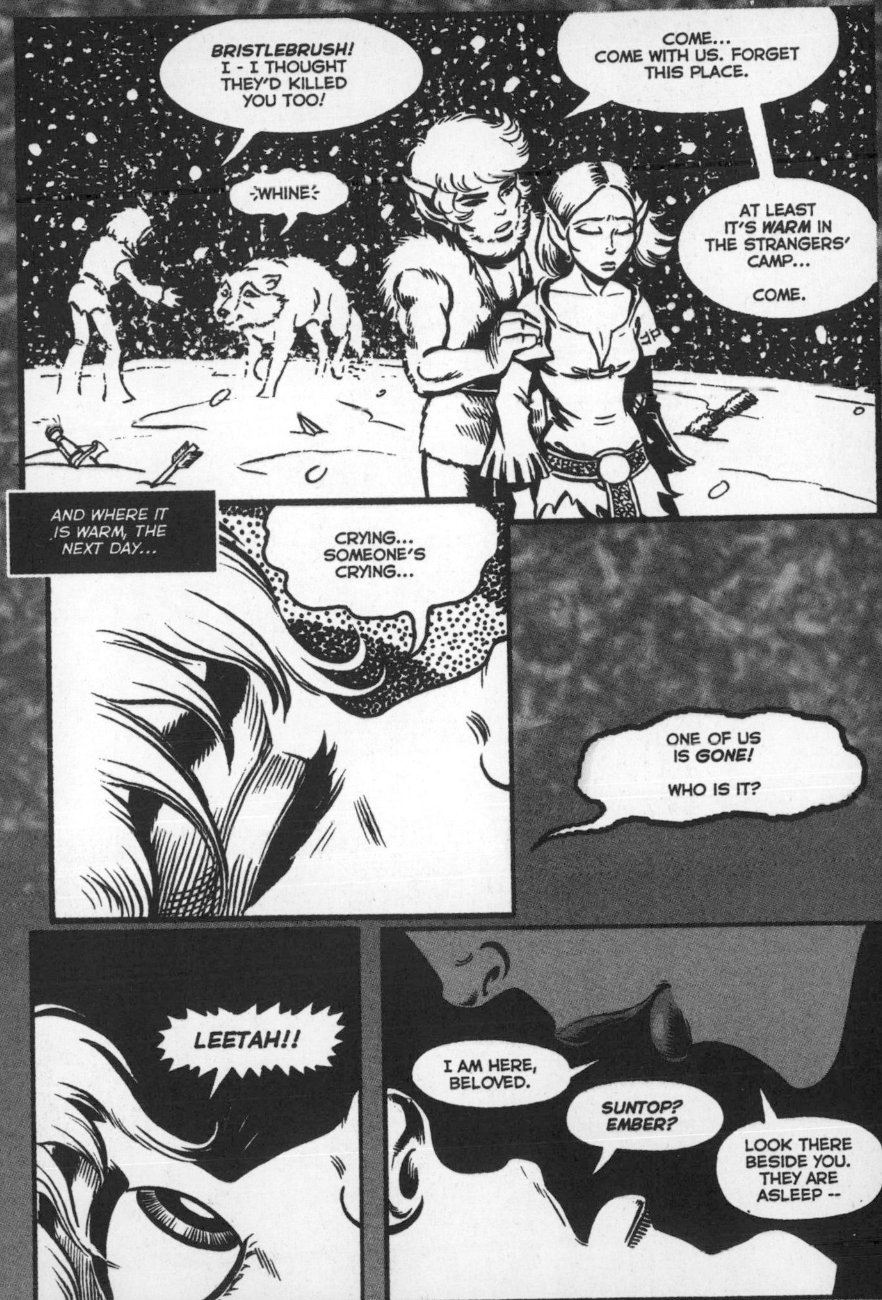

BRISTLEBRUSH! I - I THOUGHT THEY'D KILLED YOU TOO!
WHINE
COME... COME WITH US. FORGET THIS PLACE.
AT LEAST IT'S WARM IN THE STRANGERS' CAMP... COME.
AND WHERE IT IS WARM, THE NEXT DAY...
CRYING... SOMEONE'S CRYING...
ONE OF US IS GONE! WHO IS IT?
LEETAH!!
I AM HERE, BELOVED.
SUNTOP? EMBER?
LOOK THERE BESIDE YOU. THEY ARE ASLEEP --

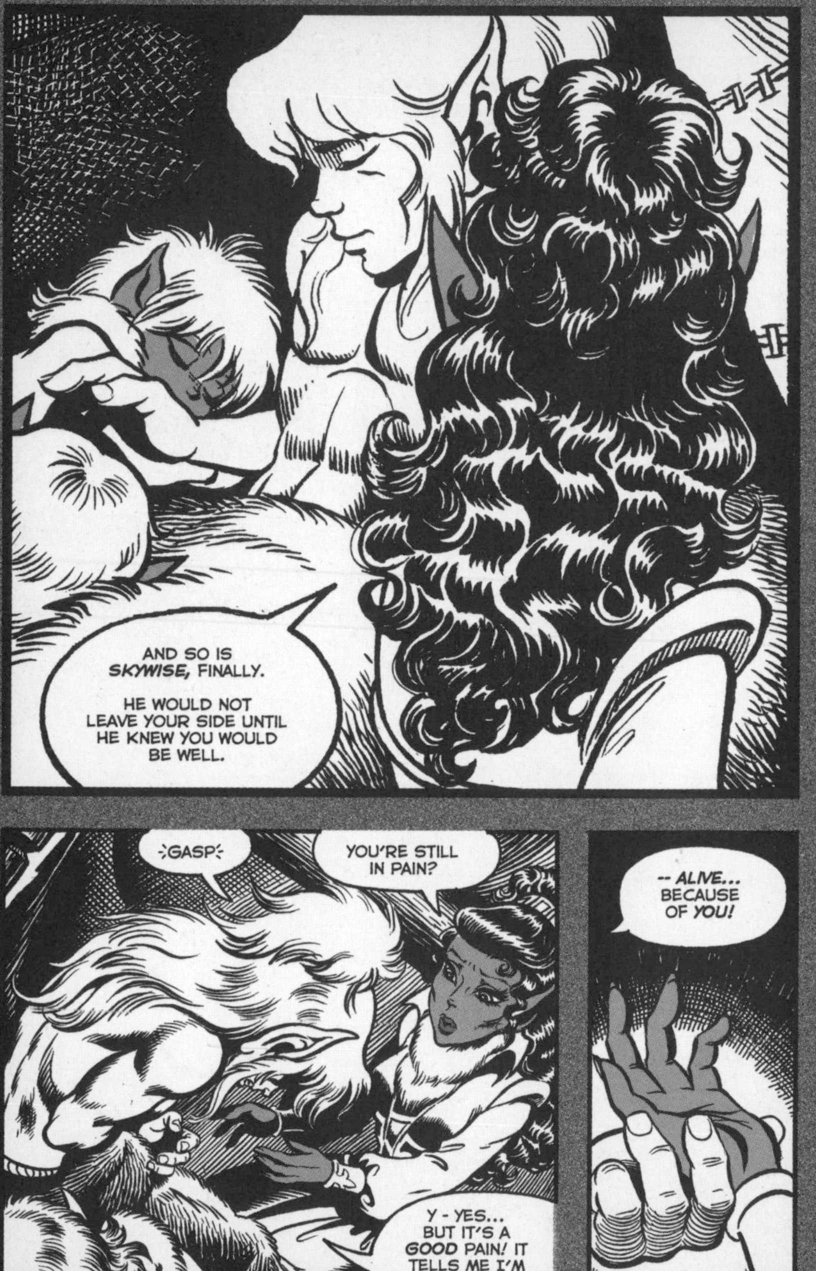
AND SO IS *SKYWISE,* FINALLY.
HE WOULD NOT LEAVE YOUR SIDE UNTIL HE KNEW YOU WOULD BE WELL.
GASP
YOU'RE STILL IN PAIN?
Y - YES... BUT IT'S A *GOOD* PAIN! IT TELLS ME I'M ALIVE --
-- *ALIVE...* BECAUSE OF *YOU!*

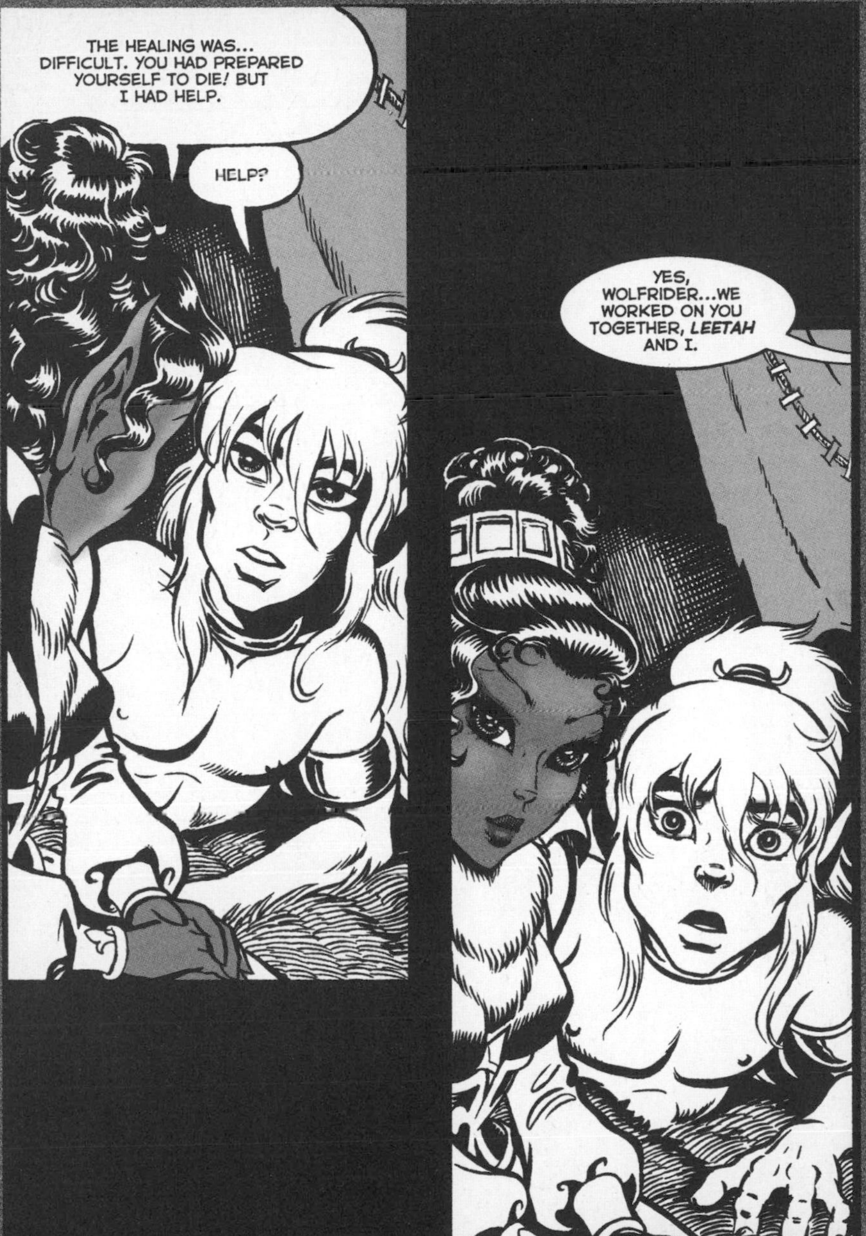
THE HEALING WAS... DIFFICULT. YOU HAD PREPARED YOURSELF TO DIE! BUT I HAD HELP.
HELP?
YES, WOLFRIDER...WE WORKED ON YOU TOGETHER, LEETAH AND I.

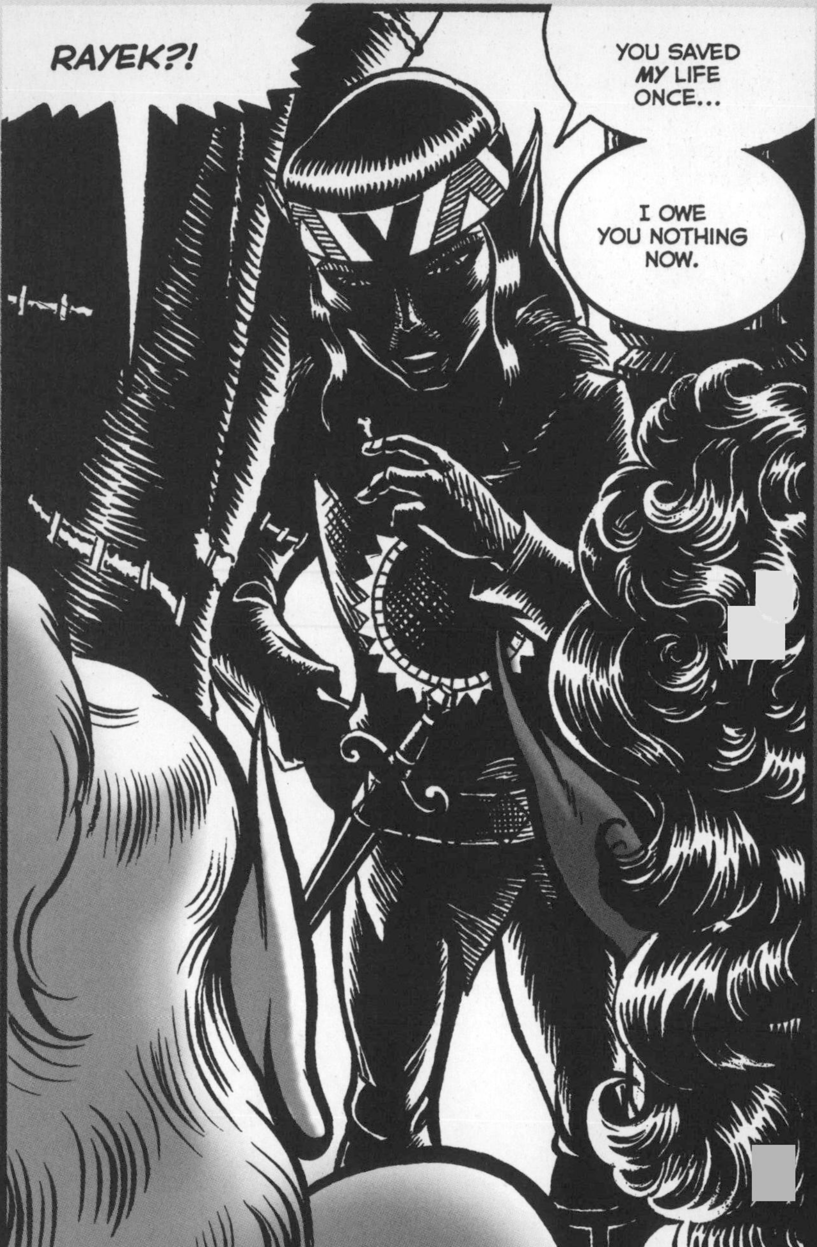
RAYEK?!
YOU SAVED *MY* LIFE ONCE...
I OWE YOU NOTHING NOW.

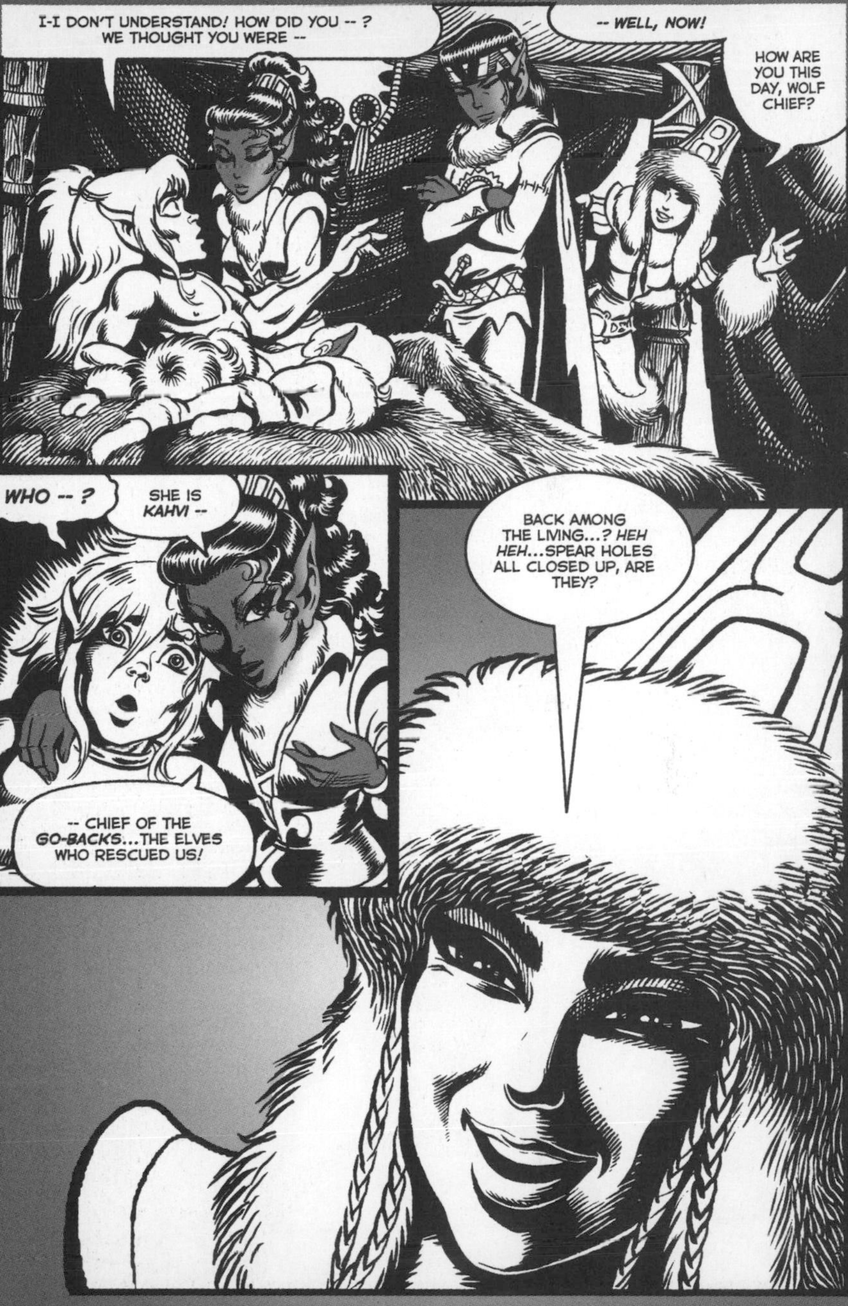
I-I DON'T UNDERSTAND! HOW DID YOU -- ? WE THOUGHT YOU WERE --
-- WELL, NOW!
HOW ARE YOU THIS DAY, WOLF CHIEF?
WHO -- ?
SHE IS KAHVI --
-- CHIEF OF THE GO-BACKS...THE ELVES WHO RESCUED US!
BACK AMONG THE LIVING...? HEH HEH...SPEAR HOLES ALL CLOSED UP, ARE THEY?

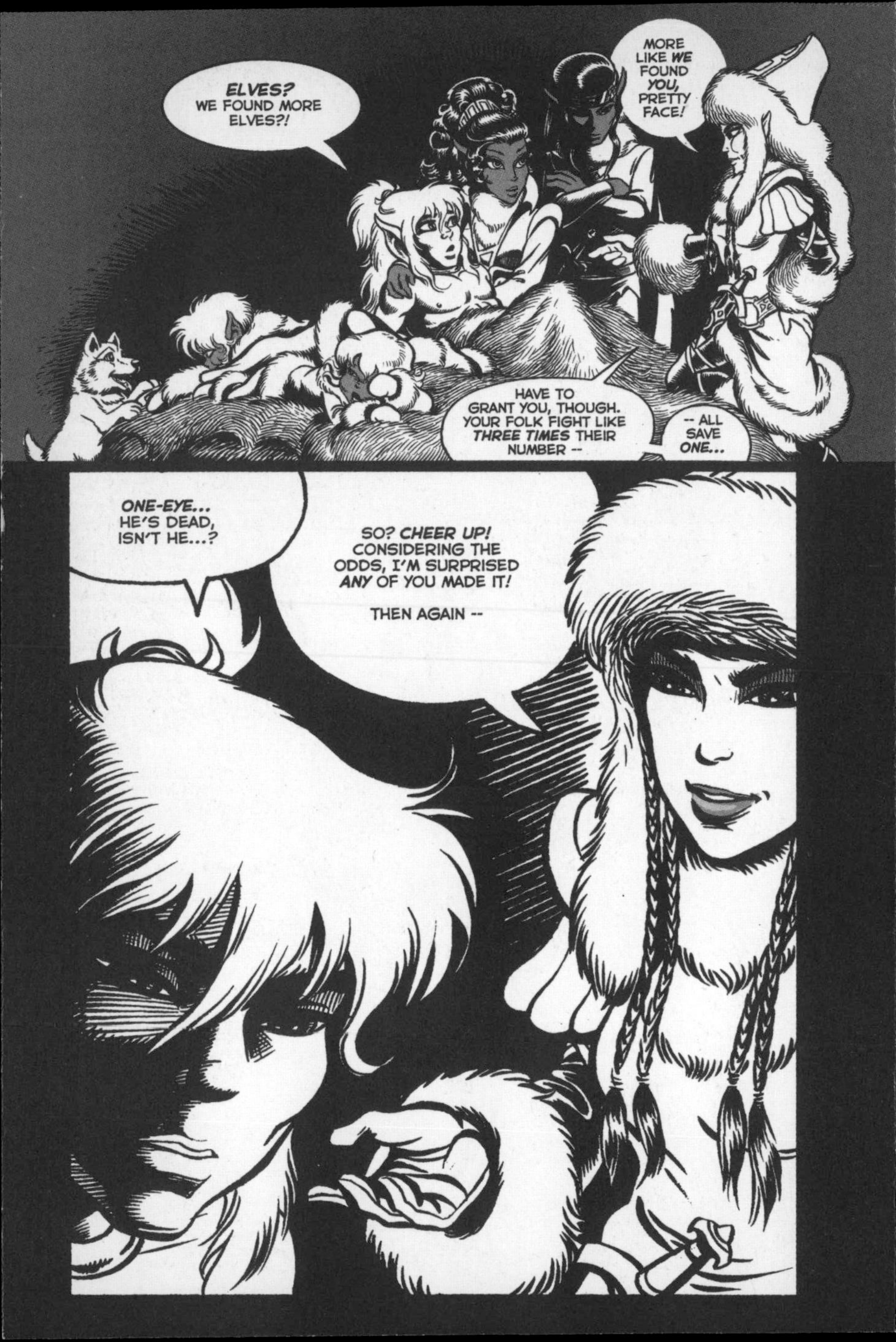
ELVES? WE FOUND MORE ELVES?!
MORE LIKE WE FOUND YOU, PRETTY FACE!
HAVE TO GRANT YOU, THOUGH. YOUR FOLK FIGHT LIKE THREE TIMES THEIR NUMBER --
-- ALL SAVE ONE...
ONE-EYE... HE'S DEAD, ISN'T HE...?
SO? CHEER UP! CONSIDERING THE ODDS, I'M SURPRISED ANY OF YOU MADE IT!
THEN AGAIN --

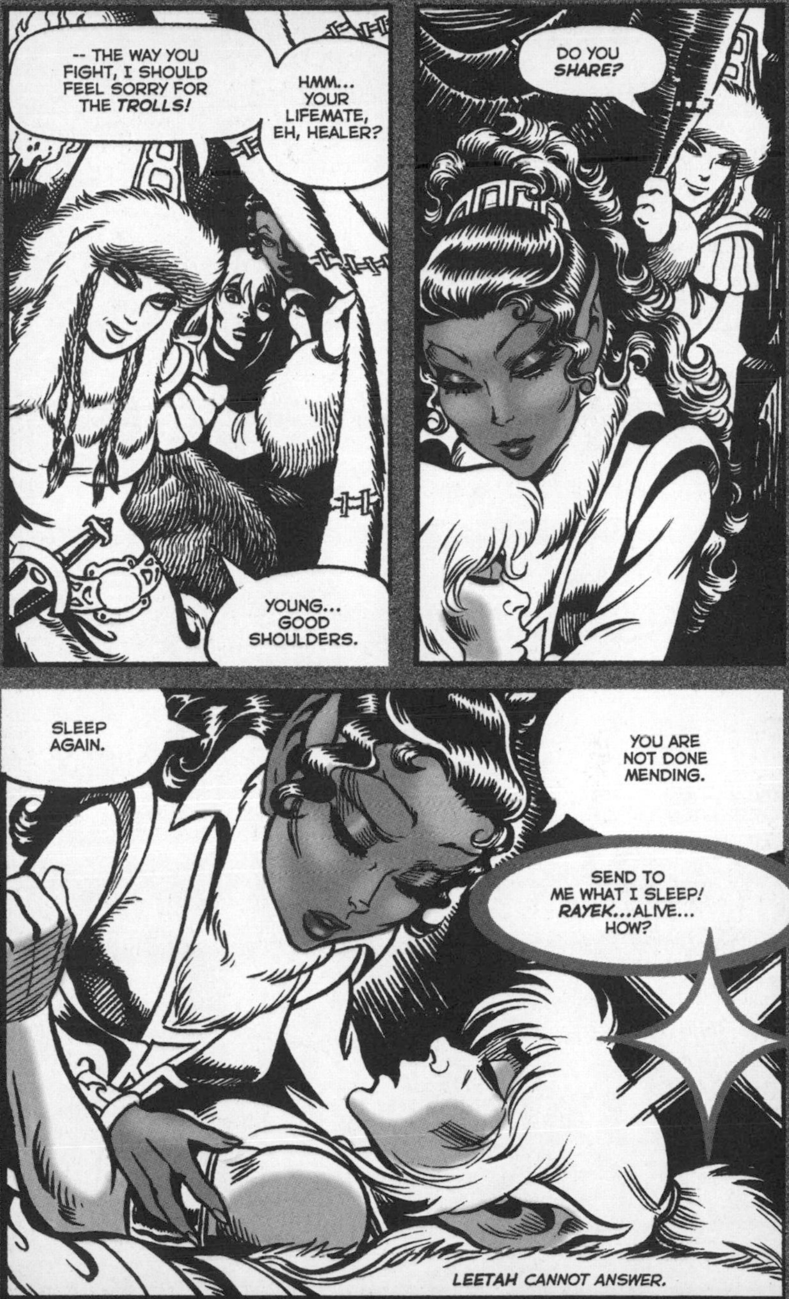
-- THE WAY YOU FIGHT, I SHOULD FEEL SORRY FOR THE TROLLS!
HMM... YOUR LIFEMATE, EH, HEALER?
YOUNG... GOOD SHOULDERS.
DO YOU SHARE?
SLEEP AGAIN.
YOU ARE NOT DONE MENDING.
SEND TO ME WHAT I SLEEP! RAYEK...ALIVE... HOW?
LEETAH CANNOT ANSWER.

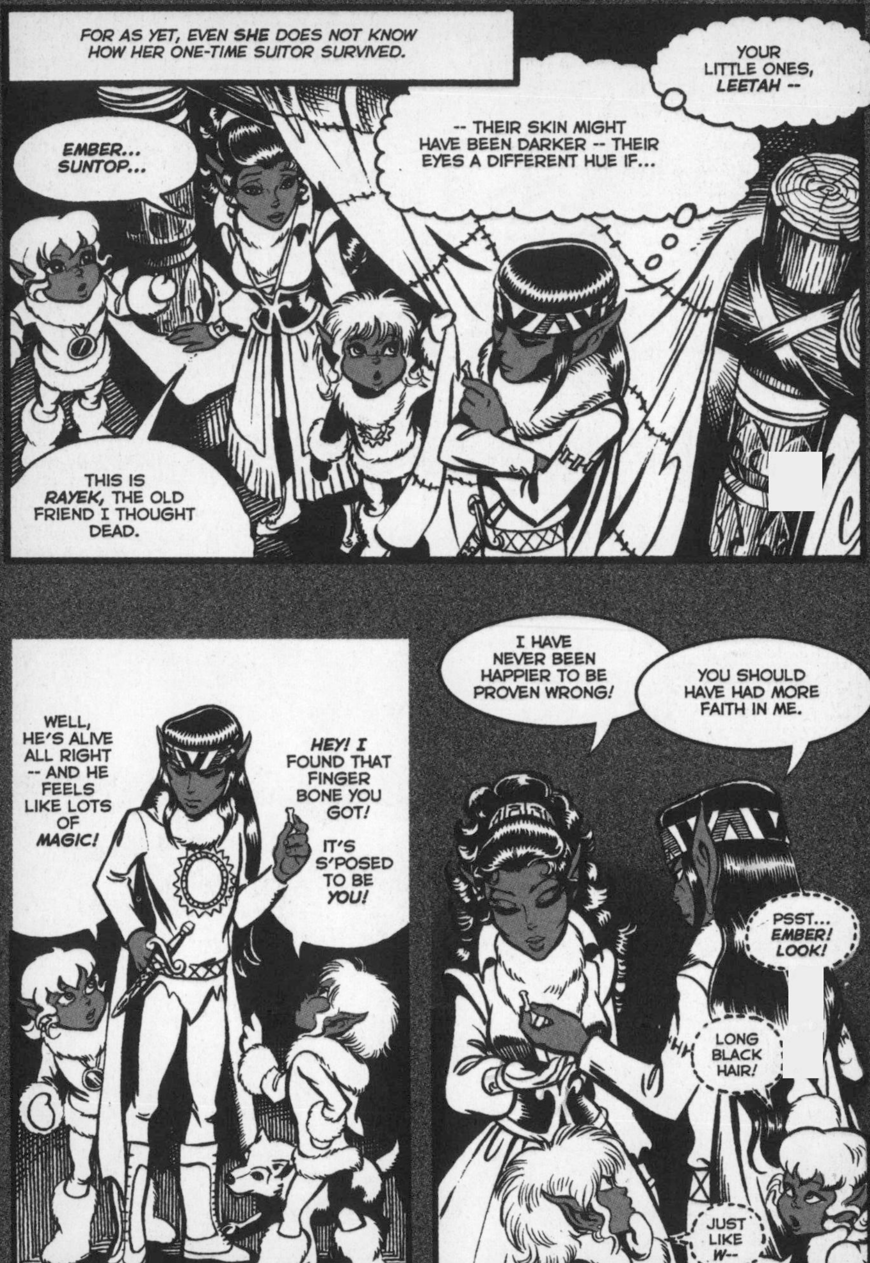
FOR AS YET, EVEN SHE DOES NOT KNOW HOW HER ONE-TIME SUITOR SURVIVED.
YOUR LITTLE ONES, LEETAH --
-- THEIR SKIN MIGHT HAVE BEEN DARKER -- THEIR EYES A DIFFERENT HUE IF...
EMBER... SUNTOP...
THIS IS RAYEK, THE OLD FRIEND I THOUGHT DEAD.
WELL, HE'S ALIVE ALL RIGHT -- AND HE FEELS LIKE LOTS OF MAGIC!
HEY! I FOUND THAT FINGER BONE YOU GOT!
IT'S S'POSED TO BE YOU!
I HAVE NEVER BEEN HAPPIER TO BE PROVEN WRONG!
YOU SHOULD HAVE HAD MORE FAITH IN ME.
PSST... EMBER! LOOK!
LONG BLACK HAIR!
JUST LIKE W--
SHH!

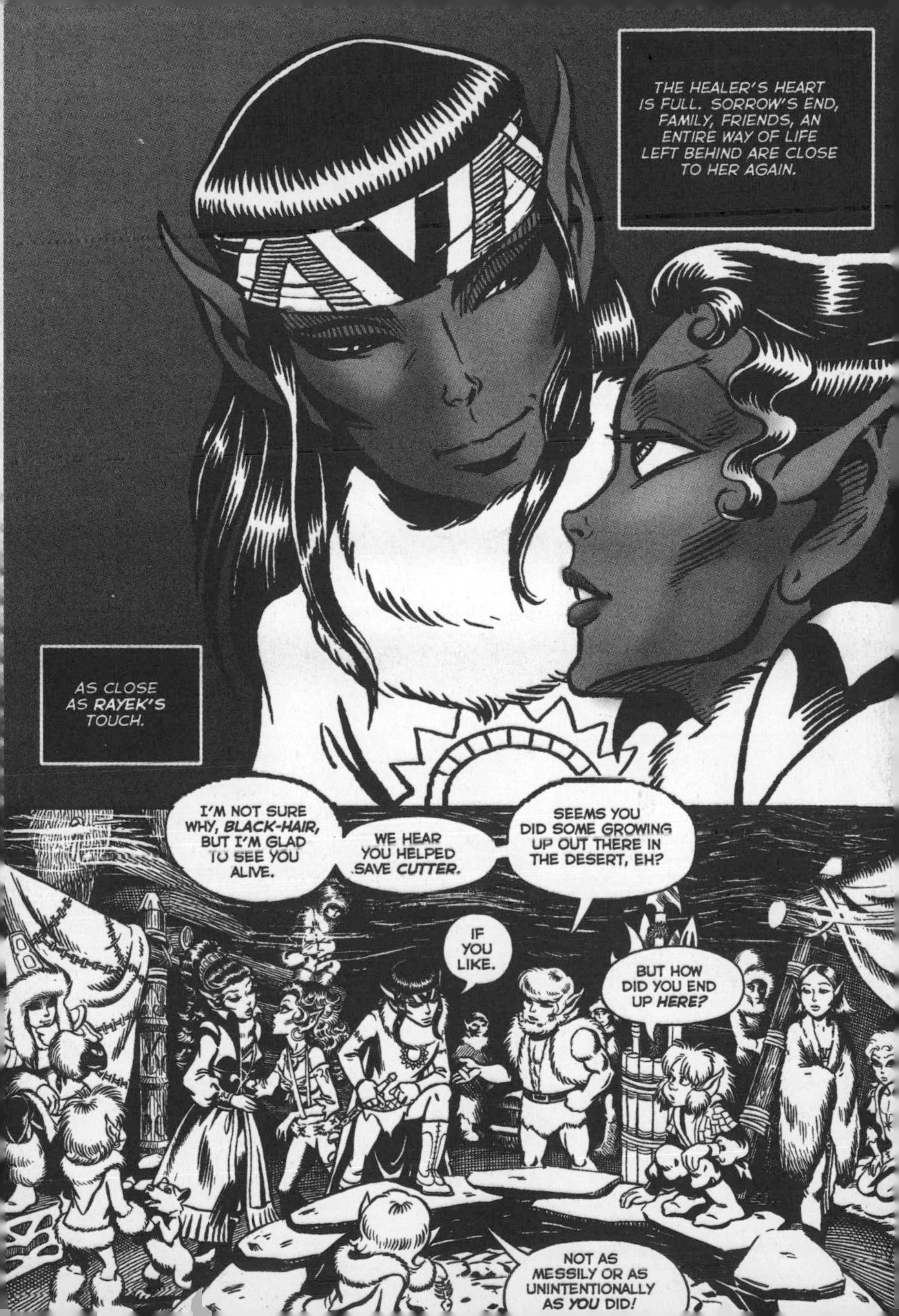

THE HEALER'S HEART IS FULL. SORROW'S END, FAMILY, FRIENDS, AN ENTIRE WAY OF LIFE LEFT BEHIND ARE CLOSE TO HER AGAIN.
AS CLOSE AS RAYEK'S TOUCH.
I'M NOT SURE WHY, BLACK-HAIR, BUT I'M GLAD TO SEE YOU ALIVE.
WE HEAR YOU HELPED SAVE CUTTER.
SEEMS YOU DID SOME GROWING UP OUT THERE IN THE DESERT, EH?
IF YOU LIKE.
BUT HOW DID YOU END UP HERE?
NOT AS MESSILY OR AS UNINTENTIONALLY AS YOU DID!

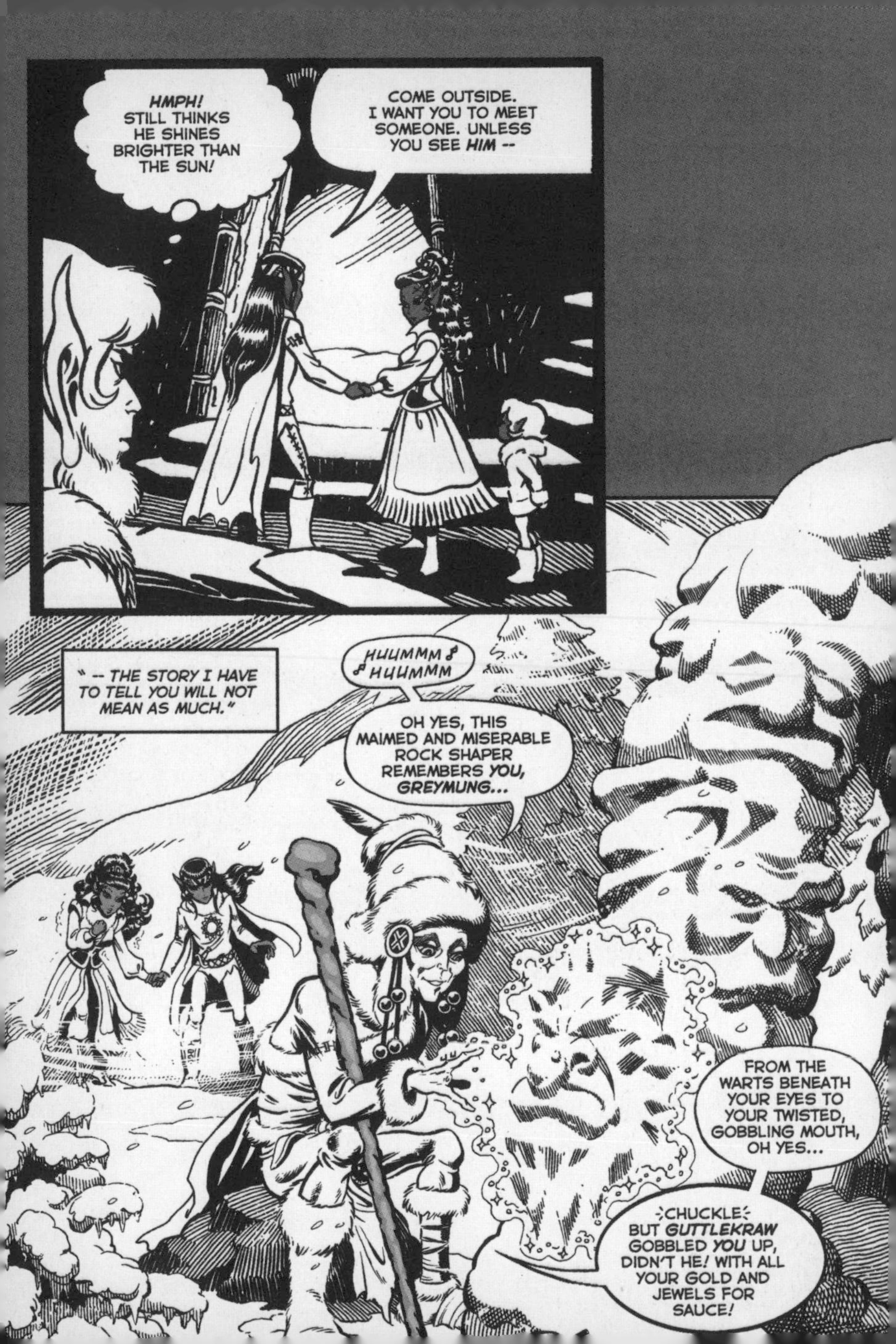
HMPH! STILL THINKS HE SHINES BRIGHTER THAN THE SUN!
COME OUTSIDE. I WANT YOU TO MEET SOMEONE. UNLESS YOU SEE HIM --
" -- THE STORY I HAVE TO TELL YOU WILL NOT MEAN AS MUCH."
HUUMMM HUUMMM
OH YES, THIS MAIMED AND MISERABLE ROCK SHAPER REMEMBERS YOU, GREYMUNG...
FROM THE WARTS BENEATH YOUR EYES TO YOUR TWISTED, GOBBLING MOUTH, OH YES...
CHUCKLE BUT GUTTLEKRAW GOBBLED YOU UP, DIDN'T HE! WITH ALL YOUR GOLD AND JEWELS FOR SAUCE!

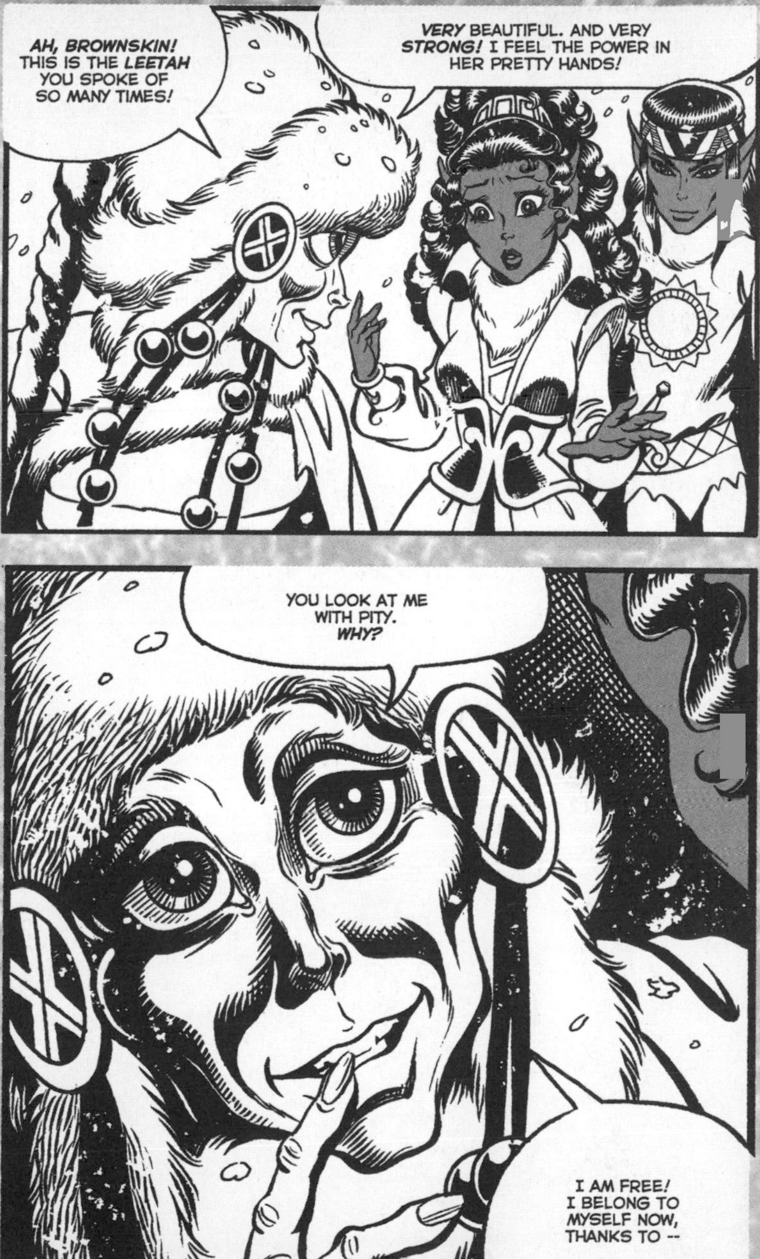
AH, BROWNSKIN! THIS IS THE LEETAH YOU SPOKE OF SO MANY TIMES!
VERY BEAUTIFUL. AND VERY STRONG! I FEEL THE POWER IN HER PRETTY HANDS!
YOU LOOK AT ME WITH PITY. WHY?
I AM FREE! I BELONG TO MYSELF NOW, THANKS TO --

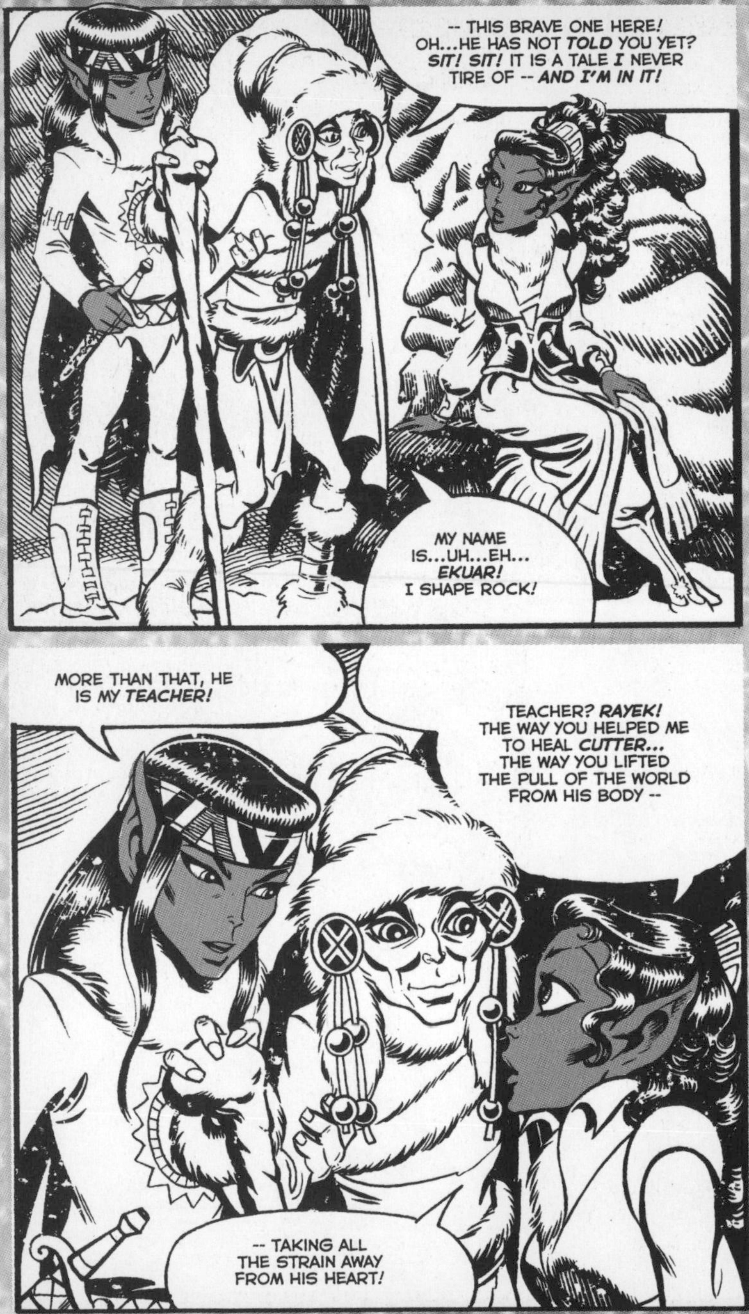
-- THIS BRAVE ONE HERE! OH...HE HAS NOT TOLD YOU YET? SIT! SIT! IT IS A TALE I NEVER TIRE OF -- AND I'M IN IT!
MY NAME IS...UH...EH... EKUAR! I SHAPE ROCK!
MORE THAN THAT, HE IS MY TEACHER!
TEACHER? RAYEK! THE WAY YOU HELPED ME TO HEAL CUTTER... THE WAY YOU LIFTED THE PULL OF THE WORLD FROM HIS BODY --
-- TAKING ALL THE STRAIN AWAY FROM HIS HEART!

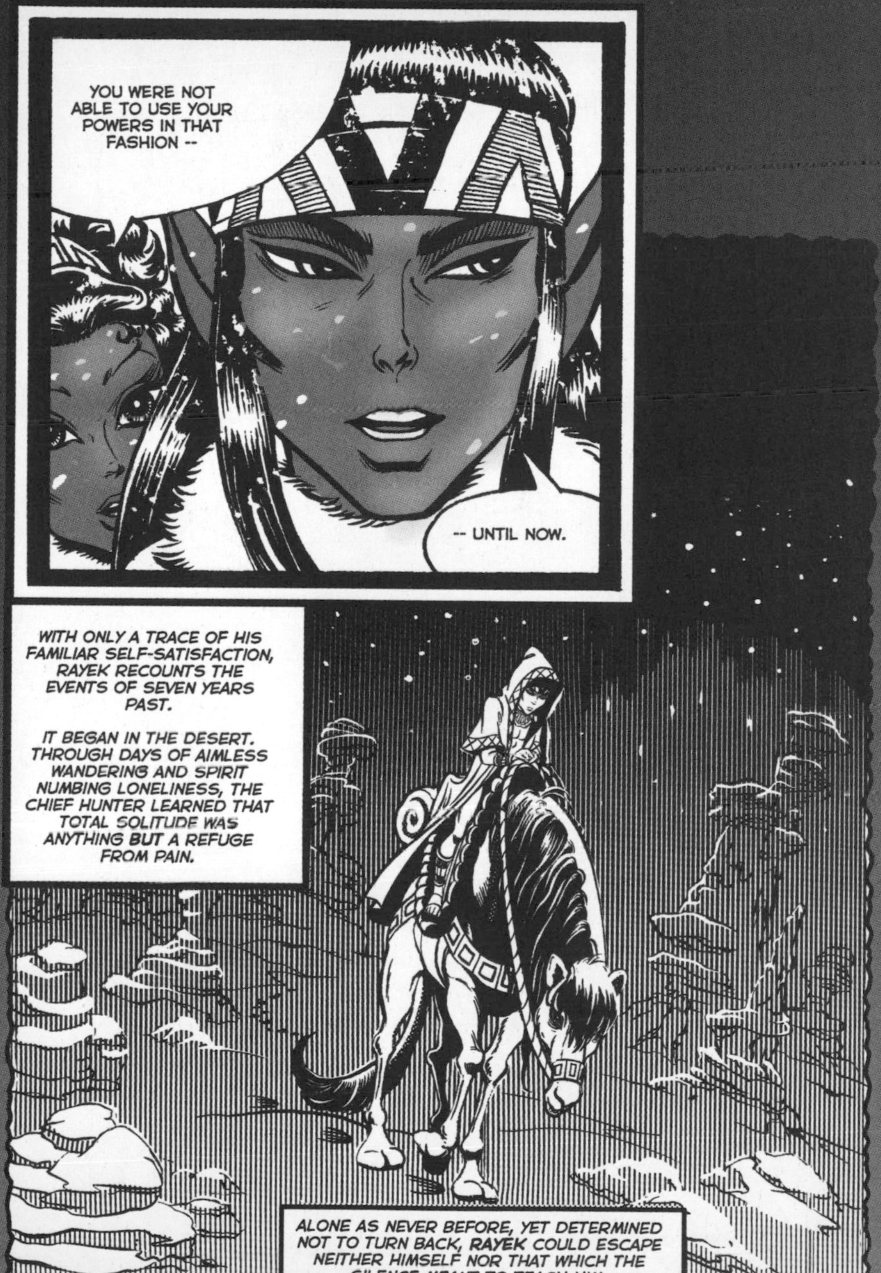

YOU WERE NOT ABLE TO USE YOUR POWERS IN THAT FASHION --
-- UNTIL NOW.
WITH ONLY A TRACE OF HIS FAMILIAR SELF-SATISFACTION, RAYEK RECOUNTS THE EVENTS OF SEVEN YEARS PAST.
IT BEGAN IN THE DESERT. THROUGH DAYS OF AIMLESS WANDERING AND SPIRIT NUMBING LONELINESS, THE CHIEF HUNTER LEARNED THAT TOTAL SOLITUDE WAS ANYTHING BUT A REFUGE FROM PAIN.
ALONE AS NEVER BEFORE, YET DETERMINED NOT TO TURN BACK, RAYEK COULD ESCAPE NEITHER HIMSELF NOR THAT WHICH THE SILENCE MEANT TO TEACH HIM.

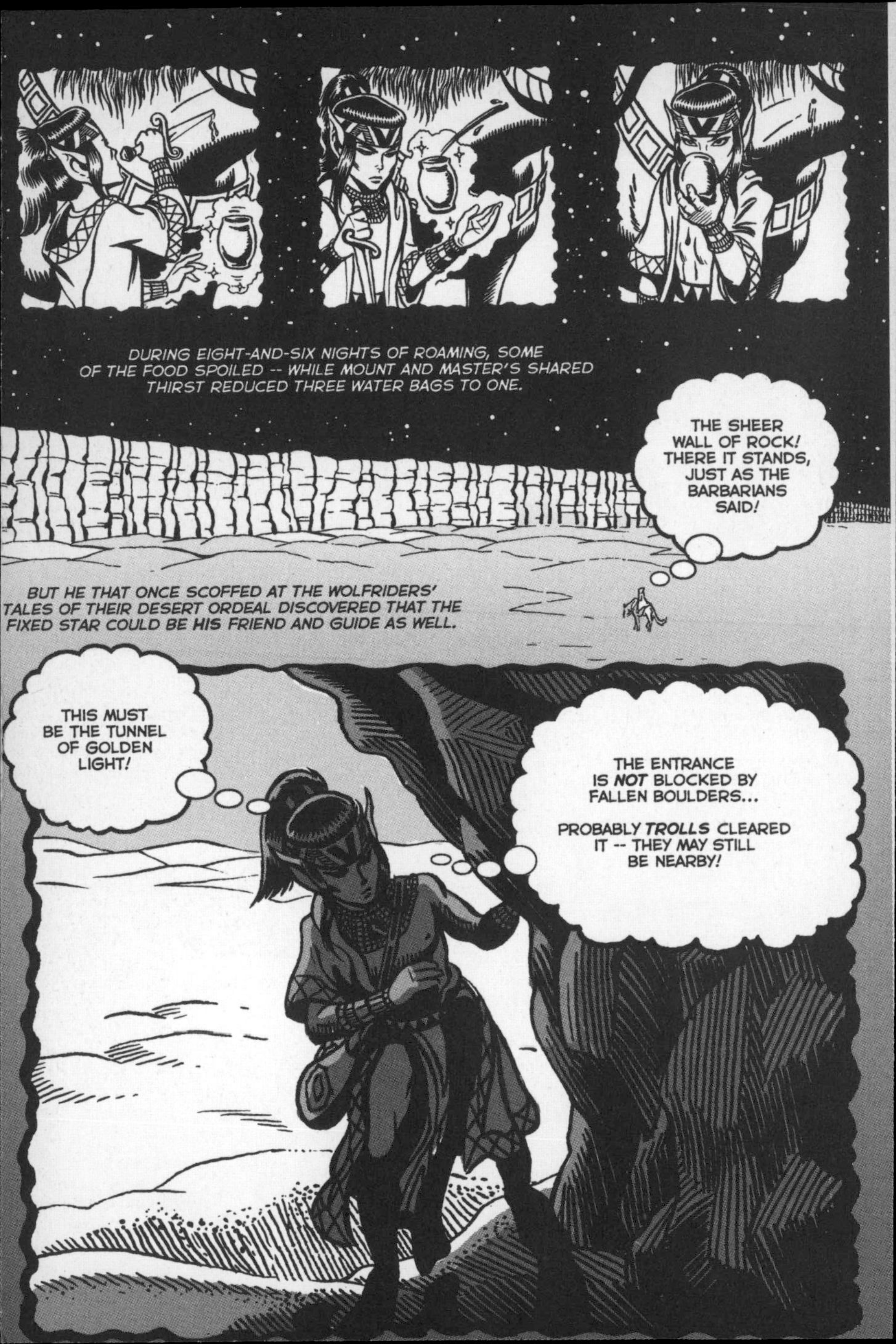

DURING EIGHT-AND-SIX NIGHTS OF ROAMING, SOME OF THE FOOD SPOILED -- WHILE MOUNT AND MASTER'S SHARED THIRST REDUCED THREE WATER BAGS TO ONE.
THE SHEER WALL OF ROCK! THERE IT STANDS, JUST AS THE BARBARIANS SAID!
BUT HE THAT ONCE SCOFFED AT THE WOLFRIDERS' TALES OF THEIR DESERT ORDEAL DISCOVERED THAT THE FIXED STAR COULD BE HIS FRIEND AND GUIDE AS WELL.
THIS MUST BE THE TUNNEL OF GOLDEN LIGHT!
THE ENTRANCE IS NOT BLOCKED BY FALLEN BOULDERS... PROBABLY TROLLS CLEARED IT -- THEY MAY STILL BE NEARBY!

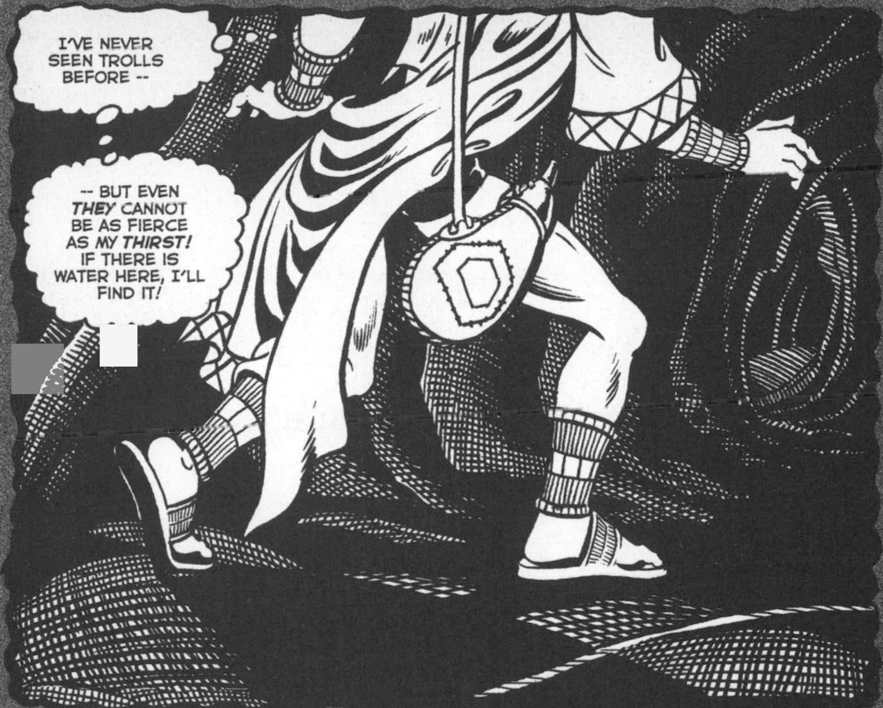
I'VE NEVER SEEN TROLLS BEFORE --
-- BUT EVEN *THEY* CANNOT BE AS FIERCE AS *MY THIRST!* IF THERE IS WATER HERE, I'LL FIND IT!

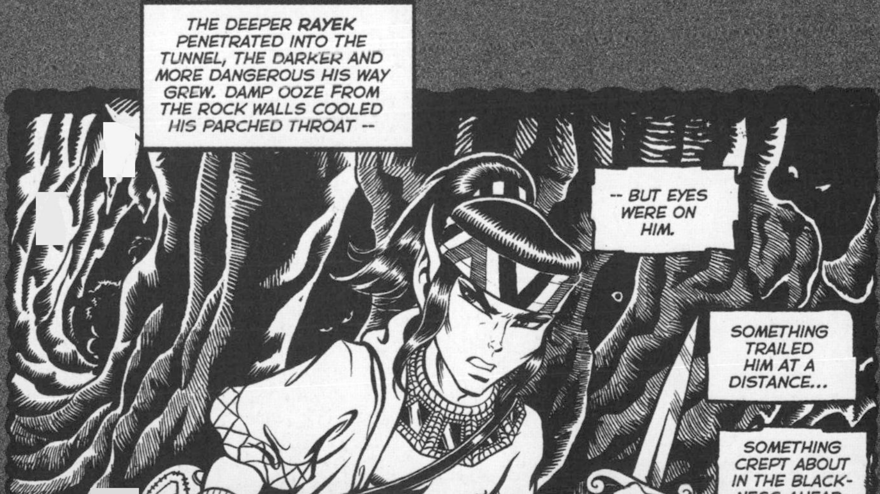
THE DEEPER **RAYEK** PENETRATED INTO THE TUNNEL, THE DARKER AND MORE DANGEROUS HIS WAY GREW. DAMP OOZE FROM THE ROCK WALLS COOLED HIS PARCHED THROAT --
-- BUT EYES WERE ON HIM.
SOMETHING TRAILED HIM AT A DISTANCE...
SOMETHING CREPT ABOUT IN THE BLACKNESS AHEAD.

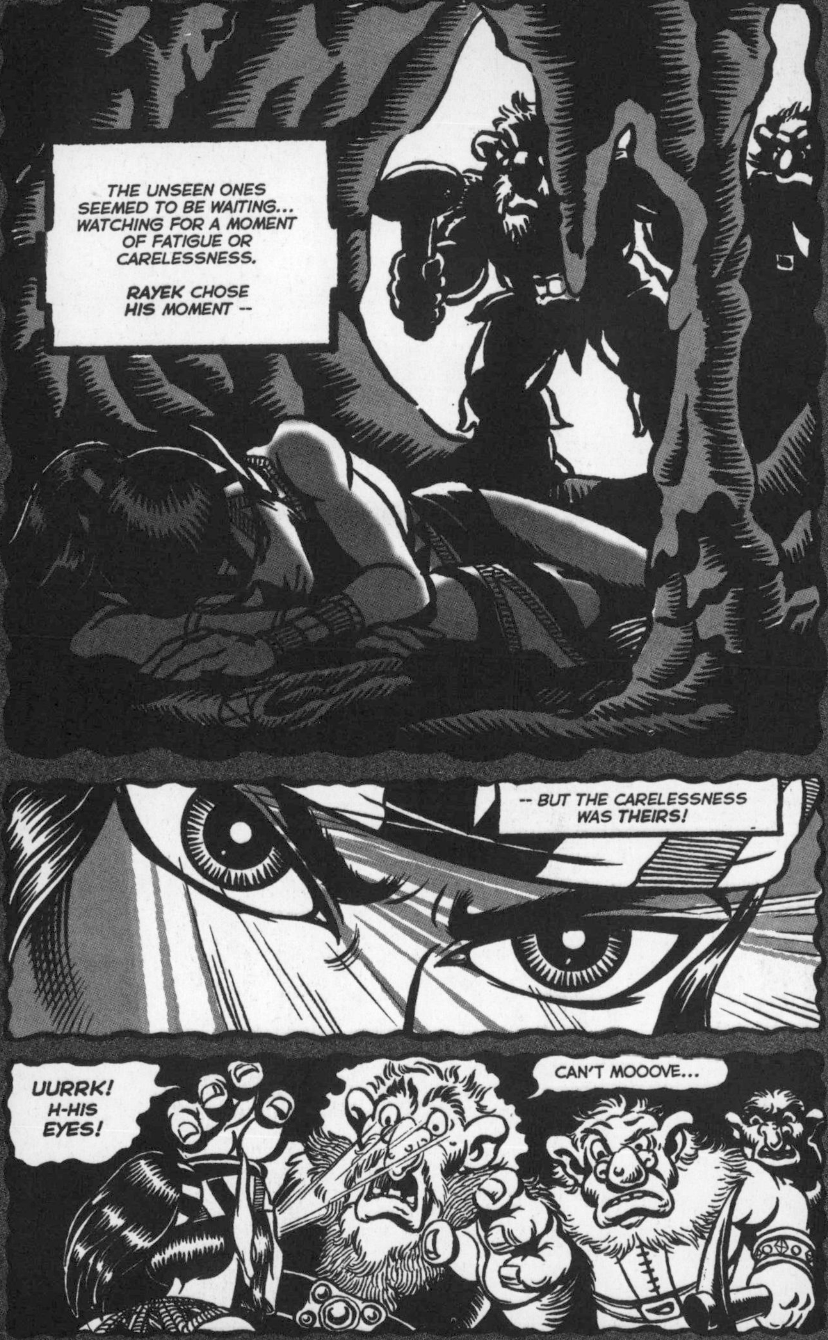
THE UNSEEN ONES SEEMED TO BE WAITING... WATCHING FOR A MOMENT OF FATIGUE OR CARELESSNESS.
RAYEK CHOSE HIS MOMENT --
-- BUT THE CARELESSNESS WAS THEIRS!
UURRK! H-HIS EYES!
CAN'T MOOOVE...

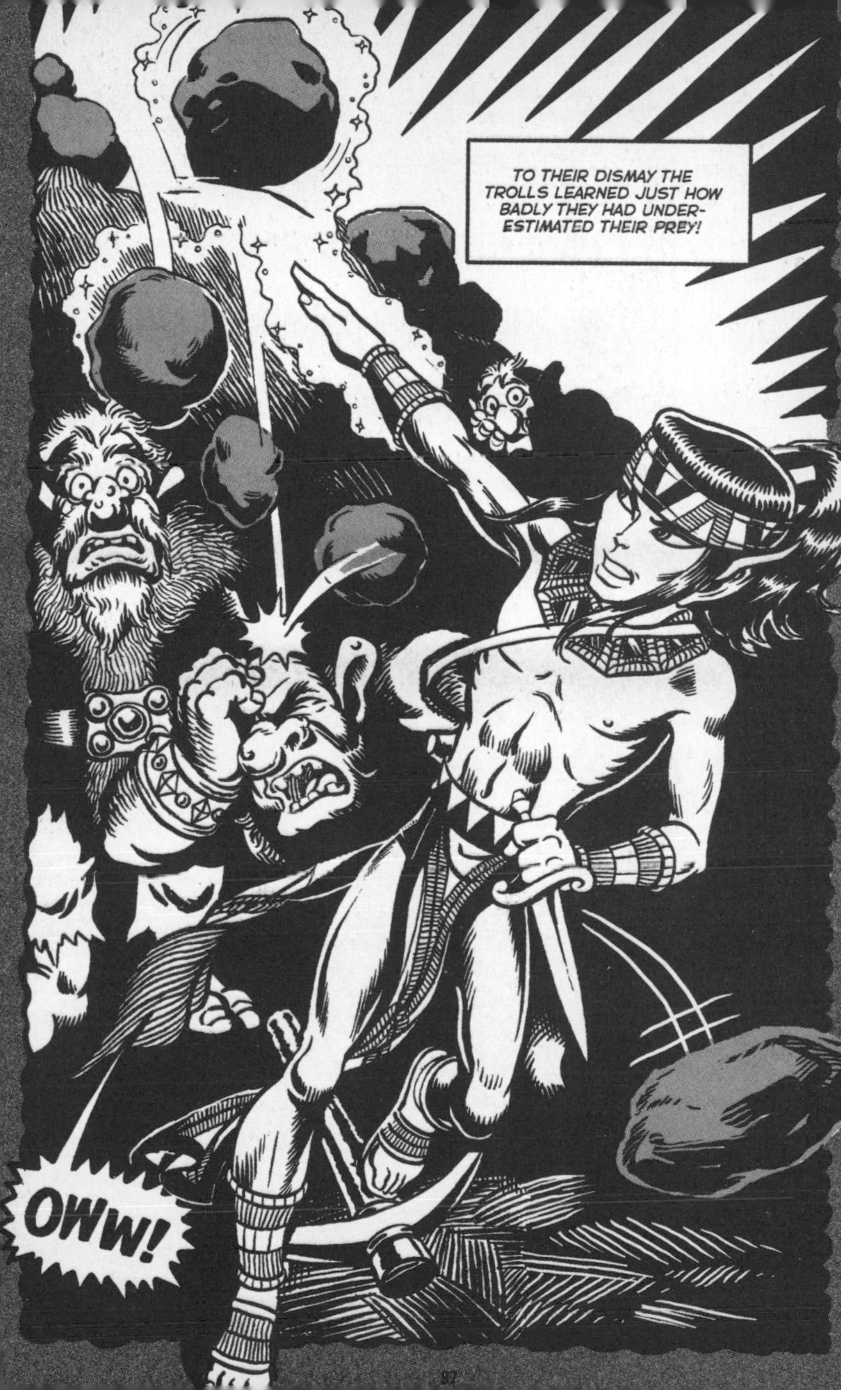
TO THEIR DISMAY THE TROLLS LEARNED JUST HOW BADLY THEY HAD UNDER-ESTIMATED THEIR PREY!
OWW!

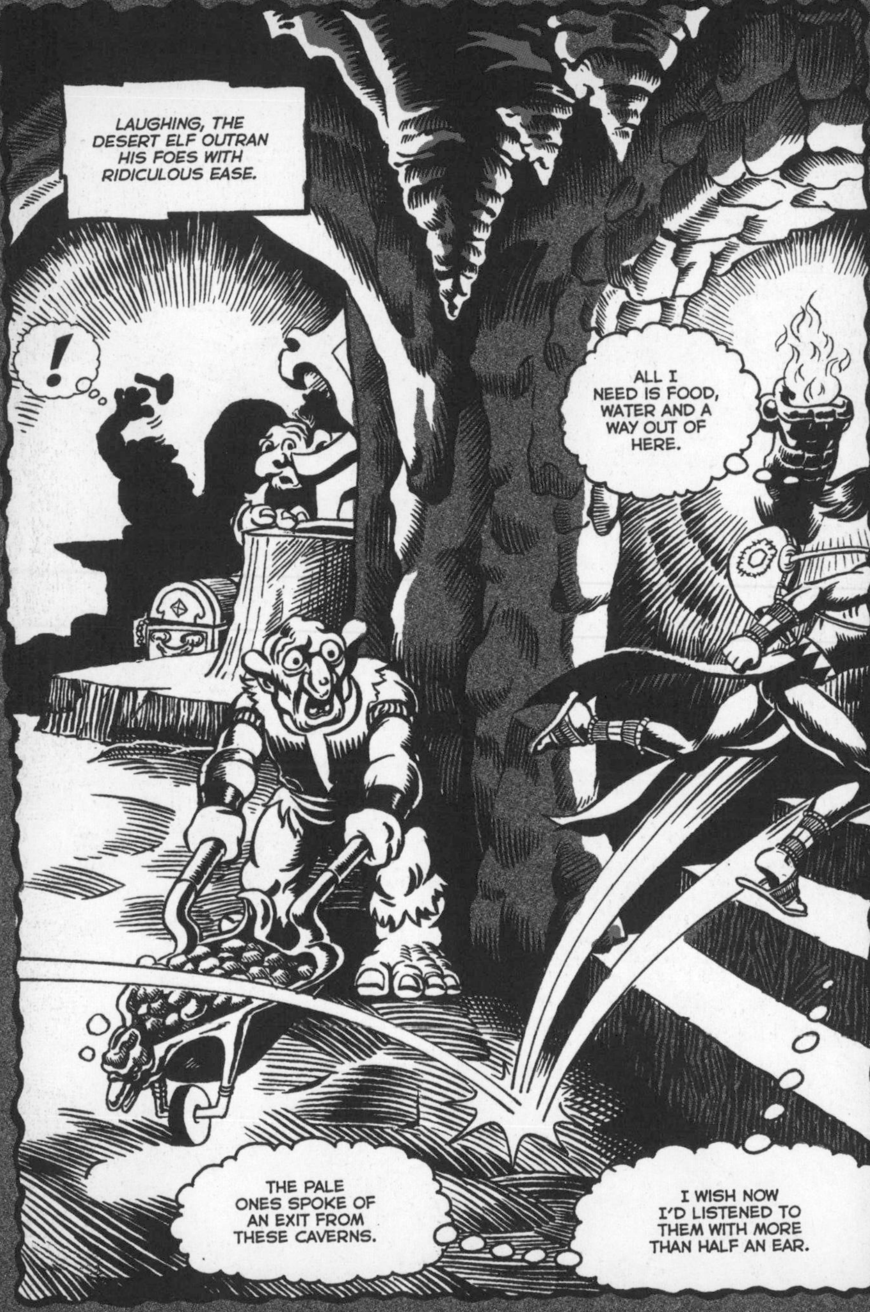
LAUGHING, THE DESERT ELF OUTRAN HIS FOES WITH RIDICULOUS EASE.
!
ALL I NEED IS FOOD, WATER AND A WAY OUT OF HERE.
THE PALE ONES SPOKE OF AN EXIT FROM THESE CAVERNS.
I WISH NOW I'D LISTENED TO THEM WITH MORE THAN HALF AN EAR.

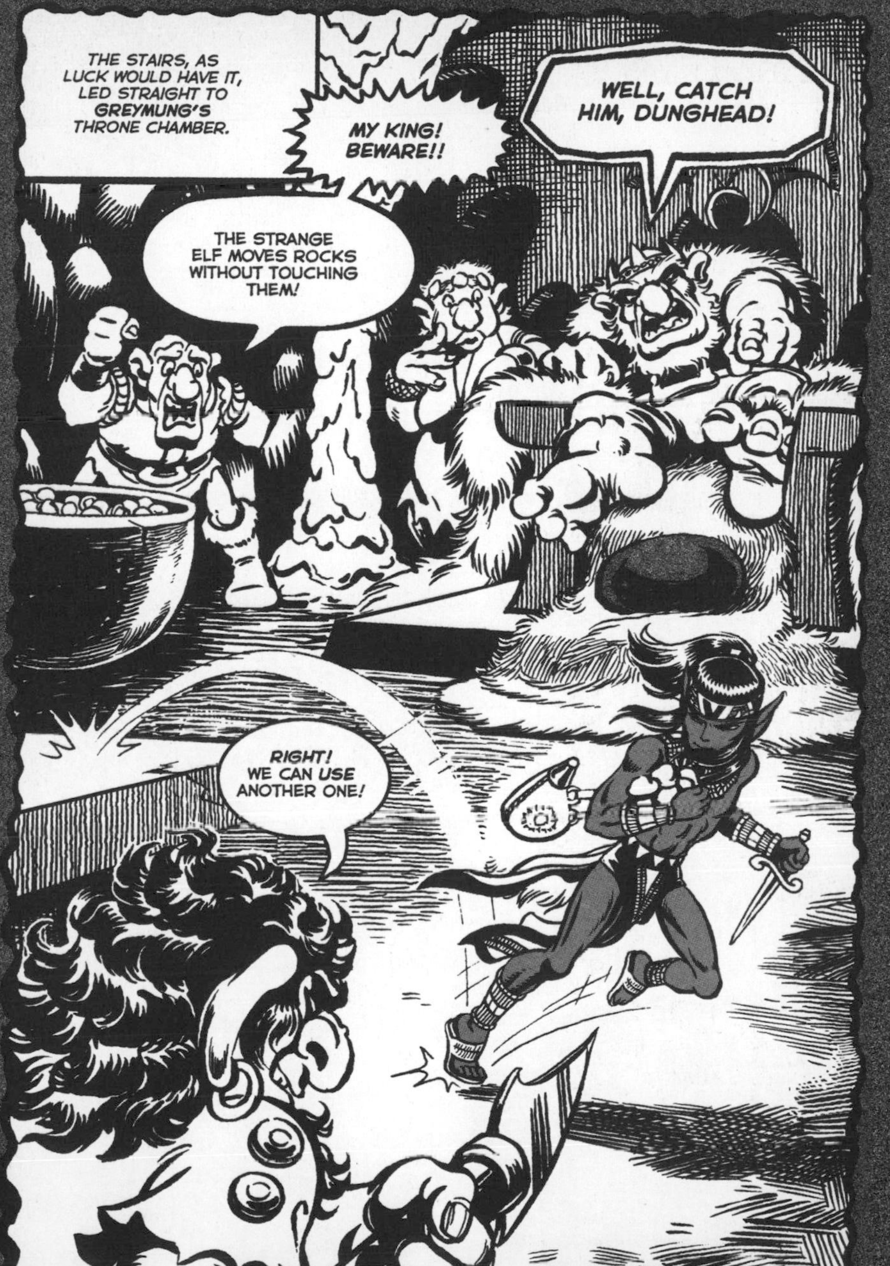

THE STAIRS, AS LUCK WOULD HAVE IT, LED STRAIGHT TO GREYMUNG'S THRONE CHAMBER.
MY KING! BEWARE!!
WELL, CATCH HIM, DUNGHEAD!
THE STRANGE ELF MOVES ROCKS WITHOUT TOUCHING THEM!
RIGHT! WE CAN USE ANOTHER ONE!

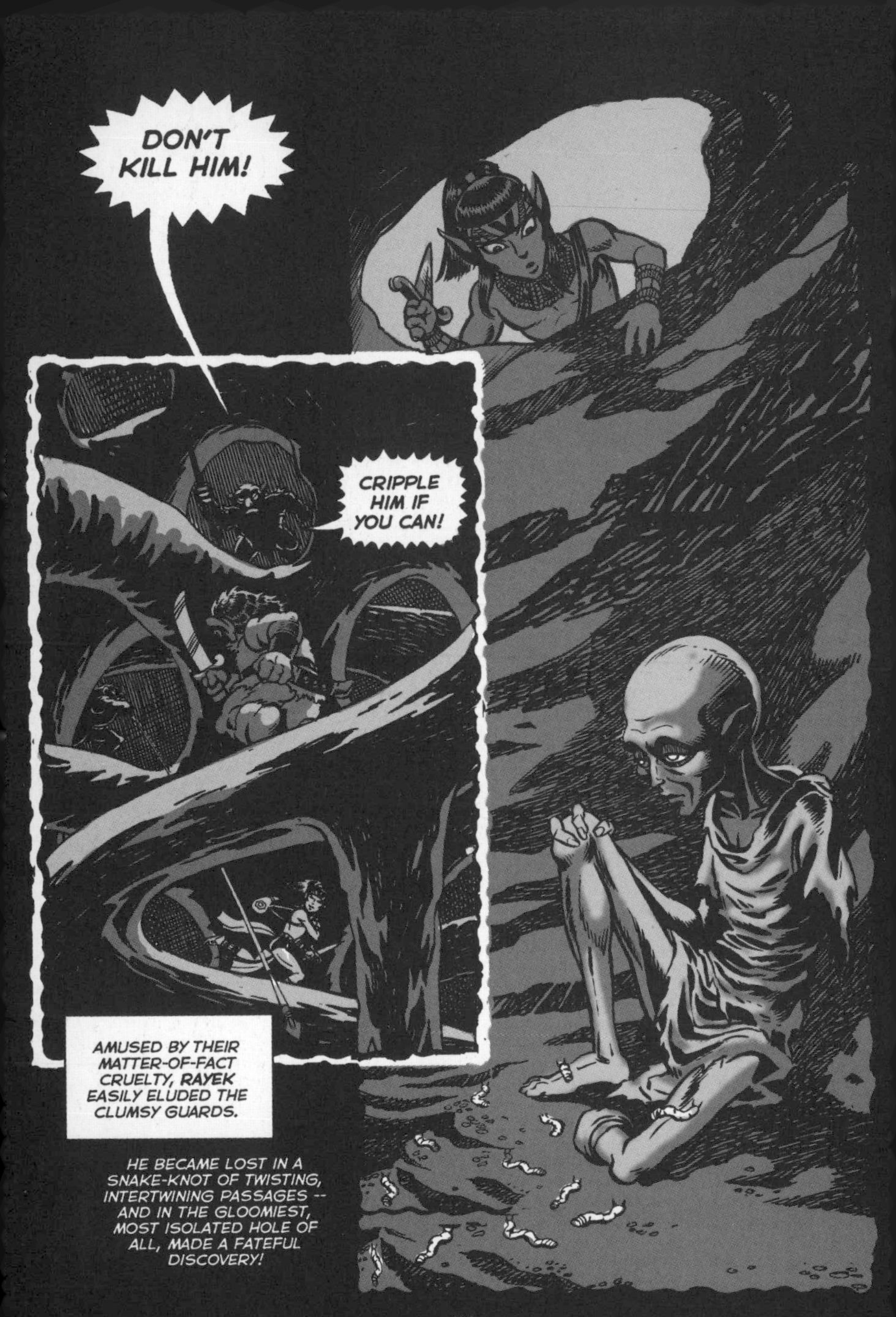
DON'T KILL HIM!
CRIPPLE HIM IF YOU CAN!
AMUSED BY THEIR MATTER-OF-FACT CRUELTY, RAYEK EASILY ELUDED THE CLUMSY GUARDS.
HE BECAME LOST IN A SNAKE-KNOT OF TWISTING, INTERTWINING PASSAGES -- AND IN THE GLOOMIEST, MOST ISOLATED HOLE OF ALL, MADE A FATEFUL DISCOVERY!

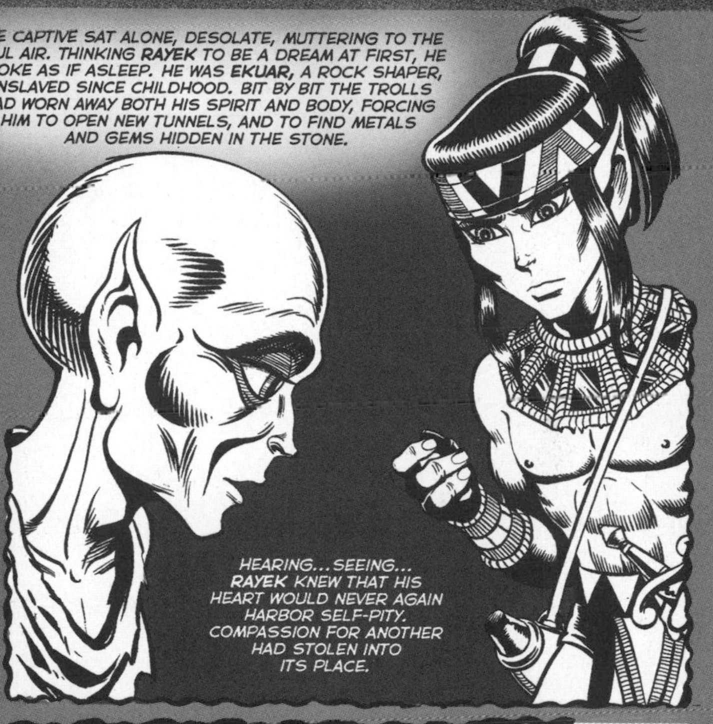
THE CAPTIVE SAT ALONE, DESOLATE, MUTTERING TO THE FOUL AIR. THINKING RAYEK TO BE A DREAM AT FIRST, HE SPOKE AS IF ASLEEP. HE WAS EKUAR, A ROCK SHAPER, ENSLAVED SINCE CHILDHOOD. BIT BY BIT THE TROLLS HAD WORN AWAY BOTH HIS SPIRIT AND BODY, FORCING HIM TO OPEN NEW TUNNELS, AND TO FIND METALS AND GEMS HIDDEN IN THE STONE.
HEARING...SEEING... RAYEK KNEW THAT HIS HEART WOULD NEVER AGAIN HARBOR SELF-PITY. COMPASSION FOR ANOTHER HAD STOLEN INTO ITS PLACE.

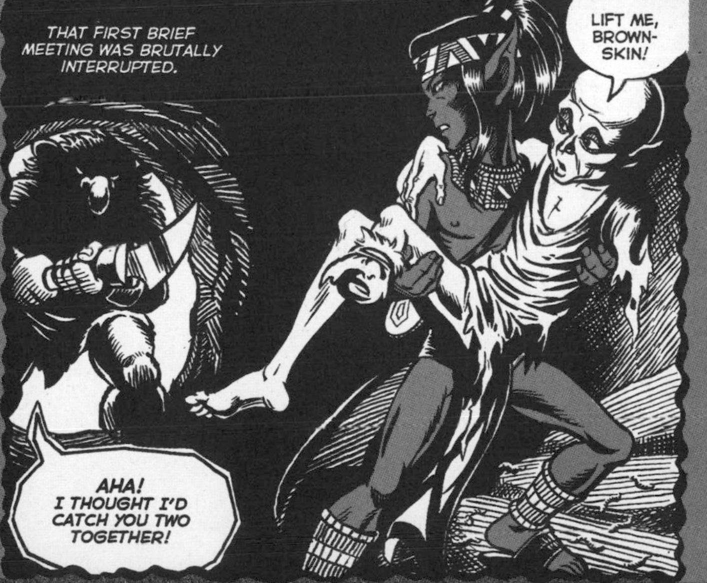
THAT FIRST BRIEF MEETING WAS BRUTALLY INTERRUPTED.
LIFT ME, BROWN-SKIN!
AHA! I THOUGHT I'D CATCH YOU TWO TOGETHER!

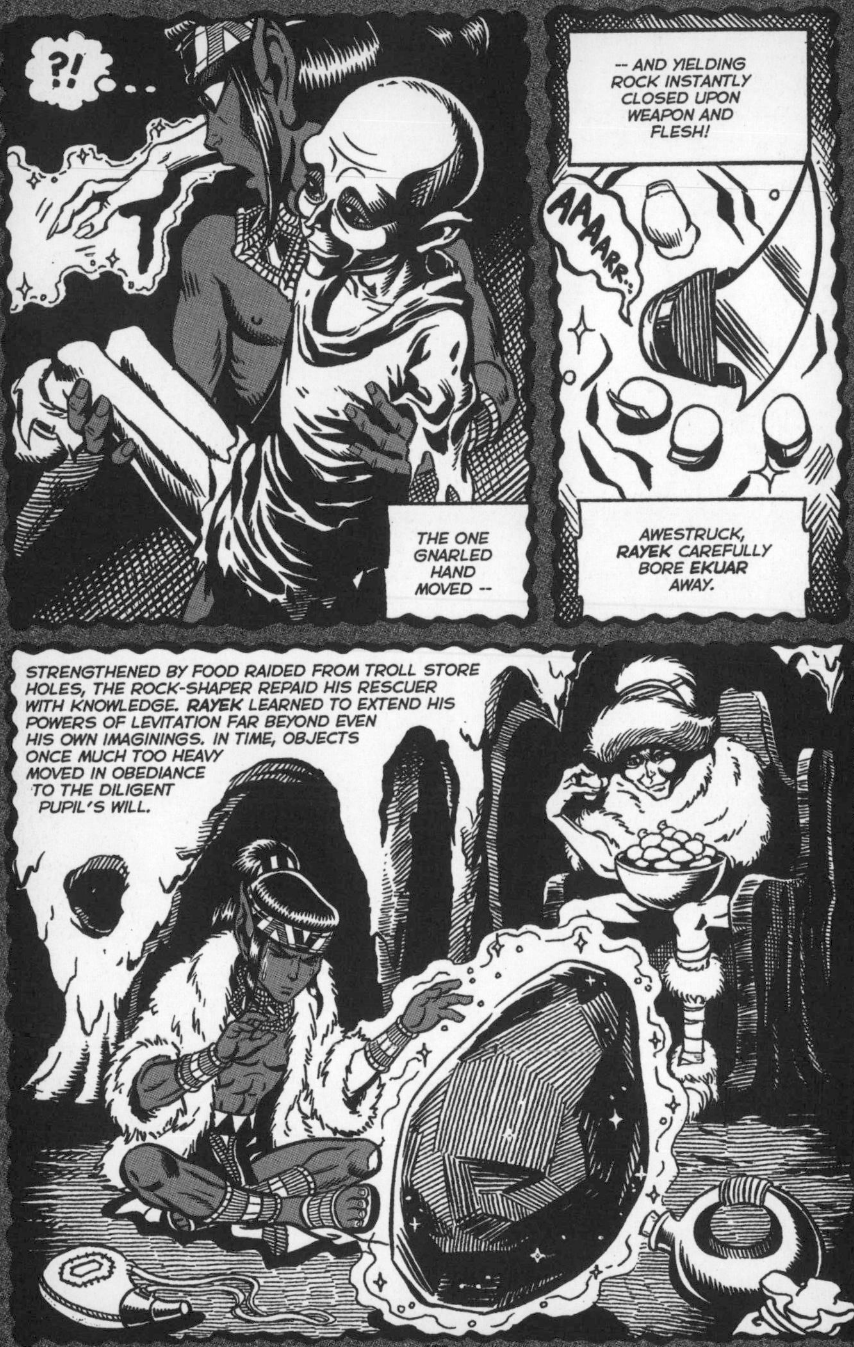
?!...
THE ONE GNARLED HAND MOVED --
-- AND YIELDING ROCK INSTANTLY CLOSED UPON WEAPON AND FLESH!
AAAAARR..
AWESTRUCK, RAYEK CAREFULLY BORE EKUAR AWAY.
STRENGTHENED BY FOOD RAIDED FROM TROLL STORE HOLES, THE ROCK-SHAPER REPAID HIS RESCUER WITH KNOWLEDGE. RAYEK LEARNED TO EXTEND HIS POWERS OF LEVITATION FAR BEYOND EVEN HIS OWN IMAGININGS. IN TIME, OBJECTS ONCE MUCH TOO HEAVY MOVED IN OBEDIANCE TO THE DILIGENT PUPIL'S WILL.

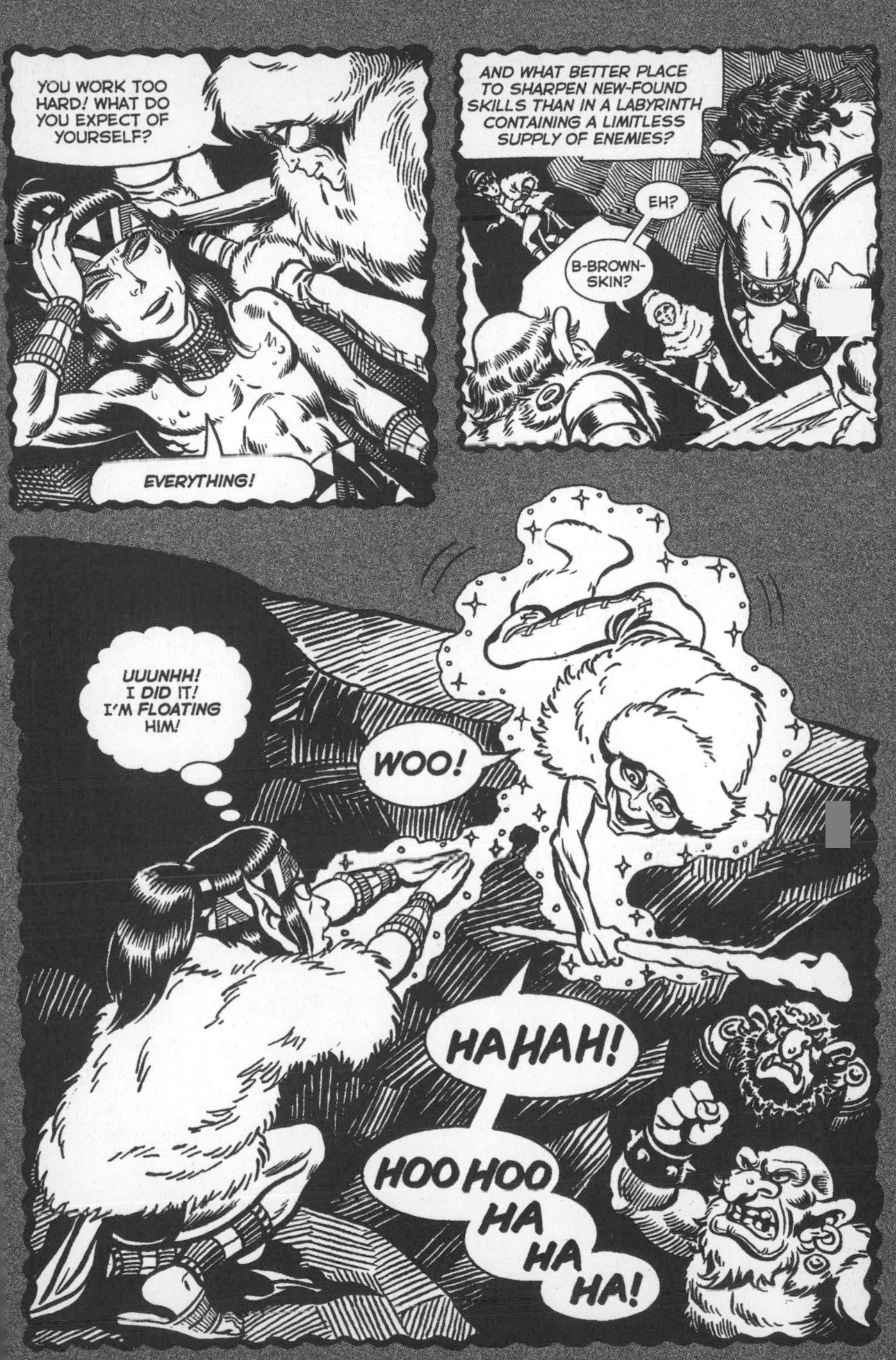

YOU WORK TOO HARD! WHAT DO YOU EXPECT OF YOURSELF?
EVERYTHING!
AND WHAT BETTER PLACE TO SHARPEN NEW-FOUND SKILLS THAN IN A LABYRINTH CONTAINING A LIMITLESS SUPPLY OF ENEMIES?
EH?
B-BROWN-SKIN?
UUUNHH! I DID IT! I'M FLOATING HIM!
WOO!
HAHAH!
HOO HOO HA HA HA!

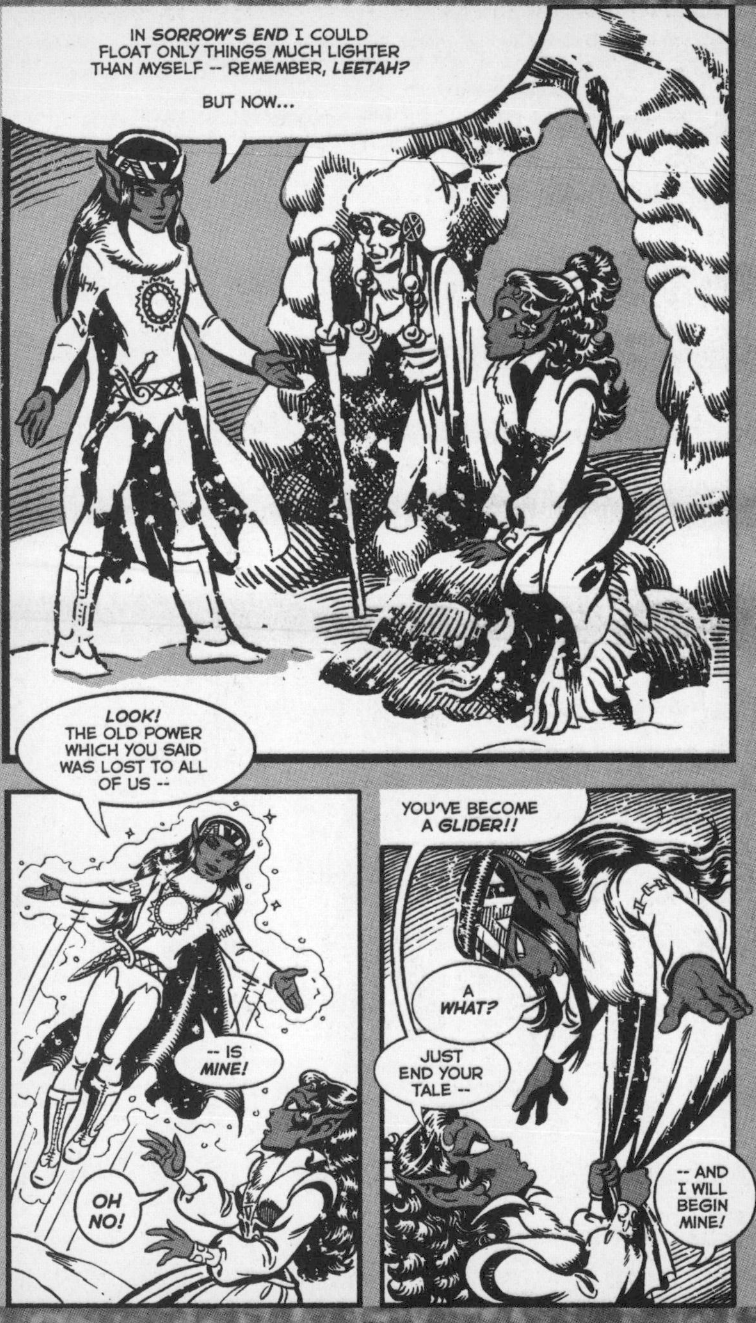

IN SORROW'S END I COULD FLOAT ONLY THINGS MUCH LIGHTER THAN MYSELF -- REMEMBER, LEETAH?
BUT NOW...
LOOK! THE OLD POWER WHICH YOU SAID WAS LOST TO ALL OF US --
-- IS MINE!
OH NO!
YOU'VE BECOME A GLIDER!!
A WHAT?
JUST END YOUR TALE --
-- AND I WILL BEGIN MINE!

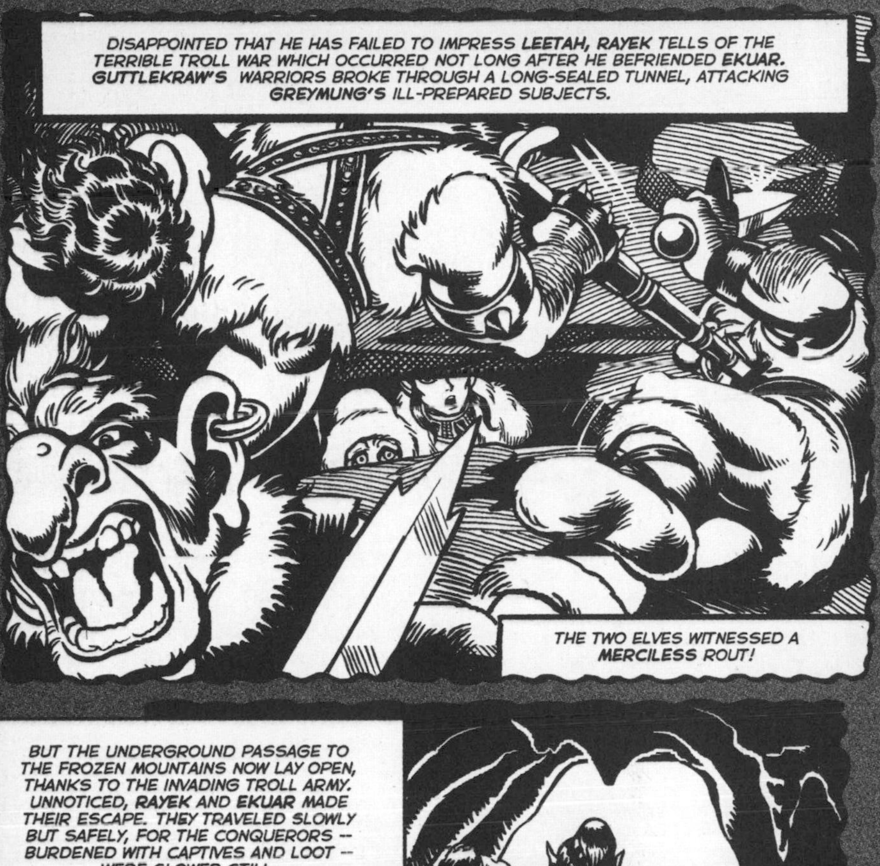
DISAPPOINTED THAT HE HAS FAILED TO IMPRESS LEETAH, RAYEK TELLS OF THE TERRIBLE TROLL WAR WHICH OCCURRED NOT LONG AFTER HE BEFRIENDED EKUAR. GUTTLEKRAW'S WARRIORS BROKE THROUGH A LONG-SEALED TUNNEL, ATTACKING GREYMUNG'S ILL-PREPARED SUBJECTS.
THE TWO ELVES WITNESSED A MERCILESS ROUT!

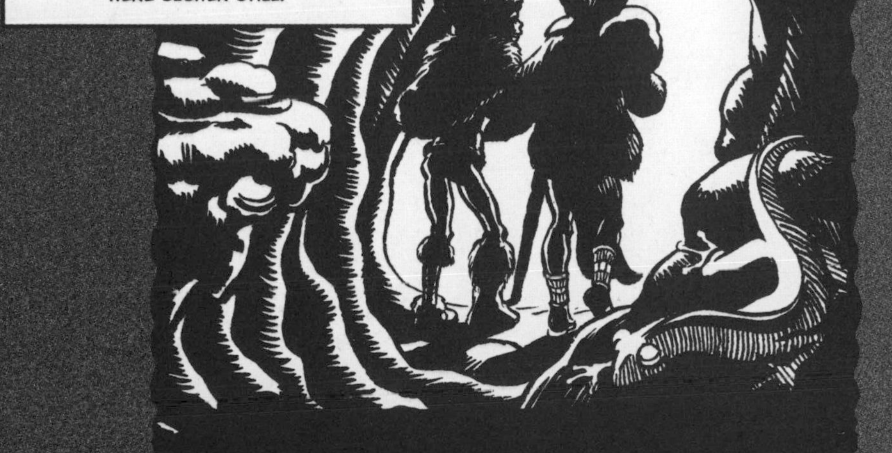
BUT THE UNDERGROUND PASSAGE TO THE FROZEN MOUNTAINS NOW LAY OPEN, THANKS TO THE INVADING TROLL ARMY. UNNOTICED, RAYEK AND EKUAR MADE THEIR ESCAPE. THEY TRAVELED SLOWLY BUT SAFELY, FOR THE CONQUERORS -- BURDENED WITH CAPTIVES AND LOOT -- WERE SLOWER STILL.

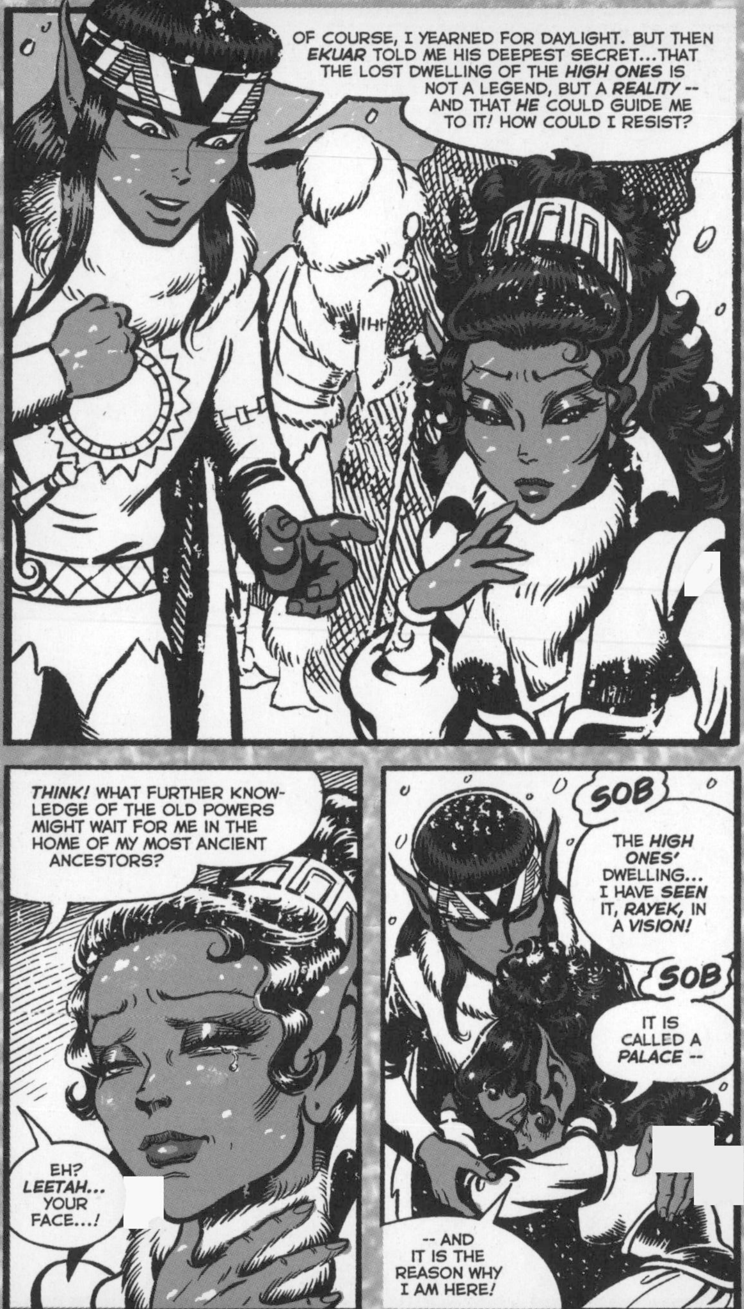
OF COURSE, I YEARNED FOR DAYLIGHT. BUT THEN EKUAR TOLD ME HIS DEEPEST SECRET...THAT THE LOST DWELLING OF THE HIGH ONES IS NOT A LEGEND, BUT A REALITY -- AND THAT HE COULD GUIDE ME TO IT! HOW COULD I RESIST?
THINK! WHAT FURTHER KNOWLEDGE OF THE OLD POWERS MIGHT WAIT FOR ME IN THE HOME OF MY MOST ANCIENT ANCESTORS?
EH? LEETAH... YOUR FACE...!
SOB
THE HIGH ONES' DWELLING... I HAVE SEEN IT, RAYEK, IN A VISION!
SOB
IT IS CALLED A PALACE --
-- AND IT IS THE REASON WHY I AM HERE!

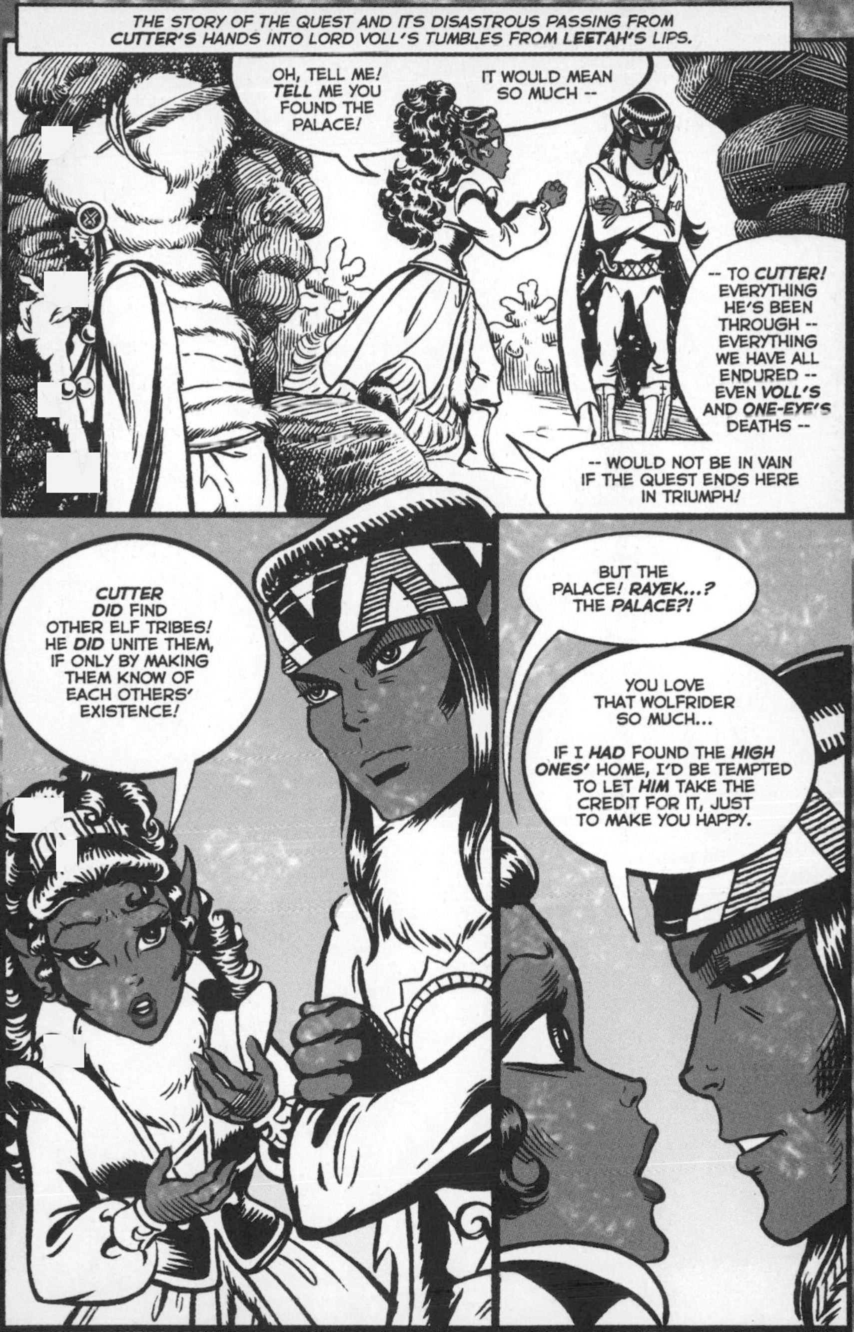

THE STORY OF THE QUEST AND ITS DISASTROUS PASSING FROM CUTTER'S HANDS INTO LORD VOLL'S TUMBLES FROM LEETAH'S LIPS.
OH, TELL ME! TELL ME YOU FOUND THE PALACE!
IT WOULD MEAN SO MUCH --
-- TO CUTTER! EVERYTHING HE'S BEEN THROUGH -- EVERYTHING WE HAVE ALL ENDURED -- EVEN VOLL'S AND ONE-EYE'S DEATHS --
-- WOULD NOT BE IN VAIN IF THE QUEST ENDS HERE IN TRIUMPH!
CUTTER DID FIND OTHER ELF TRIBES! HE DID UNITE THEM, IF ONLY BY MAKING THEM KNOW OF EACH OTHERS' EXISTENCE!
BUT THE PALACE! RAYEK...? THE PALACE?!
YOU LOVE THAT WOLFRIDER SO MUCH...
IF I HAD FOUND THE HIGH ONES' HOME, I'D BE TEMPTED TO LET HIM TAKE THE CREDIT FOR IT, JUST TO MAKE YOU HAPPY.

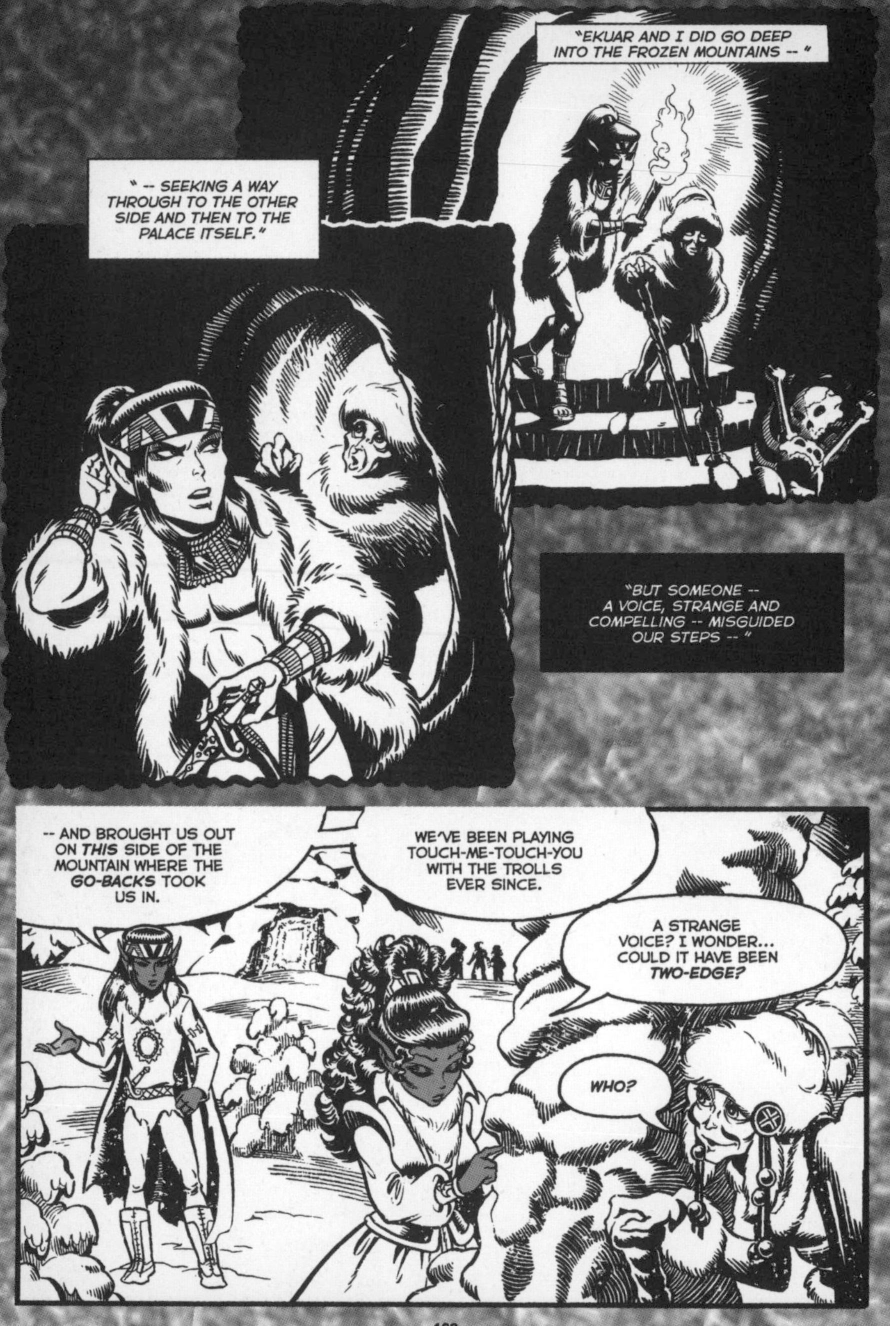
"EKUAR AND I DID GO DEEP INTO THE FROZEN MOUNTAINS -- "
" -- SEEKING A WAY THROUGH TO THE OTHER SIDE AND THEN TO THE PALACE ITSELF."
"BUT SOMEONE -- A VOICE, STRANGE AND COMPELLING -- MISGUIDED OUR STEPS -- "
-- AND BROUGHT US OUT ON *THIS* SIDE OF THE MOUNTAIN WHERE THE *GO-BACKS* TOOK US IN.
WE'VE BEEN PLAYING TOUCH-ME-TOUCH-YOU WITH THE TROLLS EVER SINCE.
A STRANGE VOICE? I WONDER... COULD IT HAVE BEEN *TWO-EDGE?*
WHO?

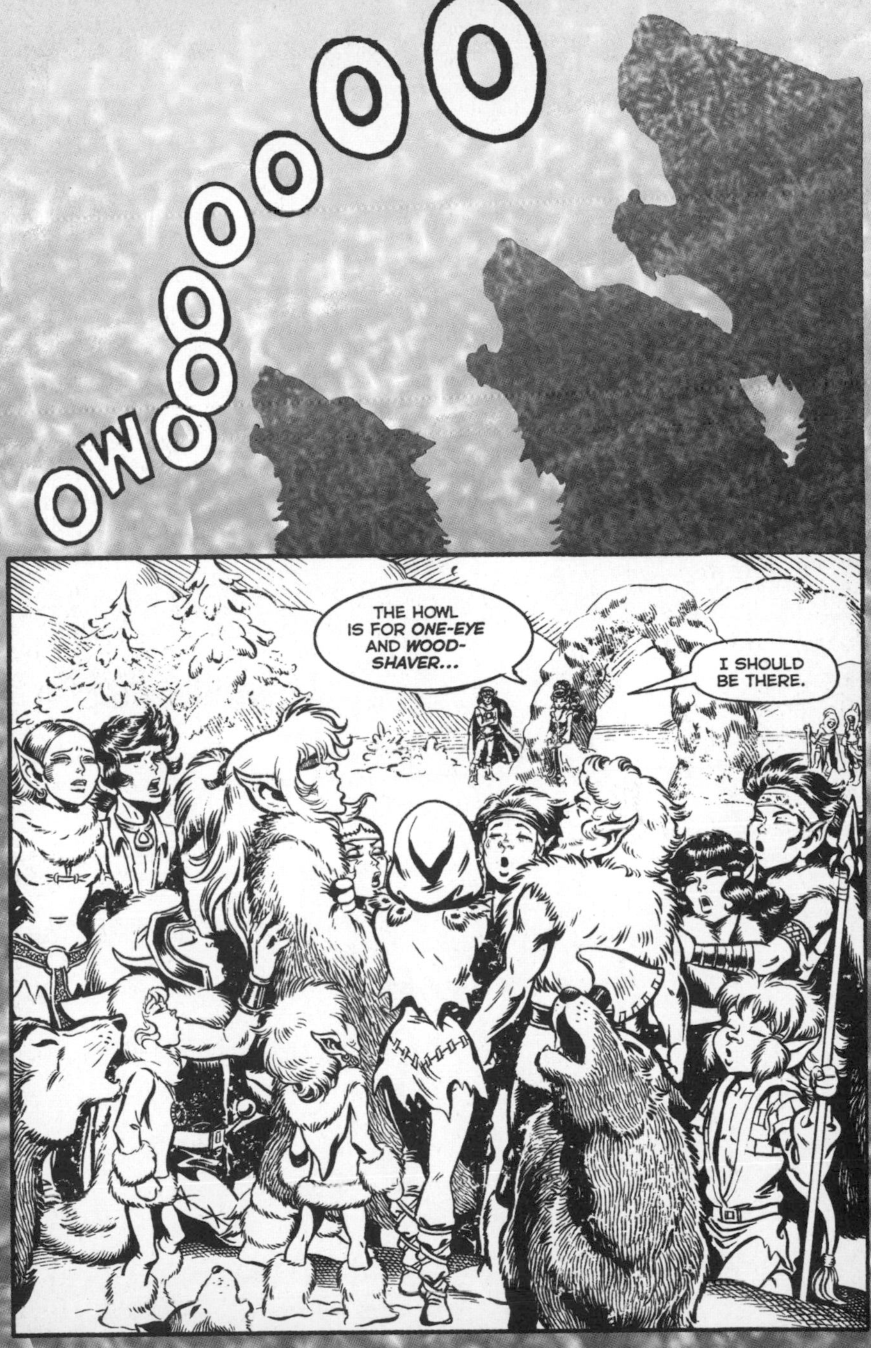
OWOOOOOOOOOO
THE HOWL IS FOR ONE-EYE AND WOOD-SHAVER...
I SHOULD BE THERE.

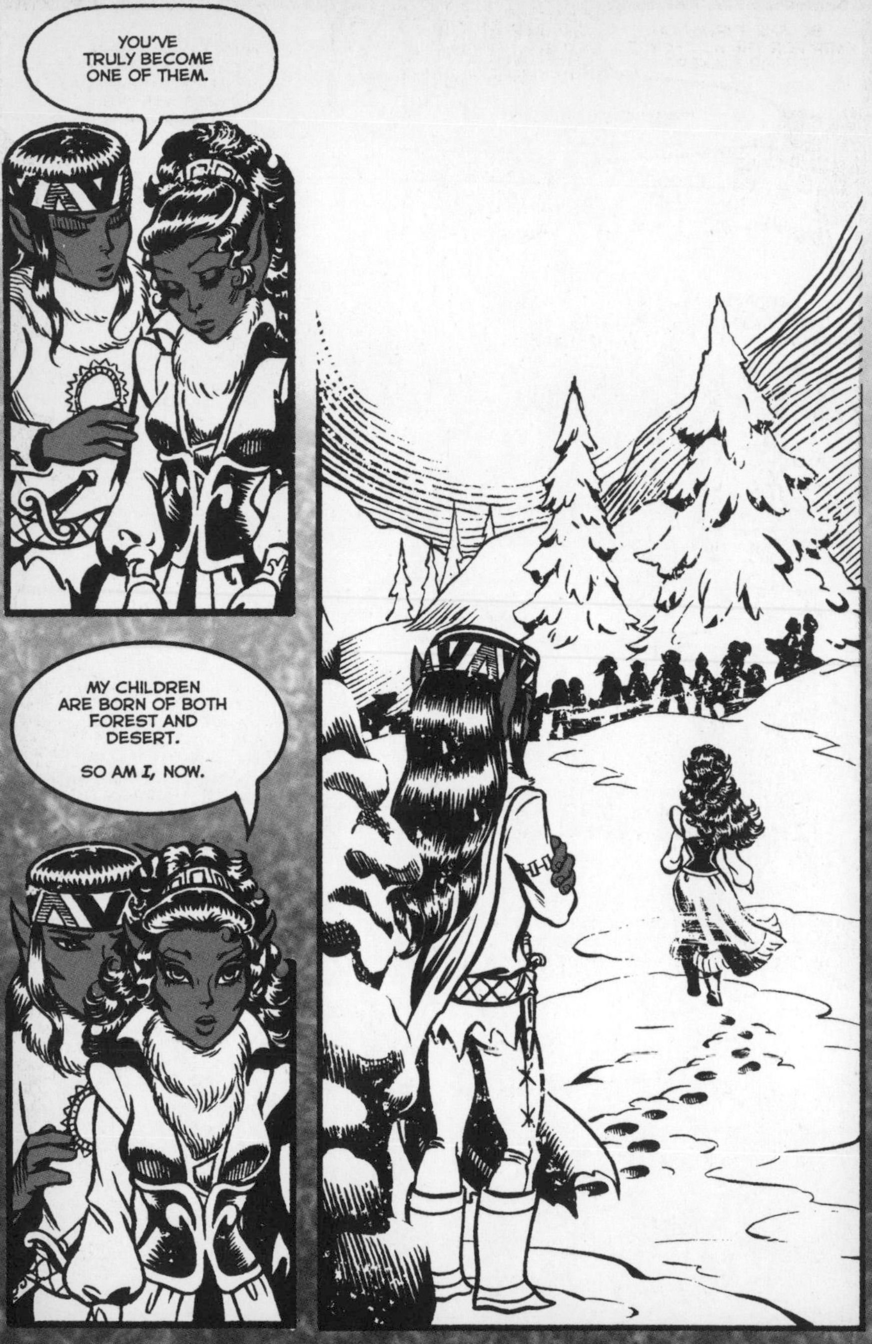
YOU'VE TRULY BECOME ONE OF THEM.
MY CHILDREN ARE BORN OF BOTH FOREST AND DESERT.
SO AM *I*, NOW.

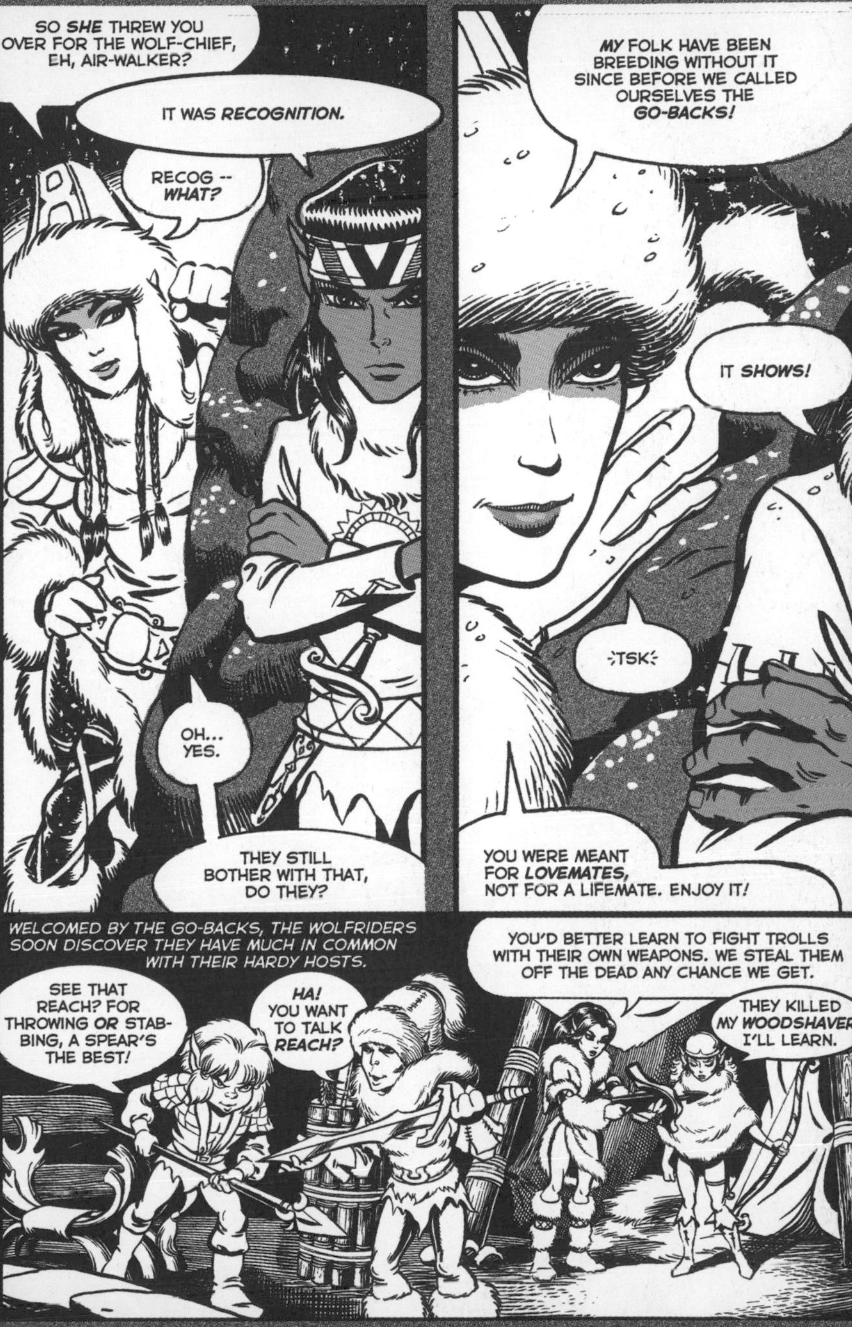
SO SHE THREW YOU OVER FOR THE WOLF-CHIEF, EH, AIR-WALKER?
IT WAS RECOGNITION.
RECOG -- WHAT?
OH... YES.
THEY STILL BOTHER WITH THAT, DO THEY?
MY FOLK HAVE BEEN BREEDING WITHOUT IT SINCE BEFORE WE CALLED OURSELVES THE GO-BACKS!
IT SHOWS!
TSK
YOU WERE MEANT FOR LOVEMATES, NOT FOR A LIFEMATE. ENJOY IT!
WELCOMED BY THE GO-BACKS, THE WOLFRIDERS SOON DISCOVER THEY HAVE MUCH IN COMMON WITH THEIR HARDY HOSTS.
SEE THAT REACH? FOR THROWING OR STABBING, A SPEAR'S THE BEST!
HA! YOU WANT TO TALK REACH?
YOU'D BETTER LEARN TO FIGHT TROLLS WITH THEIR OWN WEAPONS. WE STEAL THEM OFF THE DEAD ANY CHANCE WE GET.
THEY KILLED MY WOODSHAVER. I'LL LEARN.

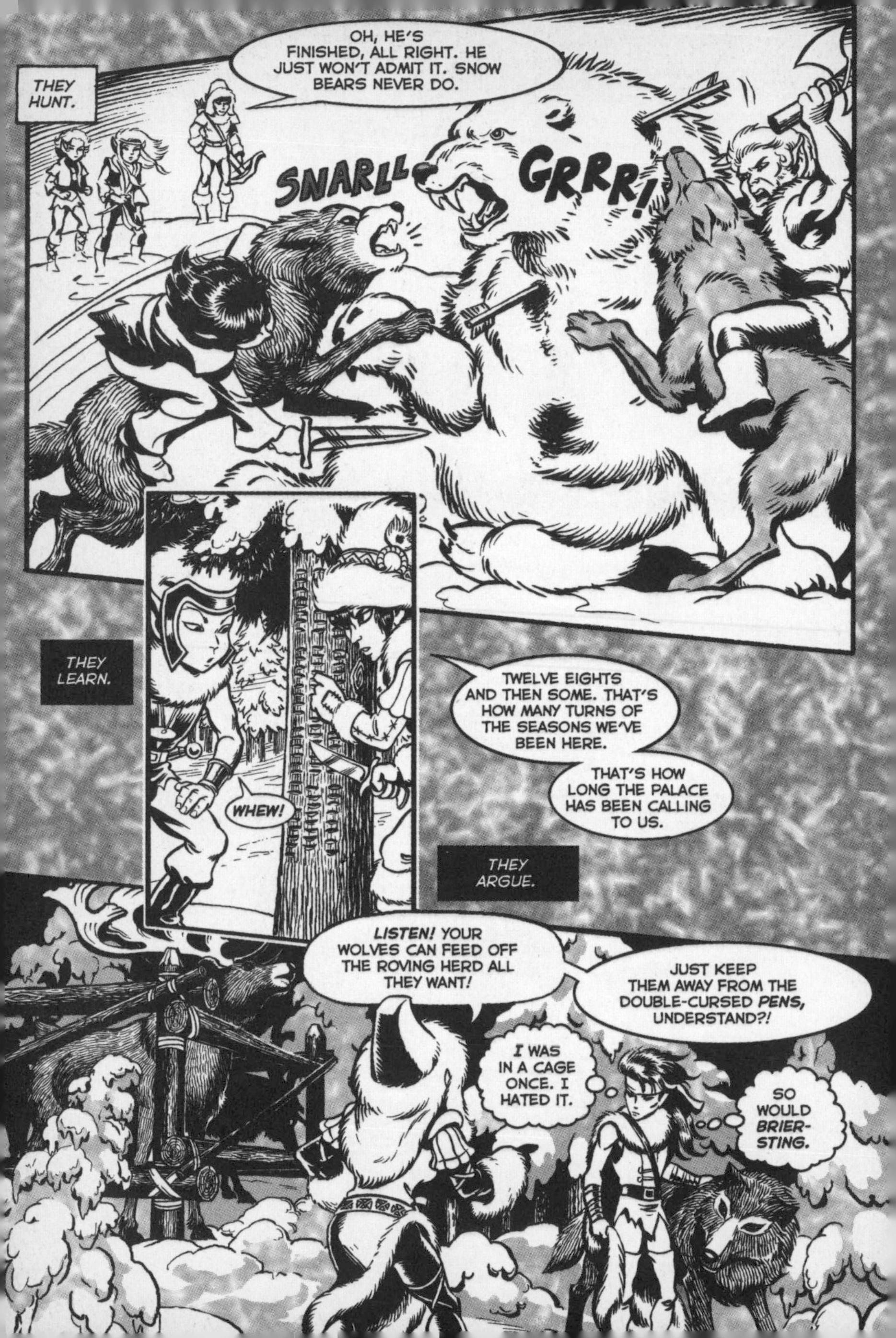
THEY HUNT.
OH, HE'S FINISHED, ALL RIGHT. HE JUST WON'T ADMIT IT. SNOW BEARS NEVER DO.
SNARLLL
GRRRR!
THEY LEARN.
WHEW!
TWELVE EIGHTS AND THEN SOME. THAT'S HOW MANY TURNS OF THE SEASONS WE'VE BEEN HERE.
THAT'S HOW LONG THE PALACE HAS BEEN CALLING TO US.
THEY ARGUE.
LISTEN! YOUR WOLVES CAN FEED OFF THE ROVING HERD ALL THEY WANT!
JUST KEEP THEM AWAY FROM THE DOUBLE-CURSED PENS, UNDERSTAND?!
I WAS IN A CAGE ONCE. I HATED IT.
SO WOULD BRIER-STING.

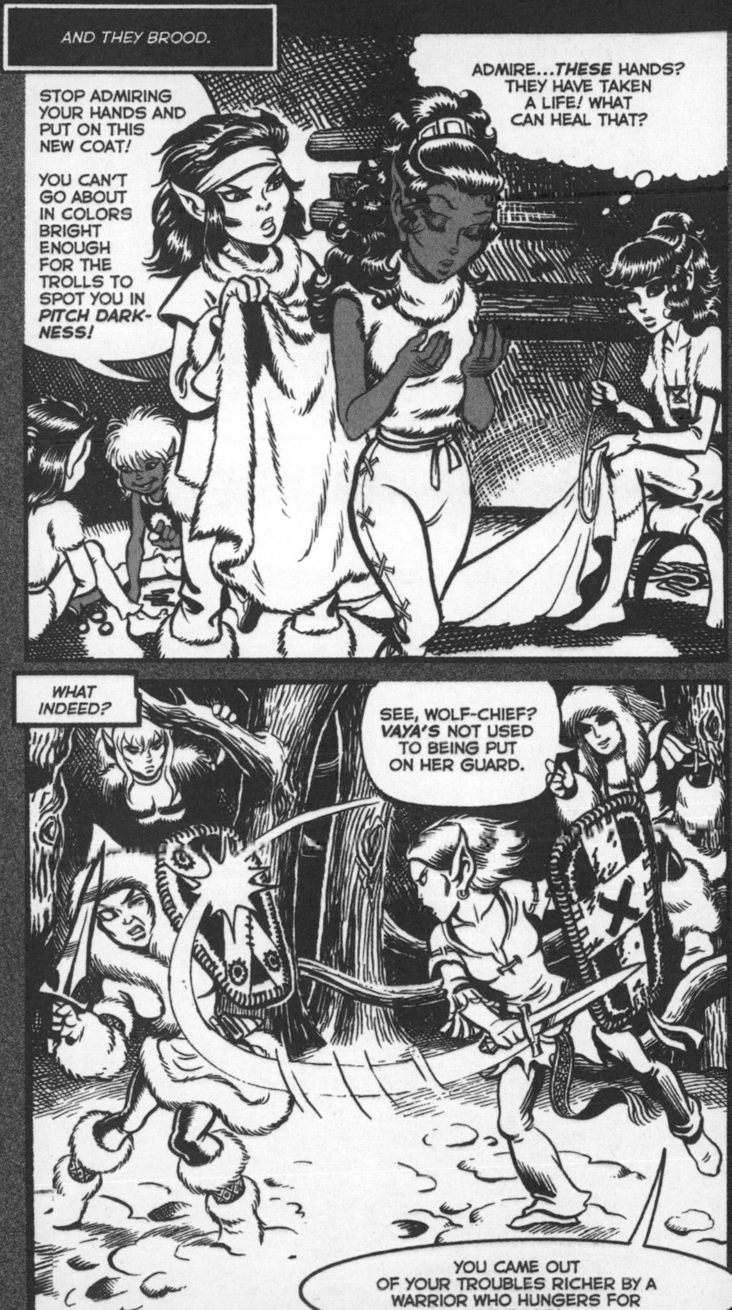
AND THEY BROOD.
STOP ADMIRING YOUR HANDS AND PUT ON THIS NEW COAT!
YOU CAN'T GO ABOUT IN COLORS BRIGHT ENOUGH FOR THE TROLLS TO SPOT YOU IN *PITCH DARKNESS!*
ADMIRE...*THESE* HANDS? THEY HAVE TAKEN A LIFE! WHAT CAN HEAL THAT?
WHAT INDEED?
SEE, WOLF-CHIEF? *VAYA'S* NOT USED TO BEING PUT ON HER GUARD.
YOU CAME OUT OF YOUR TROUBLES RICHER BY A WARRIOR WHO HUNGERS FOR *REVENGE!*

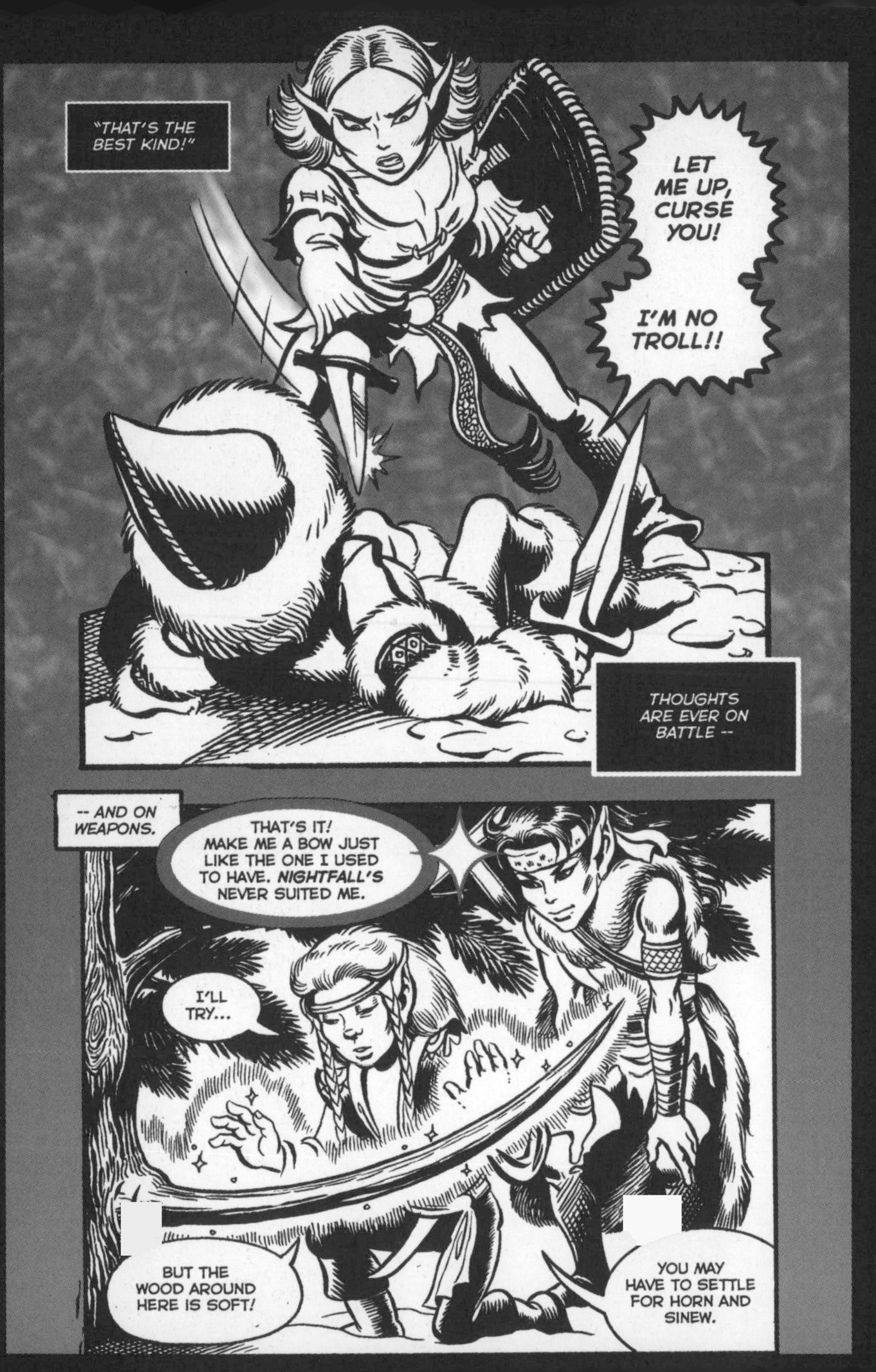
"THAT'S THE BEST KIND!"
LET ME UP, CURSE YOU!
I'M NO TROLL!!
THOUGHTS ARE EVER ON BATTLE --
-- AND ON WEAPONS.
THAT'S IT! MAKE ME A BOW JUST LIKE THE ONE I USED TO HAVE. NIGHTFALL'S NEVER SUITED ME.
I'LL TRY...
BUT THE WOOD AROUND HERE IS SOFT!
YOU MAY HAVE TO SETTLE FOR HORN AND SINEW.

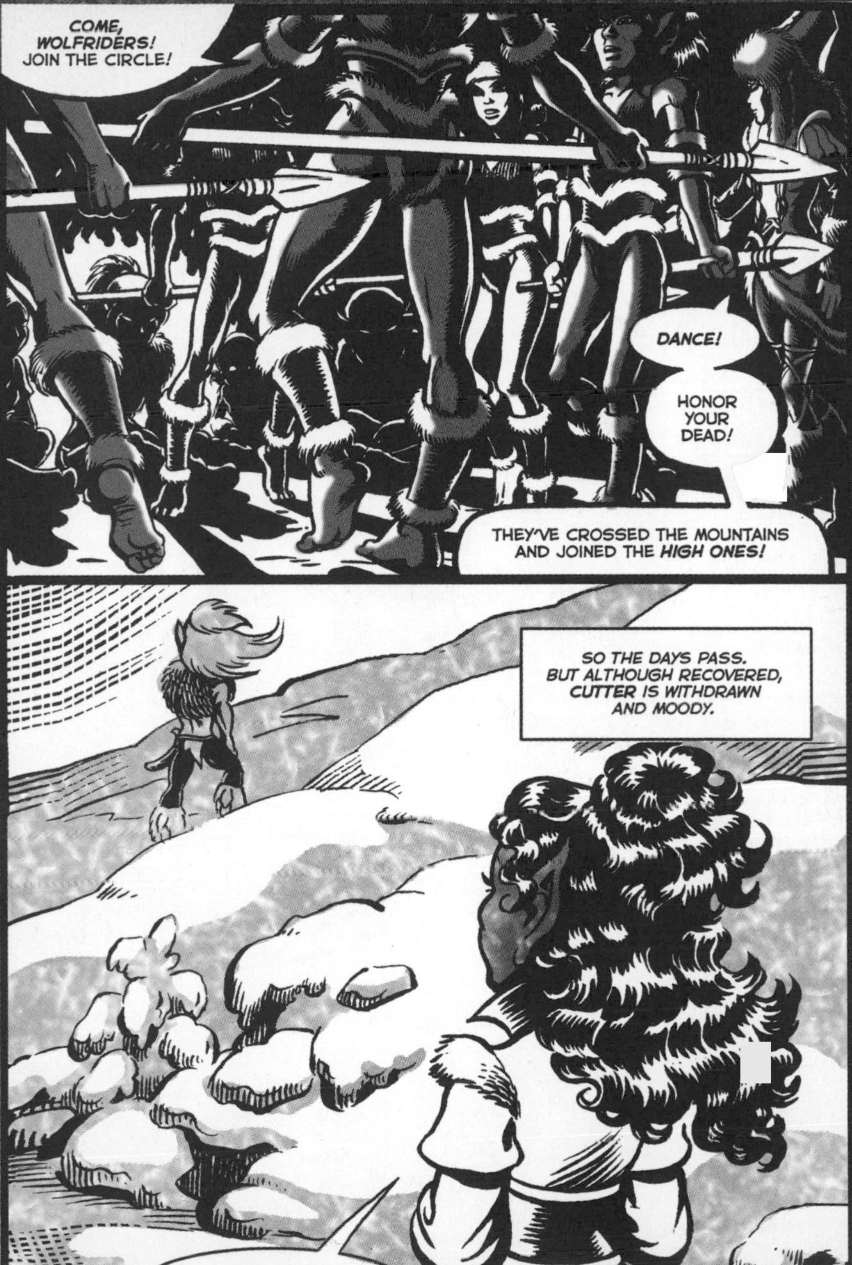

COME, WOLFRIDERS! JOIN THE CIRCLE!
DANCE!
HONOR YOUR DEAD!
THEY'VE CROSSED THE MOUNTAINS AND JOINED THE HIGH ONES!
SO THE DAYS PASS. BUT ALTHOUGH RECOVERED, CUTTER IS WITHDRAWN AND MOODY.
BELOVED...?

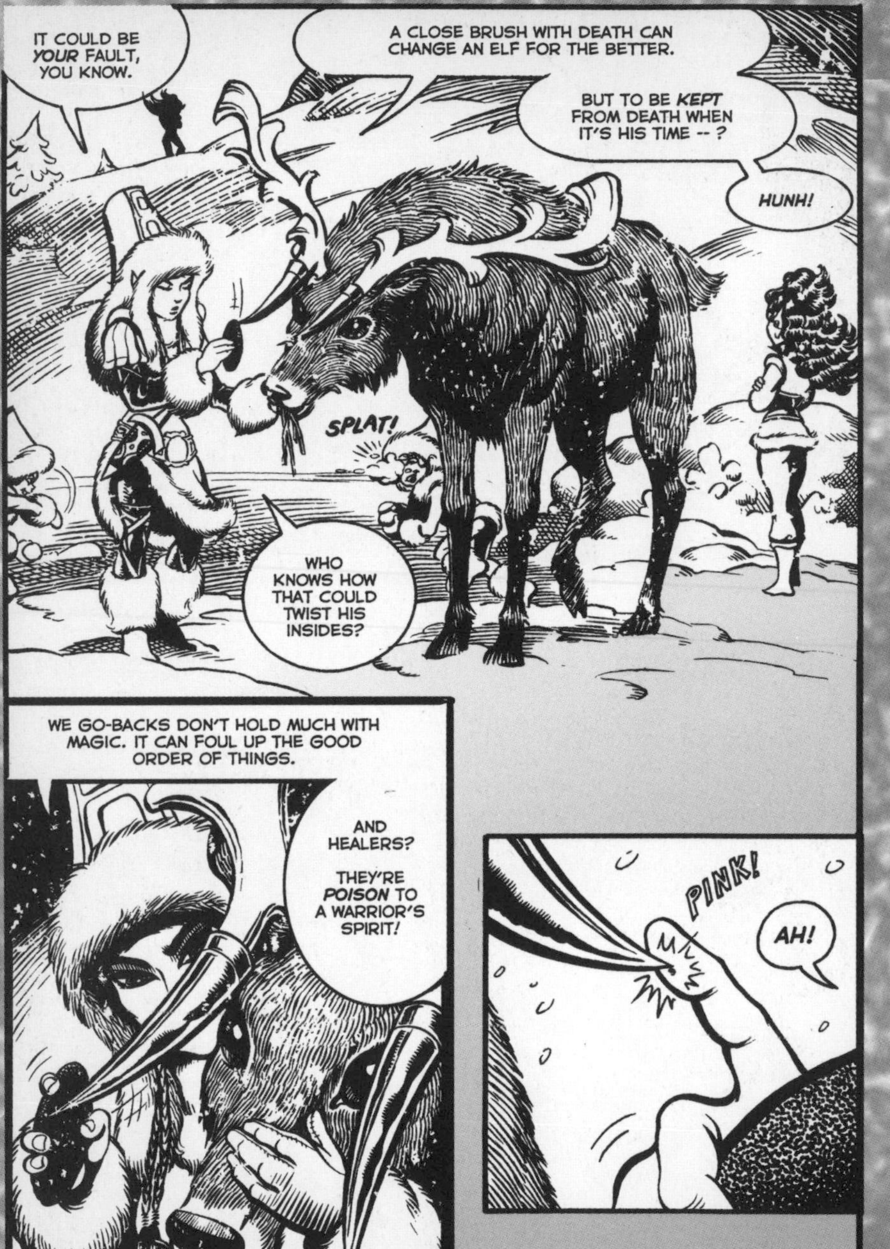
IT COULD BE YOUR FAULT, YOU KNOW.
A CLOSE BRUSH WITH DEATH CAN CHANGE AN ELF FOR THE BETTER.
BUT TO BE KEPT FROM DEATH WHEN IT'S HIS TIME -- ?
HUNH!
SPLAT!
WHO KNOWS HOW THAT COULD TWIST HIS INSIDES?
WE GO-BACKS DON'T HOLD MUCH WITH MAGIC. IT CAN FOUL UP THE GOOD ORDER OF THINGS.
AND HEALERS?
THEY'RE POISON TO A WARRIOR'S SPIRIT!
PINK!
AH!

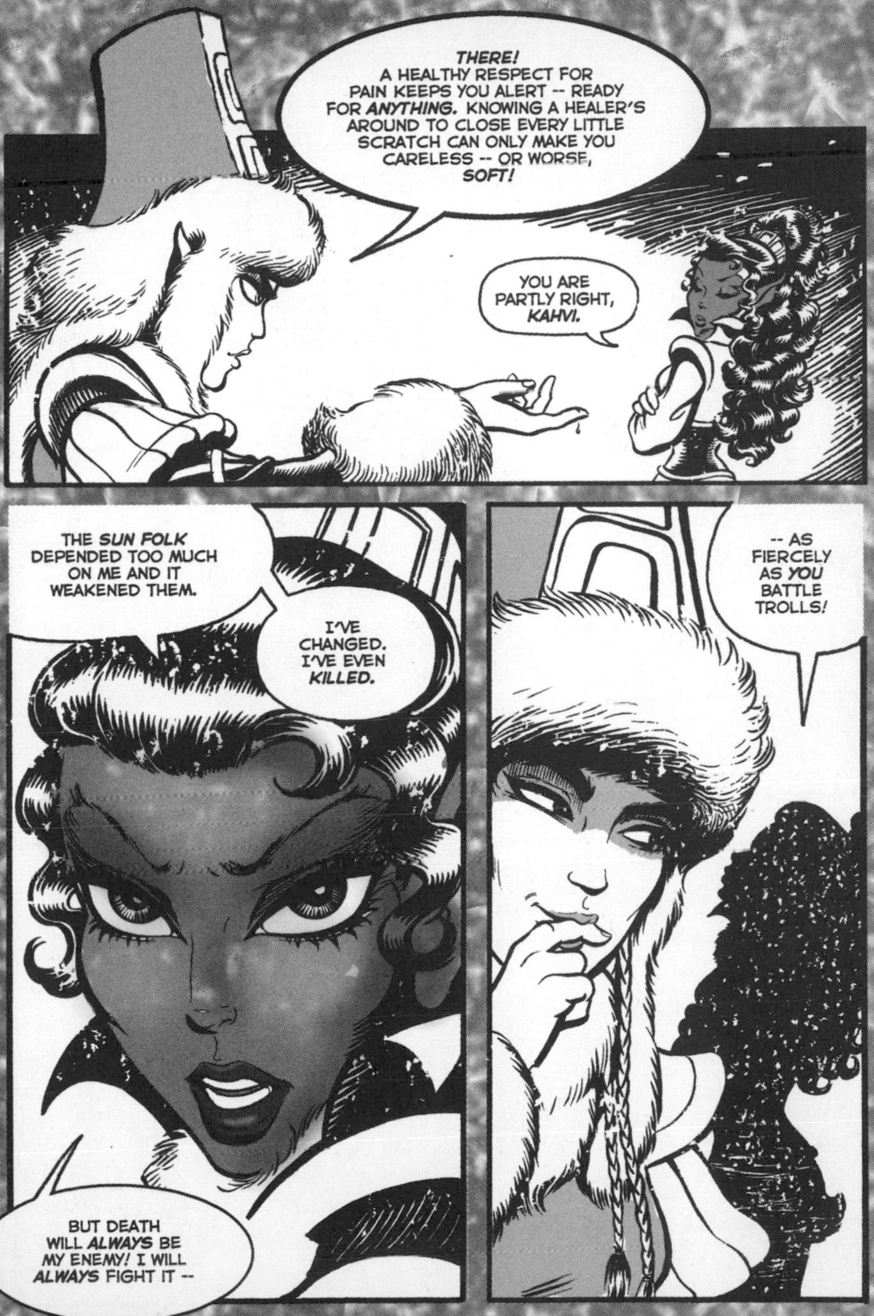
THERE! A HEALTHY RESPECT FOR PAIN KEEPS YOU ALERT -- READY FOR ANYTHING. KNOWING A HEALER'S AROUND TO CLOSE EVERY LITTLE SCRATCH CAN ONLY MAKE YOU CARELESS -- OR WORSE, SOFT!
YOU ARE PARTLY RIGHT, KAHVI.
THE SUN FOLK DEPENDED TOO MUCH ON ME AND IT WEAKENED THEM.
I'VE CHANGED. I'VE EVEN KILLED.
BUT DEATH WILL ALWAYS BE MY ENEMY! I WILL ALWAYS FIGHT IT --
-- AS FIERCELY AS YOU BATTLE TROLLS!

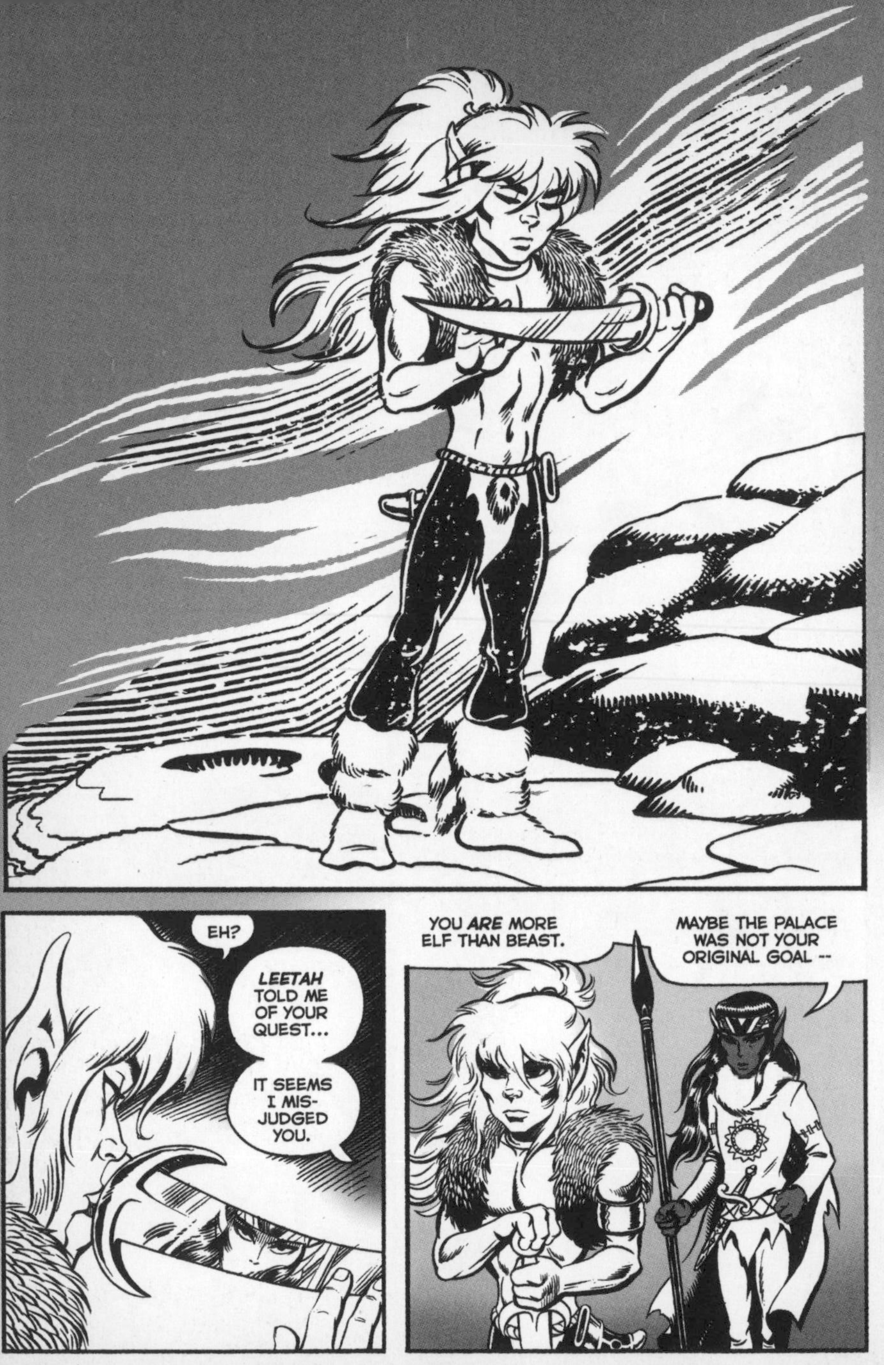
EH?
LEETAH TOLD ME OF YOUR QUEST...
IT SEEMS I MIS-JUDGED YOU.
YOU *ARE* MORE ELF THAN BEAST.
MAYBE THE PALACE WAS NOT YOUR ORIGINAL GOAL --

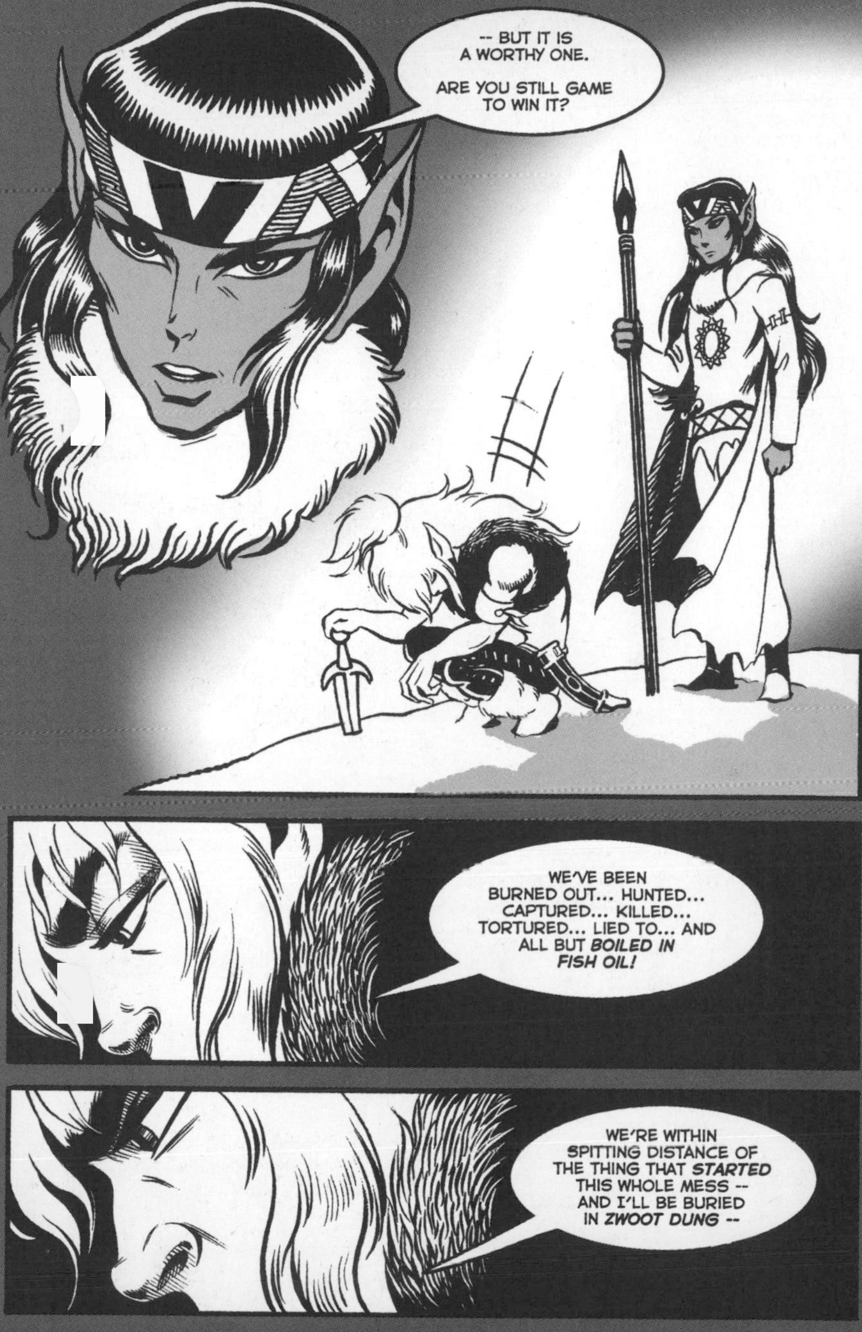
-- BUT IT IS A WORTHY ONE.
ARE YOU STILL GAME TO WIN IT?
WE'VE BEEN BURNED OUT... HUNTED... CAPTURED... KILLED... TORTURED... LIED TO... AND ALL BUT BOILED IN FISH OIL!
WE'RE WITHIN SPITTING DISTANCE OF THE THING THAT STARTED THIS WHOLE MESS -- AND I'LL BE BURIED IN ZWOOT DUNG --

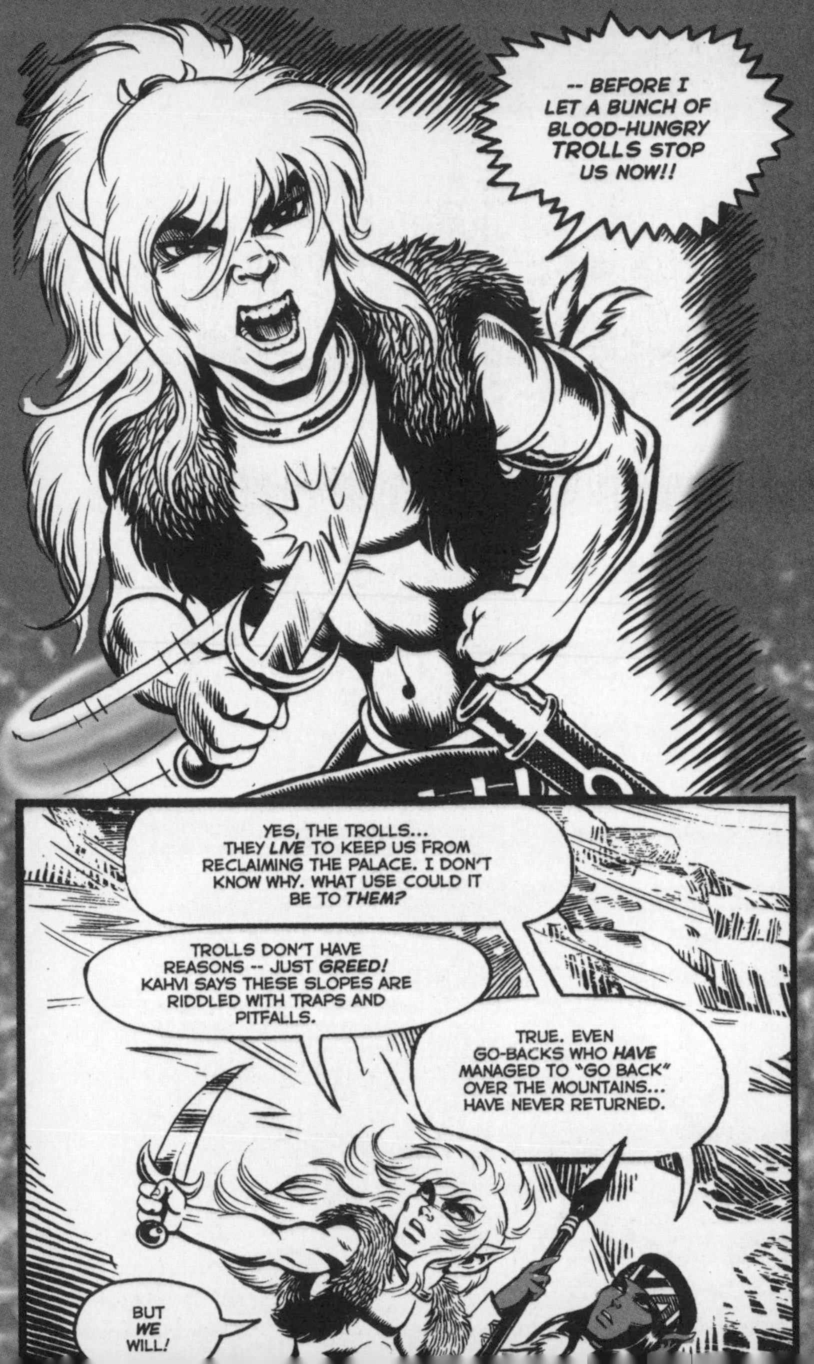
-- BEFORE I LET A BUNCH OF BLOOD-HUNGRY TROLLS STOP US NOW!!
YES, THE TROLLS... THEY LIVE TO KEEP US FROM RECLAIMING THE PALACE. I DON'T KNOW WHY. WHAT USE COULD IT BE TO THEM?
TROLLS DON'T HAVE REASONS -- JUST GREED! KAHVI SAYS THESE SLOPES ARE RIDDLED WITH TRAPS AND PITFALLS.
TRUE. EVEN GO-BACKS WHO HAVE MANAGED TO "GO BACK" OVER THE MOUNTAINS... HAVE NEVER RETURNED.
BUT WE WILL!

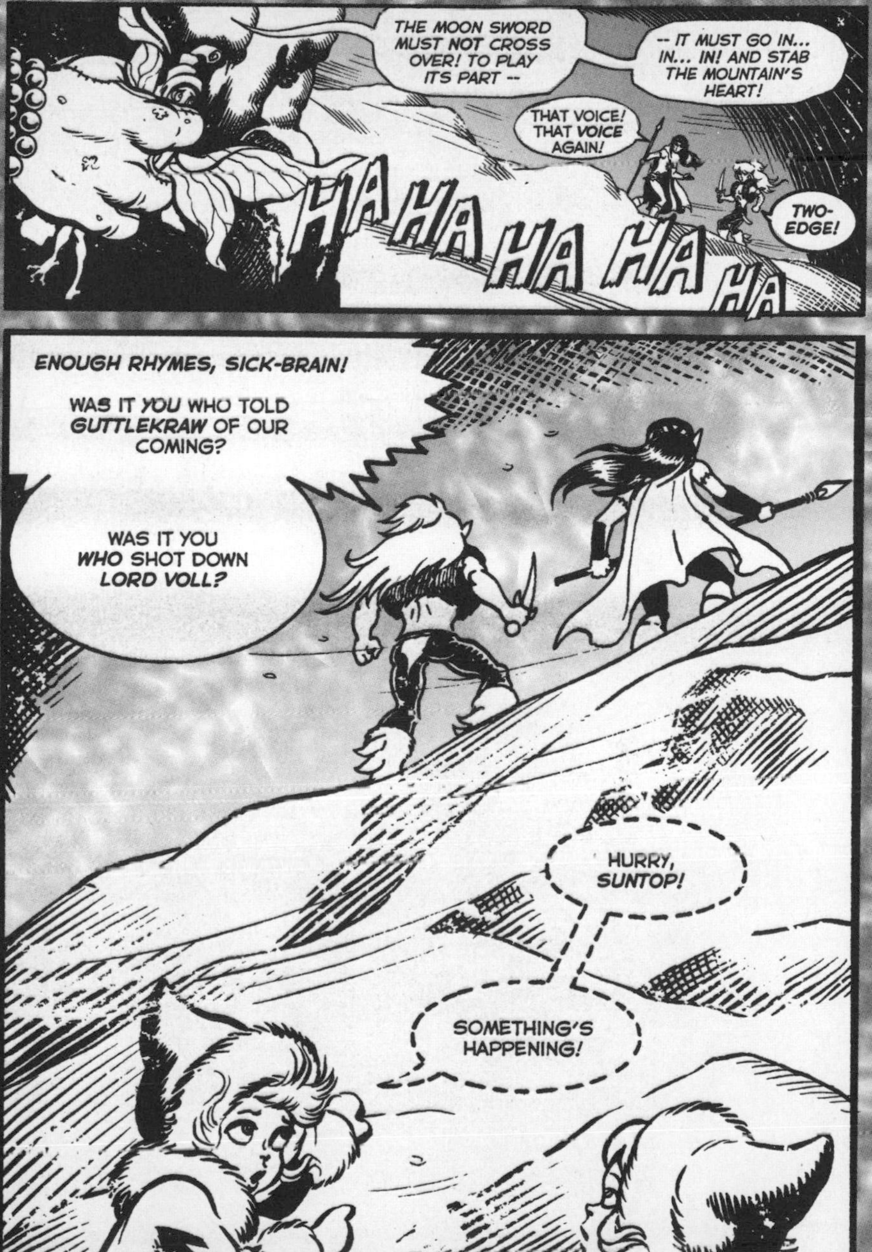
THE MOON SWORD MUST NOT CROSS OVER! TO PLAY ITS PART --
-- IT MUST GO IN... IN... IN! AND STAB THE MOUNTAIN'S HEART!
THAT VOICE! THAT VOICE AGAIN!
HA HA HA HA HA HA HA HA
TWO-EDGE!
ENOUGH RHYMES, SICK-BRAIN!
WAS IT YOU WHO TOLD GUTTLEKRAW OF OUR COMING?
WAS IT YOU WHO SHOT DOWN LORD VOLL?
HURRY, SUNTOP!
SOMETHING'S HAPPENING!

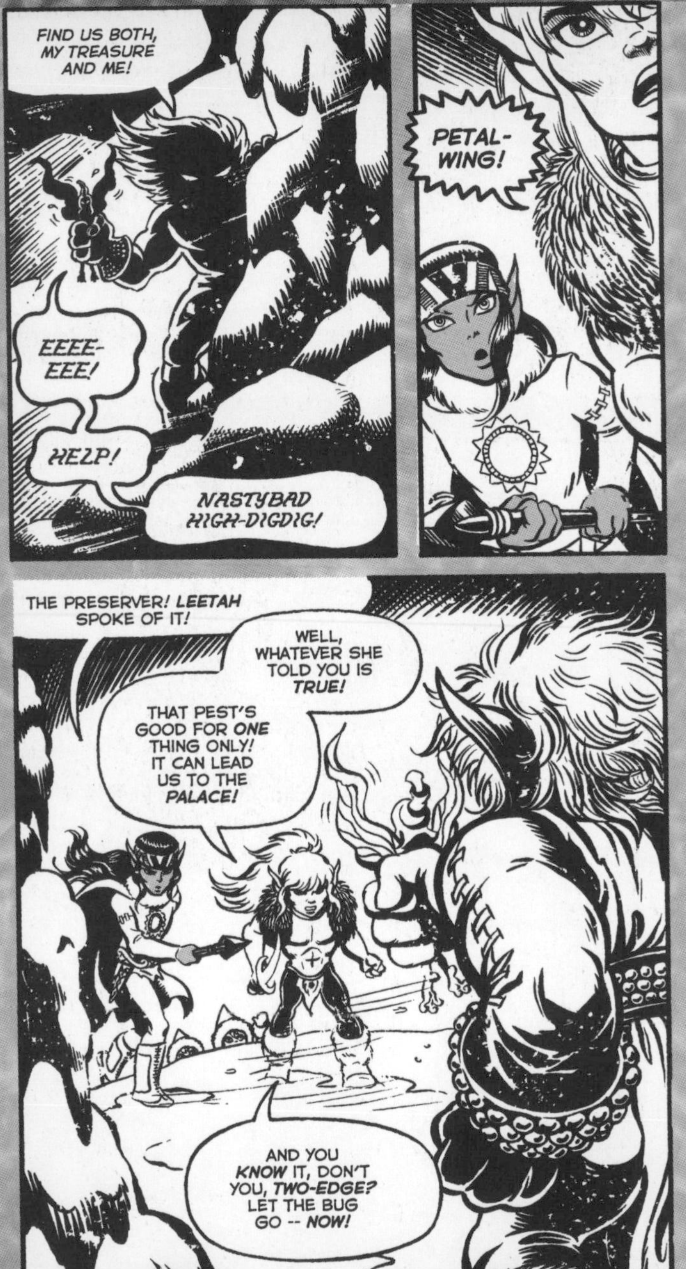
FIND US BOTH, MY TREASURE AND ME!
EEEE-EEE!
HELP!
NASTYBAD HIGH-DIGDIG!
PETAL-WING!
THE PRESERVER! LEETAH SPOKE OF IT!
WELL, WHATEVER SHE TOLD YOU IS TRUE!
THAT PEST'S GOOD FOR ONE THING ONLY! IT CAN LEAD US TO THE PALACE!
AND YOU KNOW IT, DON'T YOU, TWO-EDGE? LET THE BUG GO -- NOW!

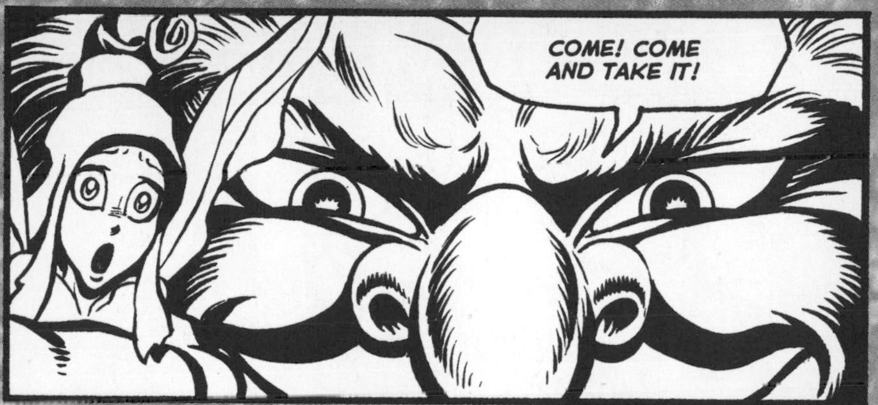
COME! COME AND TAKE IT!

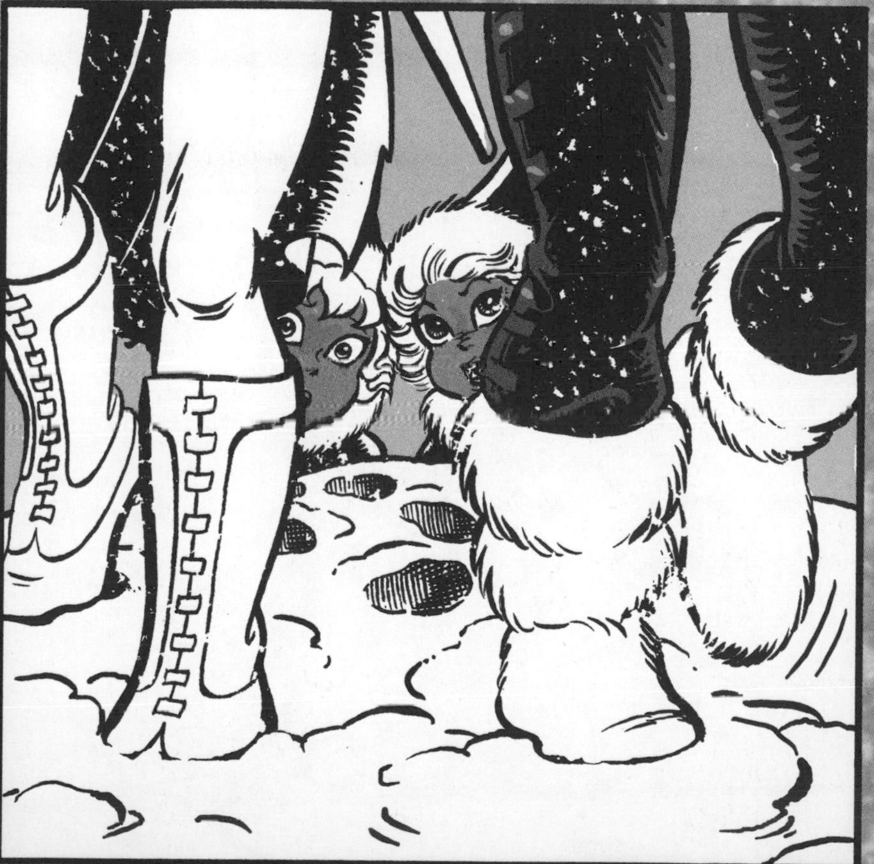

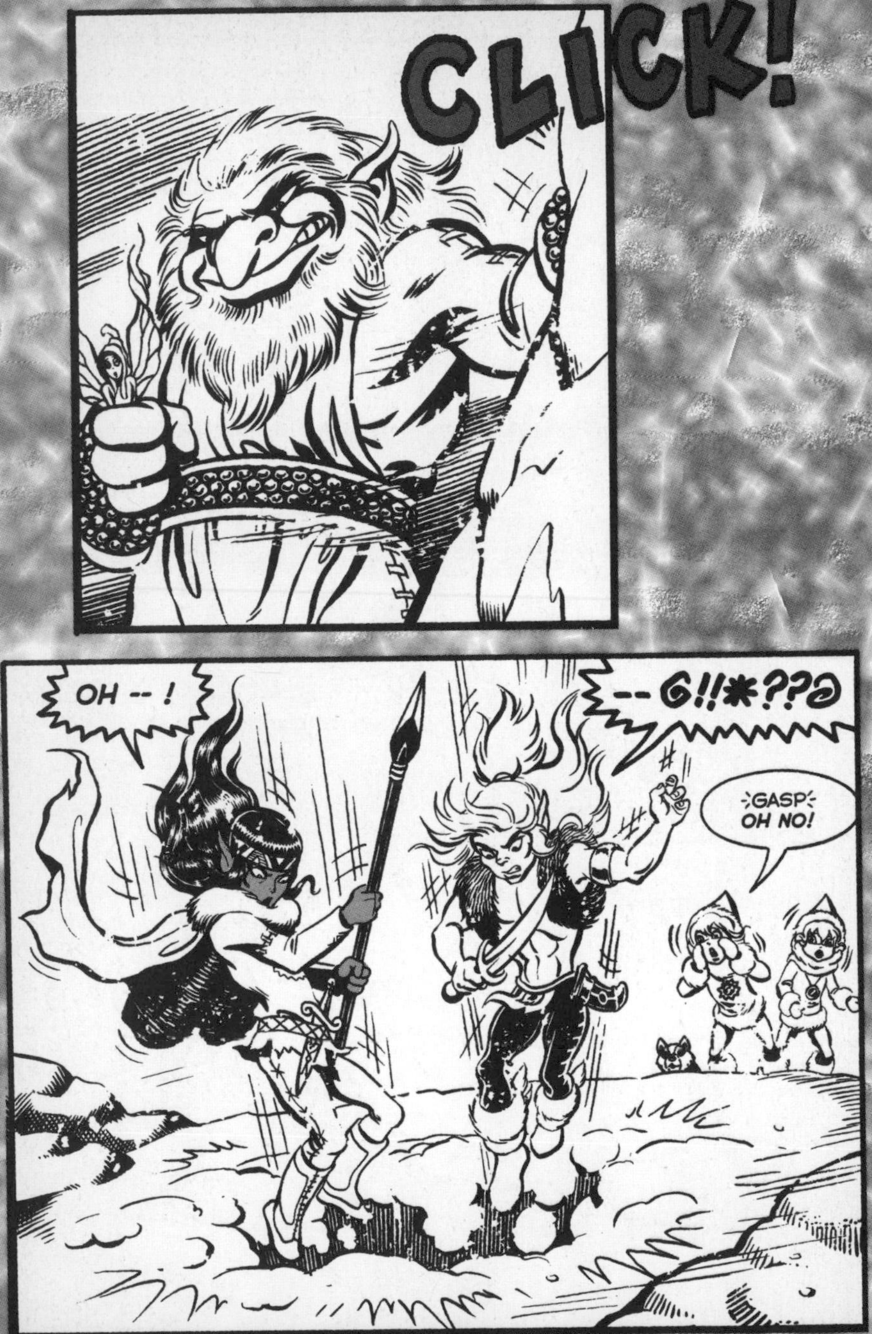
CLICK!
OH -- !
-- G!!*??@
GASP
OH NO!

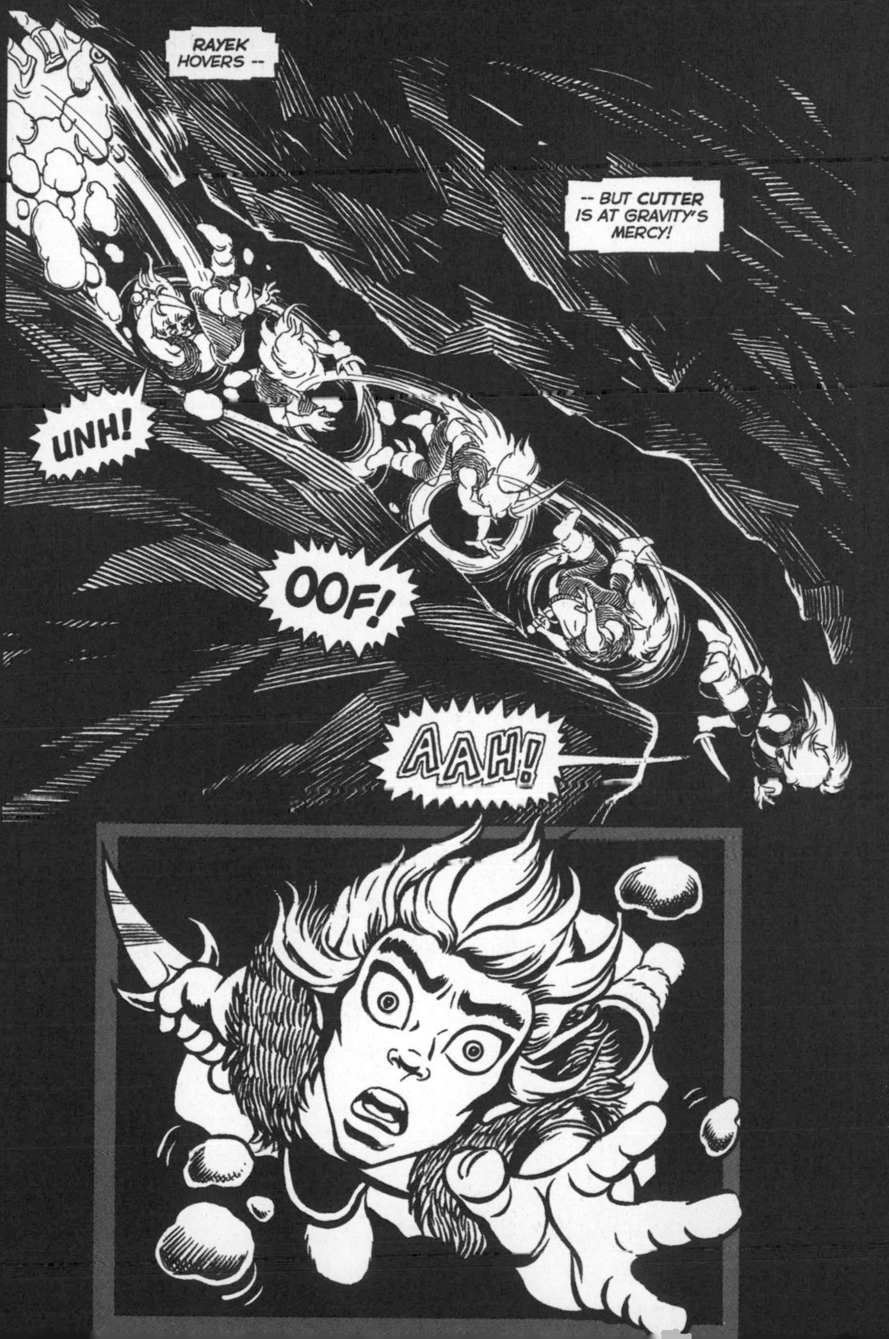
RAYEK HOVERS --
-- BUT CUTTER IS AT GRAVITY'S MERCY!
UNH!
OOF!
AAH!

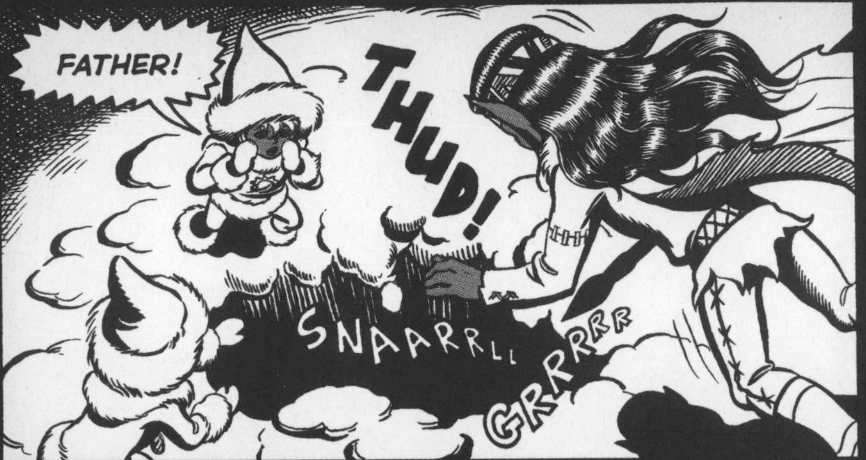
FATHER!
THUD!
SNAARRLL
GRRRRR

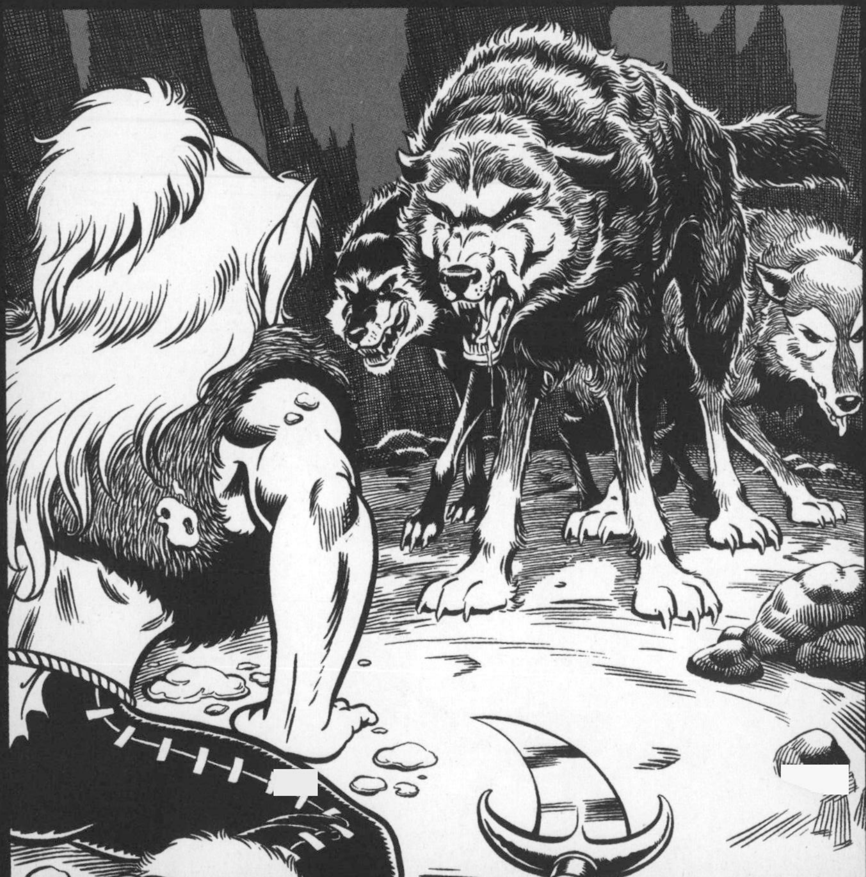

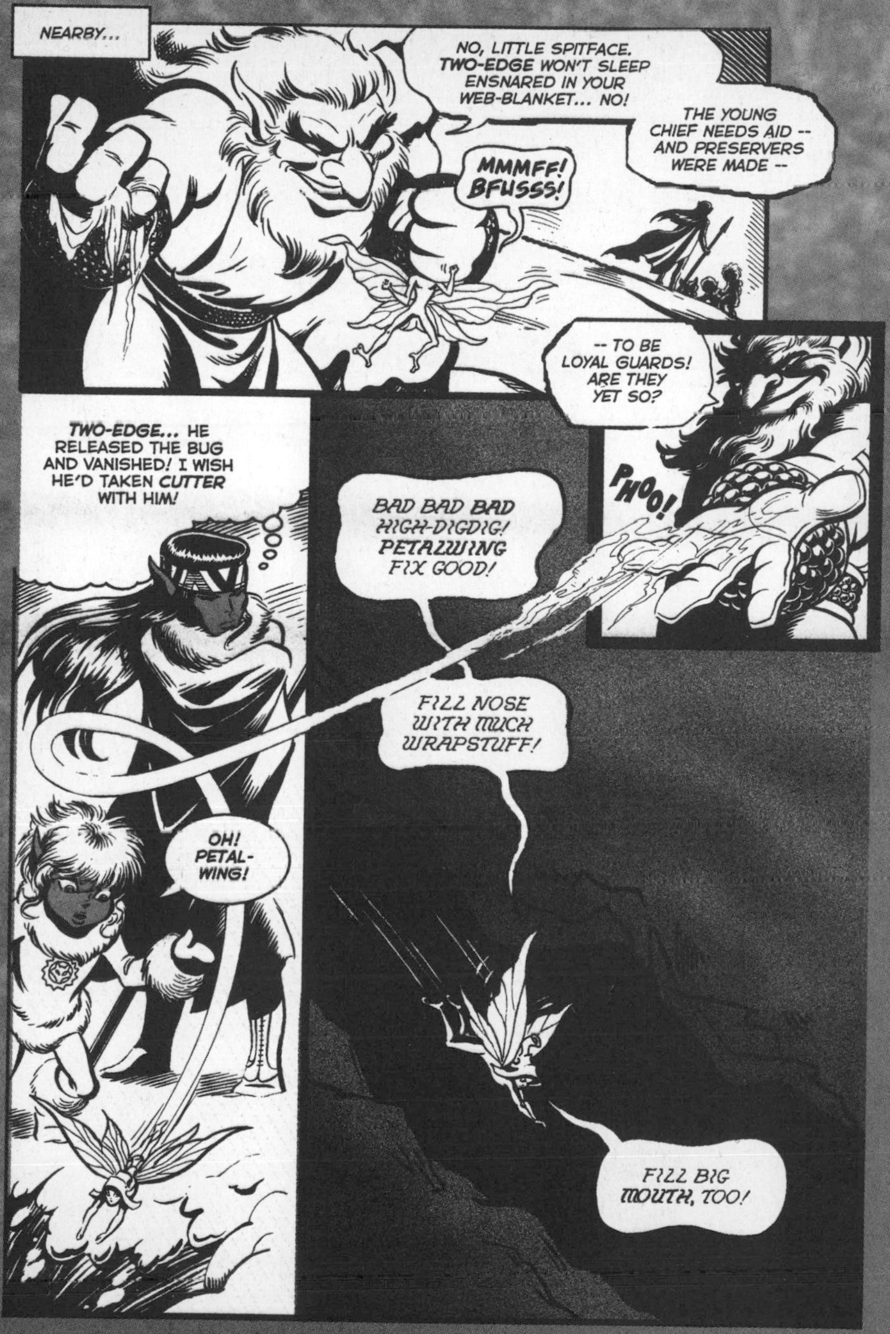
NEARBY...
NO, LITTLE SPITFACE. TWO-EDGE WON'T SLEEP ENSNARED IN YOUR WEB-BLANKET... NO!
MMMFF! BFUSSS!
THE YOUNG CHIEF NEEDS AID -- AND PRESERVERS WERE MADE --
-- TO BE LOYAL GUARDS! ARE THEY YET SO?
PHOO!
TWO-EDGE... HE RELEASED THE BUG AND VANISHED! I WISH HE'D TAKEN CUTTER WITH HIM!
BAD BAD BAD HIGH-DIGDIG! PETALWING FIX GOOD!
FILL NOSE WITH MUCH WRAPSTUFF!
OH! PETAL-WING!
FILL BIG MOUTH, TOO!

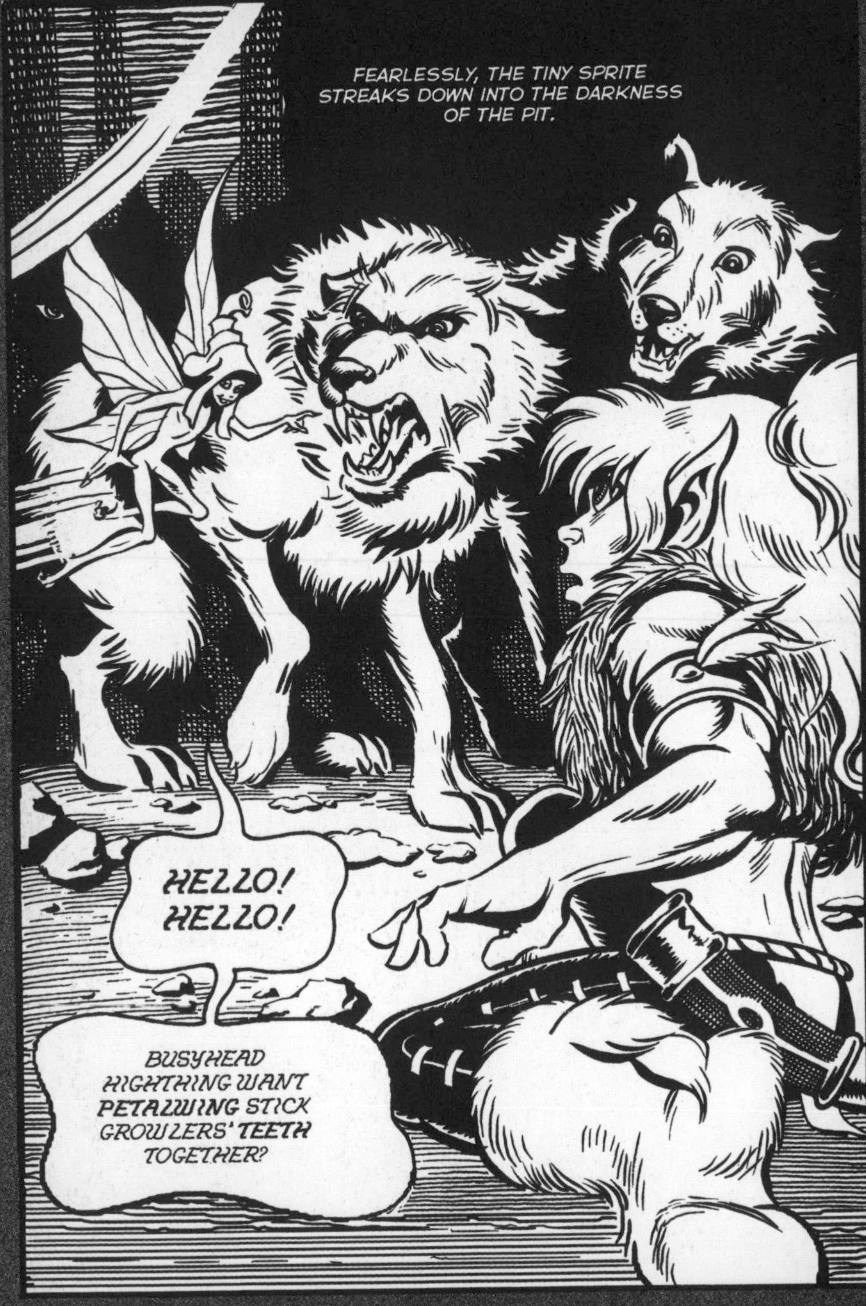
FEARLESSLY, THE TINY SPRITE STREAKS DOWN INTO THE DARKNESS OF THE PIT.
HELLO! HELLO!
BUSYHEAD HIGHTHING WANT PETALWING STICK GROWLERS' TEETH TOGETHER?

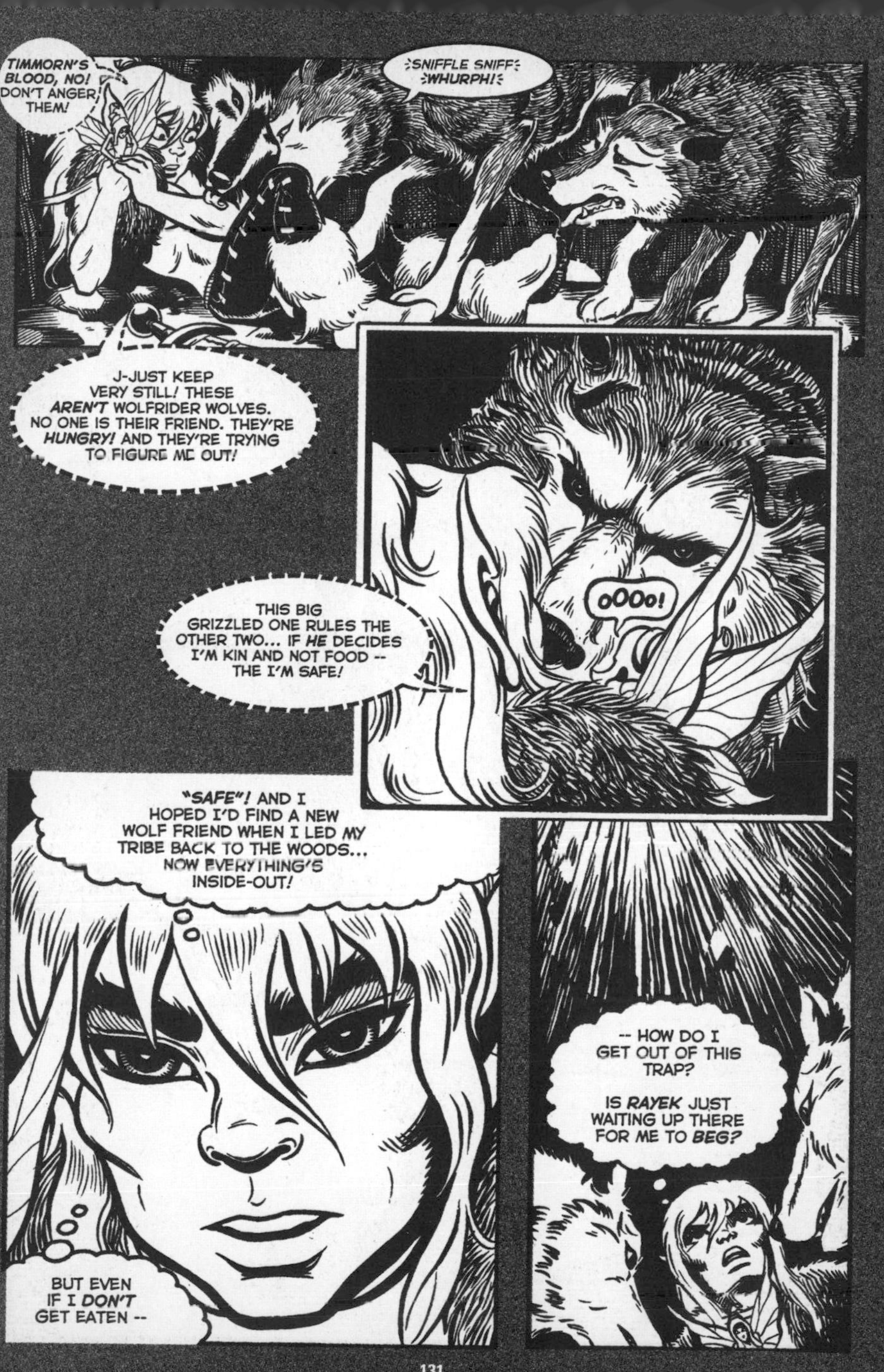

TIMMORN'S BLOOD, NO! DON'T ANGER THEM!
SNIFFLE SNIFF WHURPH!
J-JUST KEEP VERY STILL! THESE AREN'T WOLFRIDER WOLVES. NO ONE IS THEIR FRIEND. THEY'RE HUNGRY! AND THEY'RE TRYING TO FIGURE ME OUT!
OOOo!
THIS BIG GRIZZLED ONE RULES THE OTHER TWO... IF HE DECIDES I'M KIN AND NOT FOOD -- THE I'M SAFE!
"SAFE"! AND I HOPED I'D FIND A NEW WOLF FRIEND WHEN I LED MY TRIBE BACK TO THE WOODS... NOW EVERYTHING'S INSIDE-OUT!
BUT EVEN IF I DON'T GET EATEN --
-- HOW DO I GET OUT OF THIS TRAP?
IS RAYEK JUST WAITING UP THERE FOR ME TO BEG?

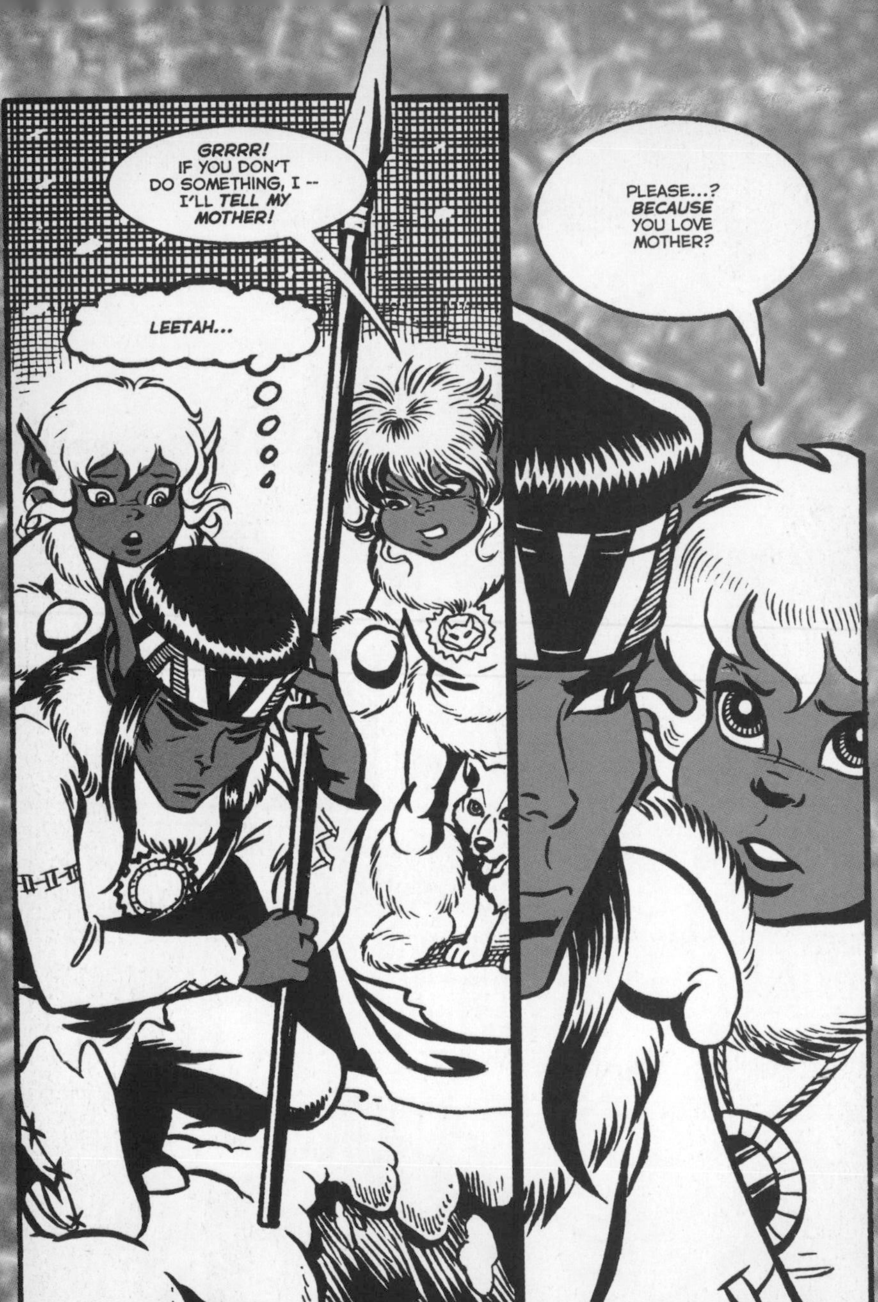
GRRRR! IF YOU DON'T DO SOMETHING, I -- I'LL *TELL MY MOTHER!*
LEETAH...
PLEASE...? *BECAUSE* YOU LOVE MOTHER?

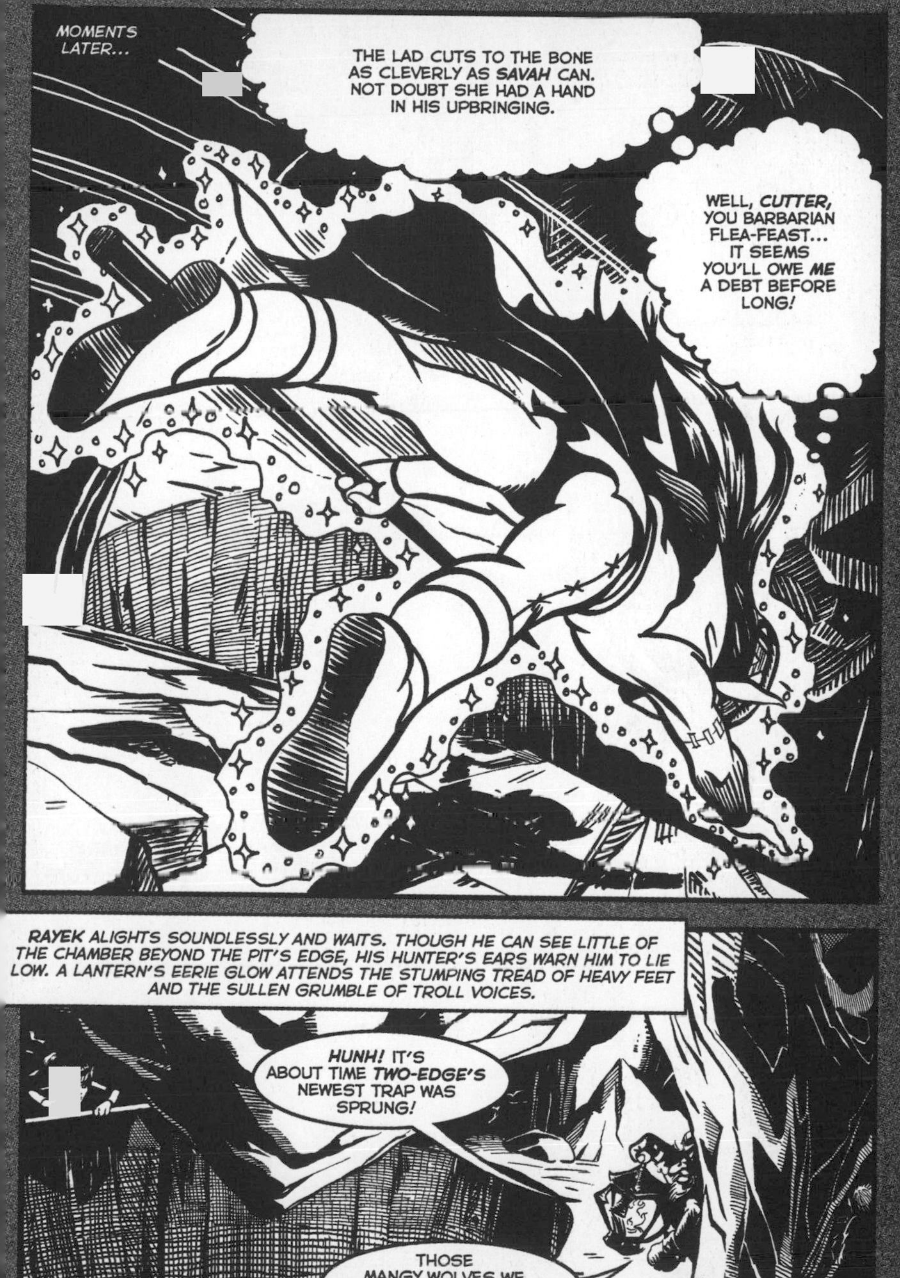
MOMENTS LATER...
THE LAD CUTS TO THE BONE AS CLEVERLY AS SAVAH CAN. NOT DOUBT SHE HAD A HAND IN HIS UPBRINGING.
WELL, CUTTER, YOU BARBARIAN FLEA-FEAST... IT SEEMS YOU'LL OWE ME A DEBT BEFORE LONG!
RAYEK ALIGHTS SOUNDLESSLY AND WAITS. THOUGH HE CAN SEE LITTLE OF THE CHAMBER BEYOND THE PIT'S EDGE, HIS HUNTER'S EARS WARN HIM TO LIE LOW. A LANTERN'S EERIE GLOW ATTENDS THE STUMPING TREAD OF HEAVY FEET AND THE SULLEN GRUMBLE OF TROLL VOICES.
HUNH! IT'S ABOUT TIME TWO-EDGE'S NEWEST TRAP WAS SPRUNG!
THOSE MANGY WOLVES WE CAUGHT ARE ABOUT TO EARN THEIR KEEP!

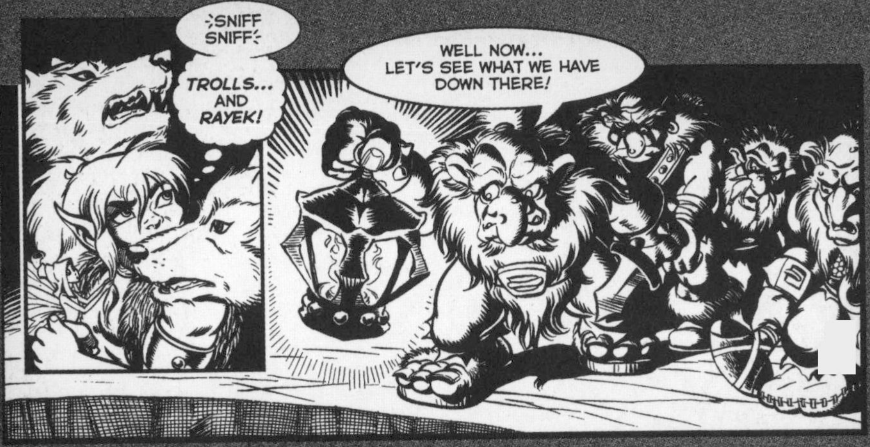

SNIFF SNIFF
TROLLS... AND RAYEK!
WELL NOW... LET'S SEE WHAT WE HAVE DOWN THERE!

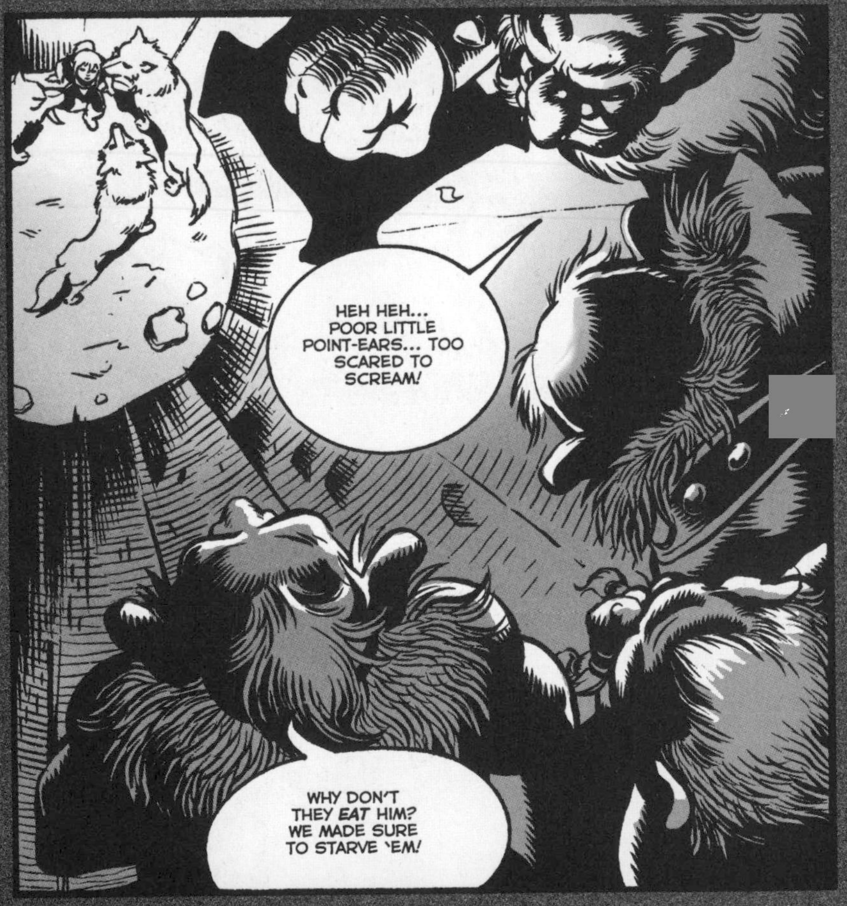

HEH HEH... POOR LITTLE POINT-EARS... TOO SCARED TO SCREAM!
WHY DON'T THEY *EAT* HIM? WE MADE SURE TO STARVE 'EM!

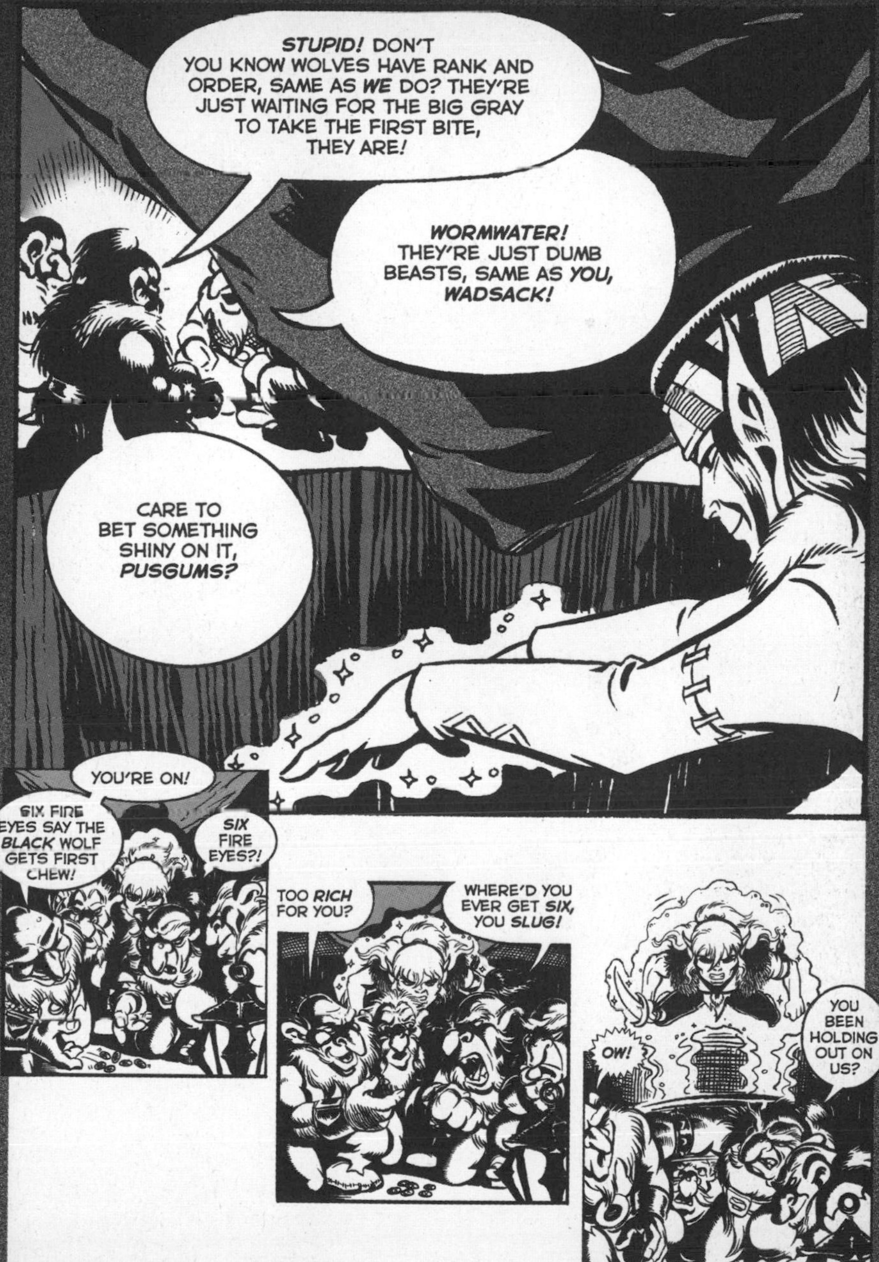
STUPID! DON'T YOU KNOW WOLVES HAVE RANK AND ORDER, SAME AS WE DO? THEY'RE JUST WAITING FOR THE BIG GRAY TO TAKE THE FIRST BITE, THEY ARE!
WORMWATER! THEY'RE JUST DUMB BEASTS, SAME AS YOU, WADSACK!
CARE TO BET SOMETHING SHINY ON IT, PUSGUMS?
YOU'RE ON!
SIX FIRE EYES SAY THE BLACK WOLF GETS FIRST CHEW!
SIX FIRE EYES?!
TOO RICH FOR YOU?
WHERE'D YOU EVER GET SIX, YOU SLUG!
OW!
YOU BEEN HOLDING OUT ON US?

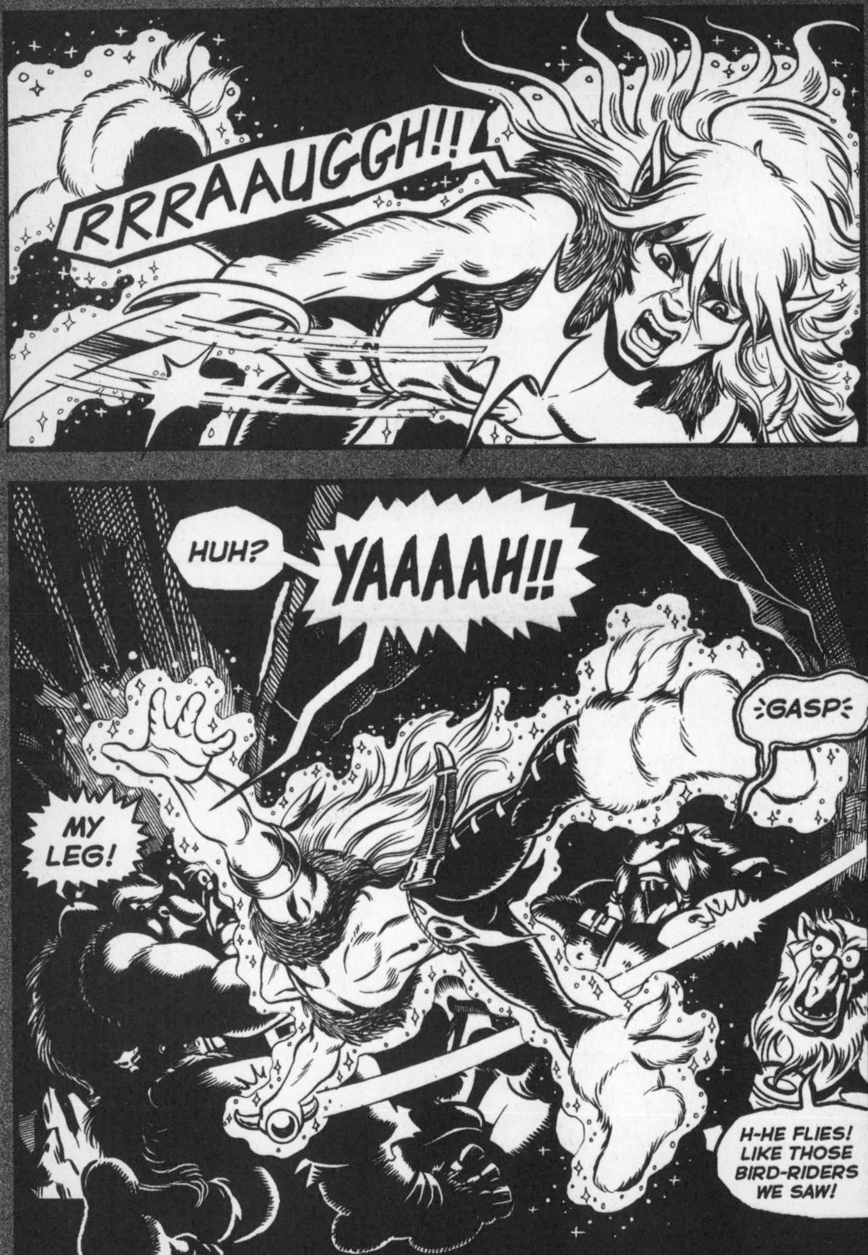
RRRAAUGGH!!
HUH?
YAAAAH!!
MY LEG!
:GASP:
H-HE FLIES! LIKE THOSE BIRD-RIDERS WE SAW!

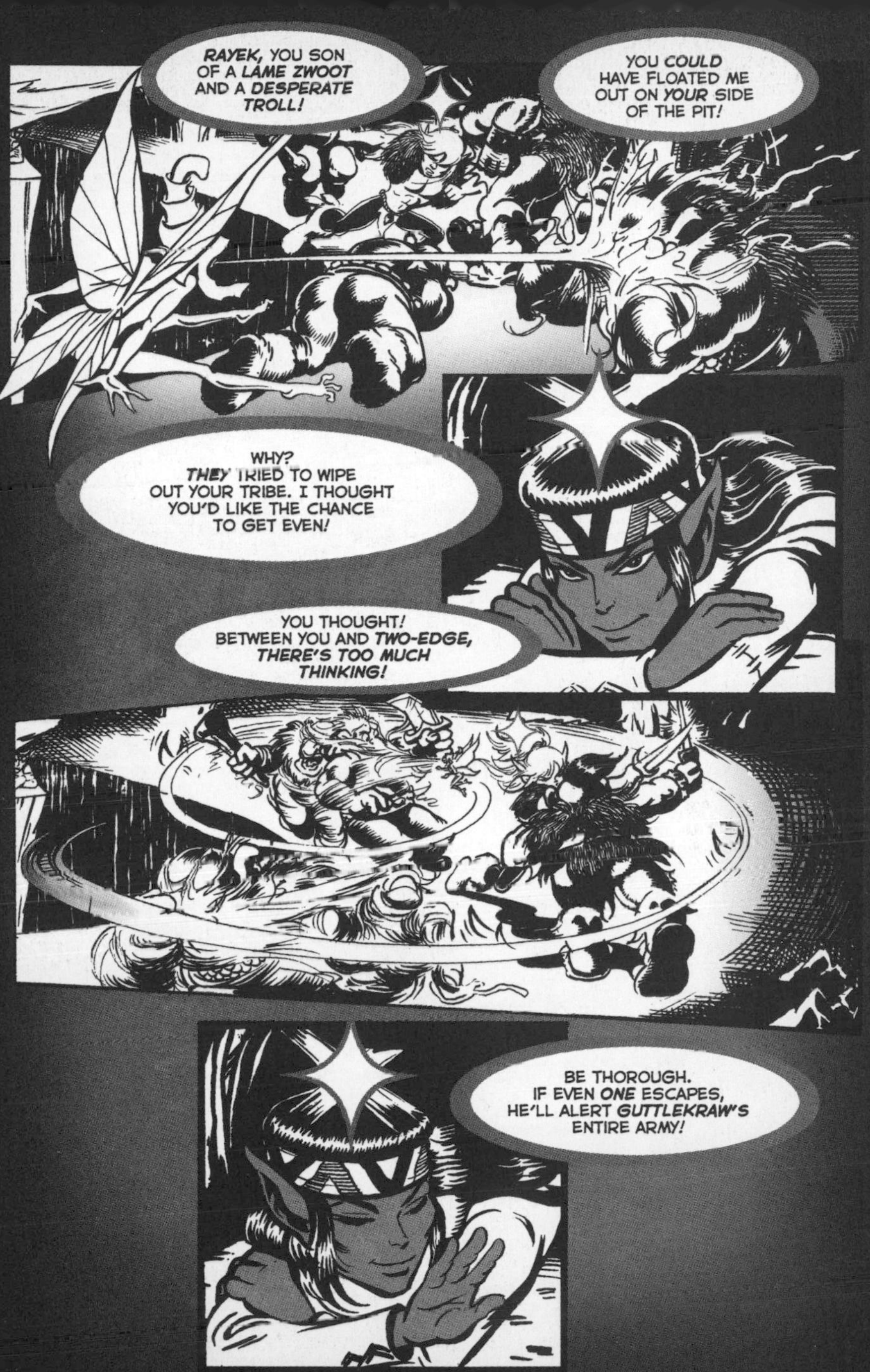
RAYEK, YOU SON OF A LAME ZWOOT AND A DESPERATE TROLL!
YOU COULD HAVE FLOATED ME OUT ON YOUR SIDE OF THE PIT!
WHY? THEY TRIED TO WIPE OUT YOUR TRIBE. I THOUGHT YOU'D LIKE THE CHANCE TO GET EVEN!
YOU THOUGHT! BETWEEN YOU AND TWO-EDGE, THERE'S TOO MUCH THINKING!
BE THOROUGH. IF EVEN ONE ESCAPES, HE'LL ALERT GUTTLEKRAW'S ENTIRE ARMY!

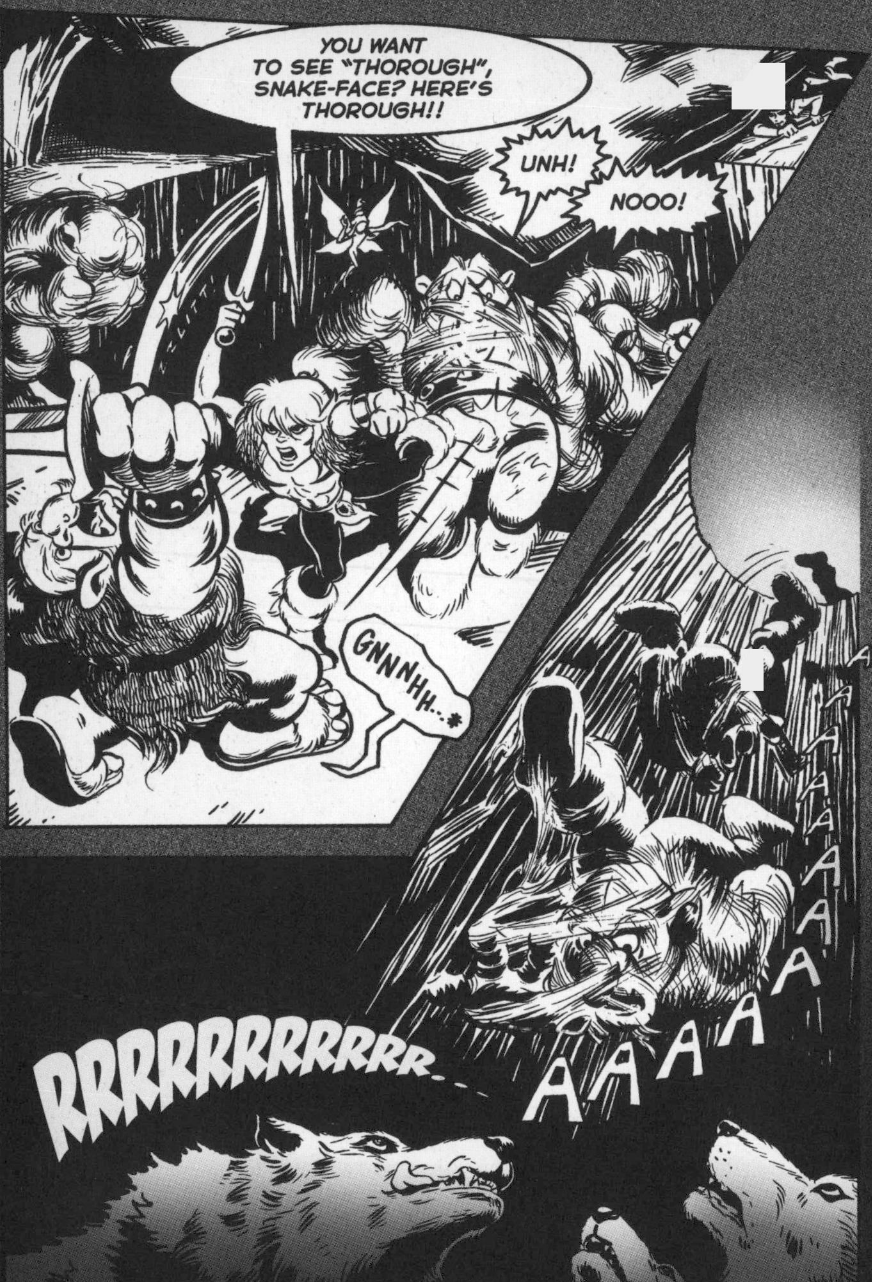
YOU WANT TO SEE "THOROUGH", SNAKE-FACE? HERE'S THOROUGH!!
UNH!
NOOO!
GNNNHH...*
AAAAAAAAAAAAAAA
RRRRRRRRRRRRRR...

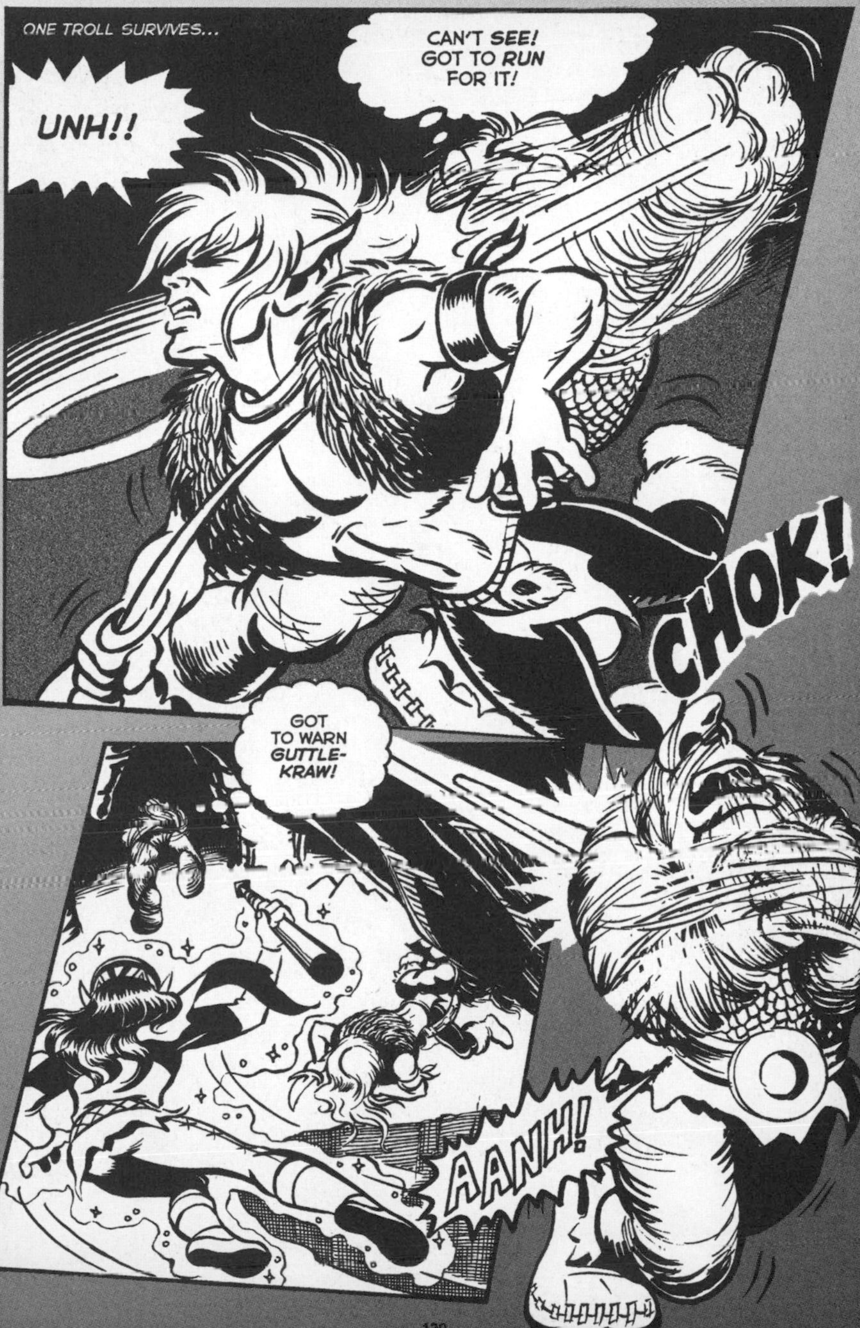
ONE TROLL SURVIVES...
UNH!!
CAN'T SEE! GOT TO RUN FOR IT!
CHOK!
GOT TO WARN GUTTLE-KRAW!
AANH!

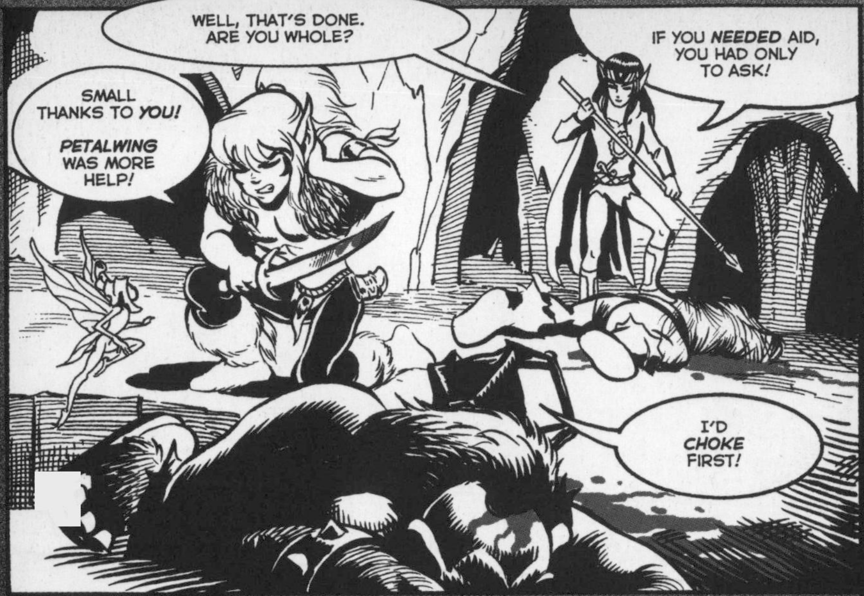
WELL, THAT'S DONE. ARE YOU WHOLE?
SMALL THANKS TO *YOU!*
PETALWING WAS MORE HELP!
IF YOU *NEEDED* AID, YOU HAD ONLY TO ASK!
I'D *CHOKE* FIRST!

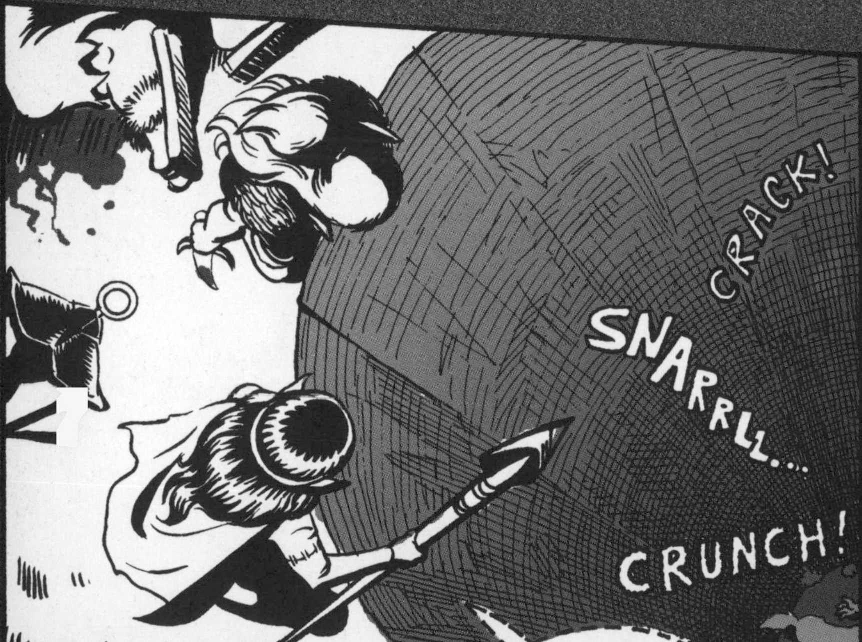
CRACK!
SNARRLL....
CRUNCH!
LET'S GO...

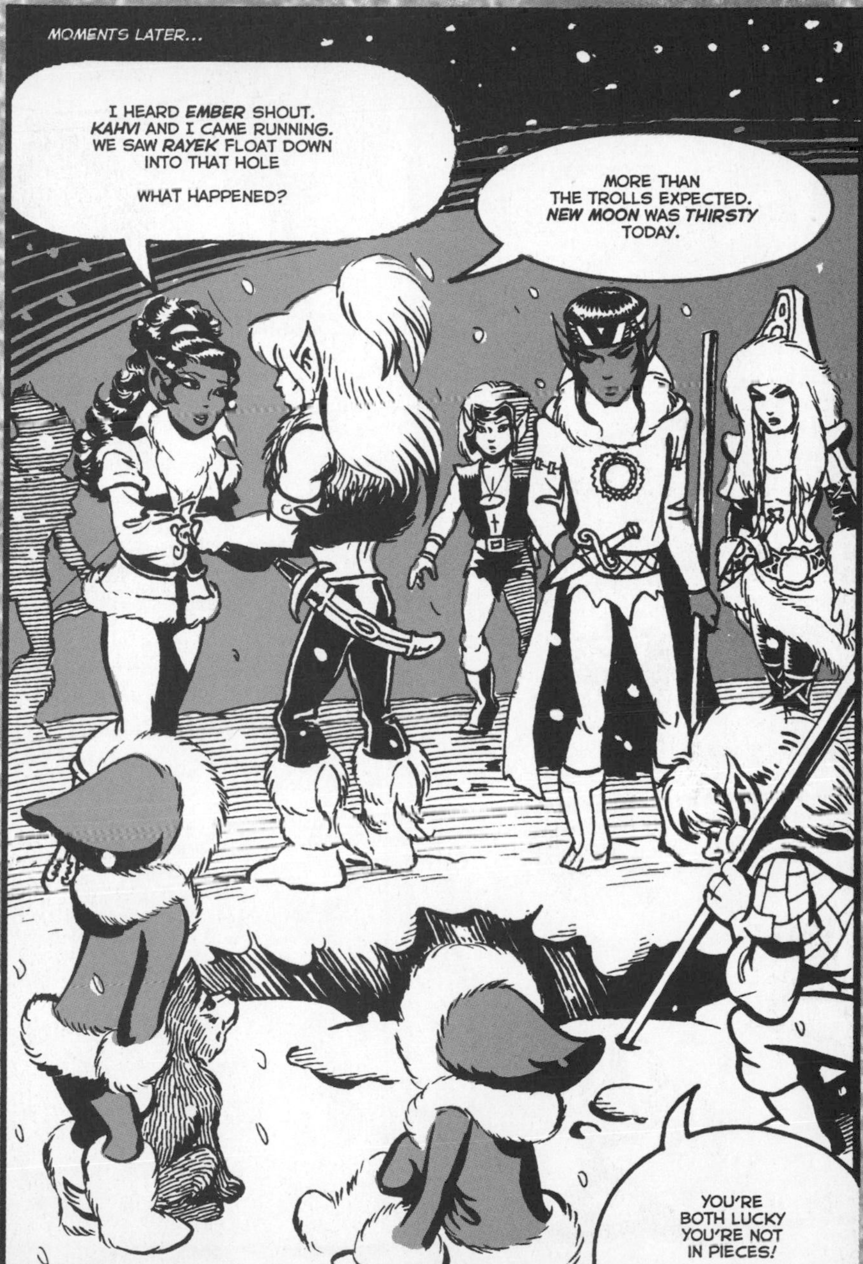
MOMENTS LATER...
I HEARD EMBER SHOUT. KAHVI AND I CAME RUNNING. WE SAW RAYEK FLOAT DOWN INTO THAT HOLE
WHAT HAPPENED?
MORE THAN THE TROLLS EXPECTED. NEW MOON WAS THIRSTY TODAY.
YOU'RE BOTH LUCKY YOU'RE NOT IN PIECES!

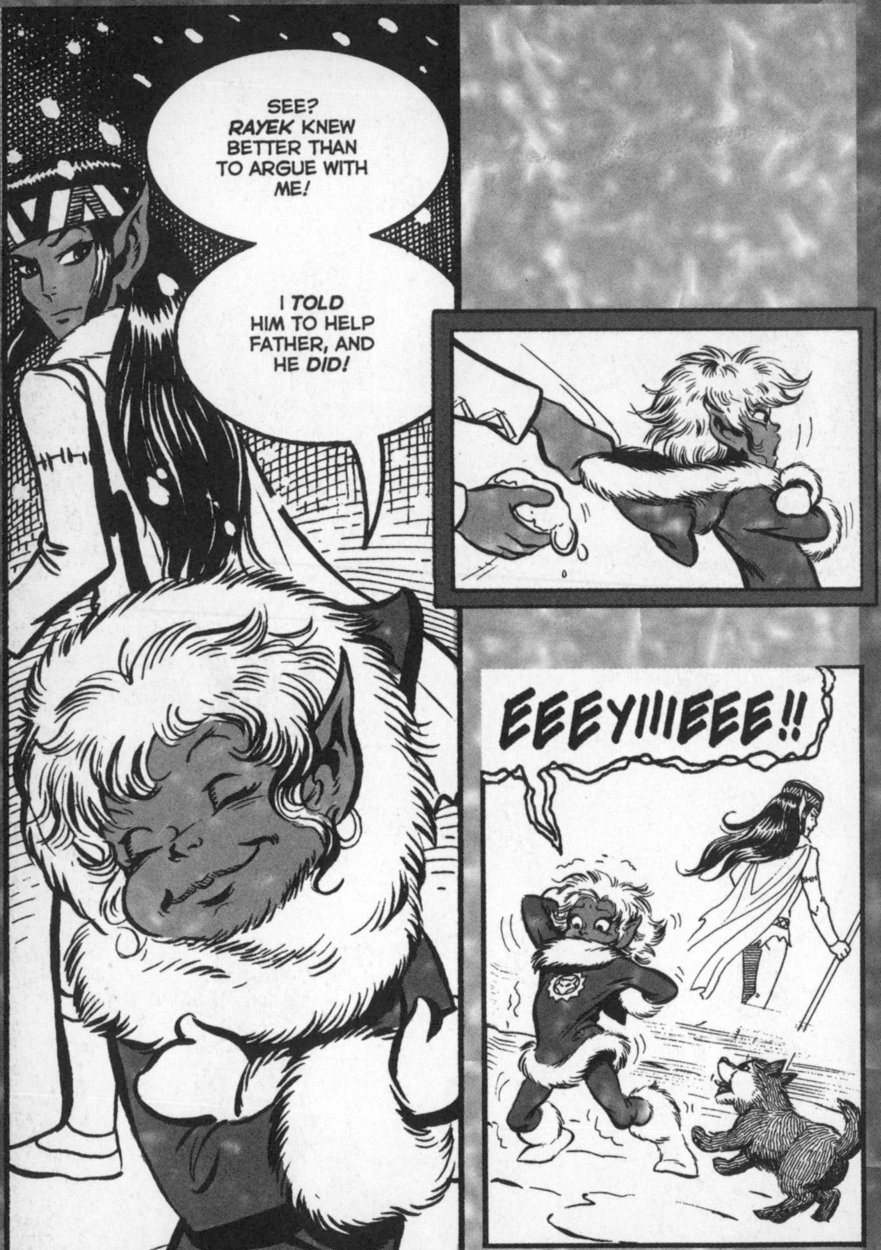
SEE? *RAYEK* KNEW BETTER THAN TO ARGUE WITH *ME!*
I *TOLD* HIM TO HELP FATHER, AND HE *DID!*
EEEYIIIIEEE!!

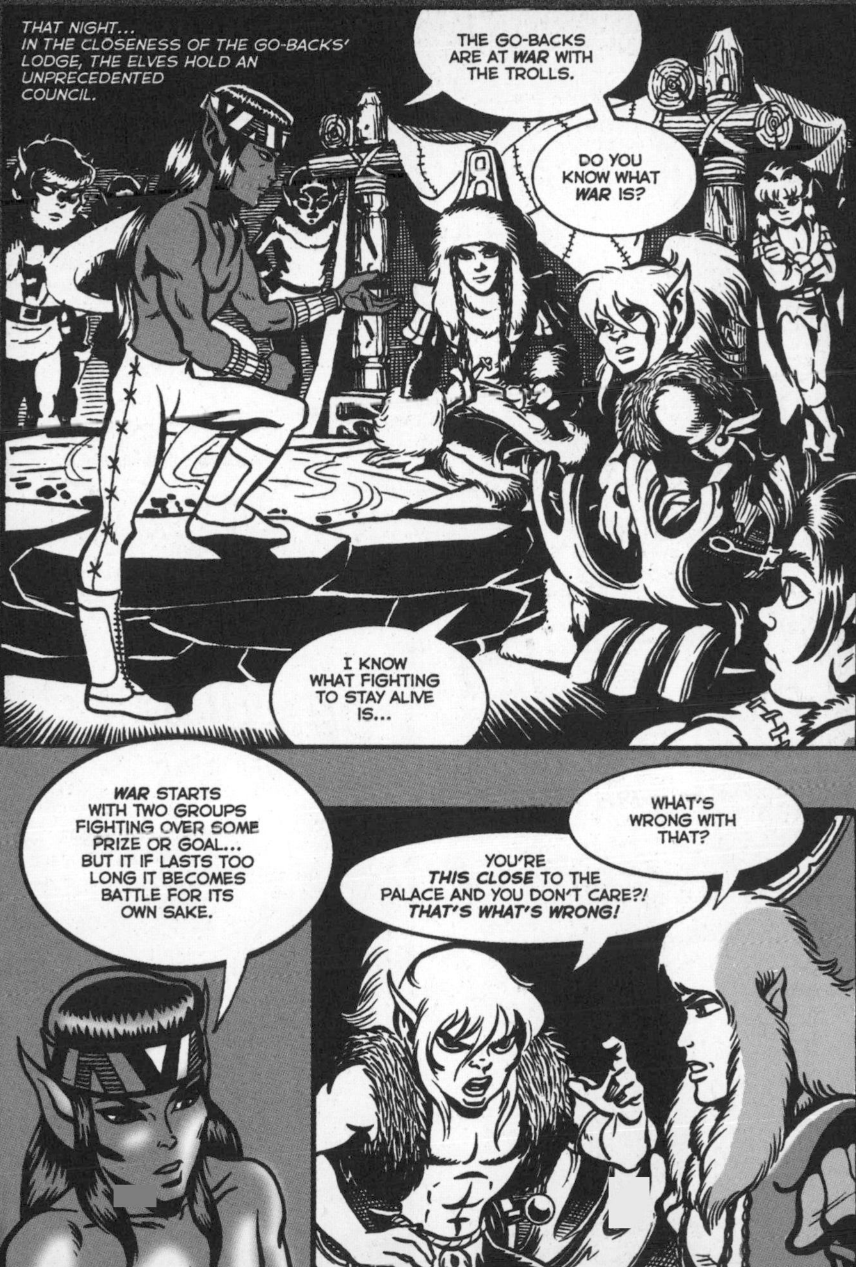
THAT NIGHT... IN THE CLOSENESS OF THE GO-BACKS' LODGE, THE ELVES HOLD AN UNPRECEDENTED COUNCIL.
THE GO-BACKS ARE AT WAR WITH THE TROLLS.
DO YOU KNOW WHAT WAR IS?
I KNOW WHAT FIGHTING TO STAY ALIVE IS...
WAR STARTS WITH TWO GROUPS FIGHTING OVER SOME PRIZE OR GOAL... BUT IT IF LASTS TOO LONG IT BECOMES BATTLE FOR ITS OWN SAKE.
WHAT'S WRONG WITH THAT?
YOU'RE THIS CLOSE TO THE PALACE AND YOU DON'T CARE?! THAT'S WHAT'S WRONG!

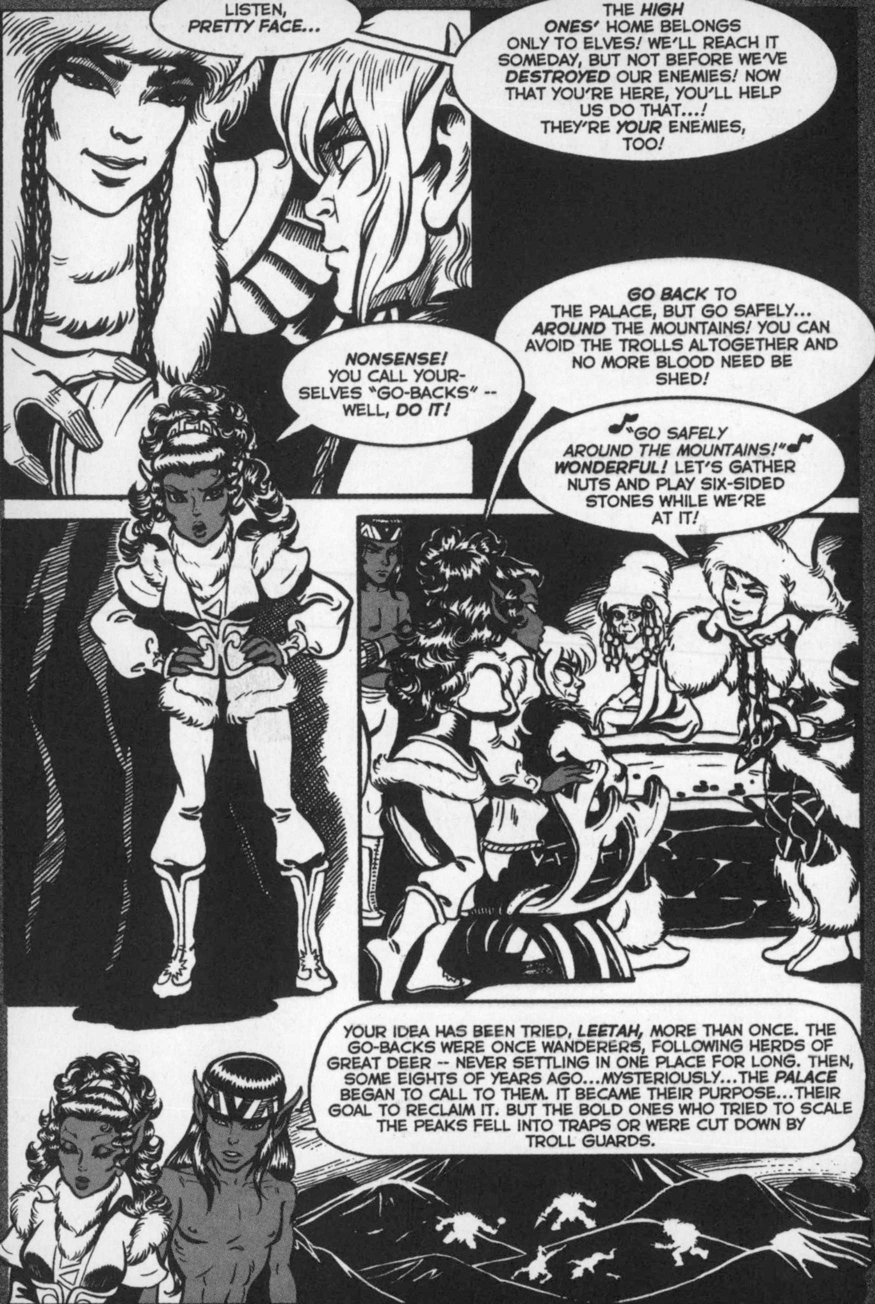

LISTEN, PRETTY FACE...
THE HIGH ONES' HOME BELONGS ONLY TO ELVES! WE'LL REACH IT SOMEDAY, BUT NOT BEFORE WE'VE DESTROYED OUR ENEMIES! NOW THAT YOU'RE HERE, YOU'LL HELP US DO THAT...! THEY'RE YOUR ENEMIES, TOO!
NONSENSE! YOU CALL YOURSELVES "GO-BACKS" -- WELL, DO IT!
GO BACK TO THE PALACE, BUT GO SAFELY... AROUND THE MOUNTAINS! YOU CAN AVOID THE TROLLS ALTOGETHER AND NO MORE BLOOD NEED BE SHED!
"GO SAFELY AROUND THE MOUNTAINS!" WONDERFUL! LET'S GATHER NUTS AND PLAY SIX-SIDED STONES WHILE WE'RE AT IT!
YOUR IDEA HAS BEEN TRIED, LEETAH, MORE THAN ONCE. THE GO-BACKS WERE ONCE WANDERERS, FOLLOWING HERDS OF GREAT DEER -- NEVER SETTLING IN ONE PLACE FOR LONG. THEN, SOME EIGHTS OF YEARS AGO...MYSTERIOUSLY...THE PALACE BEGAN TO CALL TO THEM. IT BECAME THEIR PURPOSE...THEIR GOAL TO RECLAIM IT. BUT THE BOLD ONES WHO TRIED TO SCALE THE PEAKS FELL INTO TRAPS OR WERE CUT DOWN BY TROLL GUARDS.

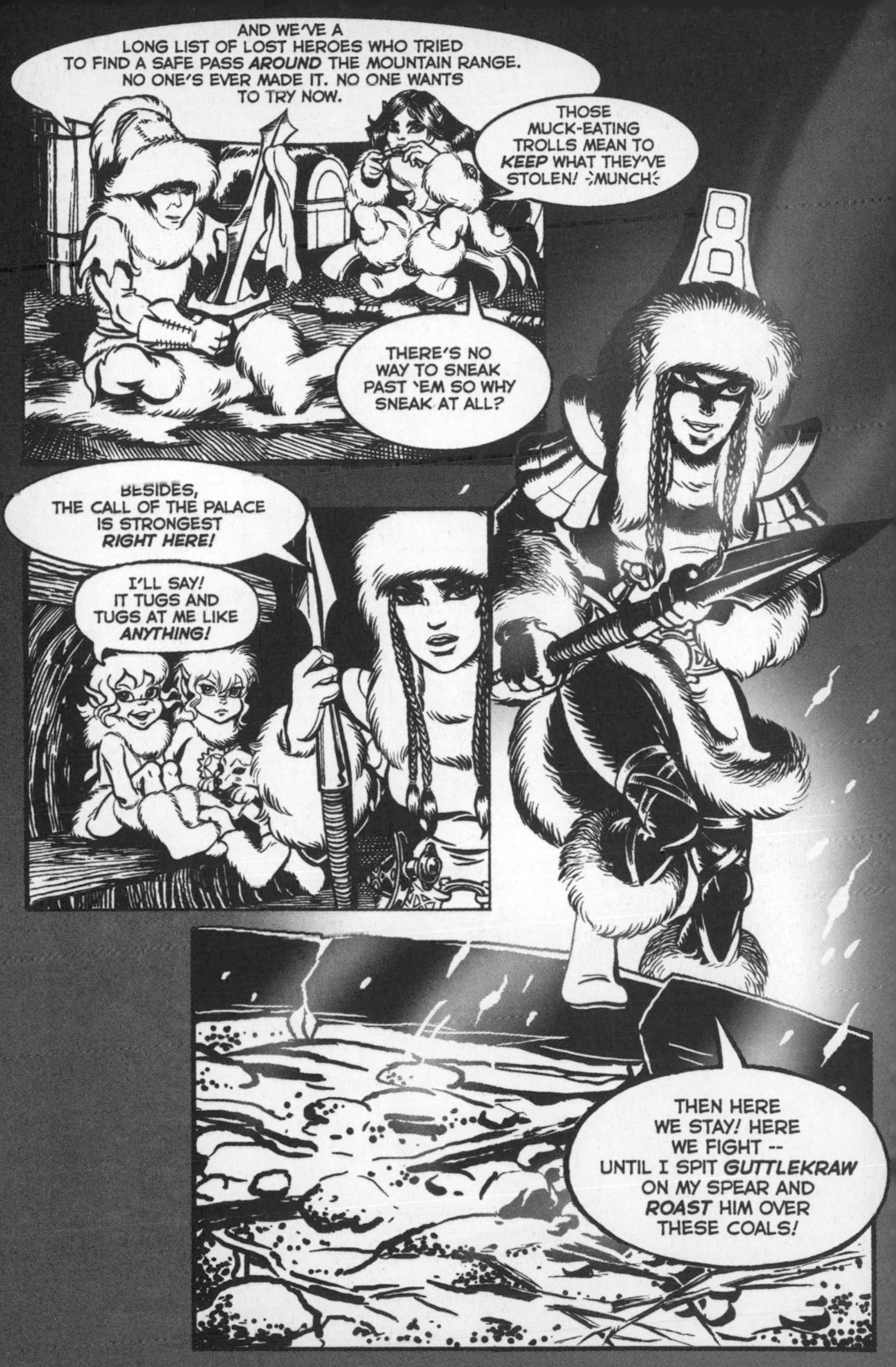
AND WE'VE A LONG LIST OF LOST HEROES WHO TRIED TO FIND A SAFE PASS *AROUND* THE MOUNTAIN RANGE. NO ONE'S EVER MADE IT. NO ONE WANTS TO TRY NOW.
THOSE MUCK-EATING TROLLS MEAN TO *KEEP* WHAT THEY'VE STOLEN! MUNCH
THERE'S NO WAY TO SNEAK PAST 'EM SO WHY SNEAK AT ALL?
BESIDES, THE CALL OF THE PALACE IS STRONGEST *RIGHT HERE!*
I'LL SAY! IT TUGS AND TUGS AT ME LIKE *ANYTHING!*
THEN HERE WE STAY! HERE WE FIGHT -- UNTIL I SPIT *GUTTLEKRAW* ON MY SPEAR AND *ROAST* HIM OVER THESE COALS!

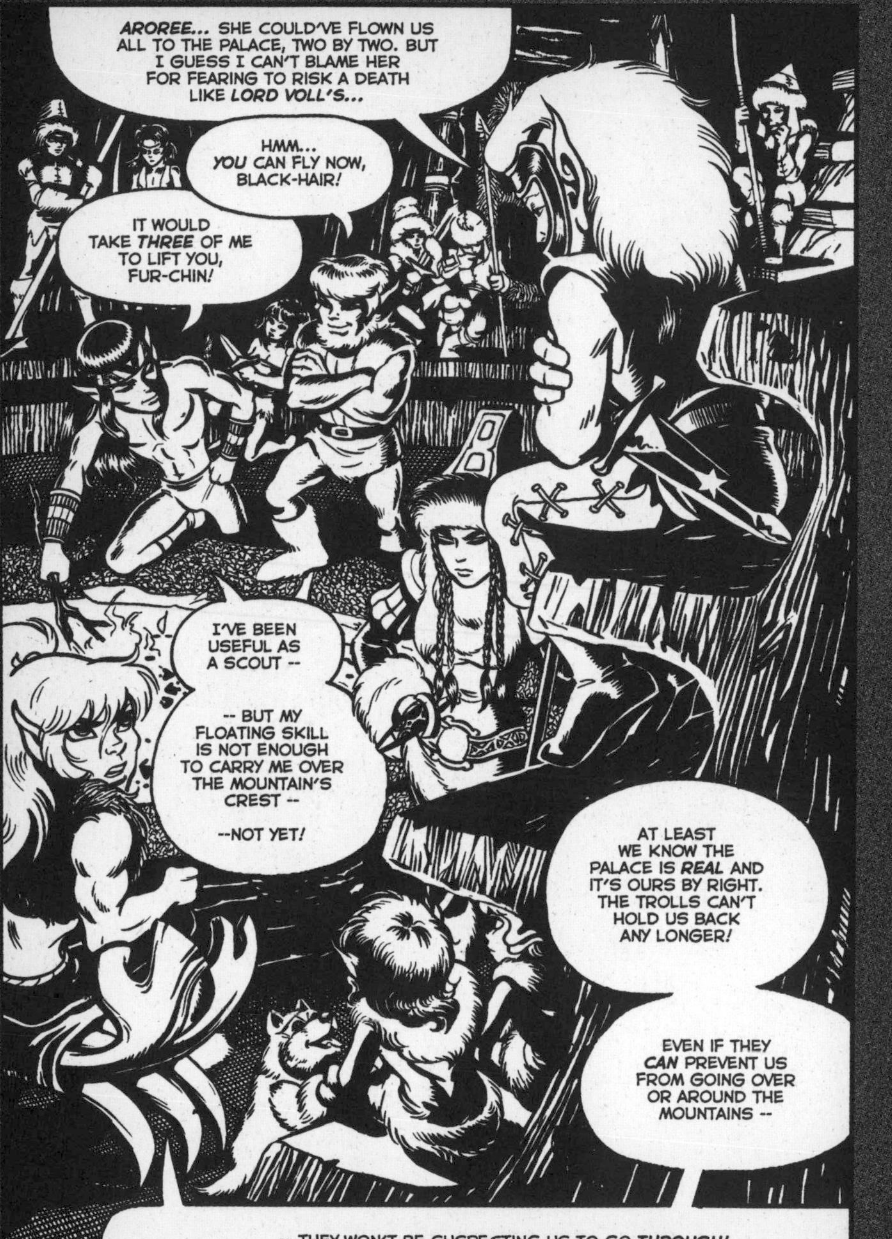
AROREE... SHE COULD'VE FLOWN US ALL TO THE PALACE, TWO BY TWO. BUT I GUESS I CAN'T BLAME HER FOR FEARING TO RISK A DEATH LIKE LORD VOLL'S...
HMM... YOU CAN FLY NOW, BLACK-HAIR!
IT WOULD TAKE THREE OF ME TO LIFT YOU, FUR-CHIN!
I'VE BEEN USEFUL AS A SCOUT --
-- BUT MY FLOATING SKILL IS NOT ENOUGH TO CARRY ME OVER THE MOUNTAIN'S CREST --
--NOT YET!
AT LEAST WE KNOW THE PALACE IS REAL AND IT'S OURS BY RIGHT. THE TROLLS CAN'T HOLD US BACK ANY LONGER!
EVEN IF THEY CAN PREVENT US FROM GOING OVER OR AROUND THE MOUNTAINS --
-- THEY WON'T BE SUSPECTING US TO GO THROUGH! THEY'RE TOO BUSY DEFENDING THE SURFACE!

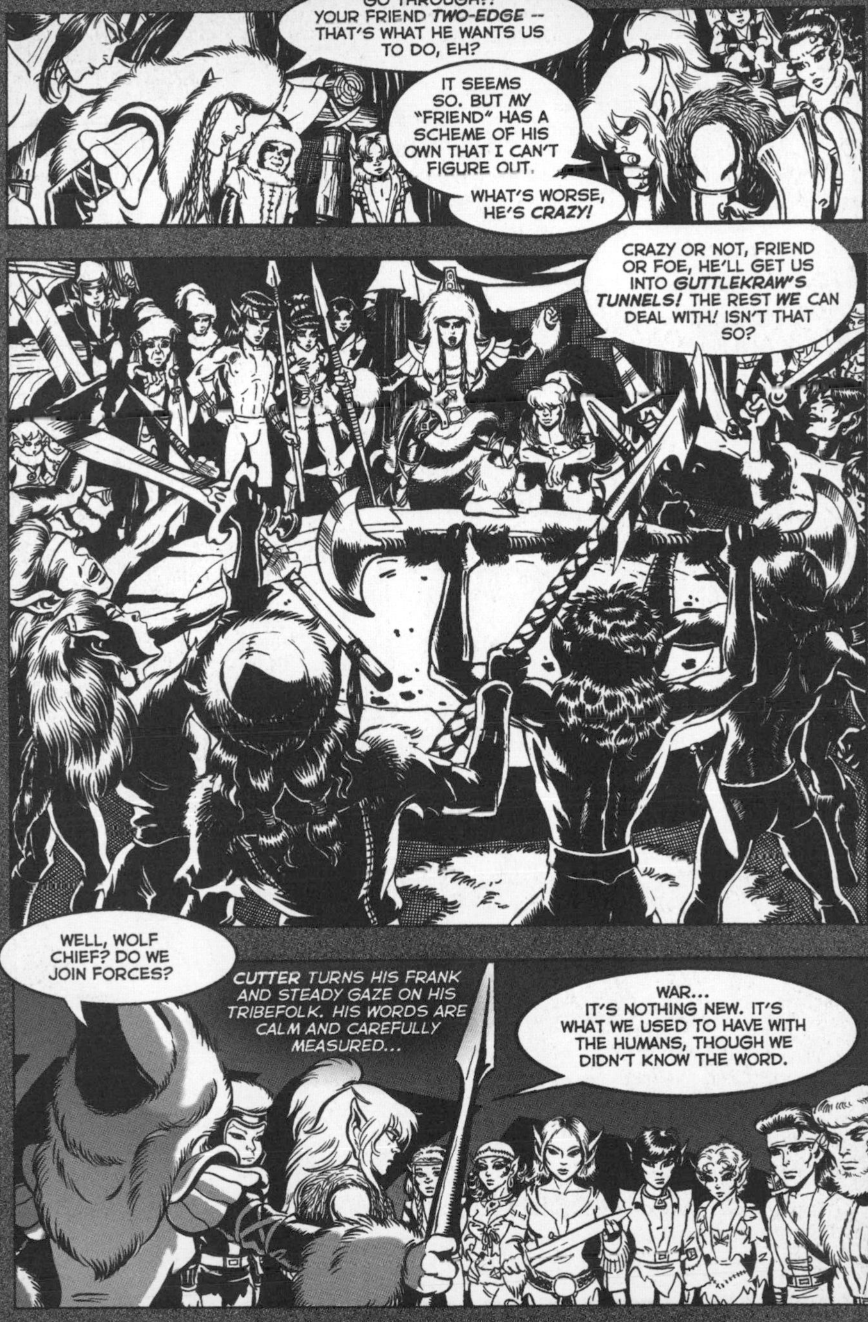
GO THROUGH?! YOUR FRIEND TWO-EDGE -- THAT'S WHAT HE WANTS US TO DO, EH?
IT SEEMS SO. BUT MY "FRIEND" HAS A SCHEME OF HIS OWN THAT I CAN'T FIGURE OUT.
WHAT'S WORSE, HE'S CRAZY!
CRAZY OR NOT, FRIEND OR FOE, HE'LL GET US INTO GUTTLEKRAW'S TUNNELS! THE REST WE CAN DEAL WITH! ISN'T THAT SO?
WELL, WOLF CHIEF? DO WE JOIN FORCES?
CUTTER TURNS HIS FRANK AND STEADY GAZE ON HIS TRIBEFOLK. HIS WORDS ARE CALM AND CAREFULLY MEASURED...
WAR... IT'S NOTHING NEW. IT'S WHAT WE USED TO HAVE WITH THE HUMANS, THOUGH WE DIDN'T KNOW THE WORD.

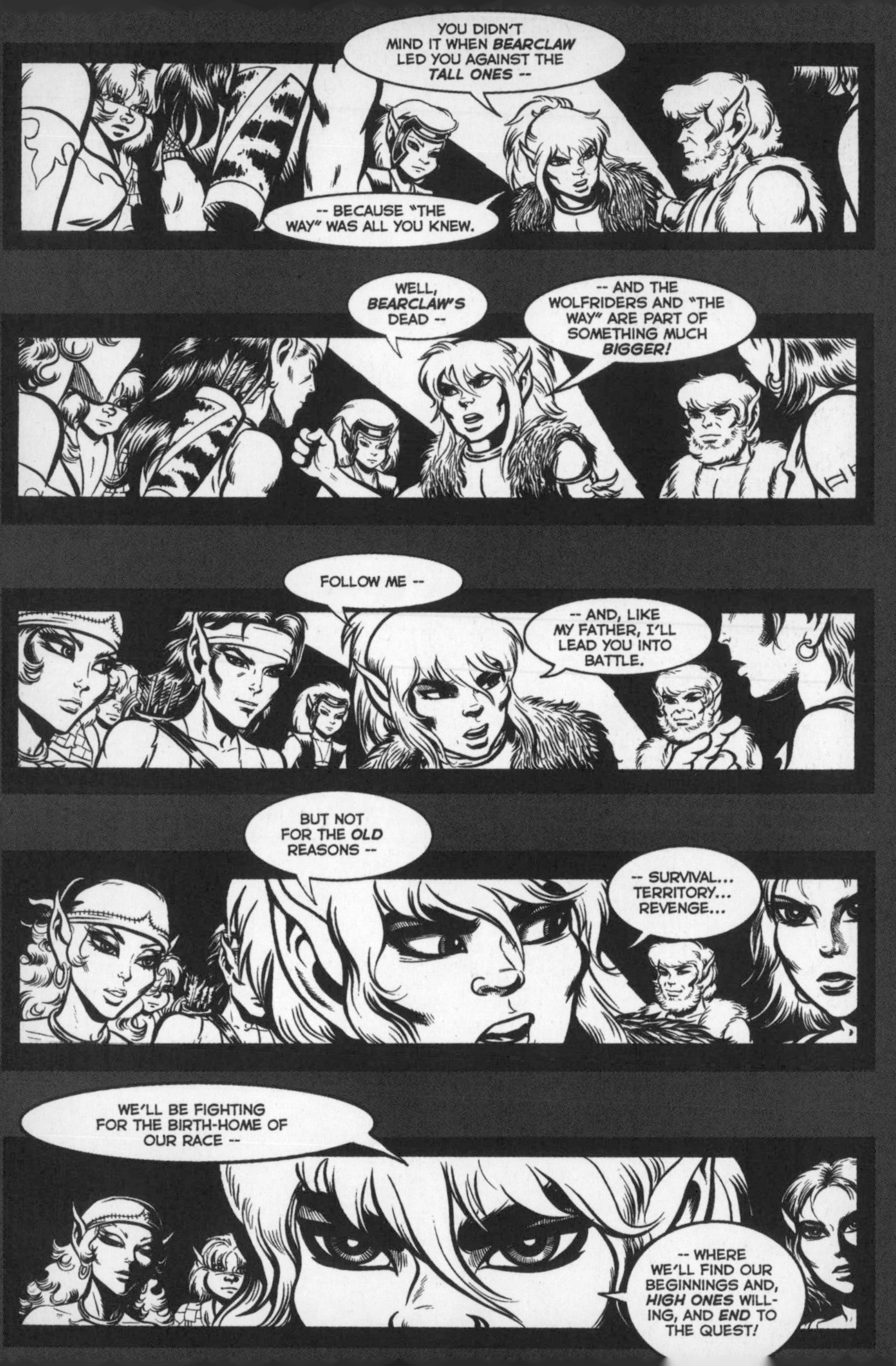
YOU DIDN'T MIND IT WHEN BEARCLAW LED YOU AGAINST THE TALL ONES --
-- BECAUSE "THE WAY" WAS ALL YOU KNEW.
WELL, BEARCLAW'S DEAD --
-- AND THE WOLFRIDERS AND "THE WAY" ARE PART OF SOMETHING MUCH BIGGER!
FOLLOW ME --
-- AND, LIKE MY FATHER, I'LL LEAD YOU INTO BATTLE.
BUT NOT FOR THE OLD REASONS --
-- SURVIVAL... TERRITORY... REVENGE...
WE'LL BE FIGHTING FOR THE BIRTH-HOME OF OUR RACE --
-- WHERE WE'LL FIND OUR BEGINNINGS AND, HIGH ONES WILL-ING, AND END TO THE QUEST!

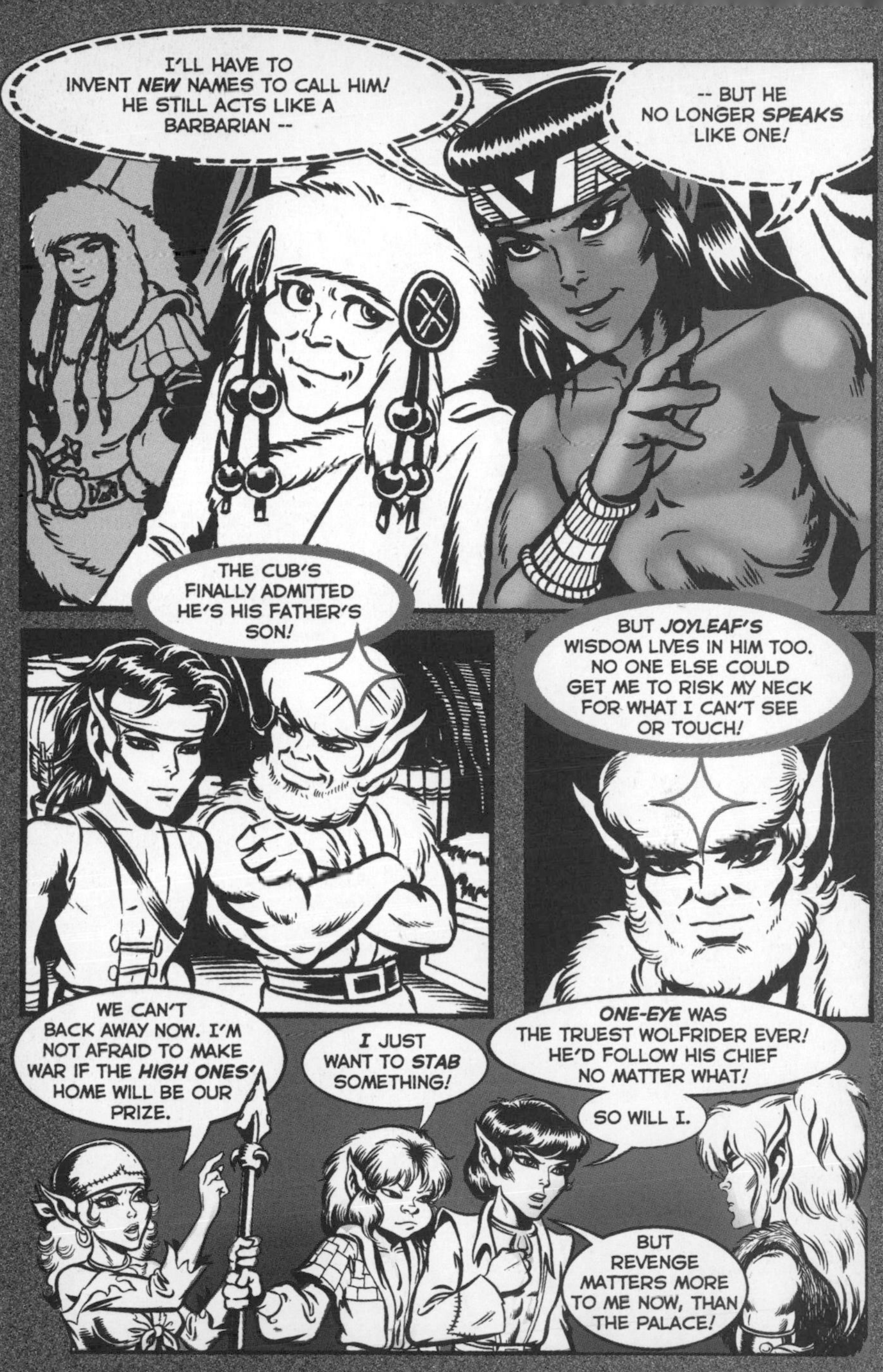
I'LL HAVE TO INVENT NEW NAMES TO CALL HIM! HE STILL ACTS LIKE A BARBARIAN --
-- BUT HE NO LONGER SPEAKS LIKE ONE!
THE CUB'S FINALLY ADMITTED HE'S HIS FATHER'S SON!
BUT JOYLEAF'S WISDOM LIVES IN HIM TOO. NO ONE ELSE COULD GET ME TO RISK MY NECK FOR WHAT I CAN'T SEE OR TOUCH!
WE CAN'T BACK AWAY NOW. I'M NOT AFRAID TO MAKE WAR IF THE HIGH ONES' HOME WILL BE OUR PRIZE.
I JUST WANT TO STAB SOMETHING!
ONE-EYE WAS THE TRUEST WOLFRIDER EVER! HE'D FOLLOW HIS CHIEF NO MATTER WHAT!
SO WILL I.
BUT REVENGE MATTERS MORE TO ME NOW, THAN THE PALACE!

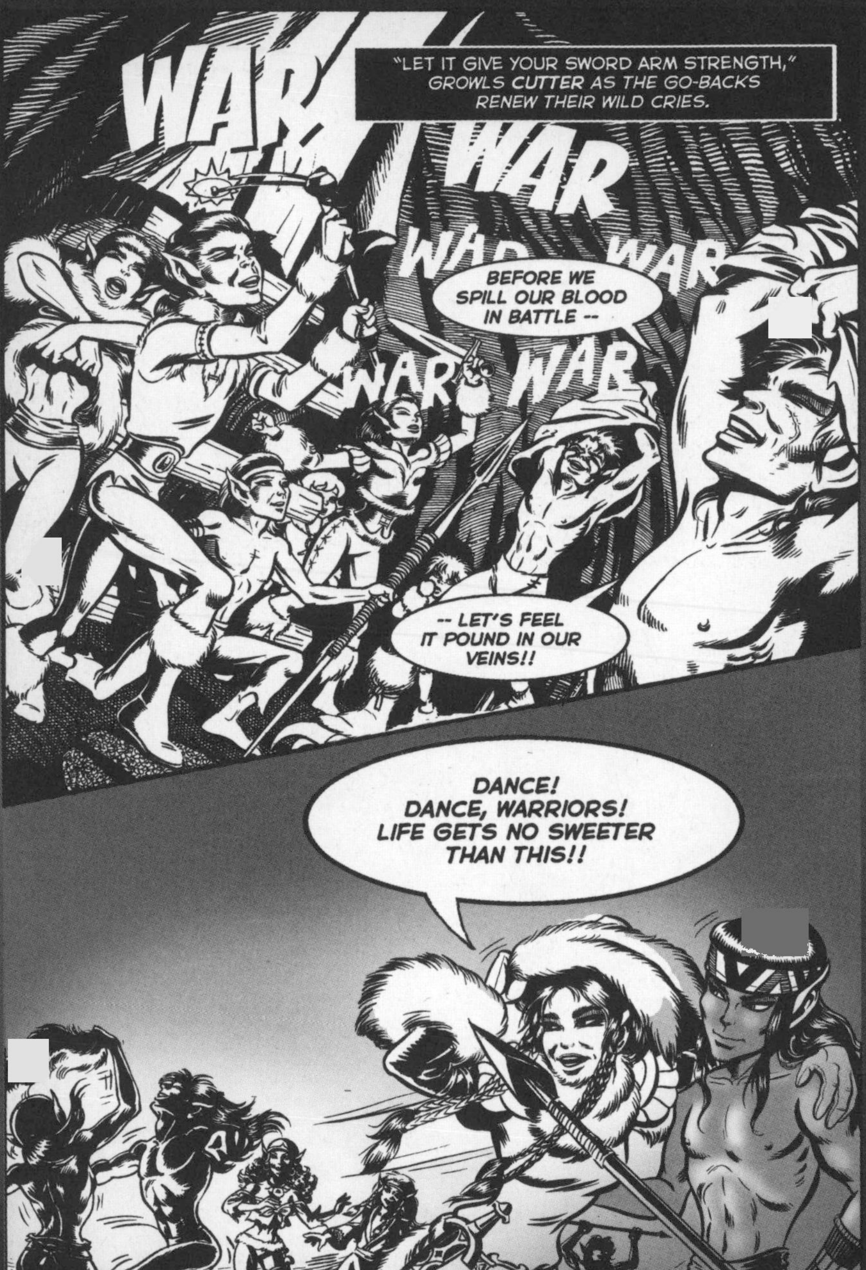

"LET IT GIVE YOUR SWORD ARM STRENGTH," GROWLS CUTTER AS THE GO-BACKS RENEW THEIR WILD CRIES.
WAR
WAR
WAR
WAR
BEFORE WE SPILL OUR BLOOD IN BATTLE --
WAR WAR
-- LET'S FEEL IT POUND IN OUR VEINS!!
DANCE! DANCE, WARRIORS! LIFE GETS NO SWEETER THAN THIS!!

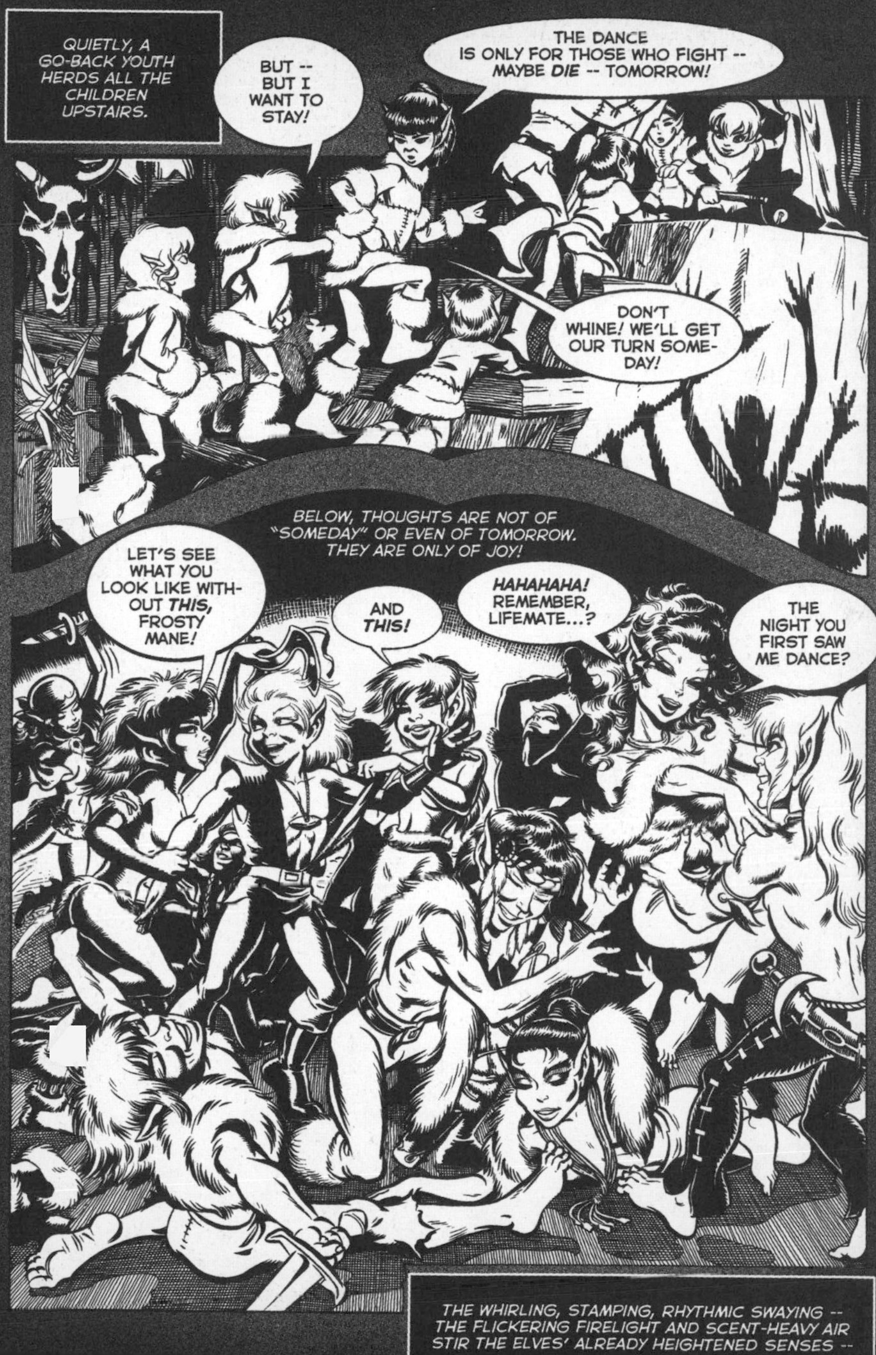
QUIETLY, A GO-BACK YOUTH HERDS ALL THE CHILDREN UPSTAIRS.
BUT -- BUT I WANT TO STAY!
THE DANCE IS ONLY FOR THOSE WHO FIGHT -- MAYBE *DIE* -- TOMORROW!
DON'T WHINE! WE'LL GET OUR TURN SOME-DAY!
BELOW, THOUGHTS ARE NOT OF "SOMEDAY" OR EVEN OF TOMORROW. THEY ARE ONLY OF JOY!
LET'S SEE WHAT YOU LOOK LIKE WITH-OUT *THIS*, FROSTY MANE!
AND *THIS*!
HAHAHAHA! REMEMBER, LIFEMATE...?
THE NIGHT YOU FIRST SAW ME DANCE?
THE WHIRLING, STAMPING, RHYTHMIC SWAYING -- THE FLICKERING FIRELIGHT AND SCENT-HEAVY AIR STIR THE ELVES' ALREADY HEIGHTENED SENSES --

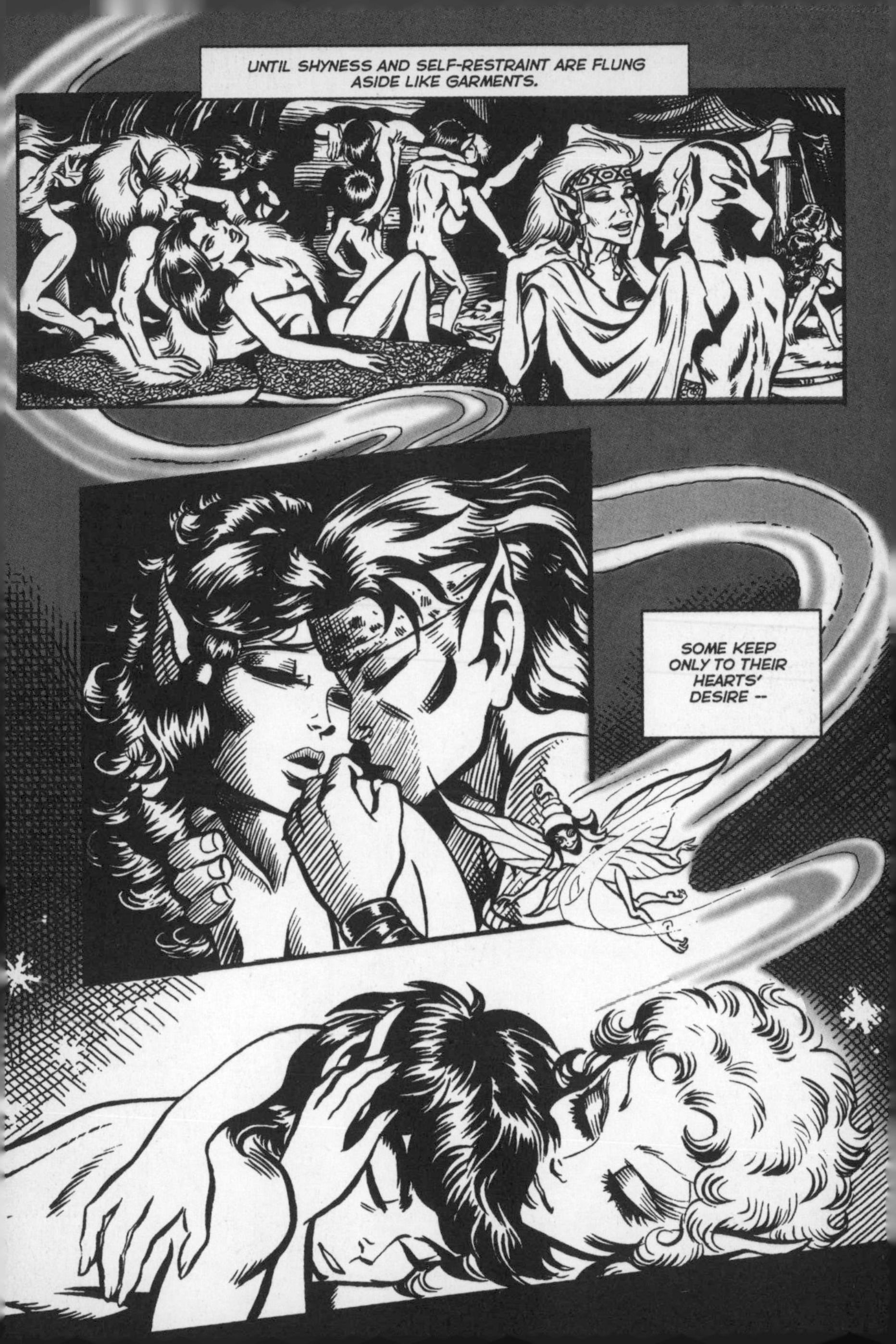
UNTIL SHYNESS AND SELF-RESTRAINT ARE FLUNG ASIDE LIKE GARMENTS.
SOME KEEP ONLY TO THEIR HEARTS' DESIRE --

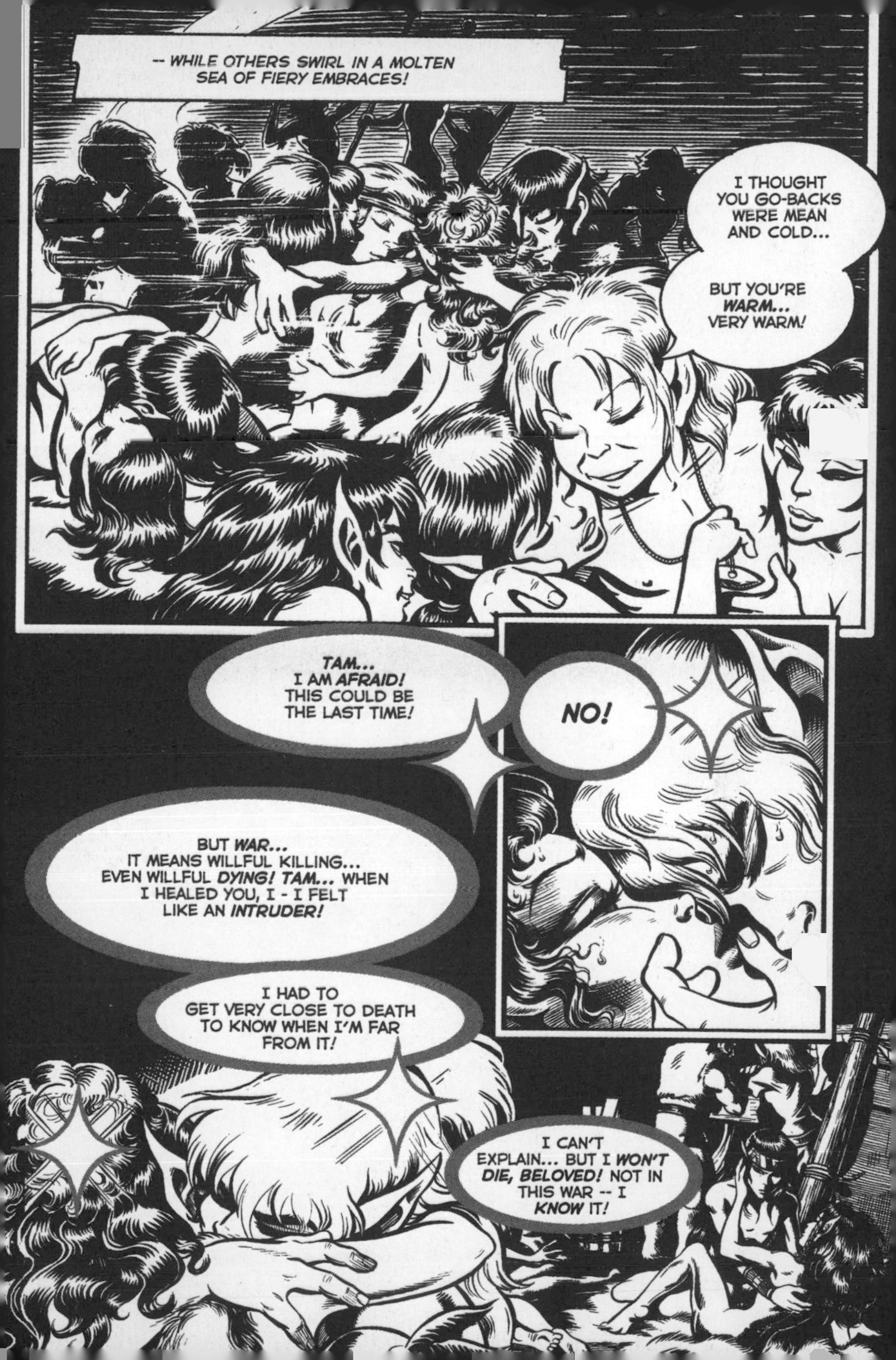
-- WHILE OTHERS SWIRL IN A MOLTEN SEA OF FIERY EMBRACES!
I THOUGHT YOU GO-BACKS WERE MEAN AND COLD...
BUT YOU'RE WARM... VERY WARM!
TAM... I AM AFRAID! THIS COULD BE THE LAST TIME!
NO!
BUT WAR... IT MEANS WILLFUL KILLING... EVEN WILLFUL DYING! TAM... WHEN I HEALED YOU, I - I FELT LIKE AN INTRUDER!
I HAD TO GET VERY CLOSE TO DEATH TO KNOW WHEN I'M FAR FROM IT!
I CAN'T EXPLAIN... BUT I WON'T DIE, BELOVED! NOT IN THIS WAR -- I KNOW IT!

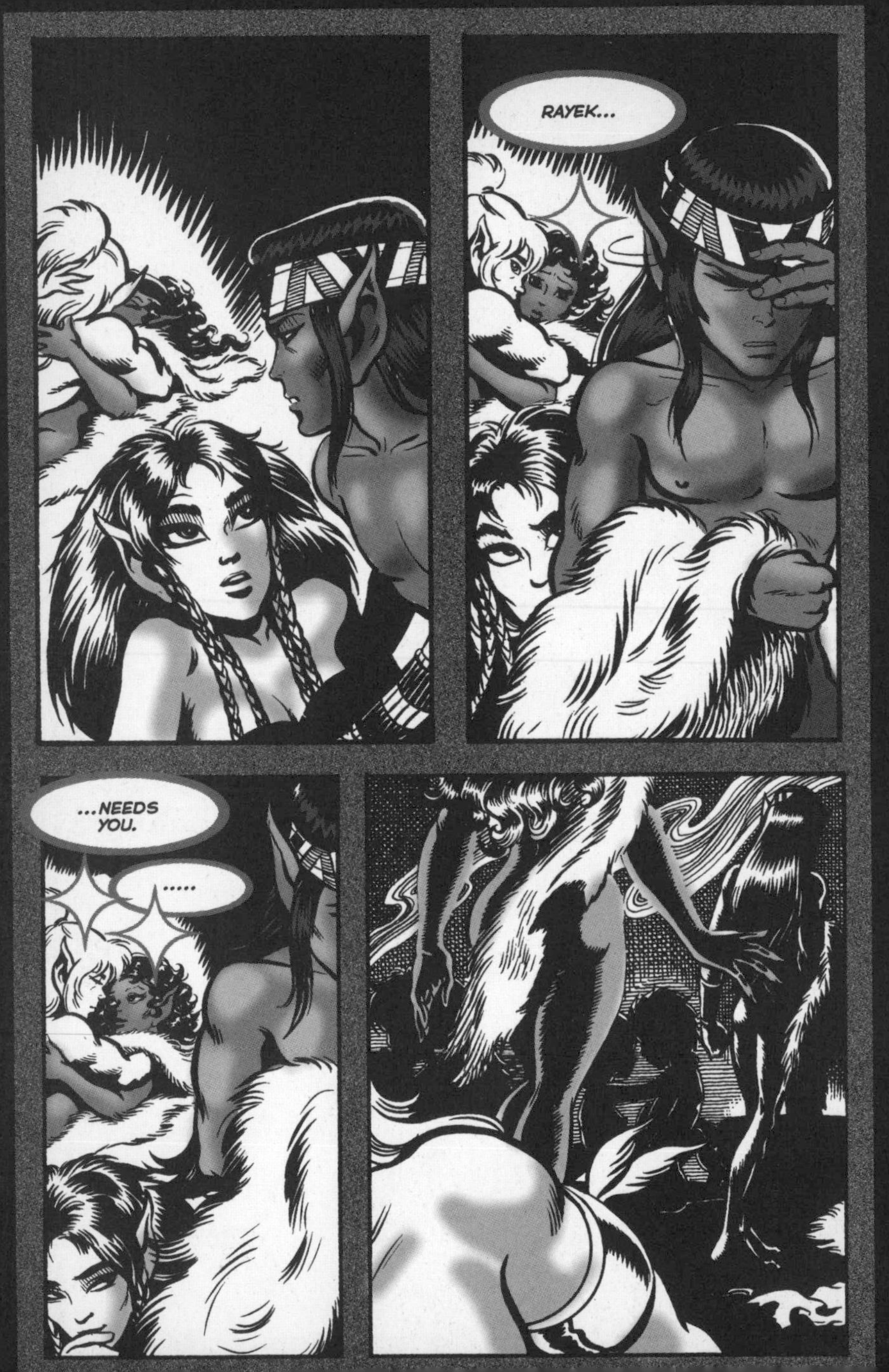
RAYEK...
...NEEDS YOU.
.....

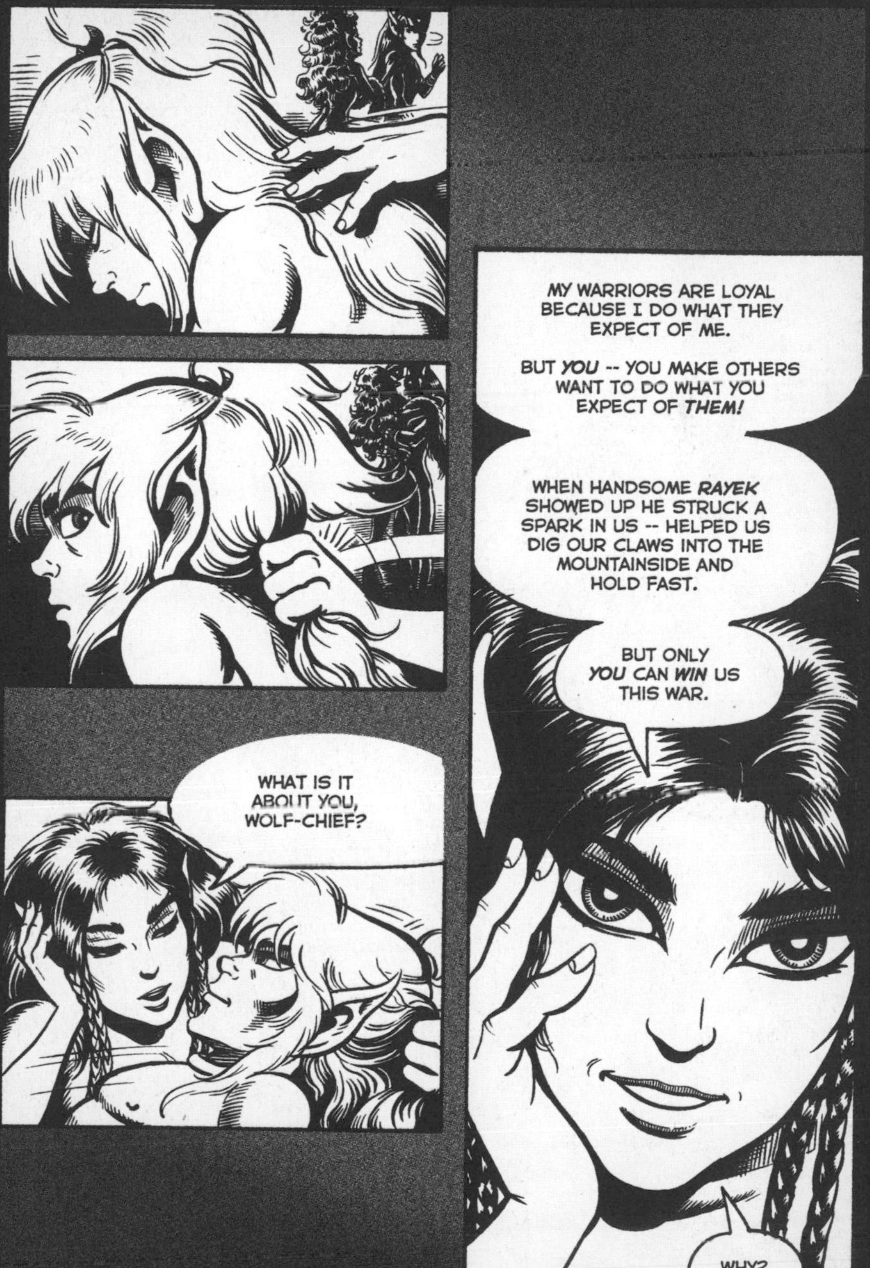
MY WARRIORS ARE LOYAL BECAUSE I DO WHAT THEY EXPECT OF ME.
BUT *YOU* -- YOU MAKE OTHERS WANT TO DO WHAT YOU EXPECT OF *THEM!*
WHEN HANDSOME *RAYEK* SHOWED UP HE STRUCK A SPARK IN US -- HELPED US DIG OUR CLAWS INTO THE MOUNTAINSIDE AND HOLD FAST.
BUT ONLY *YOU* CAN *WIN* US THIS WAR.
WHAT IS IT ABOUT YOU, WOLF-CHIEF?
WHY?

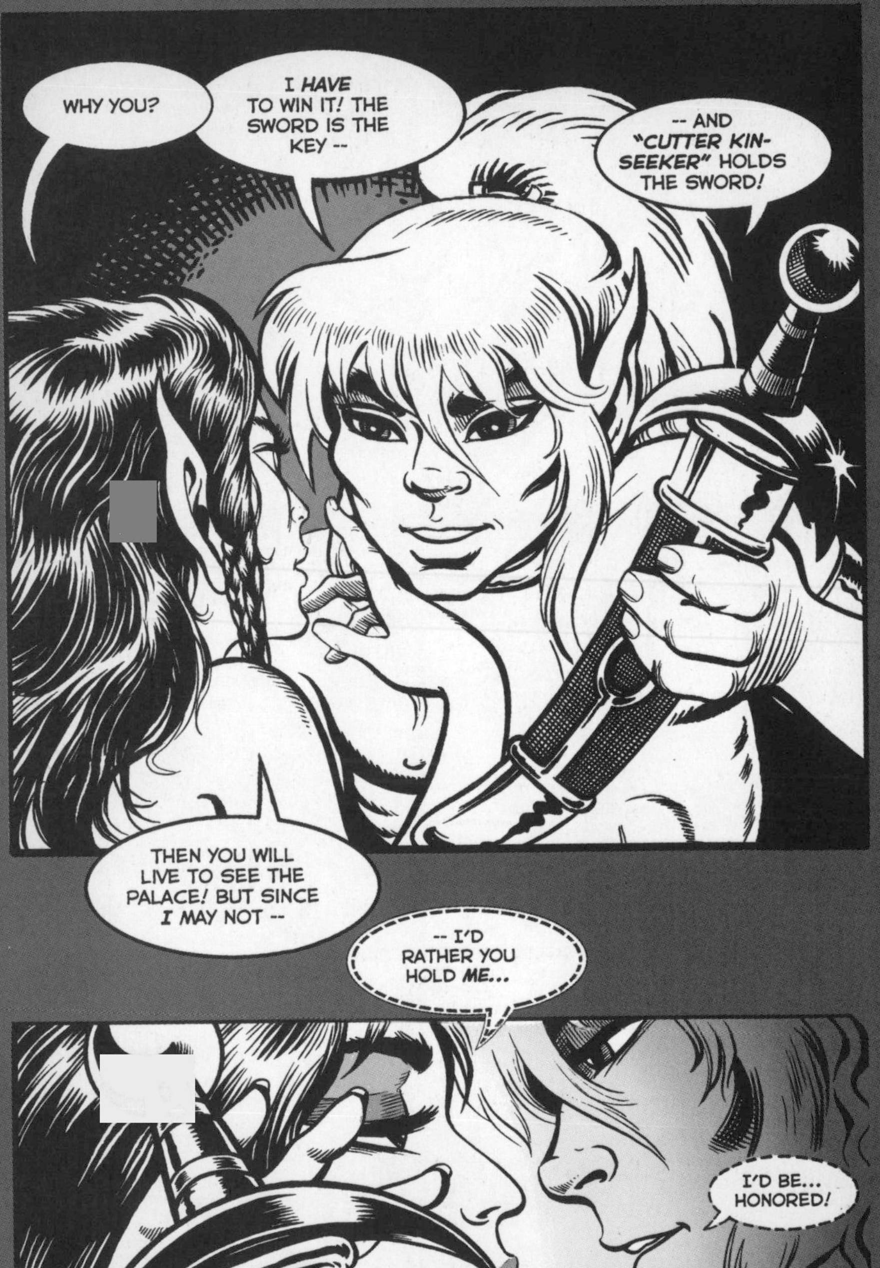
WHY YOU?
I *HAVE* TO WIN IT! THE SWORD IS THE KEY --
-- AND "CUTTER KIN-SEEKER" HOLDS THE SWORD!
THEN YOU WILL LIVE TO SEE THE PALACE! BUT SINCE *I* MAY NOT --
-- I'D RATHER YOU HOLD *ME*...
I'D BE... HONORED!

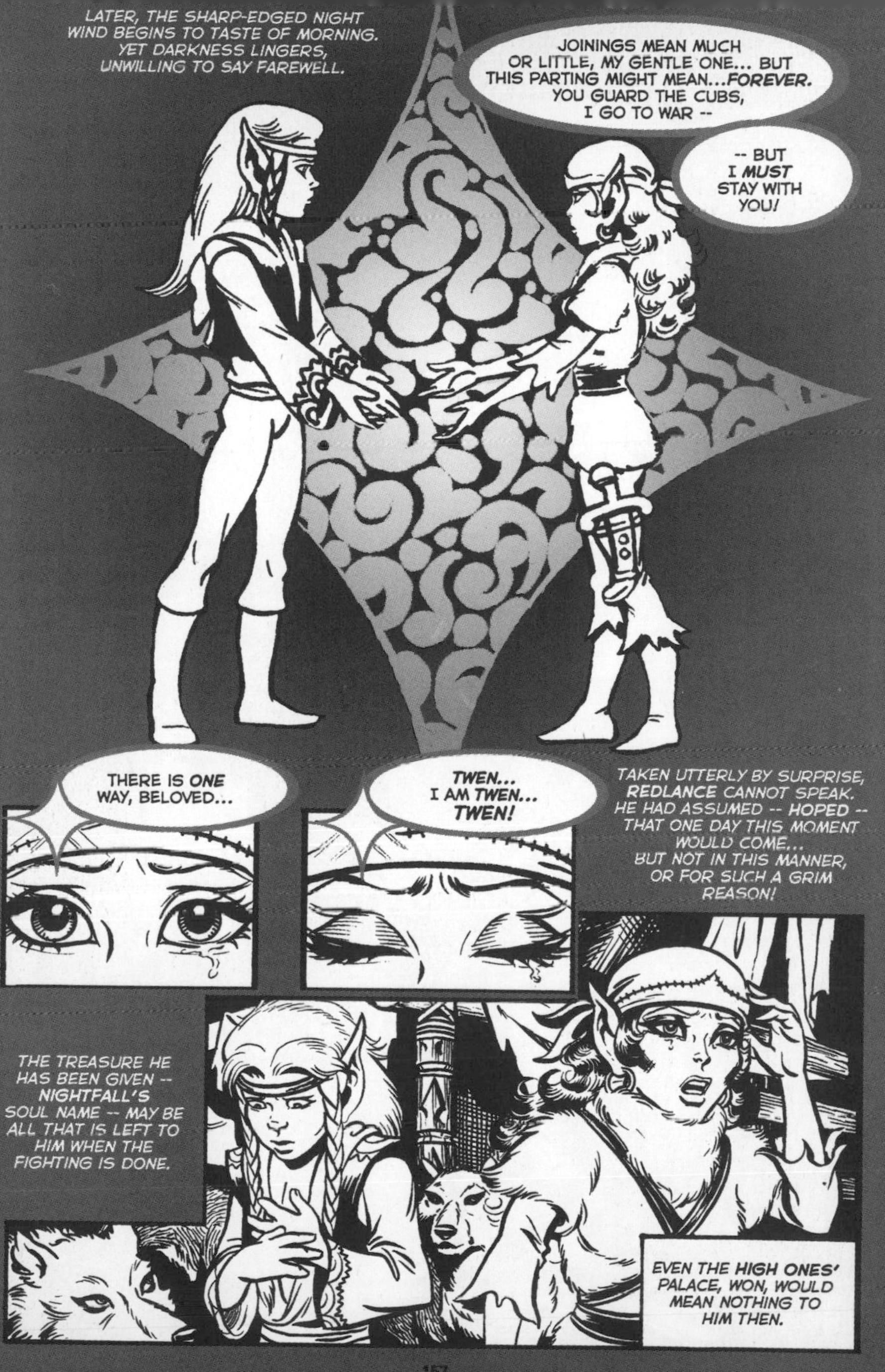

LATER, THE SHARP-EDGED NIGHT WIND BEGINS TO TASTE OF MORNING. YET DARKNESS LINGERS, UNWILLING TO SAY FAREWELL.
JOININGS MEAN MUCH OR LITTLE, MY GENTLE ONE... BUT THIS PARTING MIGHT MEAN...FOREVER. YOU GUARD THE CUBS, I GO TO WAR --
-- BUT I MUST STAY WITH YOU!
THERE IS ONE WAY, BELOVED...
TWEN... I AM TWEN... TWEN!
TAKEN UTTERLY BY SURPRISE, REDLANCE CANNOT SPEAK. HE HAD ASSUMED -- HOPED -- THAT ONE DAY THIS MOMENT WOULD COME... BUT NOT IN THIS MANNER, OR FOR SUCH A GRIM REASON!
THE TREASURE HE HAS BEEN GIVEN -- NIGHTFALL'S SOUL NAME -- MAY BE ALL THAT IS LEFT TO HIM WHEN THE FIGHTING IS DONE.
EVEN THE HIGH ONES' PALACE, WON, WOULD MEAN NOTHING TO HIM THEN.

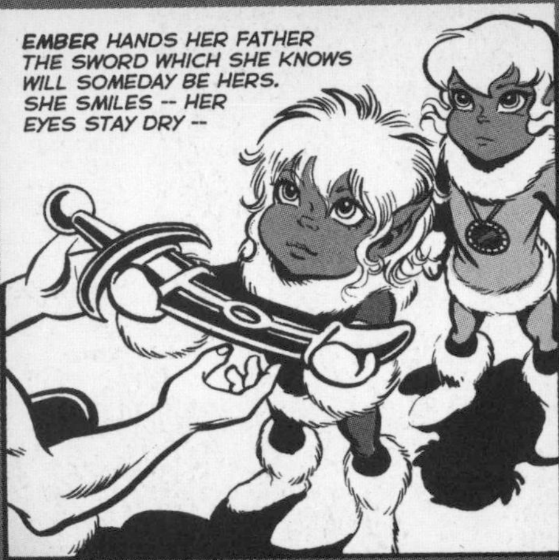
EMBER HANDS HER FATHER THE SWORD WHICH SHE KNOWS WILL SOMEDAY BE HERS. SHE SMILES -- HER EYES STAY DRY --

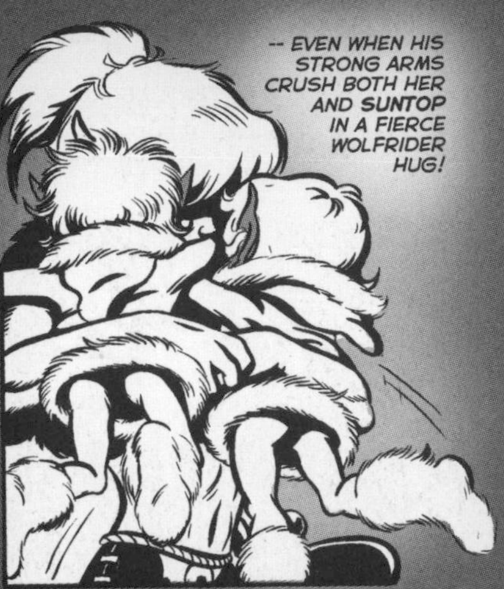
-- EVEN WHEN HIS STRONG ARMS CRUSH BOTH HER AND SUNTOP IN A FIERCE WOLFRIDER HUG!

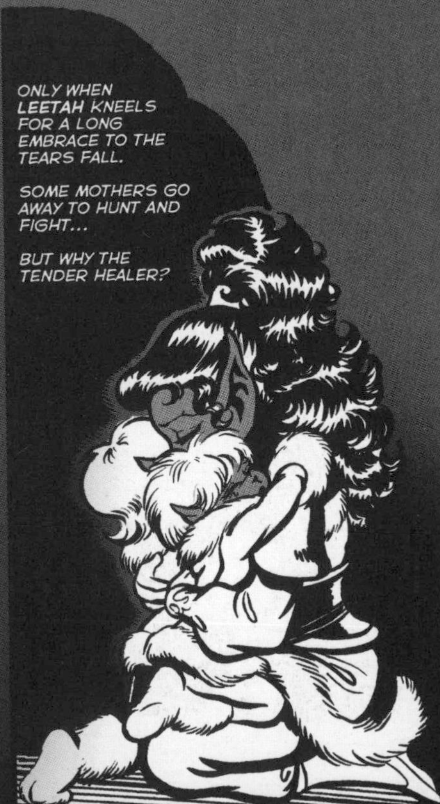
ONLY WHEN LEETAH KNEELS FOR A LONG EMBRACE TO THE TEARS FALL.
SOME MOTHERS GO AWAY TO HUNT AND FIGHT...
BUT WHY THE TENDER HEALER?

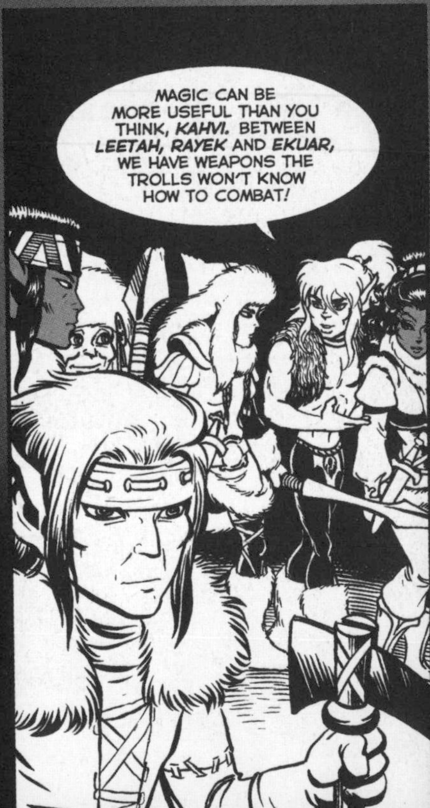
MAGIC CAN BE MORE USEFUL THAN YOU THINK, KAHVI. BETWEEN LEETAH, RAYEK AND EKUAR, WE HAVE WEAPONS THE TROLLS WON'T KNOW HOW TO COMBAT!

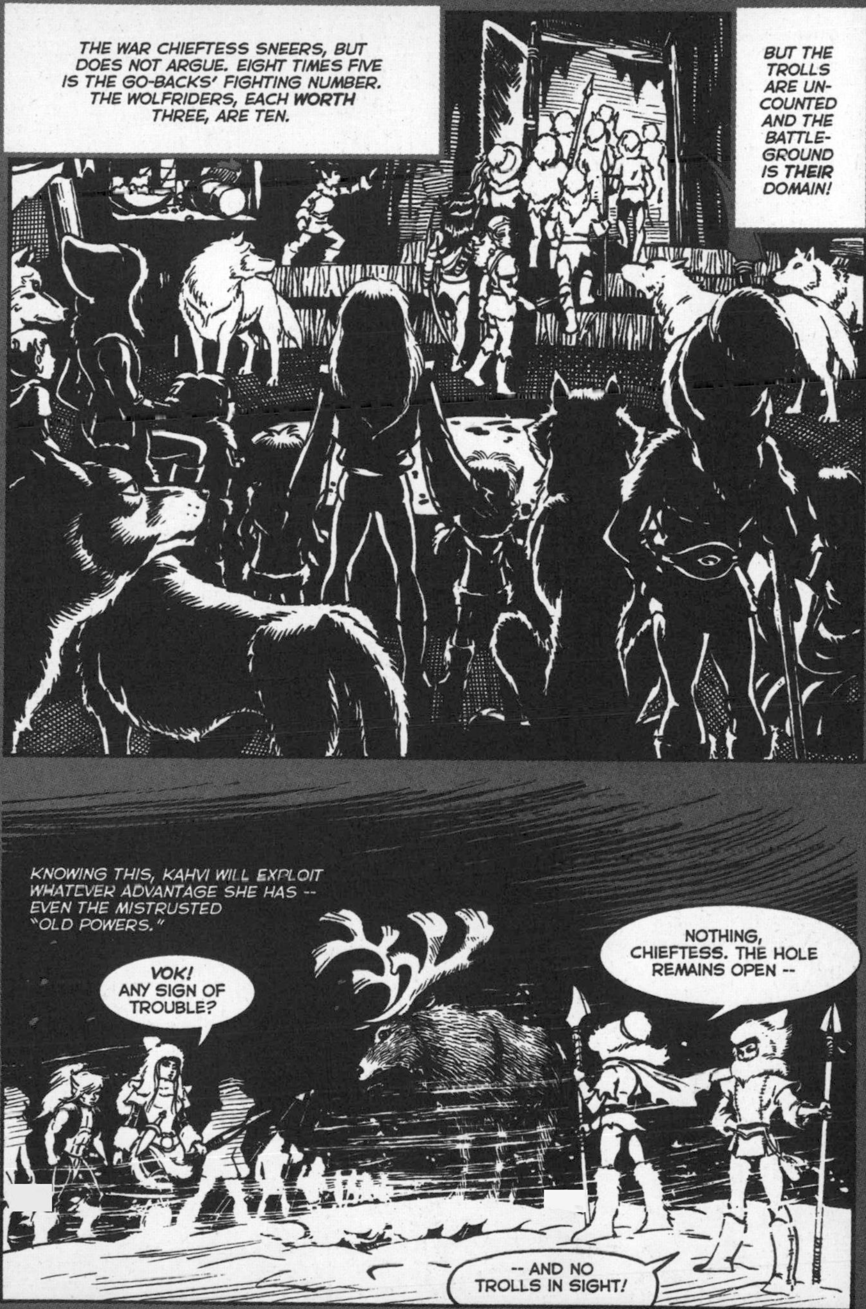
THE WAR CHIEFTESS SNEERS, BUT DOES NOT ARGUE. EIGHT TIMES FIVE IS THE GO-BACKS' FIGHTING NUMBER. THE WOLFRIDERS, EACH WORTH THREE, ARE TEN.
BUT THE TROLLS ARE UN-COUNTED AND THE BATTLE-GROUND IS THEIR DOMAIN!
KNOWING THIS, KAHVI WILL EXPLOIT WHATEVER ADVANTAGE SHE HAS -- EVEN THE MISTRUSTED "OLD POWERS."
VOK! ANY SIGN OF TROUBLE?
NOTHING, CHIEFTESS. THE HOLE REMAINS OPEN --
-- AND NO TROLLS IN SIGHT!

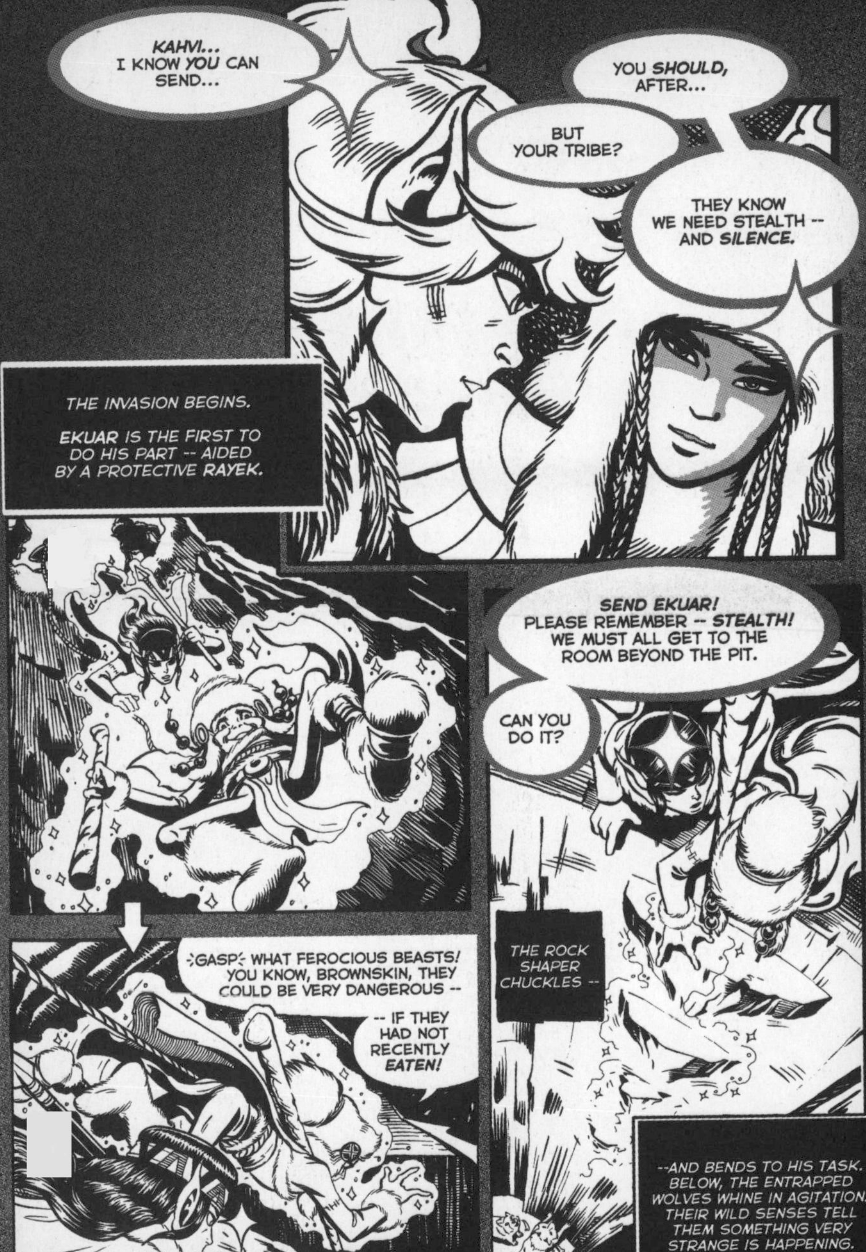
KAHVI... I KNOW YOU CAN SEND...
YOU SHOULD, AFTER...
BUT YOUR TRIBE?
THEY KNOW WE NEED STEALTH -- AND SILENCE.
THE INVASION BEGINS.
EKUAR IS THE FIRST TO DO HIS PART -- AIDED BY A PROTECTIVE RAYEK.
-GASP- WHAT FEROCIOUS BEASTS! YOU KNOW, BROWNSKIN, THEY COULD BE VERY DANGEROUS --
-- IF THEY HAD NOT RECENTLY EATEN!
SEND EKUAR! PLEASE REMEMBER -- STEALTH! WE MUST ALL GET TO THE ROOM BEYOND THE PIT.
CAN YOU DO IT?
THE ROCK SHAPER CHUCKLES --
--AND BENDS TO HIS TASK. BELOW, THE ENTRAPPED WOLVES WHINE IN AGITATION. THEIR WILD SENSES TELL THEM SOMETHING VERY STRANGE IS HAPPENING.

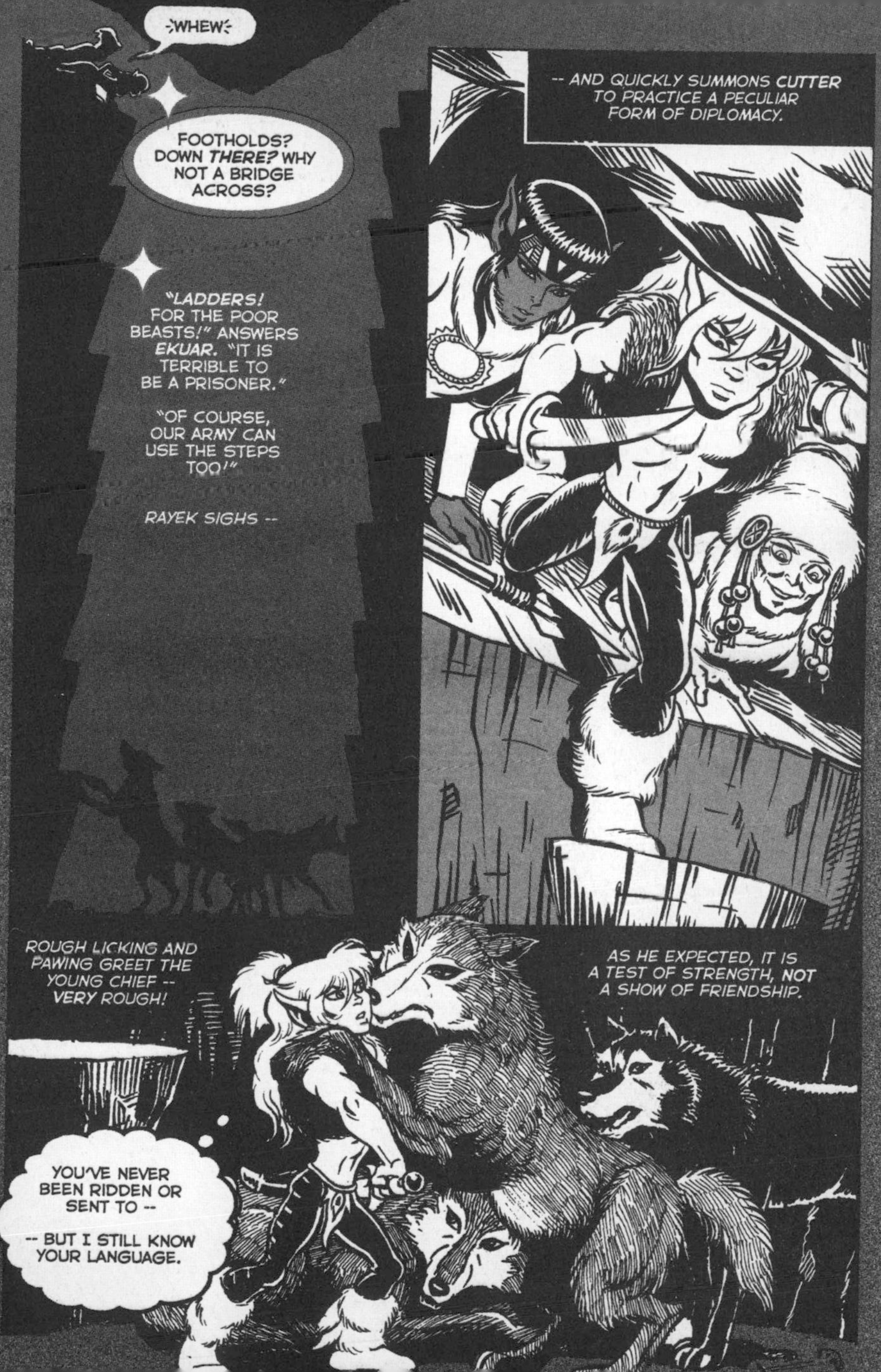
WHEW
FOOTHOLDS? DOWN THERE? WHY NOT A BRIDGE ACROSS?
"LADDERS! FOR THE POOR BEASTS!" ANSWERS EKUAR. "IT IS TERRIBLE TO BE A PRISONER."
"OF COURSE, OUR ARMY CAN USE THE STEPS TOO!"
RAYEK SIGHS --
-- AND QUICKLY SUMMONS CUTTER TO PRACTICE A PECULIAR FORM OF DIPLOMACY.
ROUGH LICKING AND PAWING GREET THE YOUNG CHIEF -- VERY ROUGH!
AS HE EXPECTED, IT IS A TEST OF STRENGTH, NOT A SHOW OF FRIENDSHIP.
YOU'VE NEVER BEEN RIDDEN OR SENT TO --
-- BUT I STILL KNOW YOUR LANGUAGE.

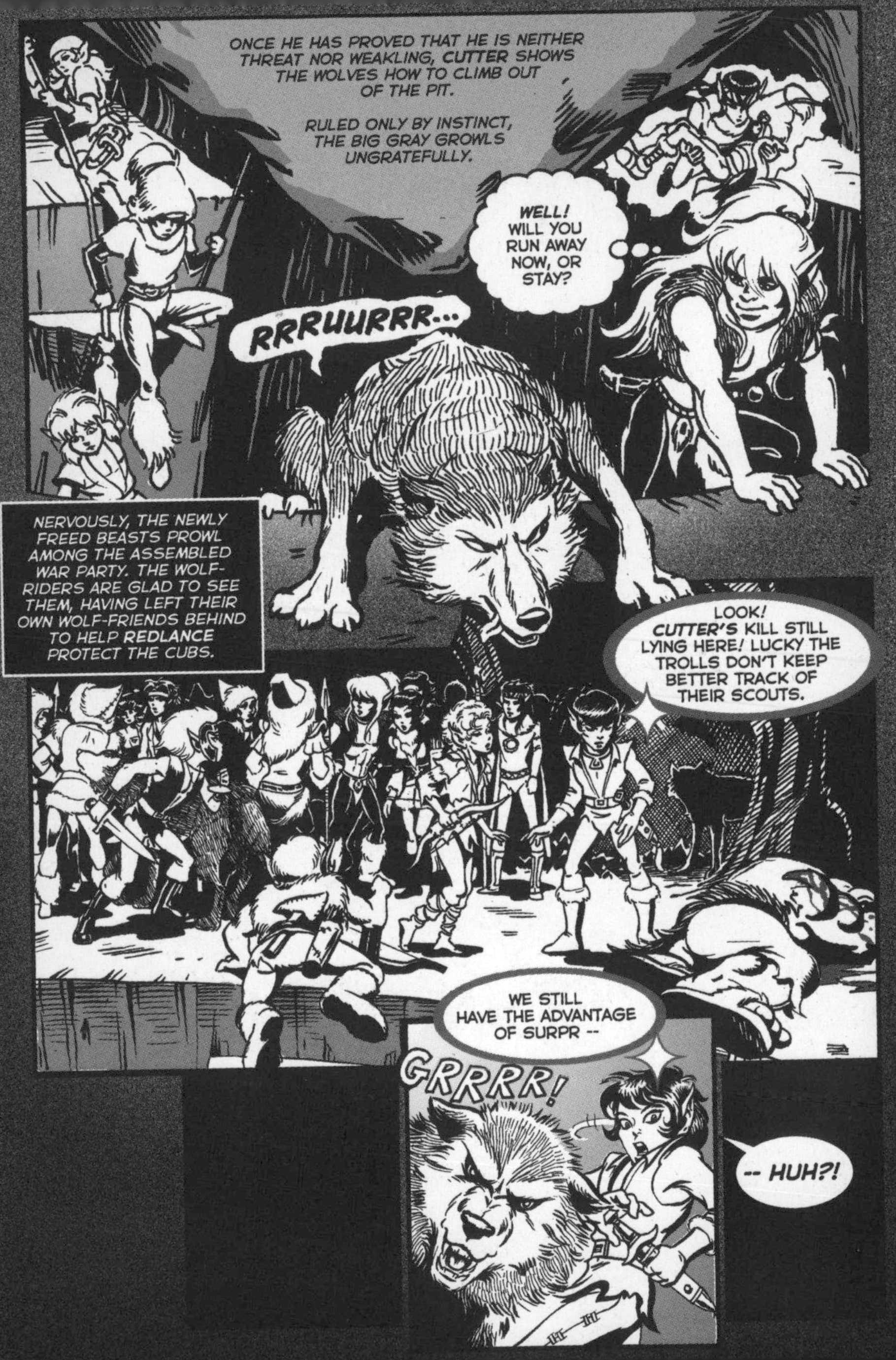
ONCE HE HAS PROVED THAT HE IS NEITHER THREAT NOR WEAKLING, CUTTER SHOWS THE WOLVES HOW TO CLIMB OUT OF THE PIT.
RULED ONLY BY INSTINCT, THE BIG GRAY GROWLS UNGRATEFULLY.
WELL! WILL YOU RUN AWAY NOW, OR STAY?
RRRUURRR...
NERVOUSLY, THE NEWLY FREED BEASTS PROWL AMONG THE ASSEMBLED WAR PARTY. THE WOLF-RIDERS ARE GLAD TO SEE THEM, HAVING LEFT THEIR OWN WOLF-FRIENDS BEHIND TO HELP REDLANCE PROTECT THE CUBS.
LOOK! CUTTER'S KILL STILL LYING HERE! LUCKY THE TROLLS DON'T KEEP BETTER TRACK OF THEIR SCOUTS.
WE STILL HAVE THE ADVANTAGE OF SURPR --
GRRRRR!
-- HUH?!

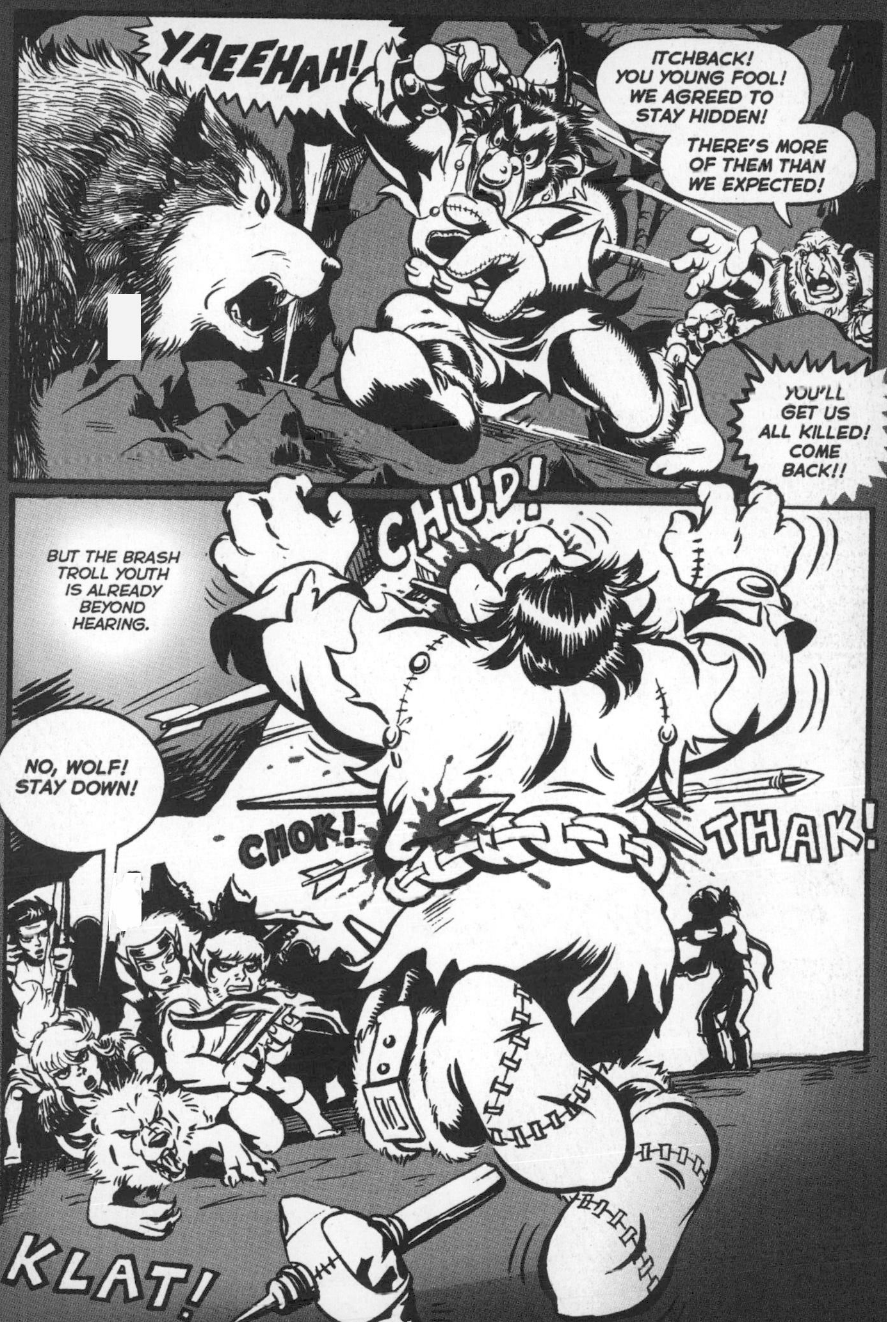
YAEEHAH!
ITCHBACK! YOU YOUNG FOOL! WE AGREED TO STAY HIDDEN!
THERE'S MORE OF THEM THAN WE EXPECTED!
YOU'LL GET US ALL KILLED! COME BACK!!
BUT THE BRASH TROLL YOUTH IS ALREADY BEYOND HEARING.
CHUD!
NO, WOLF! STAY DOWN!
CHOK!
THAK!
KLAT!

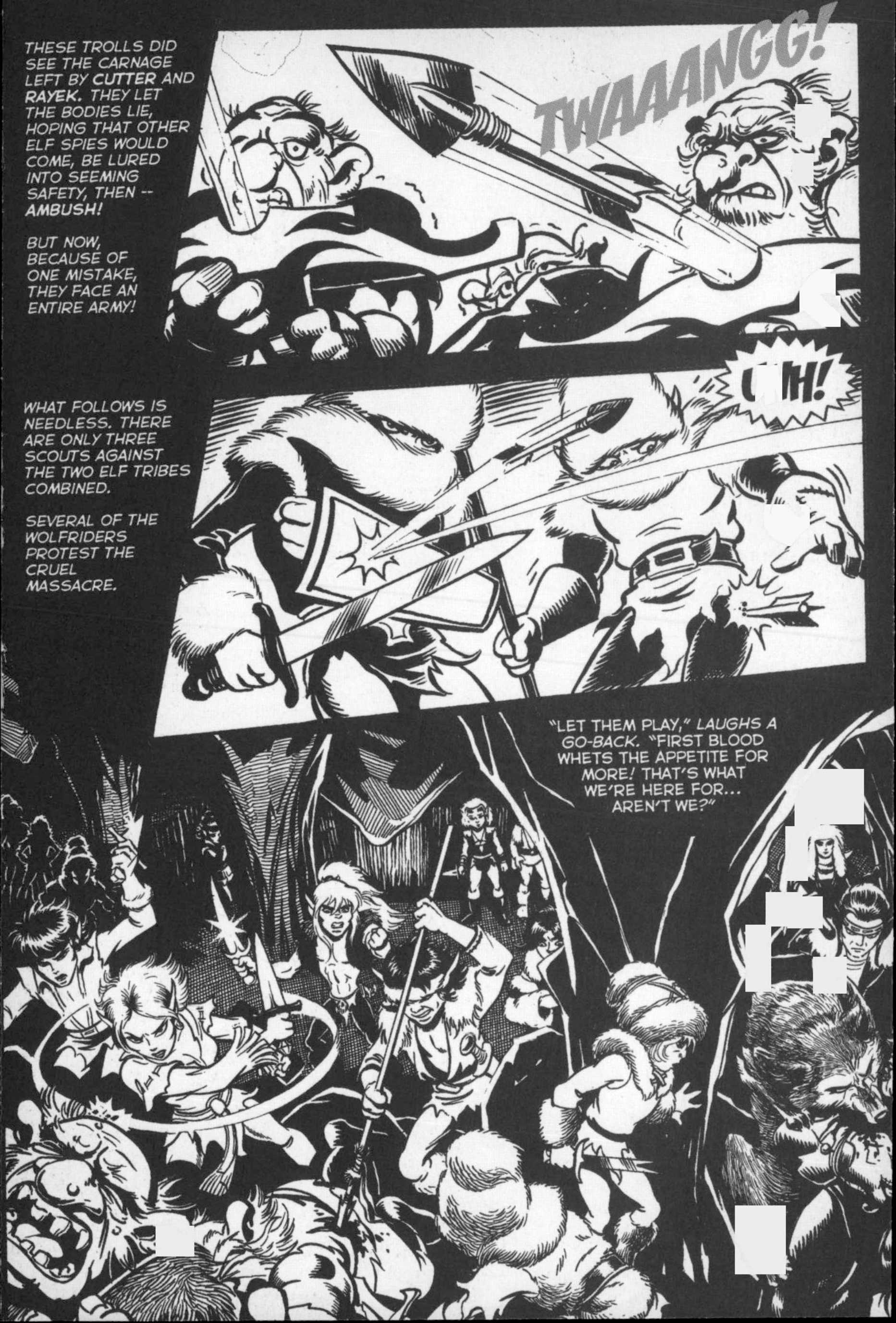
THESE TROLLS DID SEE THE CARNAGE LEFT BY CUTTER AND RAYEK. THEY LET THE BODIES LIE, HOPING THAT OTHER ELF SPIES WOULD COME, BE LURED INTO SEEMING SAFETY, THEN -- AMBUSH!
BUT NOW, BECAUSE OF ONE MISTAKE, THEY FACE AN ENTIRE ARMY!
TWAAAANGG!
WHAT FOLLOWS IS NEEDLESS. THERE ARE ONLY THREE SCOUTS AGAINST THE TWO ELF TRIBES COMBINED.
SEVERAL OF THE WOLFRIDERS PROTEST THE CRUEL MASSACRE.
H!
"LET THEM PLAY," LAUGHS A GO-BACK. "FIRST BLOOD WHETS THE APPETITE FOR MORE! THAT'S WHAT WE'RE HERE FOR... AREN'T WE?"

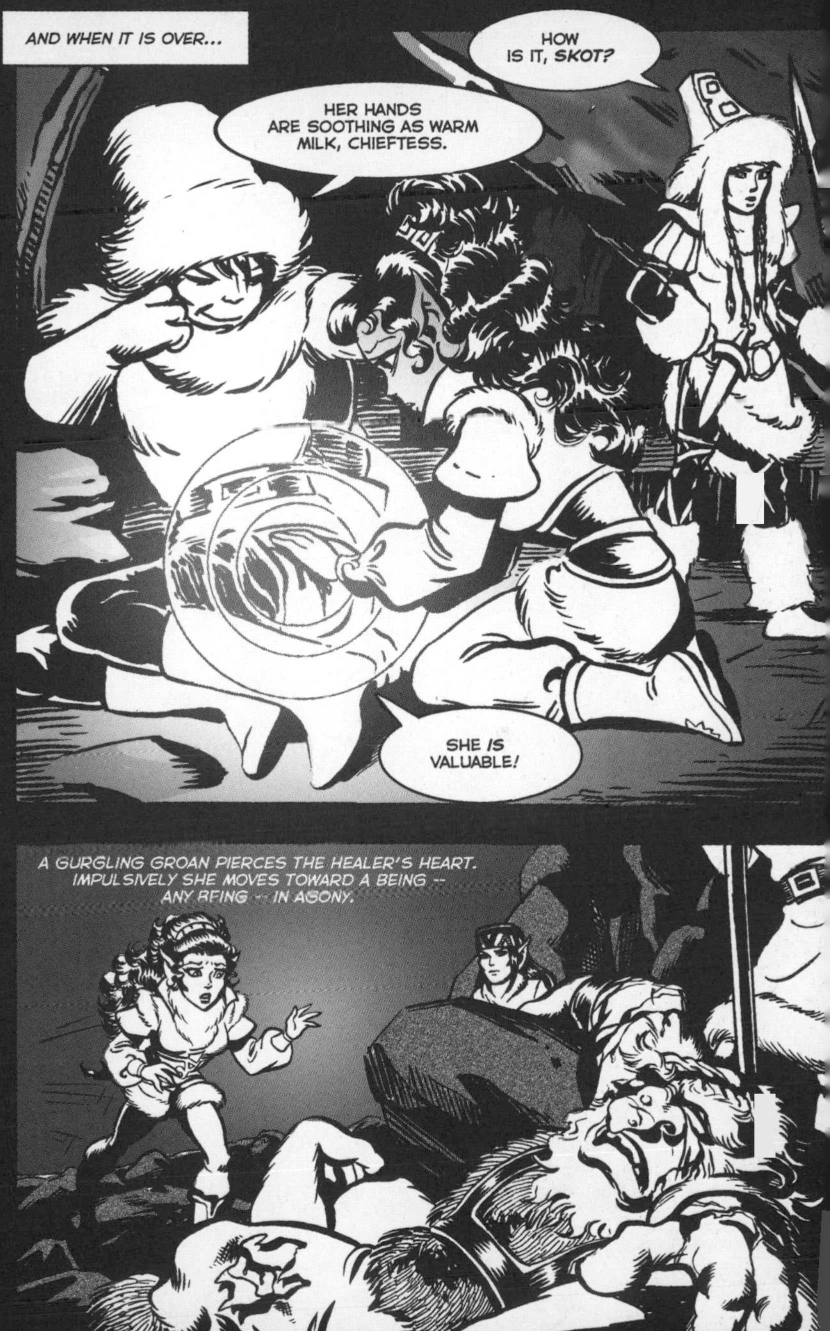
AND WHEN IT IS OVER...
HOW IS IT, SKOT?
HER HANDS ARE SOOTHING AS WARM MILK, CHIEFTESS.
SHE IS VALUABLE!
A GURGLING GROAN PIERCES THE HEALER'S HEART. IMPULSIVELY SHE MOVES TOWARD A BEING -- ANY BEING -- IN AGONY.

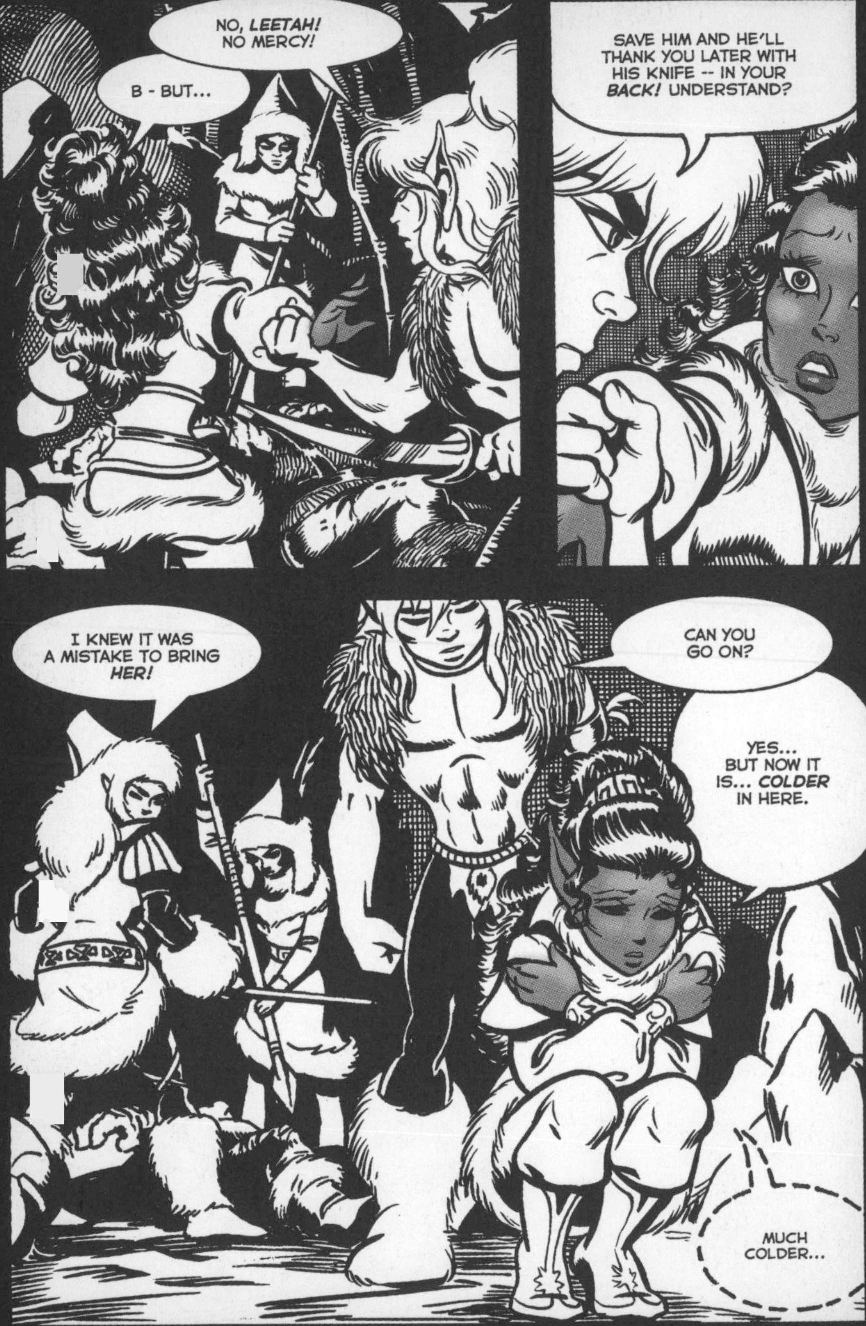
NO, LEETAH! NO MERCY!
B - BUT...
SAVE HIM AND HE'LL THANK YOU LATER WITH HIS KNIFE -- IN YOUR BACK! UNDERSTAND?
I KNEW IT WAS A MISTAKE TO BRING HER!
CAN YOU GO ON?
YES... BUT NOW IT IS... COLDER IN HERE.
MUCH COLDER...

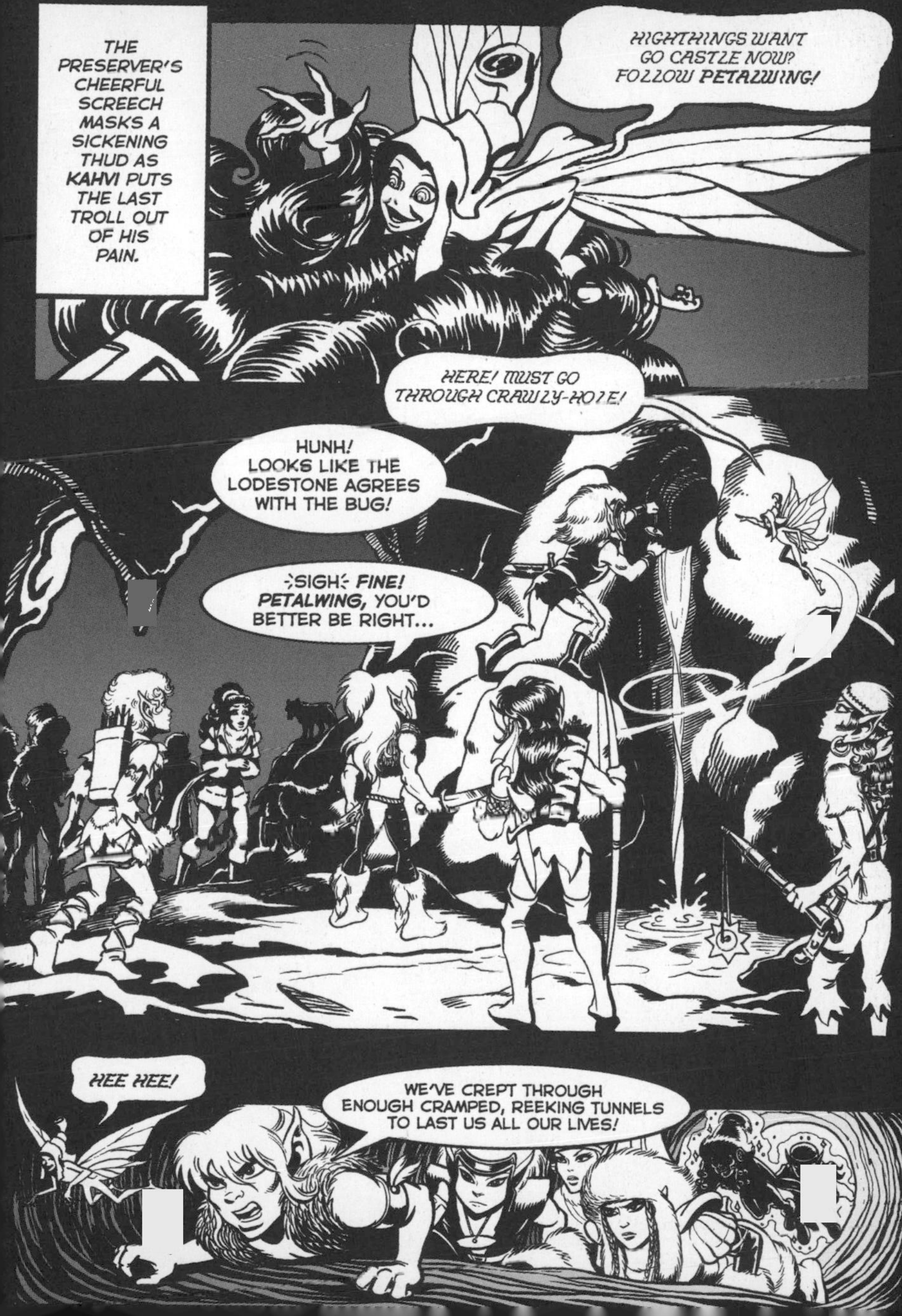
THE PRESERVER'S CHEERFUL SCREECH MASKS A SICKENING THUD AS KAHVI PUTS THE LAST TROLL OUT OF HIS PAIN.
HIGHTHINGS WANT GO CASTLE NOW? FOLLOW PETALWING!
HERE! MUST GO THROUGH CRAWLY-HOLE!
HUNH! LOOKS LIKE THE LODESTONE AGREES WITH THE BUG!
-SIGH- FINE! PETALWING, YOU'D BETTER BE RIGHT...
HEE HEE!
WE'VE CREPT THROUGH ENOUGH CRAMPED, REEKING TUNNELS TO LAST US ALL OUR LIVES!

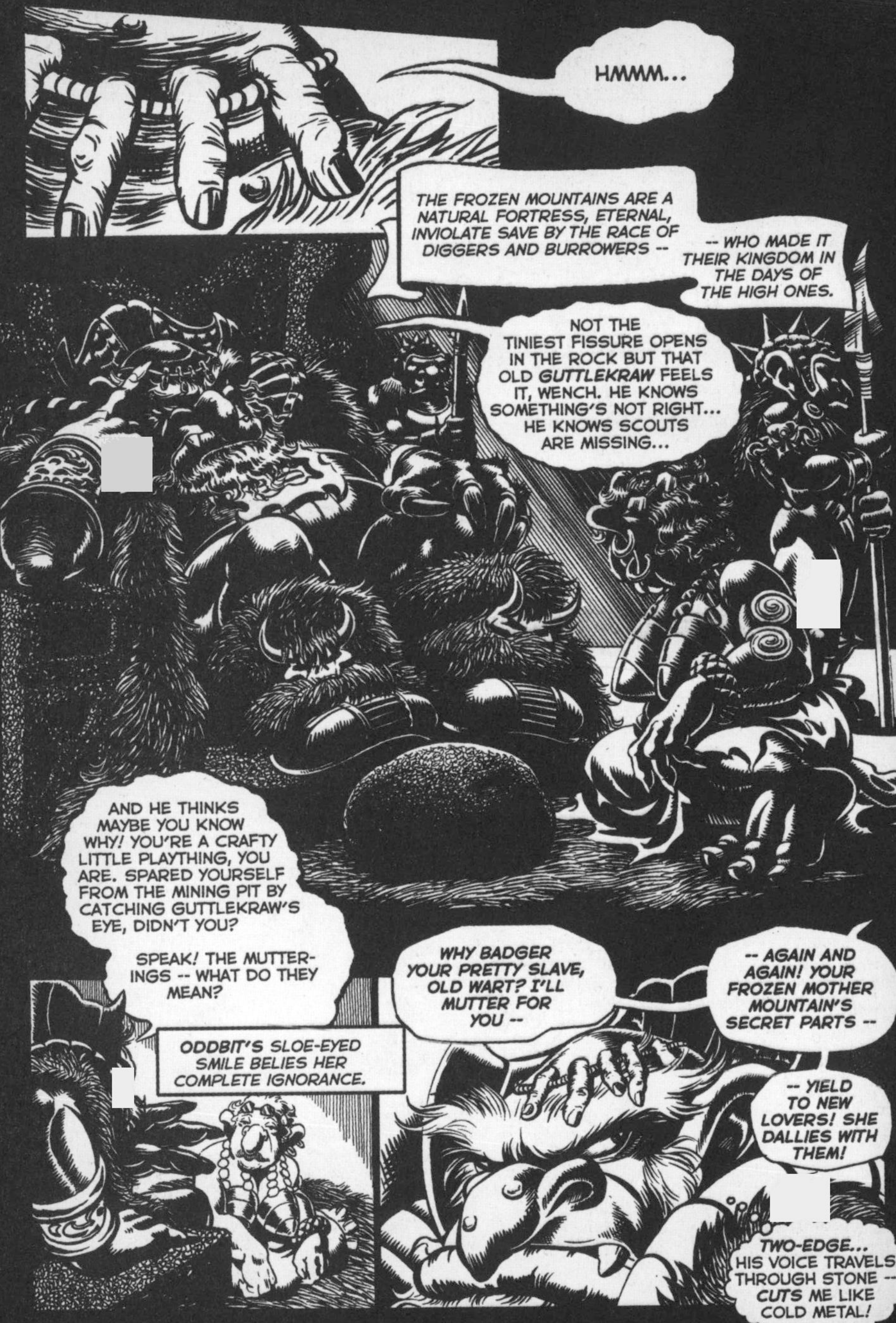
HMMM...
THE FROZEN MOUNTAINS ARE A NATURAL FORTRESS, ETERNAL, INVIOLATE SAVE BY THE RACE OF DIGGERS AND BURROWERS --
-- WHO MADE IT THEIR KINGDOM IN THE DAYS OF THE HIGH ONES.
NOT THE TINIEST FISSURE OPENS IN THE ROCK BUT THAT OLD GUTTLEKRAW FEELS IT, WENCH. HE KNOWS SOMETHING'S NOT RIGHT... HE KNOWS SCOUTS ARE MISSING...
AND HE THINKS MAYBE YOU KNOW WHY! YOU'RE A CRAFTY LITTLE PLAYTHING, YOU ARE. SPARED YOURSELF FROM THE MINING PIT BY CATCHING GUTTLEKRAW'S EYE, DIDN'T YOU?
SPEAK! THE MUTTERINGS -- WHAT DO THEY MEAN?
ODDBIT'S SLOE-EYED SMILE BELIES HER COMPLETE IGNORANCE.
WHY BADGER YOUR PRETTY SLAVE, OLD WART? I'LL MUTTER FOR YOU --
-- AGAIN AND AGAIN! YOUR FROZEN MOTHER MOUNTAIN'S SECRET PARTS --
-- YIELD TO NEW LOVERS! SHE DALLIES WITH THEM!
TWO-EDGE... HIS VOICE TRAVELS THROUGH STONE -- CUTS ME LIKE COLD METAL!

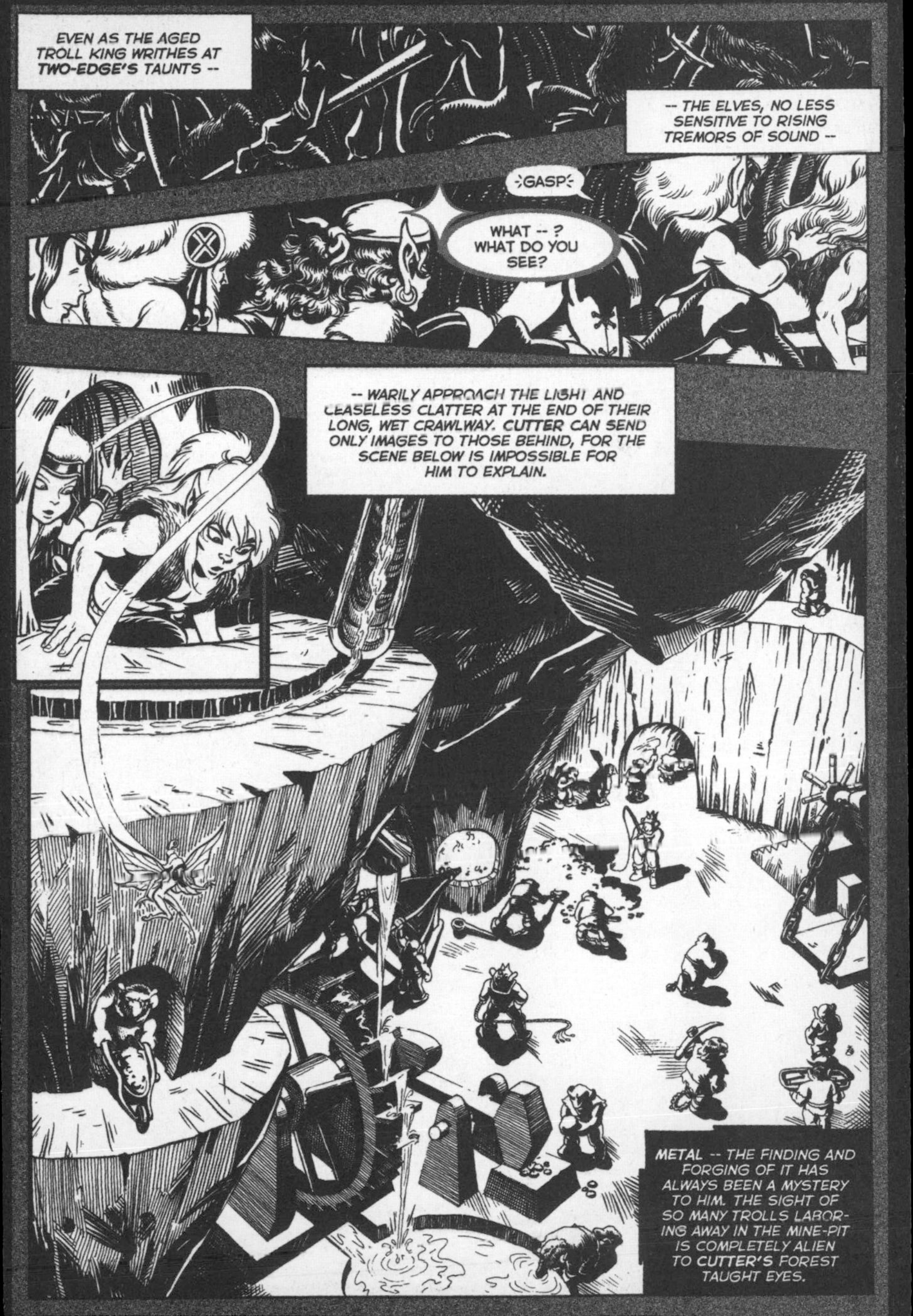
EVEN AS THE AGED TROLL KING WRITHES AT TWO-EDGE'S TAUNTS --
-- THE ELVES, NO LESS SENSITIVE TO RISING TREMORS OF SOUND --
GASP
WHAT -- ? WHAT DO YOU SEE?
-- WARILY APPROACH THE LIGHT AND CEASELESS CLATTER AT THE END OF THEIR LONG, WET CRAWLWAY. CUTTER CAN SEND ONLY IMAGES TO THOSE BEHIND, FOR THE SCENE BELOW IS IMPOSSIBLE FOR HIM TO EXPLAIN.
METAL -- THE FINDING AND FORGING OF IT HAS ALWAYS BEEN A MYSTERY TO HIM. THE SIGHT OF SO MANY TROLLS LABORING AWAY IN THE MINE-PIT IS COMPLETELY ALIEN TO CUTTER'S FOREST TAUGHT EYES.

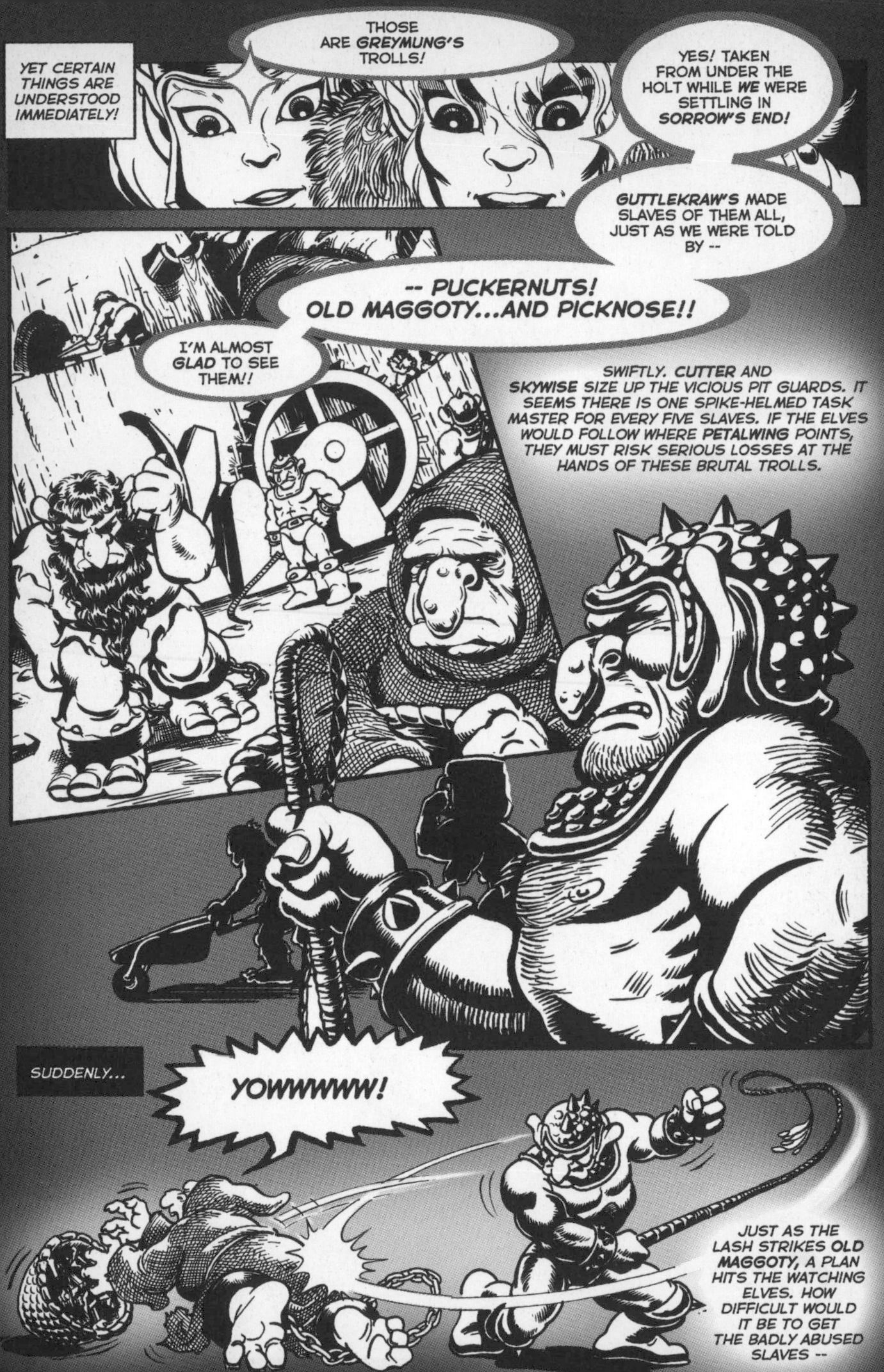
YET CERTAIN THINGS ARE UNDERSTOOD IMMEDIATELY!
THOSE ARE GREYMUNG'S TROLLS!
YES! TAKEN FROM UNDER THE HOLT WHILE WE WERE SETTLING IN SORROW'S END!
GUTTLEKRAW'S MADE SLAVES OF THEM ALL, JUST AS WE WERE TOLD BY --
-- PUCKERNUTS! OLD MAGGOTY...AND PICKNOSE!!
I'M ALMOST GLAD TO SEE THEM!!
SWIFTLY. CUTTER AND SKYWISE SIZE UP THE VICIOUS PIT GUARDS. IT SEEMS THERE IS ONE SPIKE-HELMED TASK MASTER FOR EVERY FIVE SLAVES. IF THE ELVES WOULD FOLLOW WHERE PETALWING POINTS, THEY MUST RISK SERIOUS LOSSES AT THE HANDS OF THESE BRUTAL TROLLS.
SUDDENLY...
YOWWWWW!
JUST AS THE LASH STRIKES OLD MAGGOTY, A PLAN HITS THE WATCHING ELVES. HOW DIFFICULT WOULD IT BE TO GET THE BADLY ABUSED SLAVES --

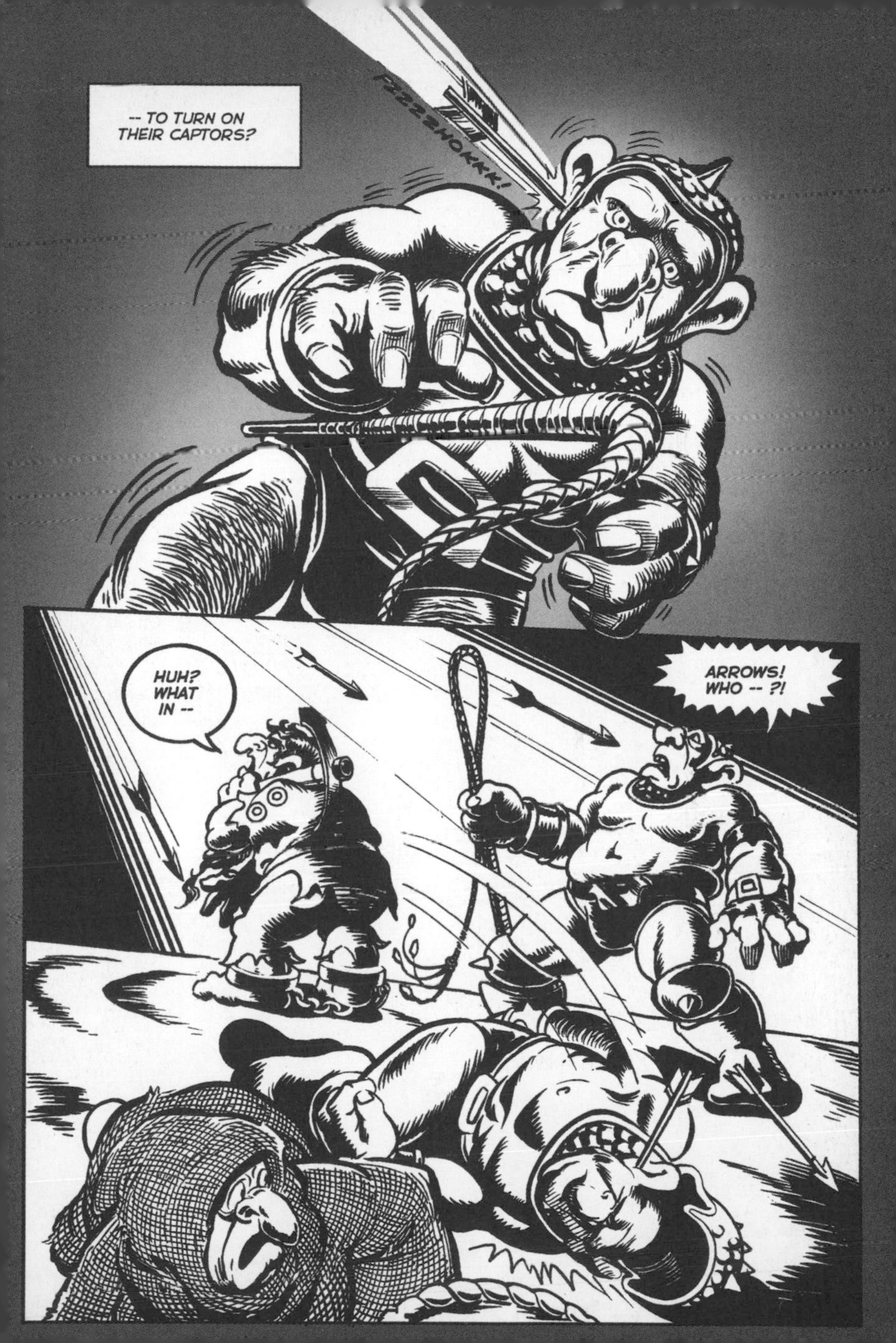
-- TO TURN ON THEIR CAPTORS?
FZZZZHOKKK!
HUH? WHAT IN --
ARROWS! WHO -- ?!

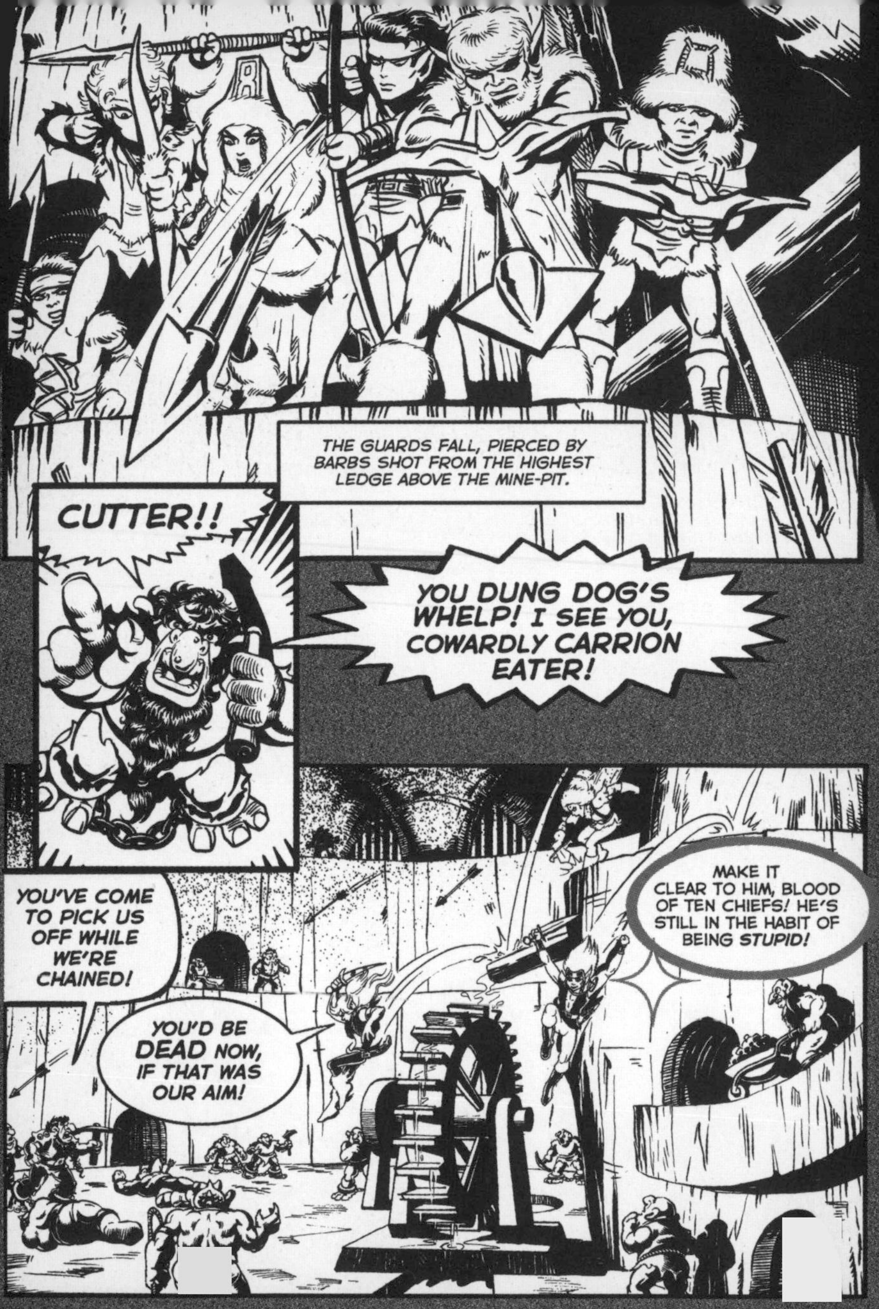
THE GUARDS FALL, PIERCED BY BARBS SHOT FROM THE HIGHEST LEDGE ABOVE THE MINE-PIT.
CUTTER!!
YOU DUNG DOG'S WHELP! I SEE YOU, COWARDLY CARRION EATER!
YOU'VE COME TO PICK US OFF WHILE WE'RE CHAINED!
YOU'D BE DEAD NOW, IF THAT WAS OUR AIM!
MAKE IT CLEAR TO HIM, BLOOD OF TEN CHIEFS! HE'S STILL IN THE HABIT OF BEING STUPID!

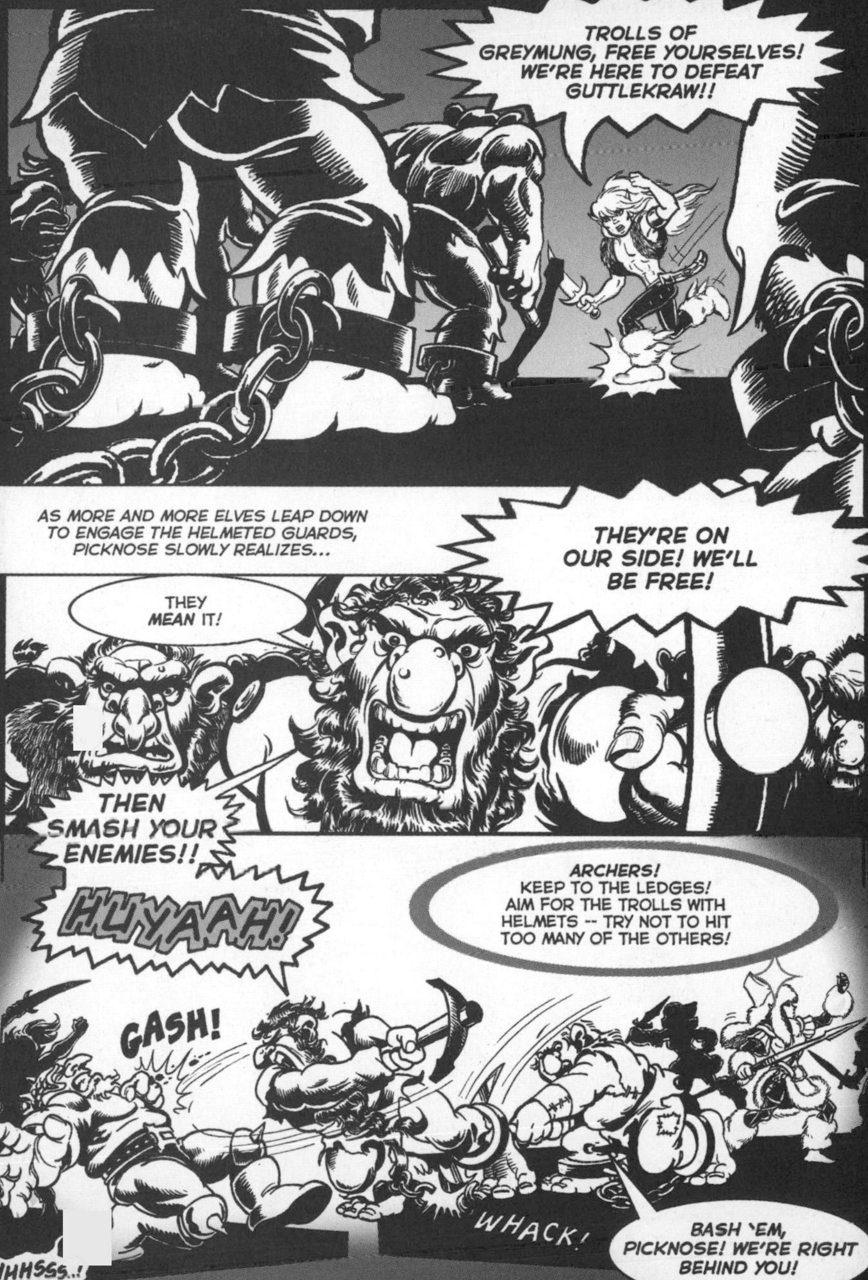

TROLLS OF GREYMUNG, FREE YOURSELVES! WE'RE HERE TO DEFEAT GUTTLEKRAW!!
AS MORE AND MORE ELVES LEAP DOWN TO ENGAGE THE HELMETED GUARDS, PICKNOSE SLOWLY REALIZES...
THEY'RE ON OUR SIDE! WE'LL BE FREE!
THEY MEAN IT!
THEN SMASH YOUR ENEMIES!!
HUYAAH!
ARCHERS! KEEP TO THE LEDGES! AIM FOR THE TROLLS WITH HELMETS -- TRY NOT TO HIT TOO MANY OF THE OTHERS!
GASH!
WHACK!
BASH 'EM, PICKNOSE! WE'RE RIGHT BEHIND YOU!
HHHSSS..!

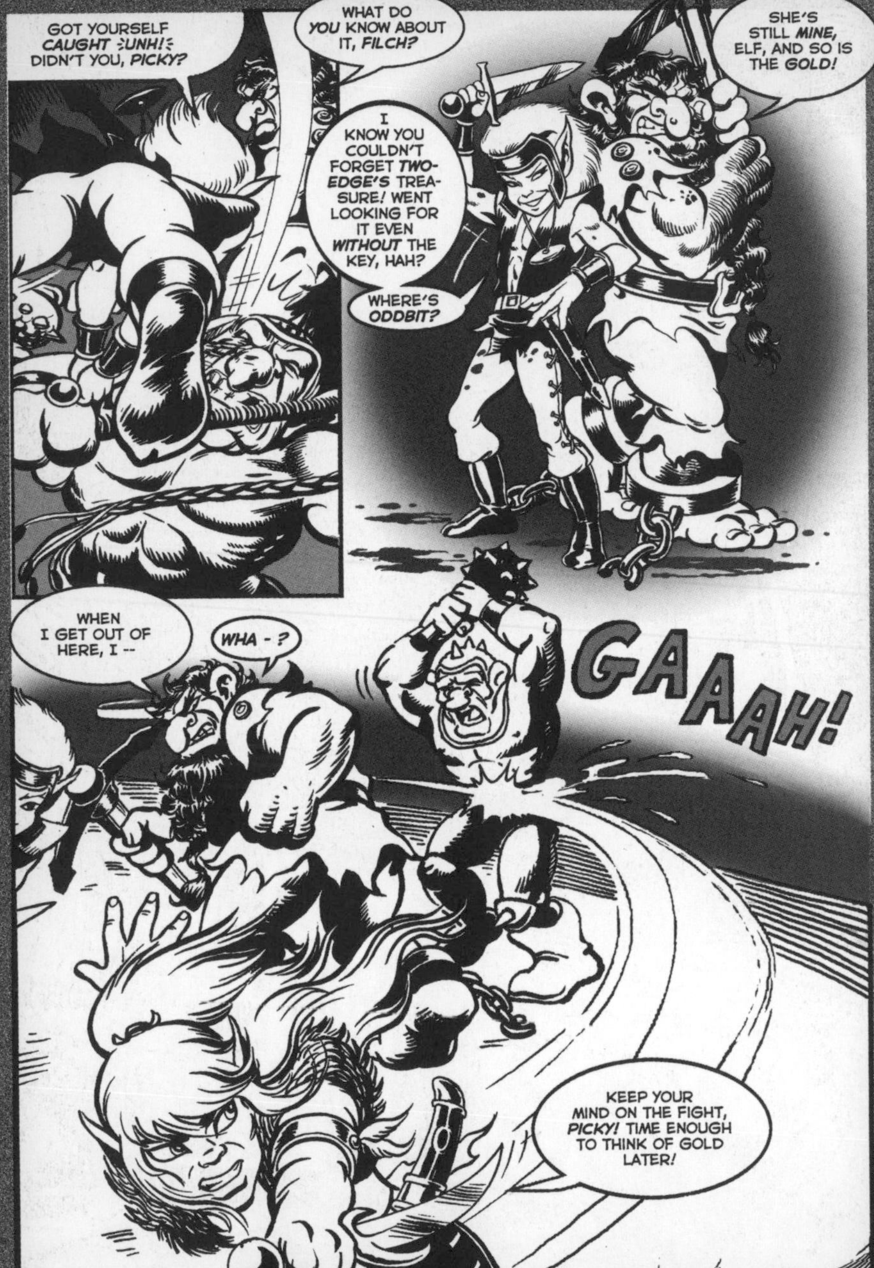
GOT YOURSELF CAUGHT -UNH!- DIDN'T YOU, PICKY?
WHAT DO YOU KNOW ABOUT IT, FILCH?
I KNOW YOU COULDN'T FORGET TWO-EDGE'S TREASURE! WENT LOOKING FOR IT EVEN WITHOUT THE KEY, HAH?
WHERE'S ODDBIT?
SHE'S STILL MINE, ELF, AND SO IS THE GOLD!
WHEN I GET OUT OF HERE, I --
WHA - ?
GAAAH!
KEEP YOUR MIND ON THE FIGHT, PICKY! TIME ENOUGH TO THINK OF GOLD LATER!

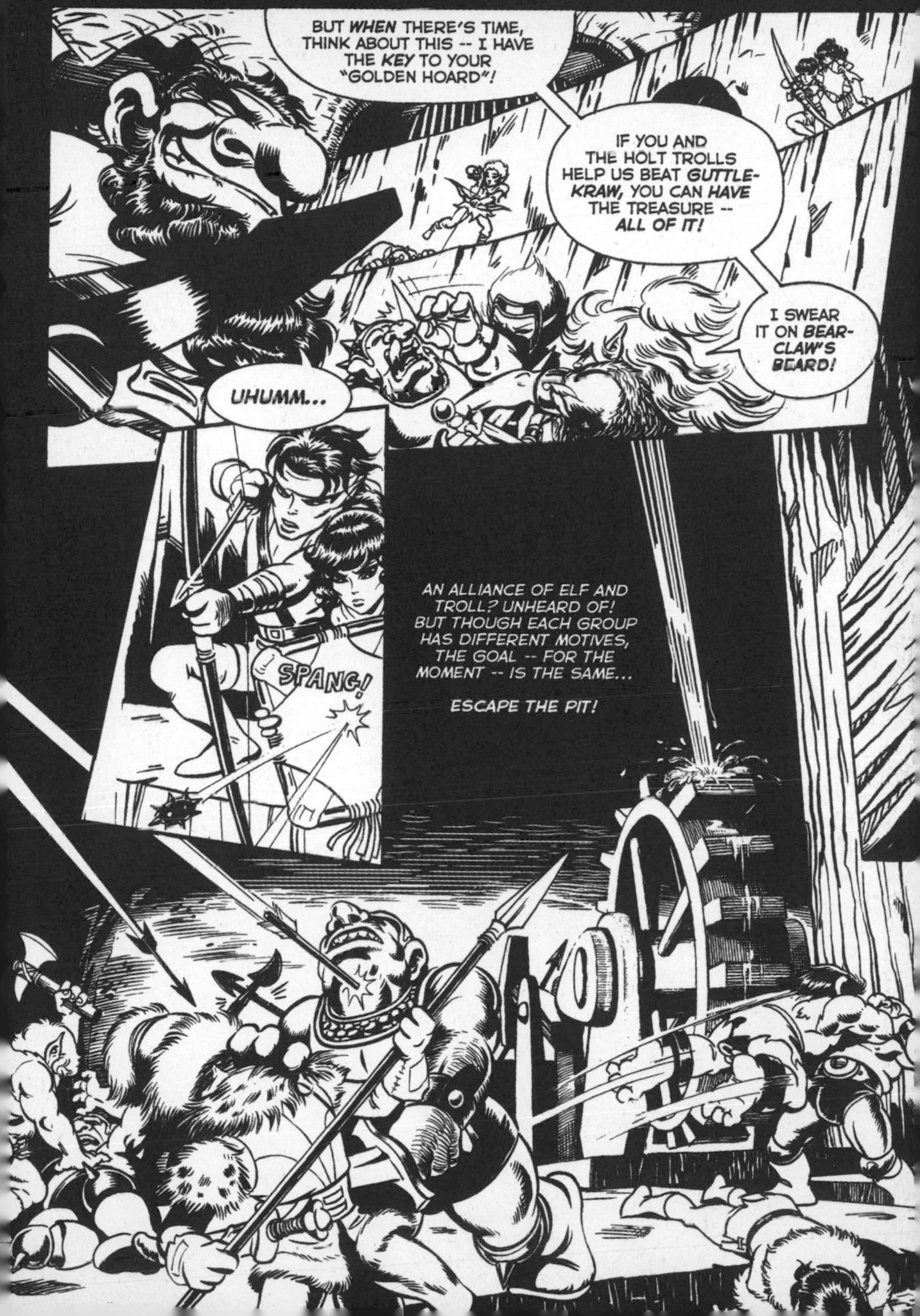
BUT WHEN THERE'S TIME, THINK ABOUT THIS -- I HAVE THE KEY TO YOUR "GOLDEN HOARD"!
IF YOU AND THE HOLT TROLLS HELP US BEAT GUTTLE-KRAW, YOU CAN HAVE THE TREASURE -- ALL OF IT!
I SWEAR IT ON BEAR-CLAW'S BEARD!
UHUMM...
SPANG!
AN ALLIANCE OF ELF AND TROLL? UNHEARD OF! BUT THOUGH EACH GROUP HAS DIFFERENT MOTIVES, THE GOAL -- FOR THE MOMENT -- IS THE SAME...
ESCAPE THE PIT!

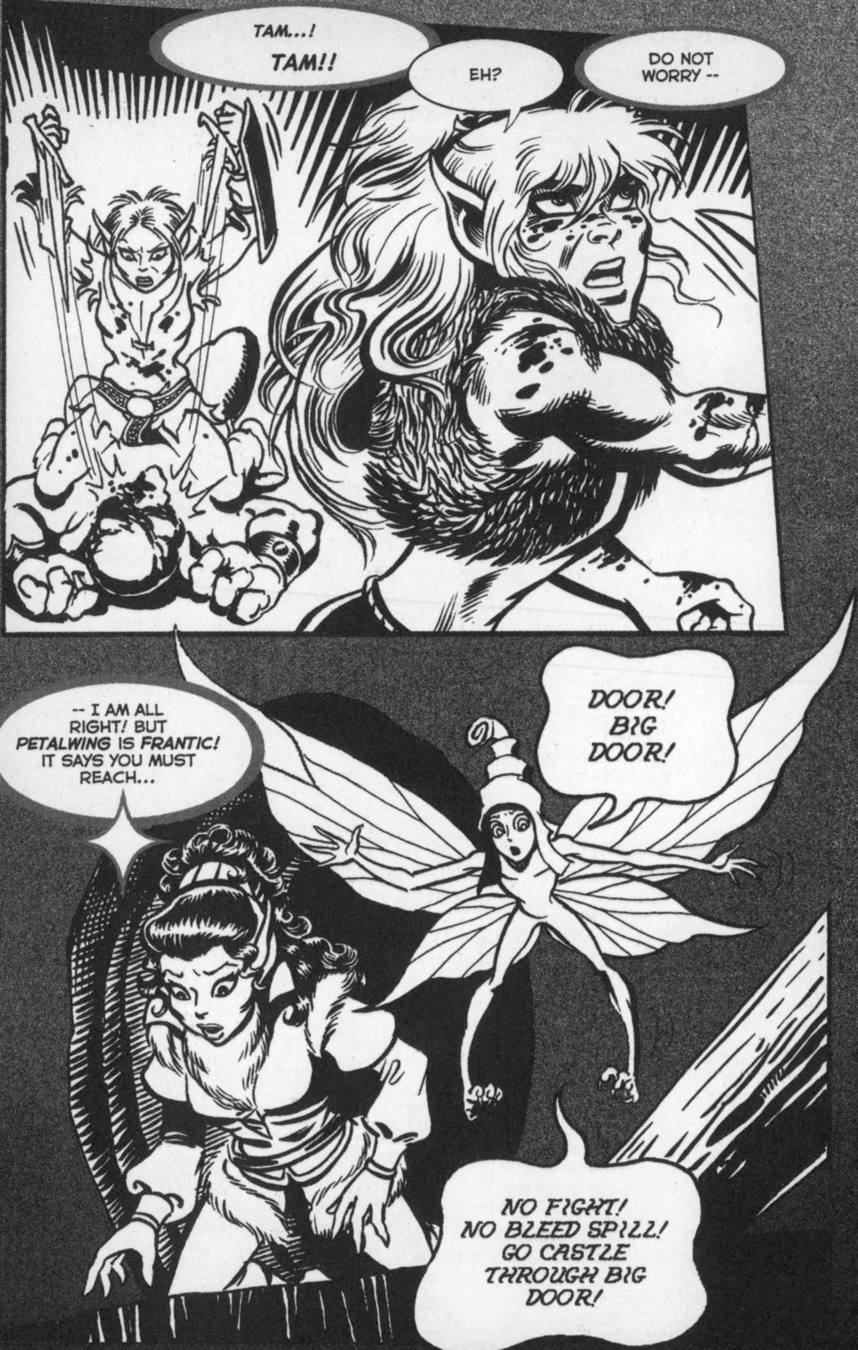
TAM...!
TAM!!
EH?
DO NOT WORRY --
-- I AM ALL RIGHT! BUT PETALWING IS FRANTIC! IT SAYS YOU MUST REACH...
DOOR! BIG DOOR!
NO FIGHT! NO BLEED SPILL! GO CASTLE THROUGH BIG DOOR!

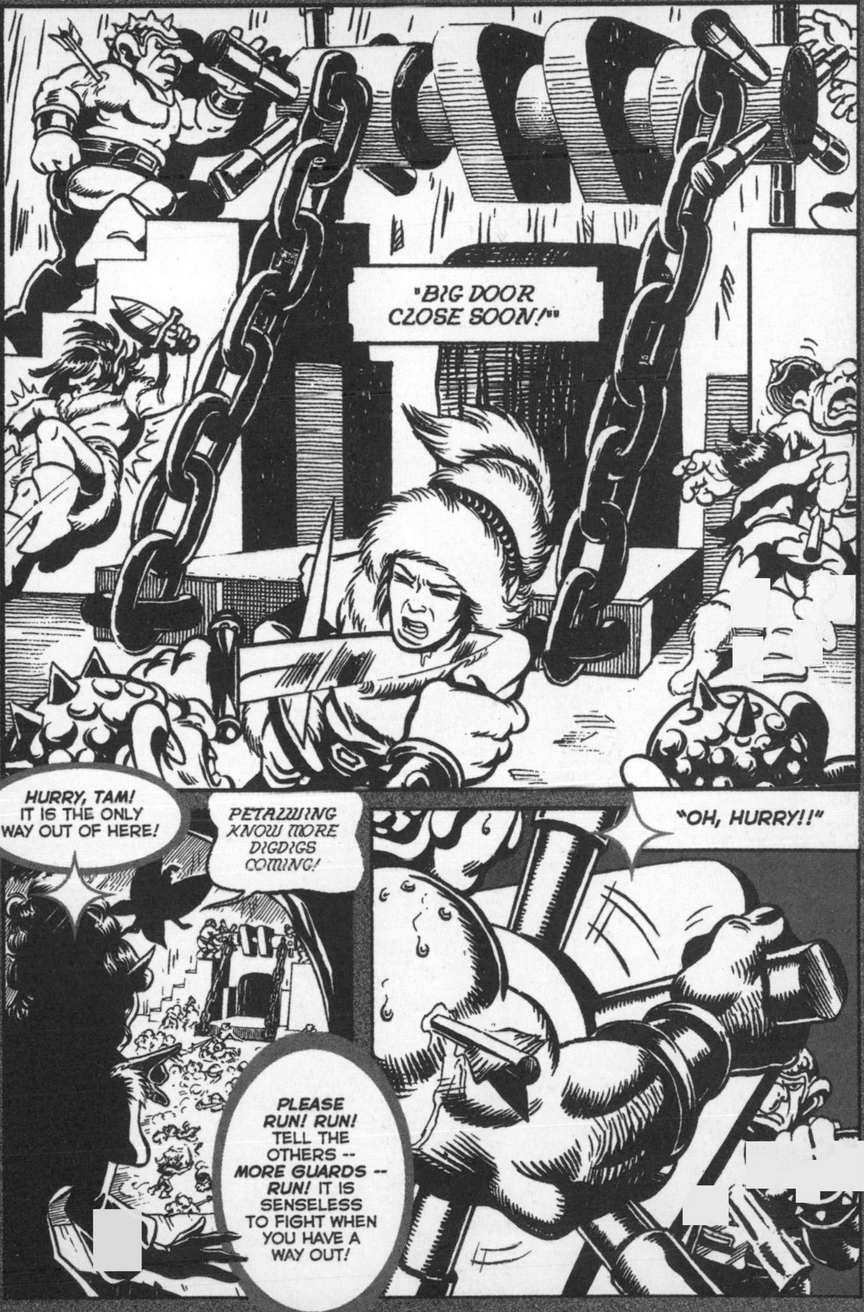
"BIG DOOR
CLOSE SOON!"
HURRY, TAM!
IT IS THE ONLY
WAY OUT OF HERE!
PETALWING
KNOW MORE
DIGDIGS
COMING!
"OH, HURRY!!"
PLEASE
RUN! RUN!
TELL THE
OTHERS --
MORE GUARDS --
RUN! IT IS
SENSELESS
TO FIGHT WHEN
YOU HAVE A
WAY OUT!

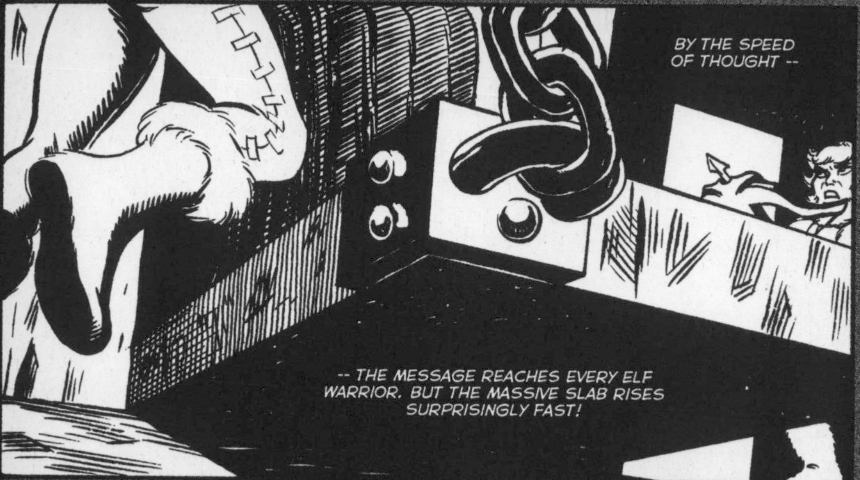

BY THE SPEED OF THOUGHT --
-- THE MESSAGE REACHES EVERY ELF WARRIOR. BUT THE MASSIVE SLAB RISES SURPRISINGLY FAST!

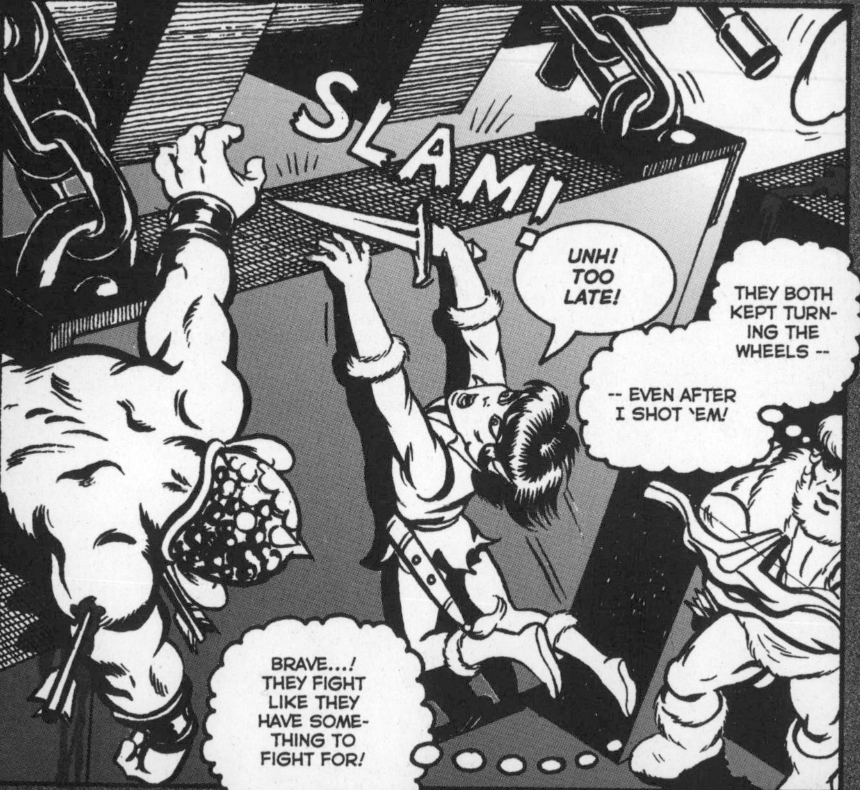

SLAM!
UNH! TOO LATE!
THEY BOTH KEPT TURNING THE WHEELS --
-- EVEN AFTER I SHOT 'EM!
BRAVE...! THEY FIGHT LIKE THEY HAVE SOMETHING TO FIGHT FOR!

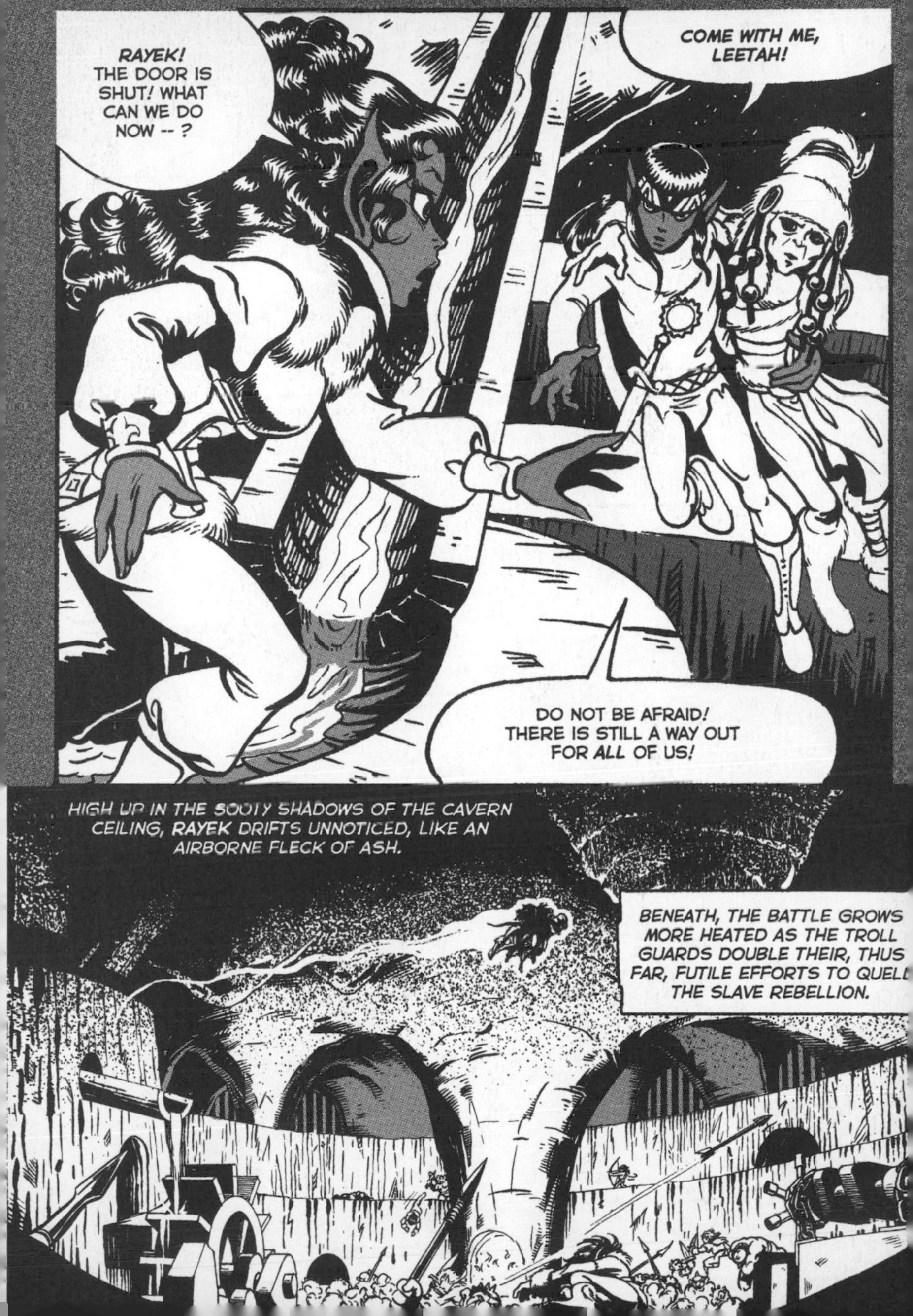
RAYEK! THE DOOR IS SHUT! WHAT CAN WE DO NOW -- ?
COME WITH ME, LEETAH!
DO NOT BE AFRAID! THERE IS STILL A WAY OUT FOR ALL OF US!
HIGH UP IN THE SOOTY SHADOWS OF THE CAVERN CEILING, RAYEK DRIFTS UNNOTICED, LIKE AN AIRBORNE FLECK OF ASH.
BENEATH, THE BATTLE GROWS MORE HEATED AS THE TROLL GUARDS DOUBLE THEIR, THUS FAR, FUTILE EFFORTS TO QUELL THE SLAVE REBELLION.

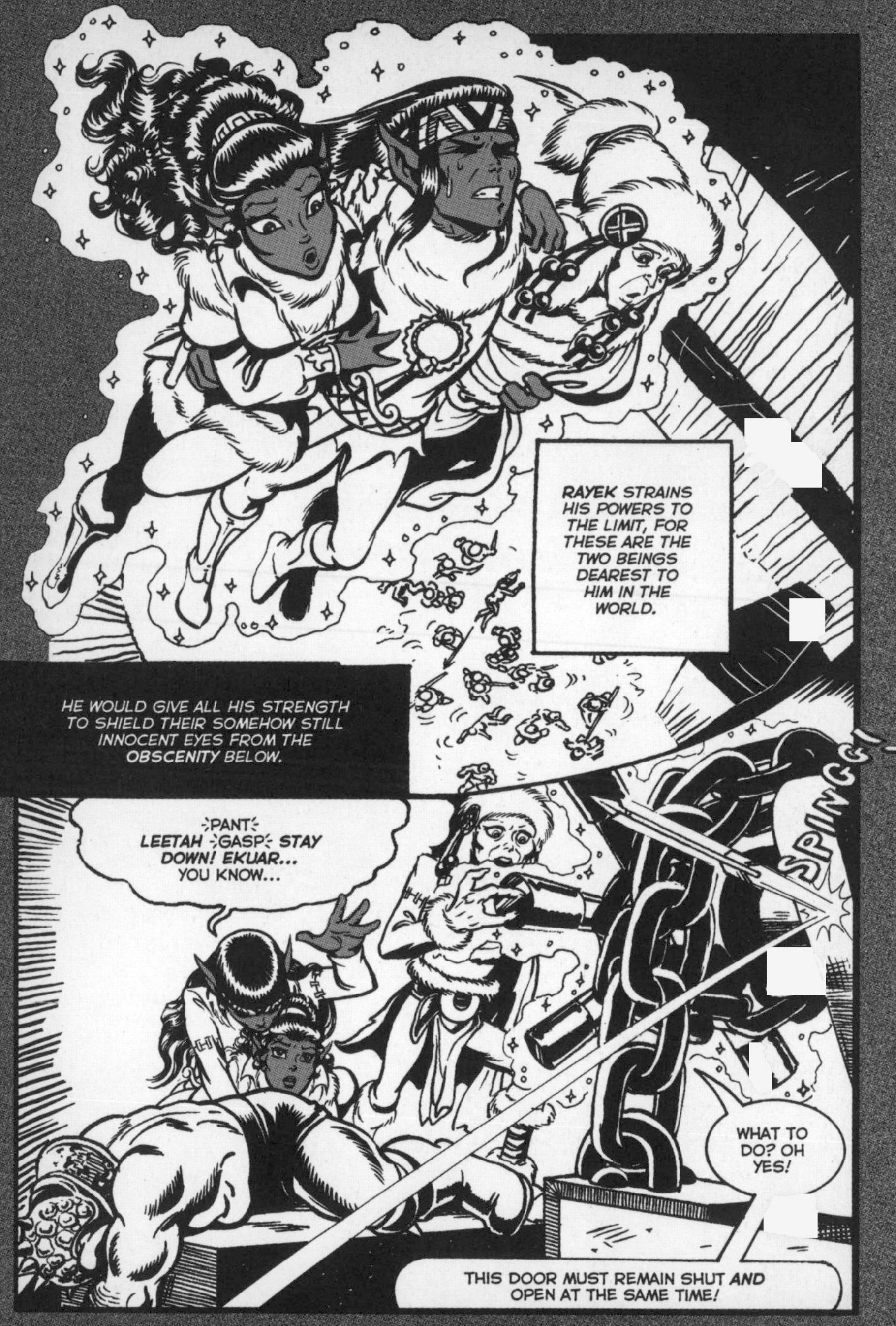
RAYEK STRAINS HIS POWERS TO THE LIMIT, FOR THESE ARE THE TWO BEINGS DEAREST TO HIM IN THE WORLD.
HE WOULD GIVE ALL HIS STRENGTH TO SHIELD THEIR SOMEHOW STILL INNOCENT EYES FROM THE OBSCENITY BELOW.
-PANT- LEETAH -GASP- STAY DOWN! EKUAR... YOU KNOW...
SPINGG!
WHAT TO DO? OH YES!
THIS DOOR MUST REMAIN SHUT AND OPEN AT THE SAME TIME!

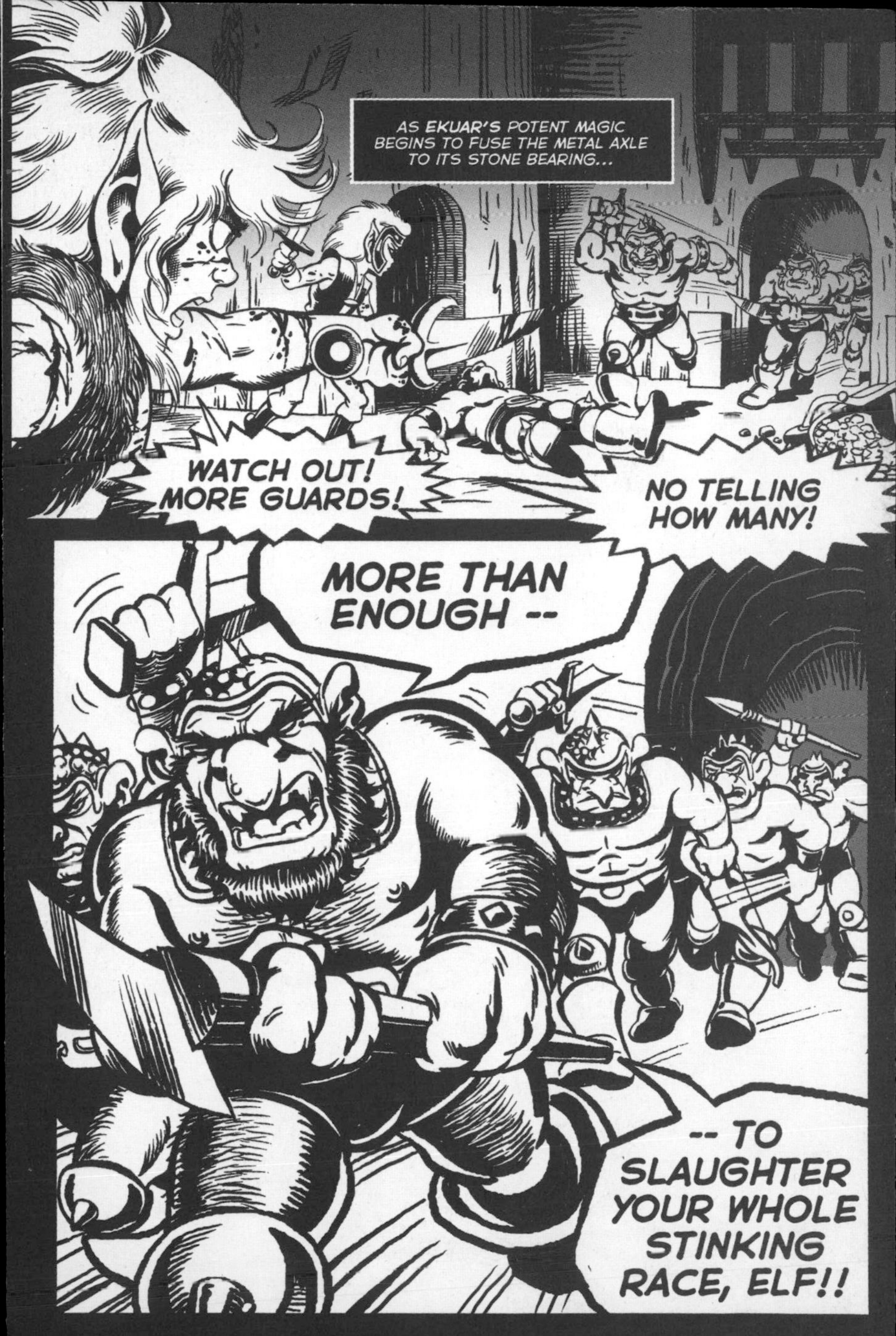
AS EKUAR'S POTENT MAGIC BEGINS TO FUSE THE METAL AXLE TO ITS STONE BEARING...
WATCH OUT! MORE GUARDS!
NO TELLING HOW MANY!
MORE THAN ENOUGH --
-- TO SLAUGHTER YOUR WHOLE STINKING RACE, ELF!!

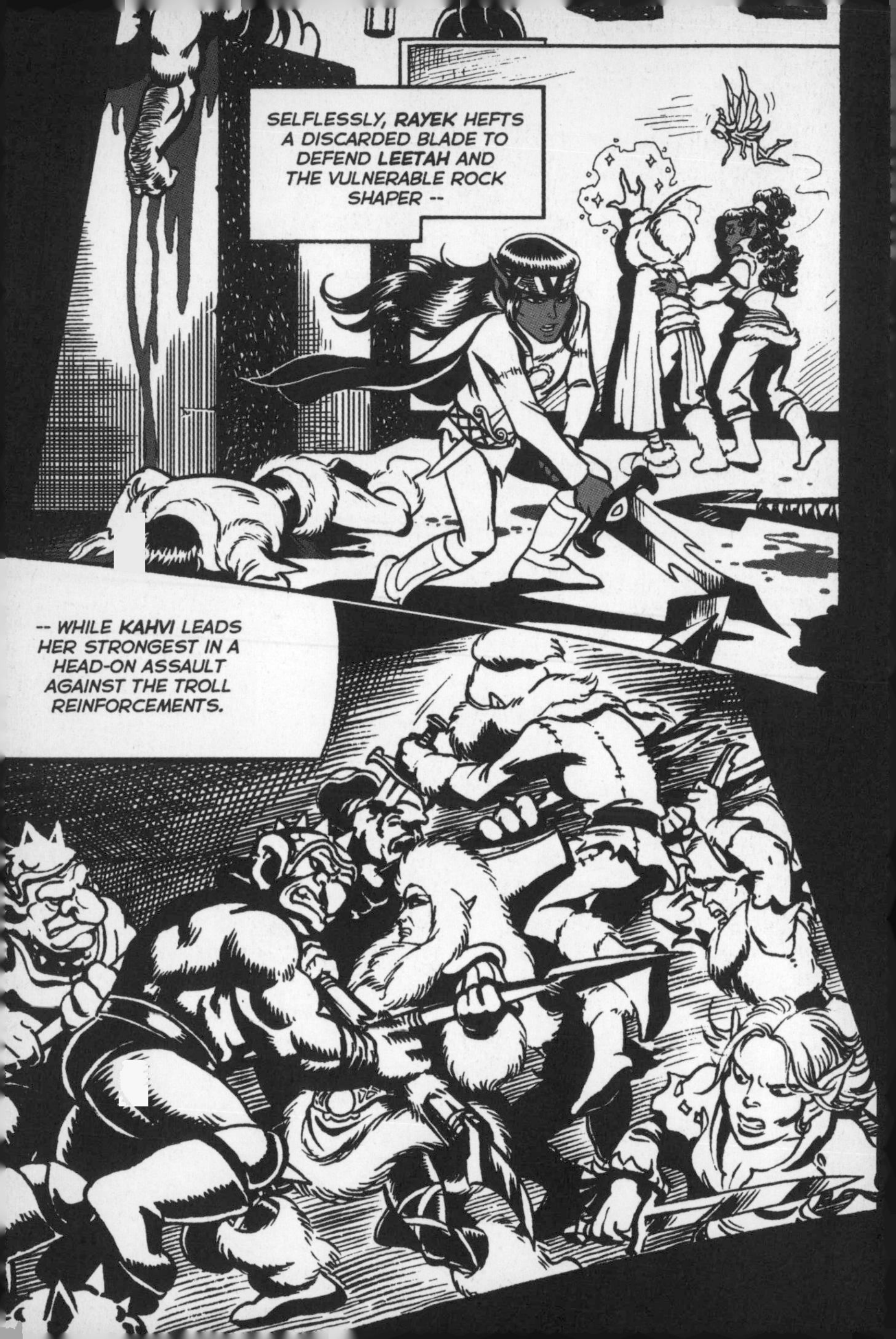
SELFLESSLY, RAYEK HEFTS A DISCARDED BLADE TO DEFEND LEETAH AND THE VULNERABLE ROCK SHAPER --
-- WHILE KAHVI LEADS HER STRONGEST IN A HEAD-ON ASSAULT AGAINST THE TROLL REINFORCEMENTS.

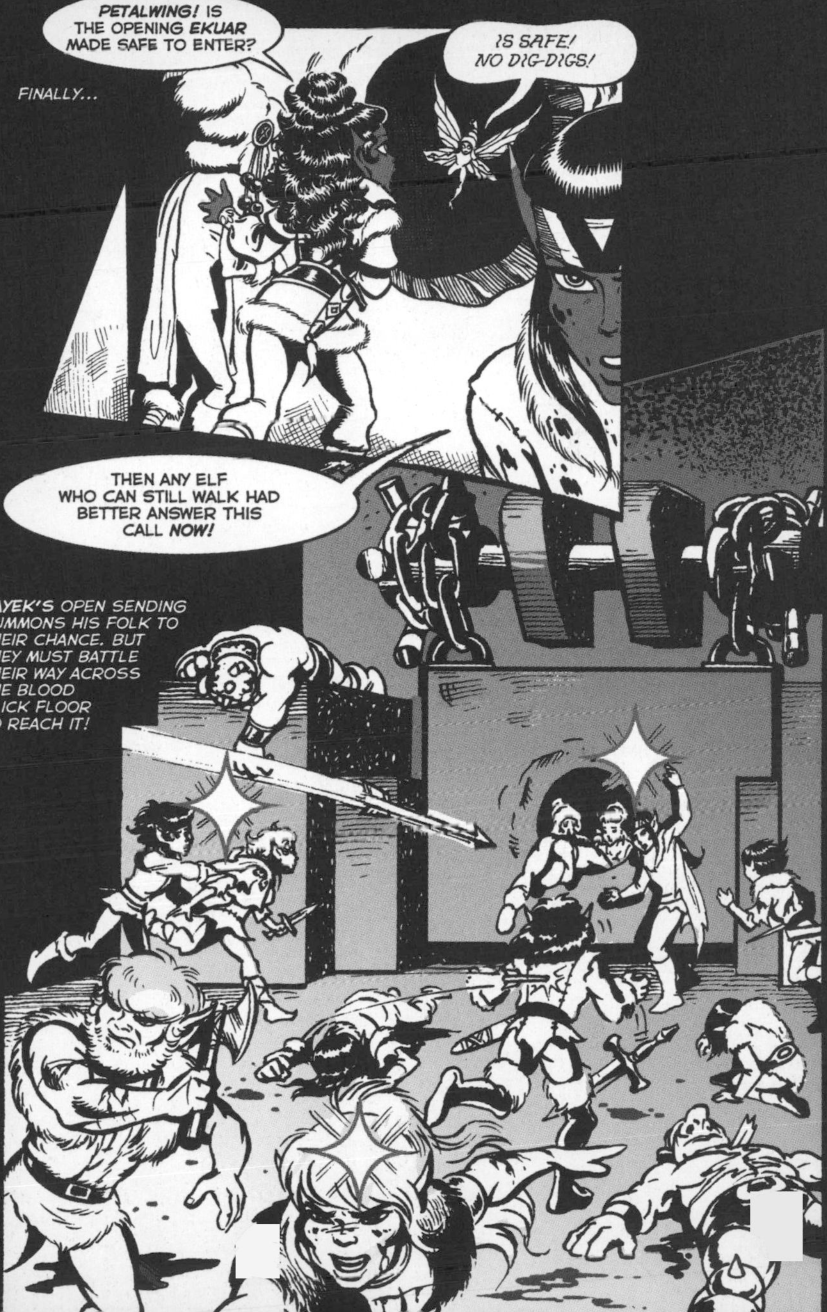
FINALLY...
PETALWING! IS THE OPENING EKUAR MADE SAFE TO ENTER?
IS SAFE! NO DIG-DIGS!
THEN ANY ELF WHO CAN STILL WALK HAD BETTER ANSWER THIS CALL NOW!
RAYEK'S OPEN SENDING SUMMONS HIS FOLK TO THEIR CHANCE. BUT THEY MUST BATTLE THEIR WAY ACROSS THE BLOOD SLICK FLOOR TO REACH IT!

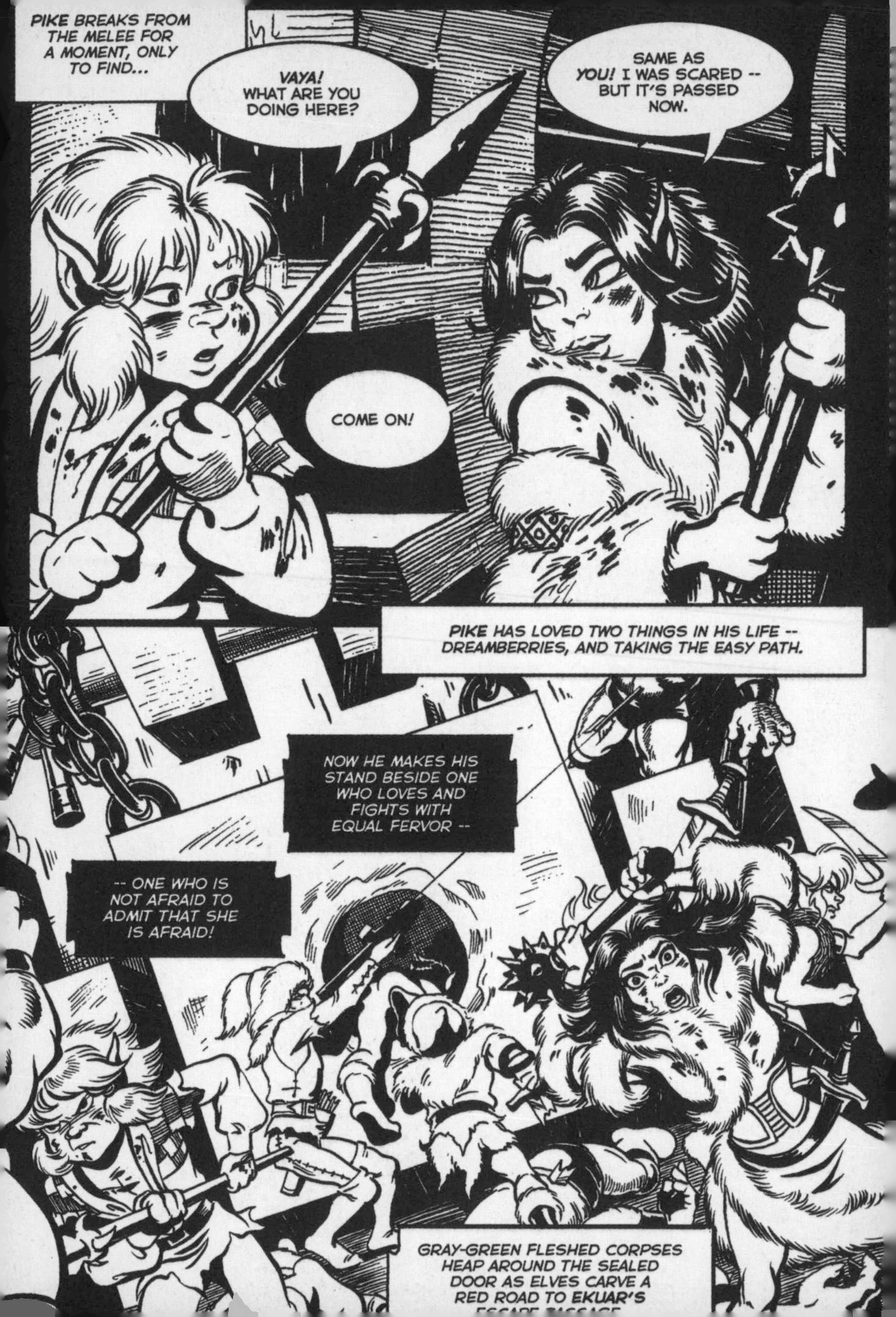
PIKE BREAKS FROM THE MELEE FOR A MOMENT, ONLY TO FIND...
VAYA! WHAT ARE YOU DOING HERE?
SAME AS YOU! I WAS SCARED -- BUT IT'S PASSED NOW.
COME ON!
PIKE HAS LOVED TWO THINGS IN HIS LIFE -- DREAMBERRIES, AND TAKING THE EASY PATH.
NOW HE MAKES HIS STAND BESIDE ONE WHO LOVES AND FIGHTS WITH EQUAL FERVOR --
-- ONE WHO IS NOT AFRAID TO ADMIT THAT SHE IS AFRAID!
GRAY-GREEN FLESHED CORPSES HEAP AROUND THE SEALED DOOR AS ELVES CARVE A RED ROAD TO EKUAR'S

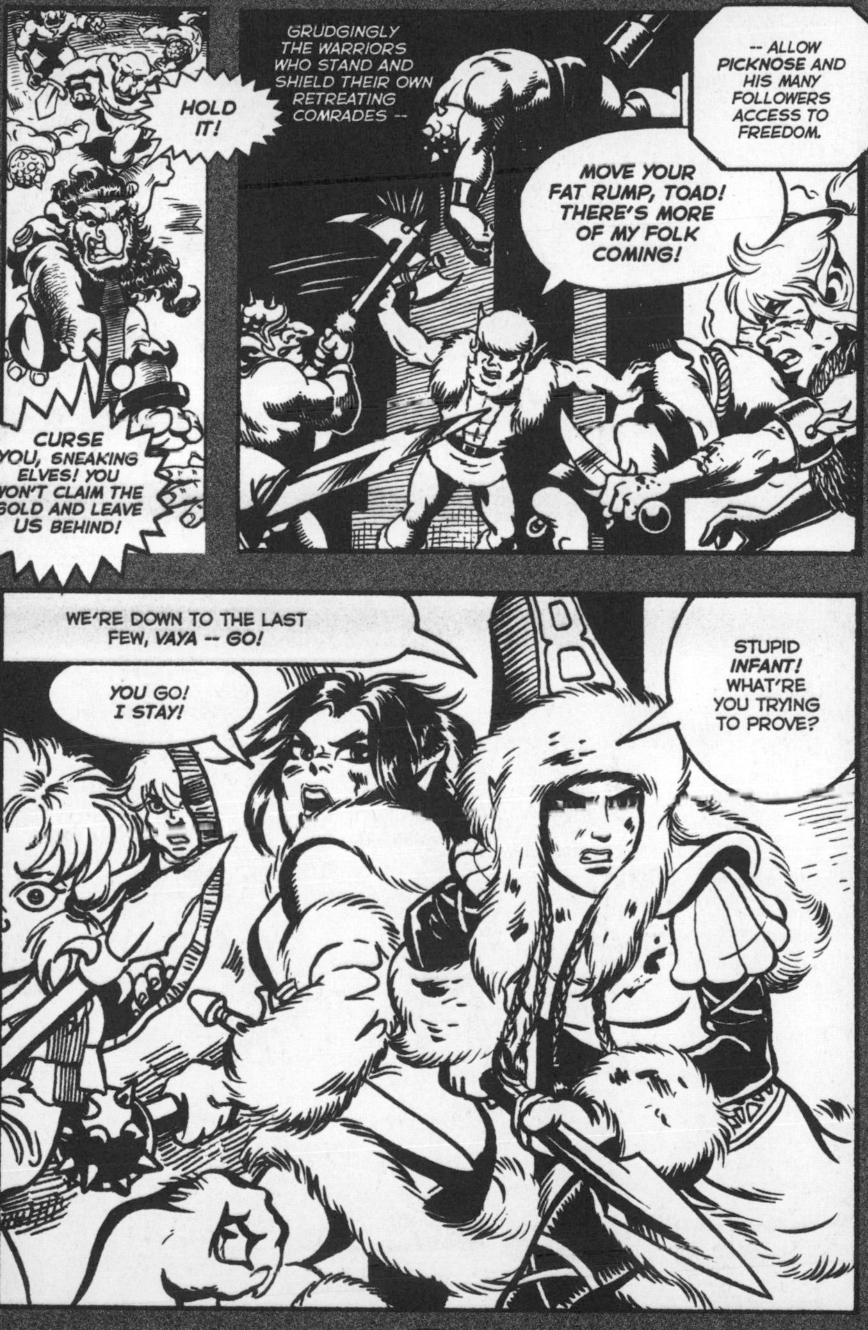
HOLD IT!
CURSE YOU, SNEAKING ELVES! YOU WON'T CLAIM THE GOLD AND LEAVE US BEHIND!
GRUDGINGLY THE WARRIORS WHO STAND AND SHIELD THEIR OWN RETREATING COMRADES --
-- ALLOW PICKNOSE AND HIS MANY FOLLOWERS ACCESS TO FREEDOM.
MOVE YOUR FAT RUMP, TOAD! THERE'S MORE OF MY FOLK COMING!
WE'RE DOWN TO THE LAST FEW, VAYA -- GO!
YOU GO! I STAY!
STUPID INFANT! WHAT'RE YOU TRYING TO PROVE?

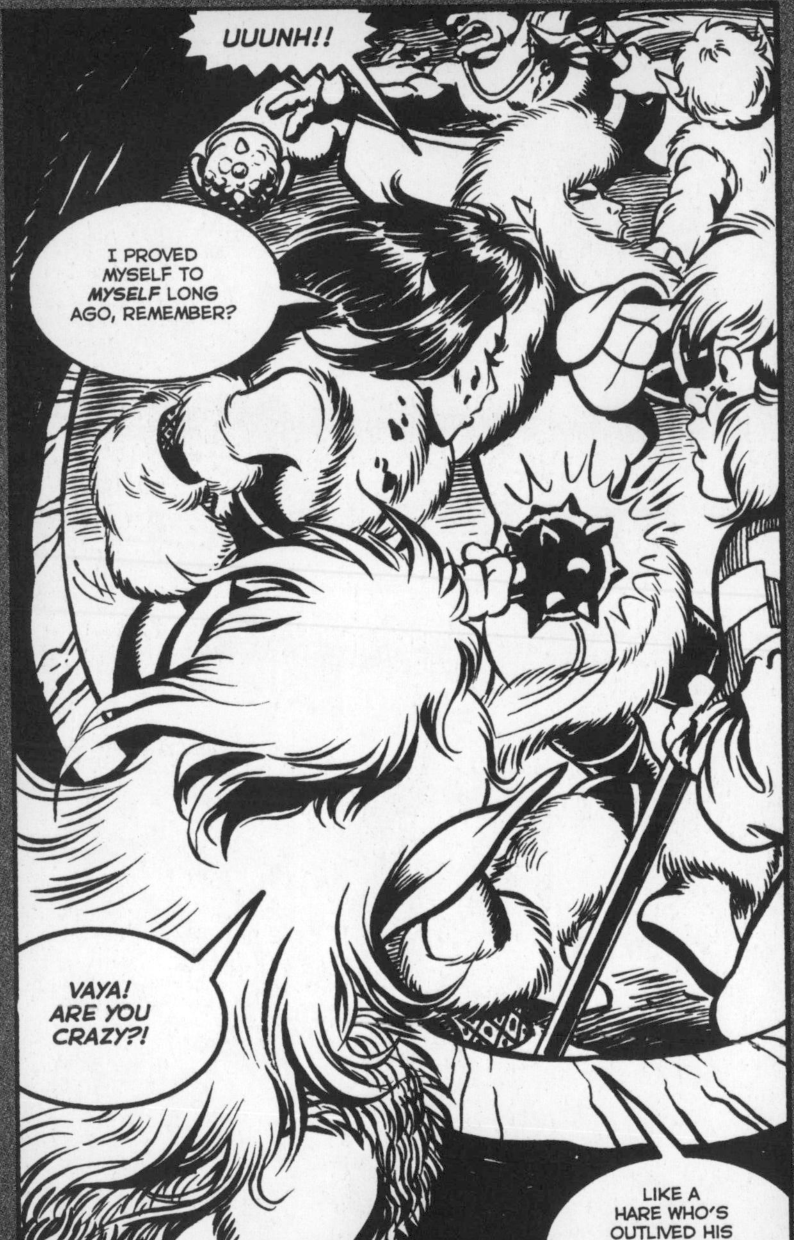
UUUNH!!
I PROVED MYSELF TO *MYSELF* LONG AGO, REMEMBER?
VAYA! ARE YOU CRAZY?!
LIKE A HARE WHO'S OUTLIVED HIS HUNTERS, WOLF CHIEF!

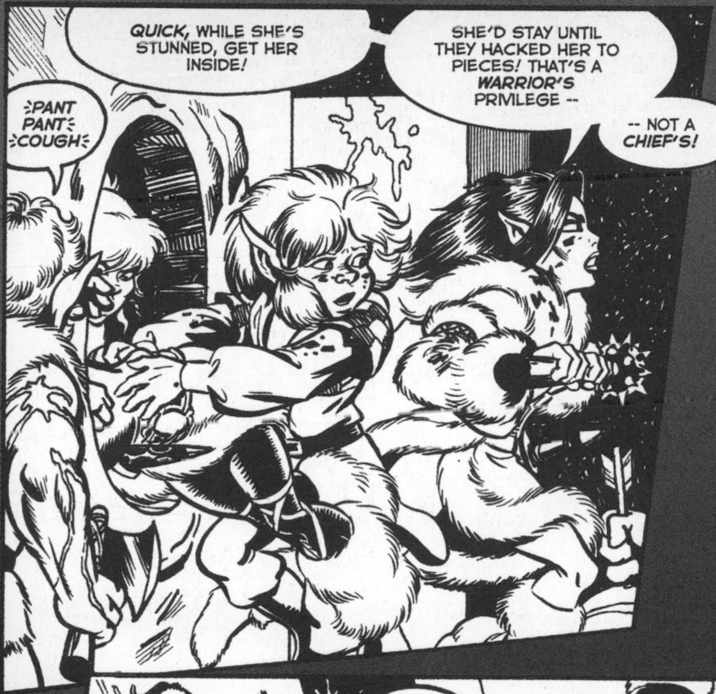
QUICK, WHILE SHE'S STUNNED, GET HER INSIDE!
PANT PANT COUGH
SHE'D STAY UNTIL THEY HACKED HER TO PIECES! THAT'S A WARRIOR'S PRIVILEGE --
-- NOT A CHIEF'S!
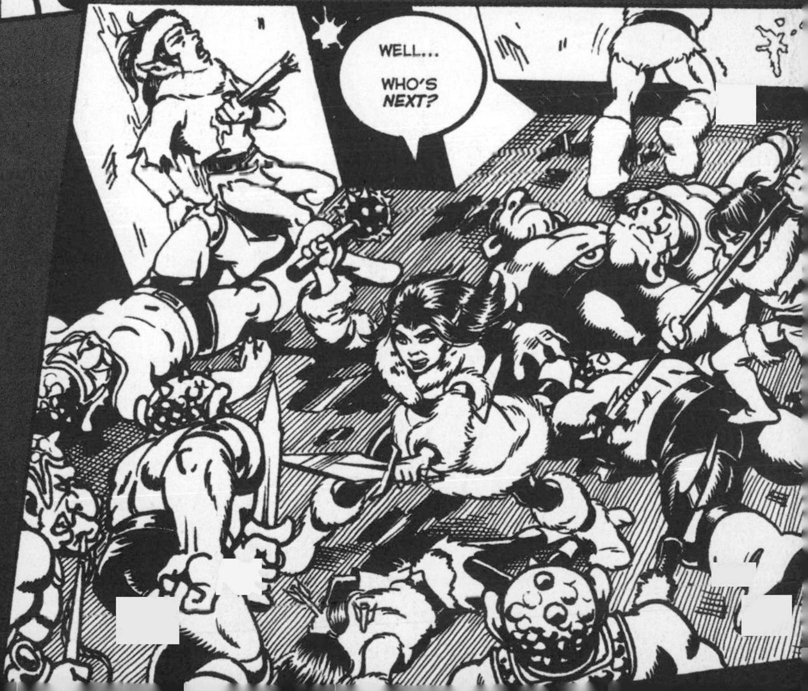
WELL...
WHO'S NEXT?

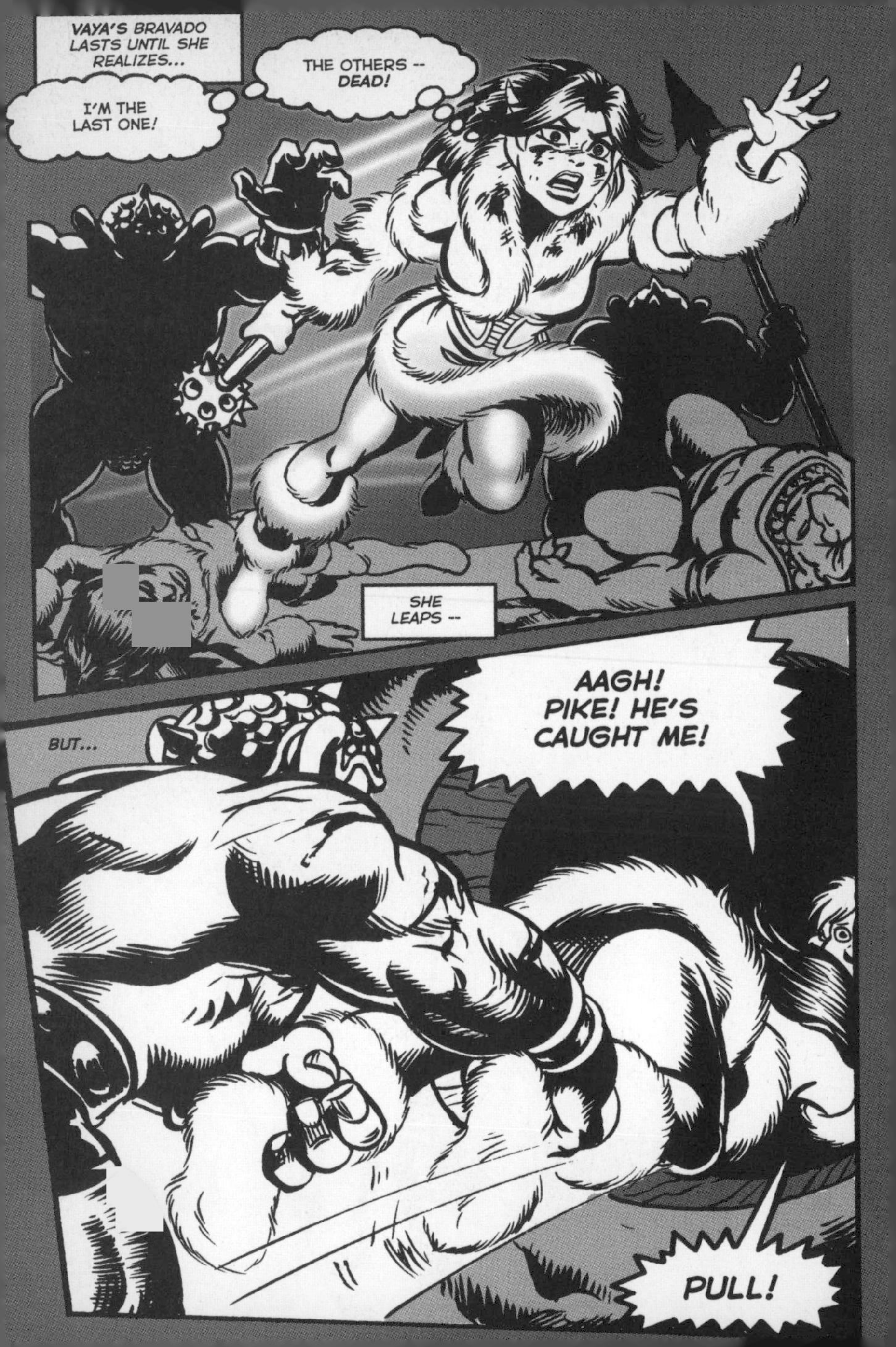
VAYA'S BRAVADO LASTS UNTIL SHE REALIZES...
THE OTHERS -- DEAD!
I'M THE LAST ONE!
SHE LEAPS --
BUT...
AAGH! PIKE! HE'S CAUGHT ME!
PULL!

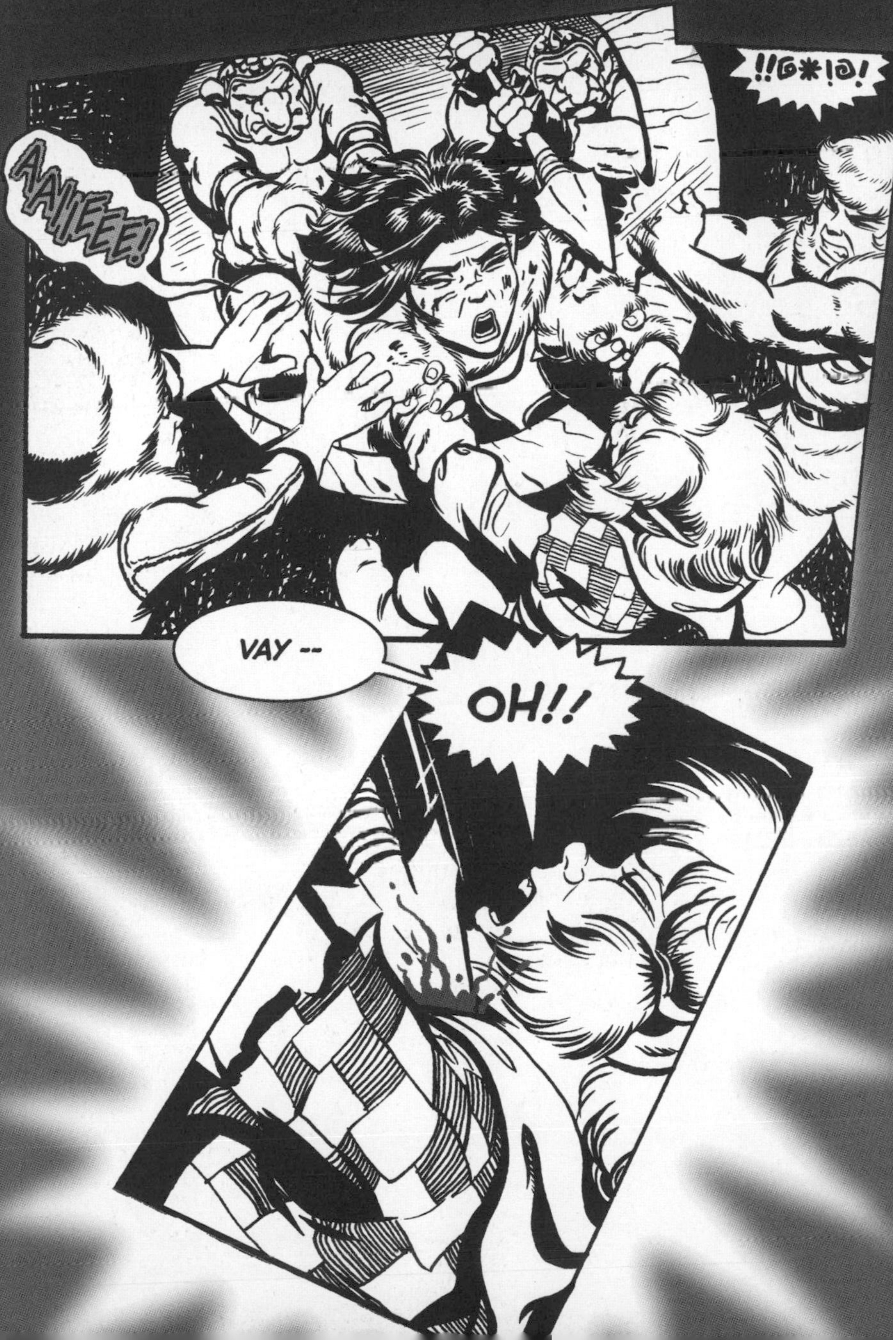

AAIIEEEE!
!@!*@!!
VAY --
OH!!

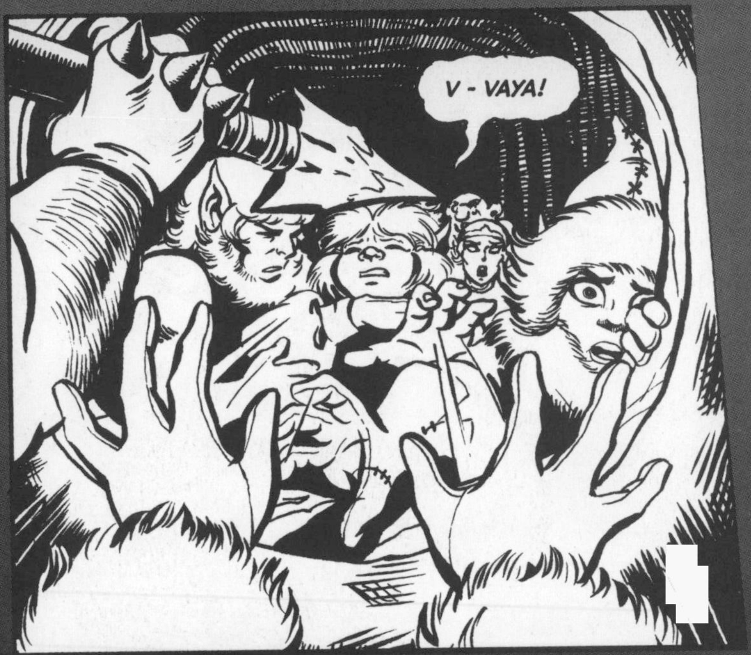
V - VAYA!

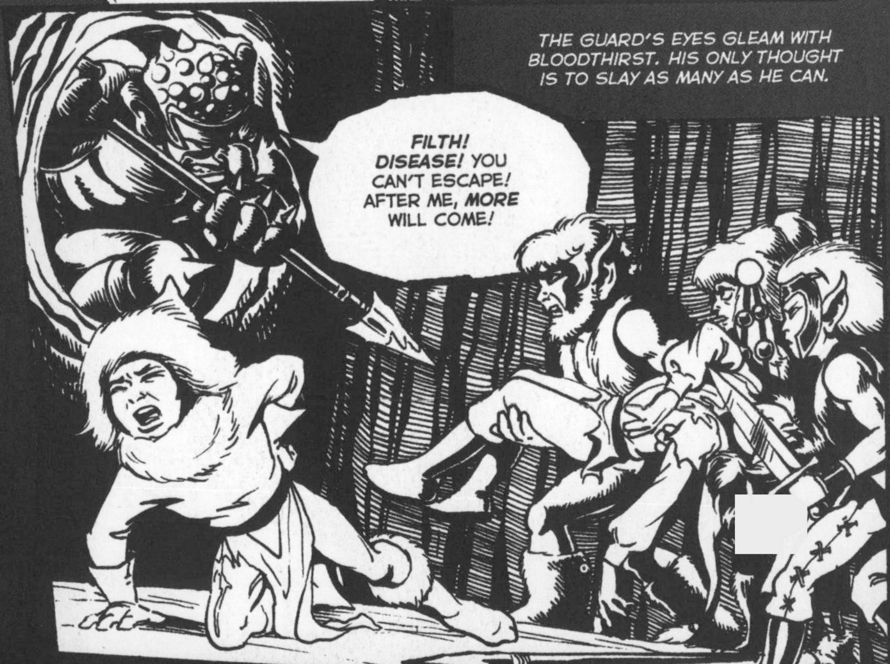
THE GUARD'S EYES GLEAM WITH BLOODTHIRST. HIS ONLY THOUGHT IS TO SLAY AS MANY AS HE CAN.
FILTH! DISEASE! YOU CAN'T ESCAPE! AFTER ME, MORE WILL COME!

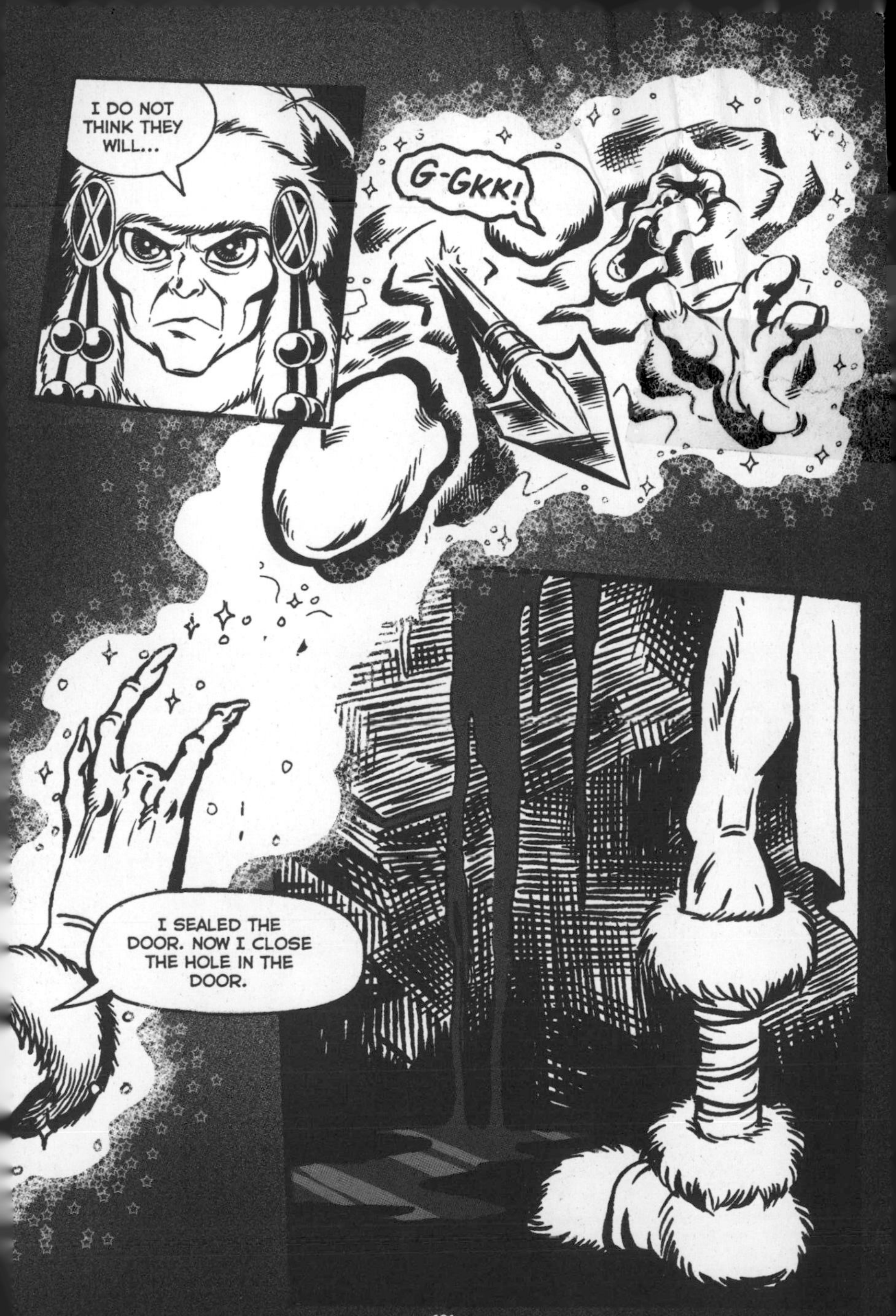
I DO NOT THINK THEY WILL...
G-GKK!
I SEALED THE DOOR. NOW I CLOSE THE HOLE IN THE DOOR.

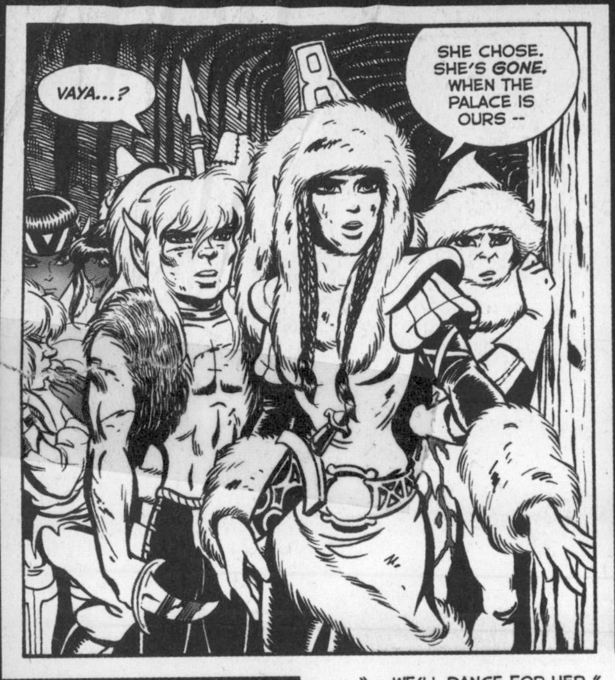
VAYA...?
SHE CHOSE. SHE'S GONE. WHEN THE PALACE IS OURS --

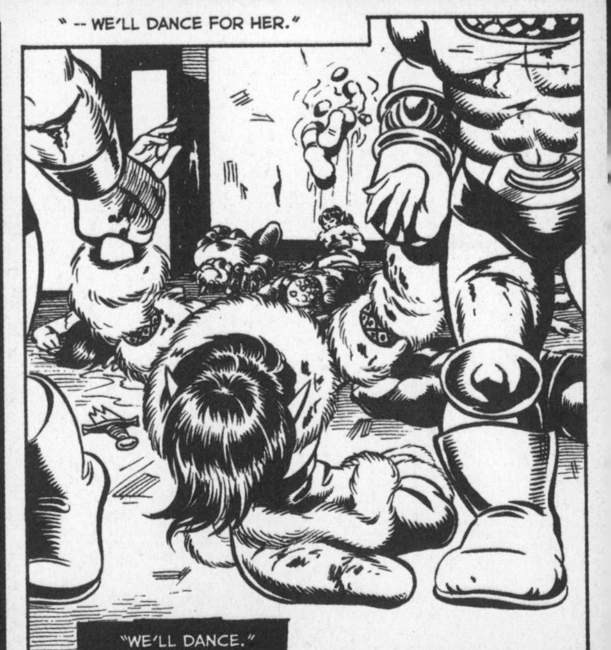
" -- WE'LL DANCE FOR HER."
"WE'LL DANCE."

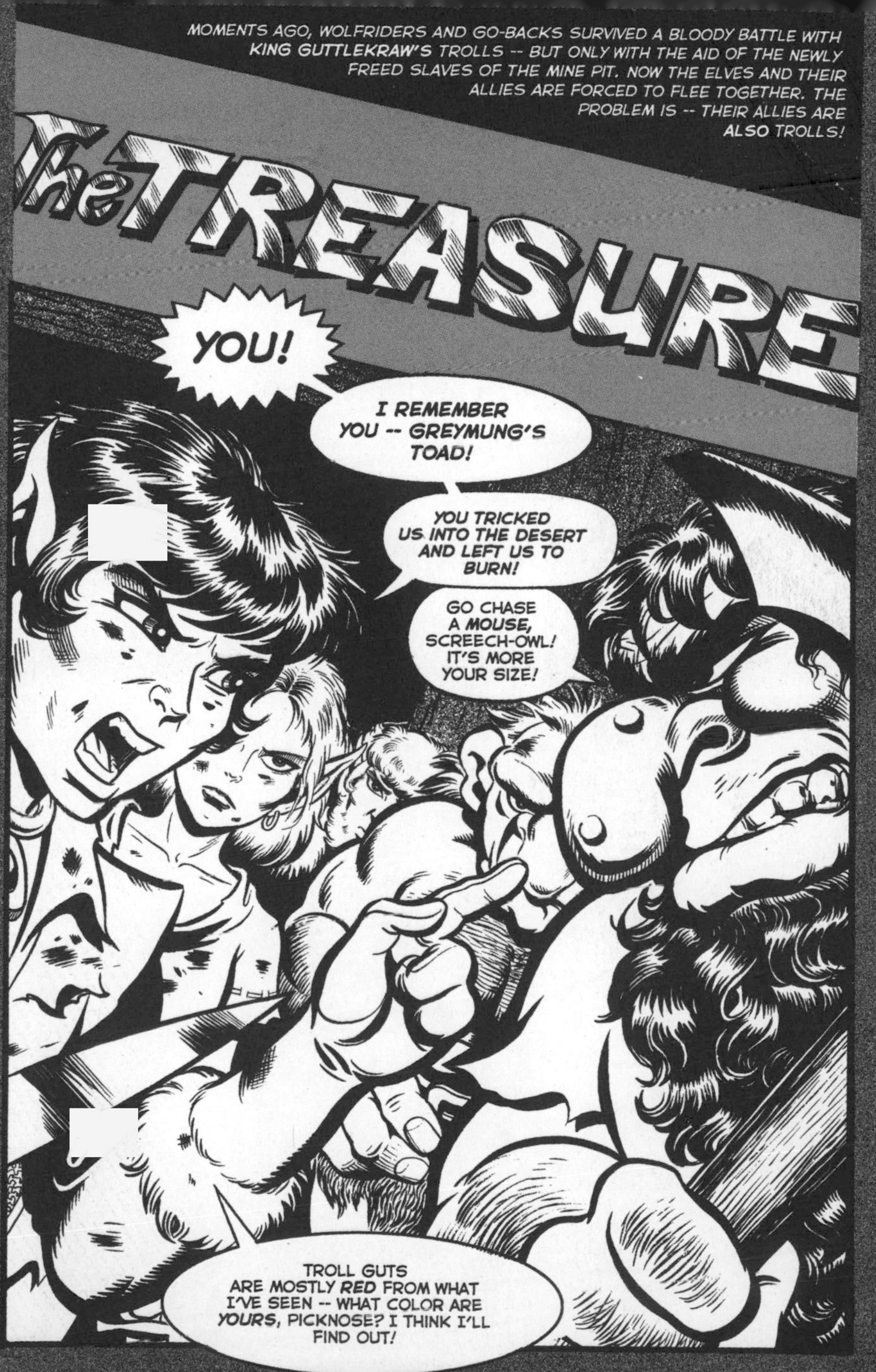
MOMENTS AGO, WOLFRIDERS AND GO-BACKS SURVIVED A BLOODY BATTLE WITH KING GUTTLEKRAW'S TROLLS -- BUT ONLY WITH THE AID OF THE NEWLY FREED SLAVES OF THE MINE PIT. NOW THE ELVES AND THEIR ALLIES ARE FORCED TO FLEE TOGETHER. THE PROBLEM IS -- THEIR ALLIES ARE ALSO TROLLS!
The TREASURE
YOU!
I REMEMBER YOU -- GREYMUNG'S TOAD!
YOU TRICKED US INTO THE DESERT AND LEFT US TO BURN!
GO CHASE A MOUSE, SCREECH-OWL! IT'S MORE YOUR SIZE!
TROLL GUTS ARE MOSTLY RED FROM WHAT I'VE SEEN -- WHAT COLOR ARE YOURS, PICKNOSE? I THINK I'LL FIND OUT!

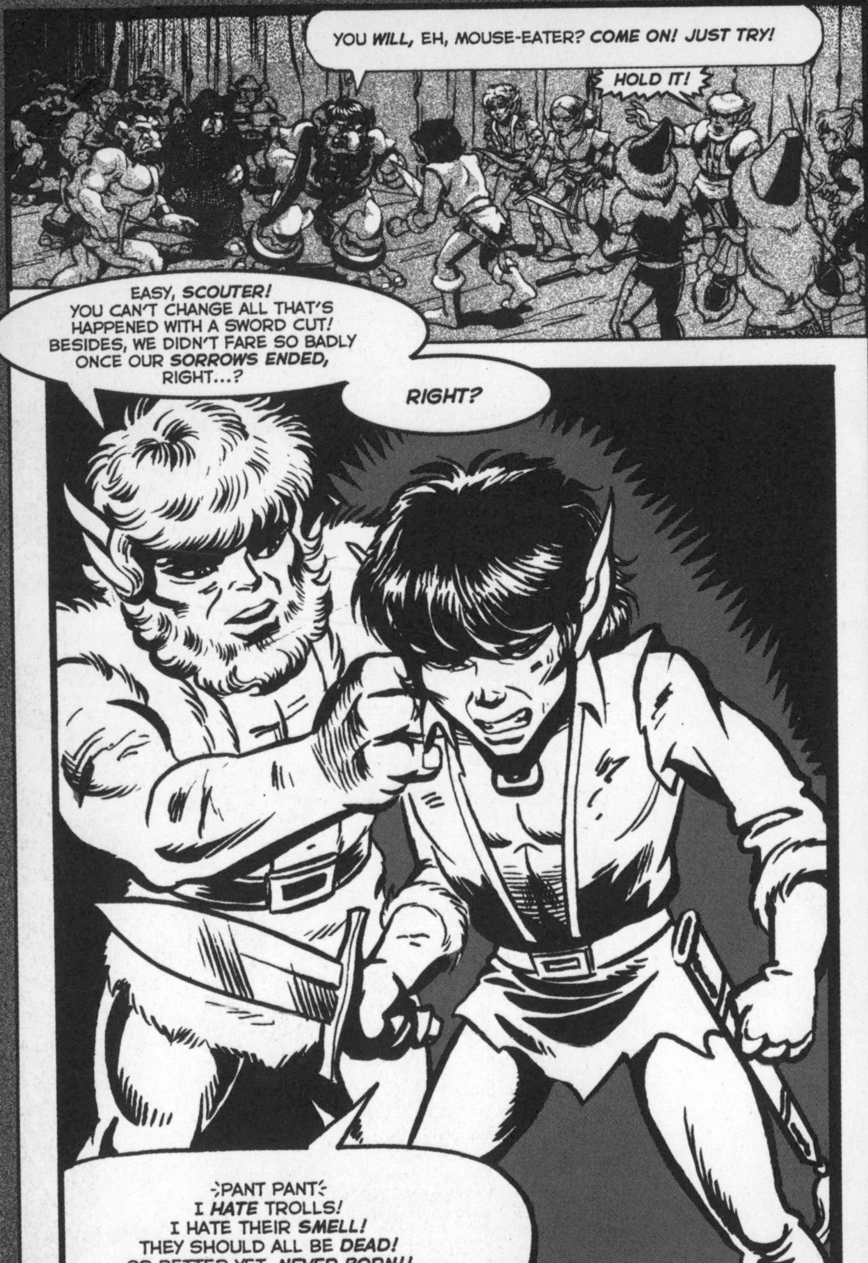

YOU WILL, EH, MOUSE-EATER? COME ON! JUST TRY!
HOLD IT!
EASY, SCOUTER! YOU CAN'T CHANGE ALL THAT'S HAPPENED WITH A SWORD CUT! BESIDES, WE DIDN'T FARE SO BADLY ONCE OUR SORROWS ENDED, RIGHT...?
RIGHT?
PANT PANT
I HATE TROLLS! I HATE THEIR SMELL! THEY SHOULD ALL BE DEAD! OR BETTER YET, NEVER BORN!!

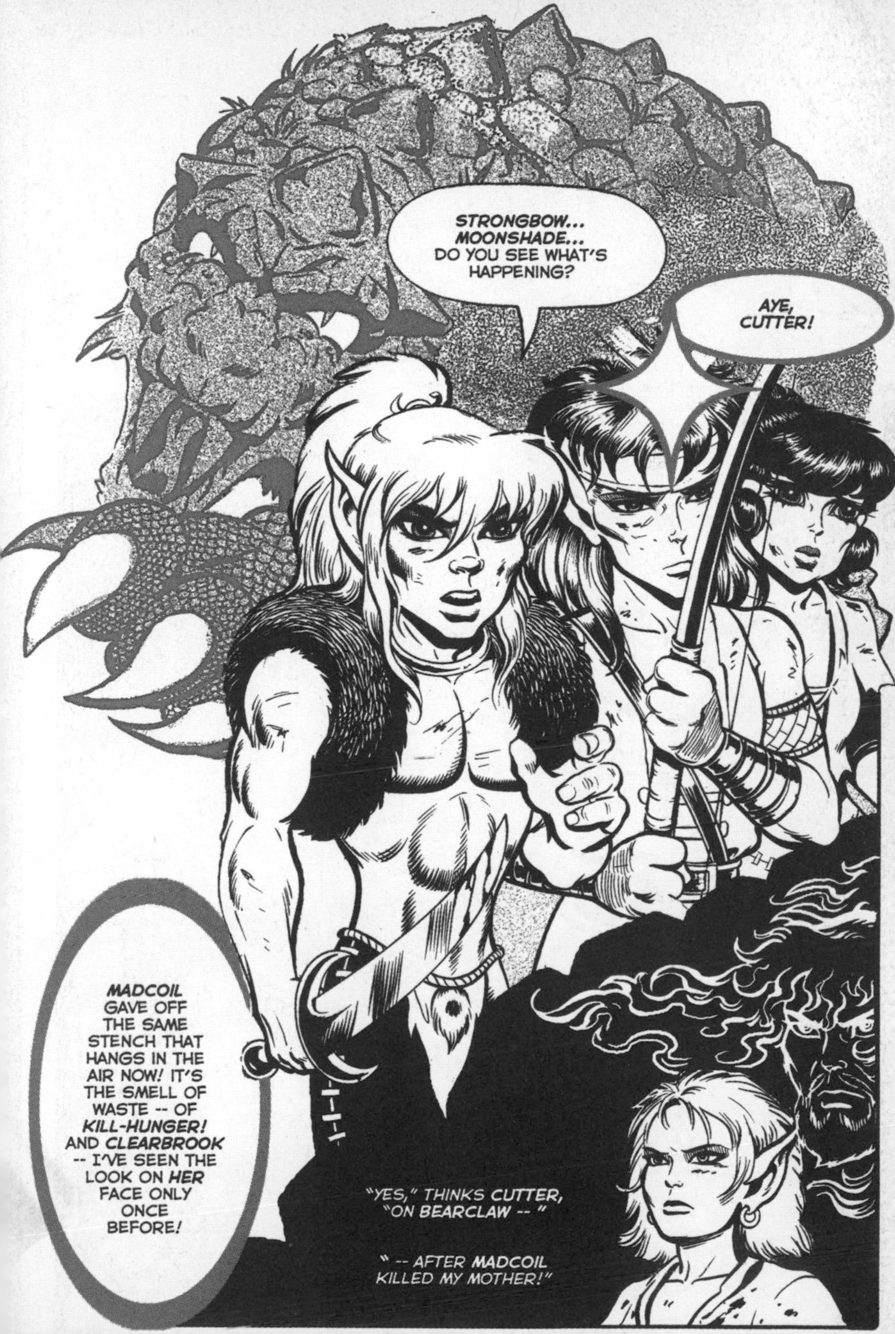
STRONGBOW... MOONSHADE... DO YOU SEE WHAT'S HAPPENING?
AYE, CUTTER!
MADCOIL GAVE OFF THE SAME STENCH THAT HANGS IN THE AIR NOW! IT'S THE SMELL OF WASTE -- OF KILL-HUNGER! AND CLEARBROOK -- I'VE SEEN THE LOOK ON HER FACE ONLY ONCE BEFORE!
"YES," THINKS CUTTER, "ON BEARCLAW -- "
" -- AFTER MADCOIL KILLED MY MOTHER!"

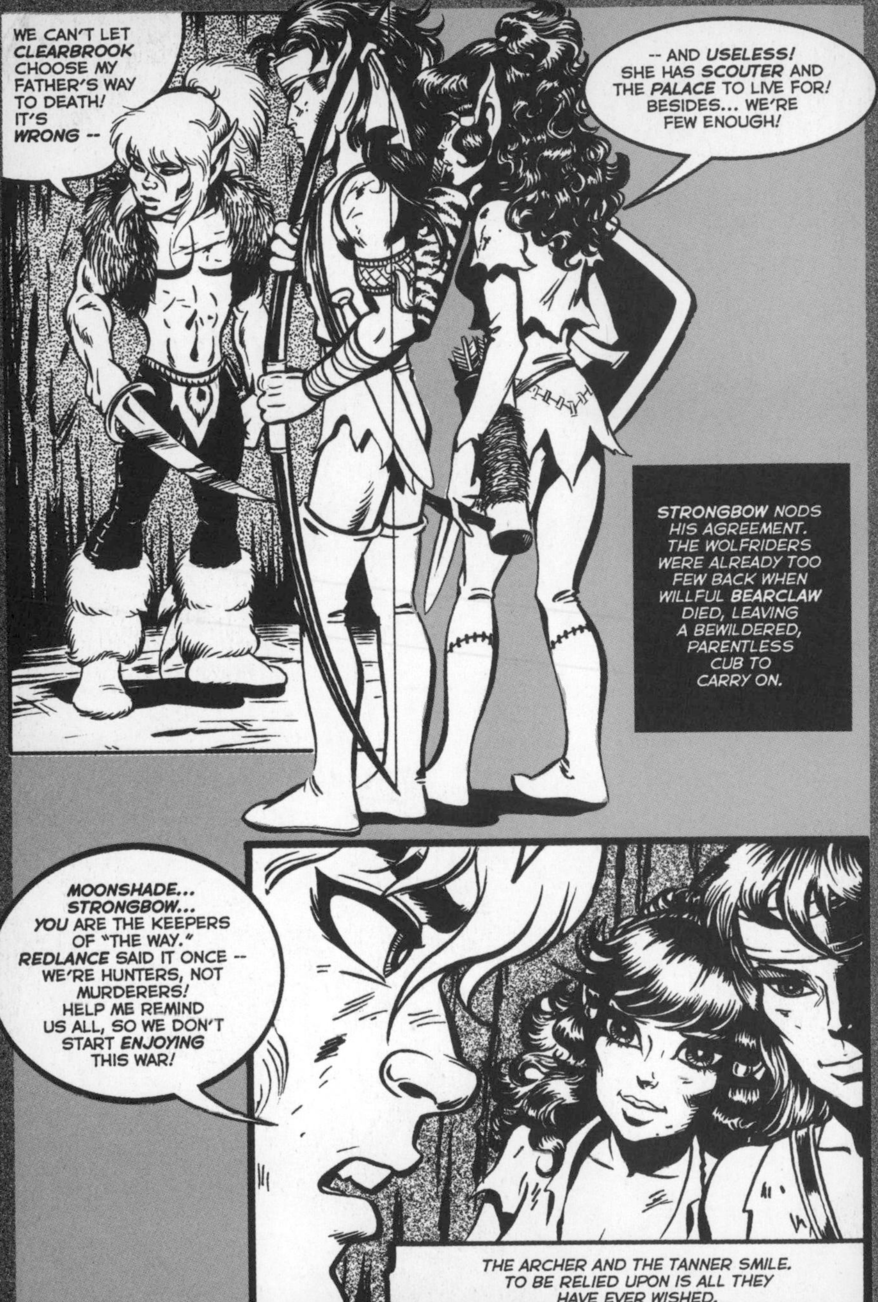

WE CAN'T LET CLEARBROOK CHOOSE MY FATHER'S WAY TO DEATH! IT'S WRONG --
-- AND USELESS! SHE HAS SCOUTER AND THE PALACE TO LIVE FOR! BESIDES... WE'RE FEW ENOUGH!
STRONGBOW NODS HIS AGREEMENT. THE WOLFRIDERS WERE ALREADY TOO FEW BACK WHEN WILLFUL BEARCLAW DIED, LEAVING A BEWILDERED, PARENTLESS CUB TO CARRY ON.
MOONSHADE... STRONGBOW... YOU ARE THE KEEPERS OF "THE WAY." REDLANCE SAID IT ONCE -- WE'RE HUNTERS, NOT MURDERERS! HELP ME REMIND US ALL, SO WE DON'T START ENJOYING THIS WAR!
THE ARCHER AND THE TANNER SMILE. TO BE RELIED UPON IS ALL THEY HAVE EVER WISHED.

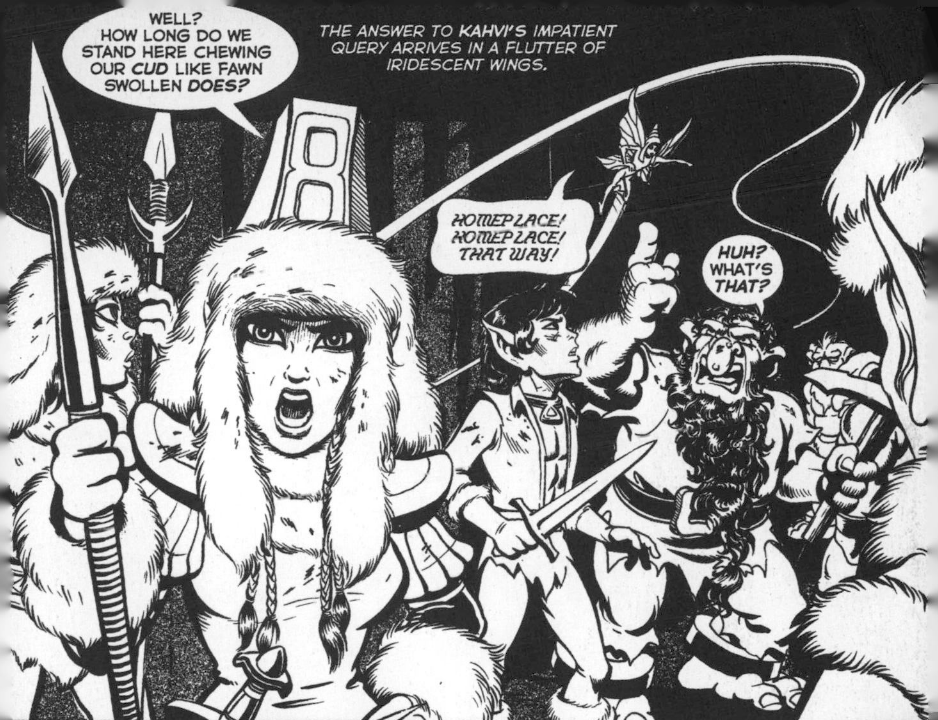

WELL? HOW LONG DO WE STAND HERE CHEWING OUR CUD LIKE FAWN SWOLLEN DOES?
THE ANSWER TO KAHVI'S IMPATIENT QUERY ARRIVES IN A FLUTTER OF IRIDESCENT WINGS.
HOMEPLACE! HOMEPLACE! THAT WAY!
HUH? WHAT'S THAT?

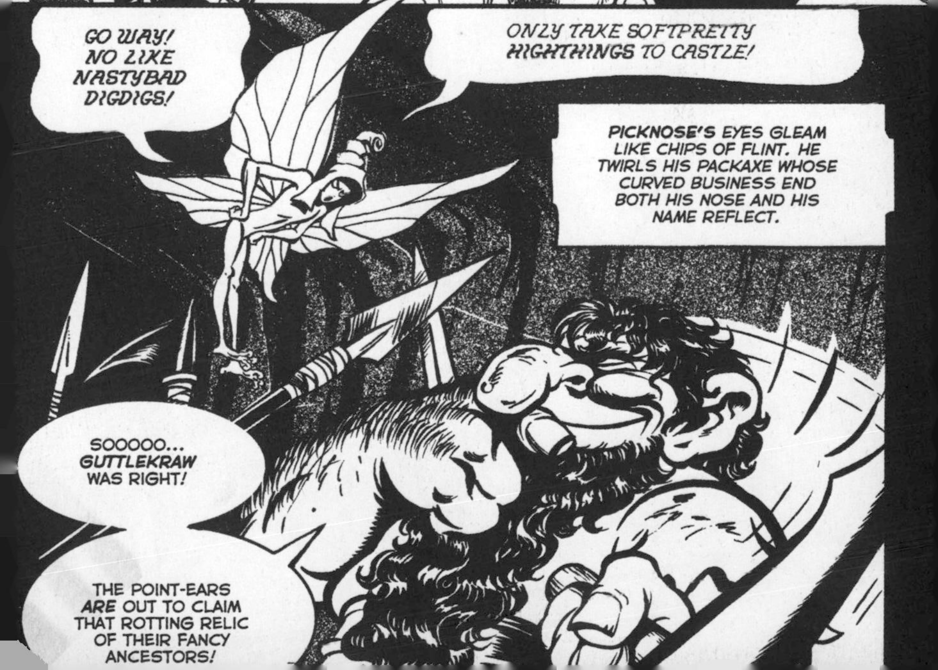

GO WAY! NO LIKE NASTYBAD DIGDIGS!
ONLY TAKE SOFTPRETTY HIGHTHINGS TO CASTLE!
PICKNOSE'S EYES GLEAM LIKE CHIPS OF FLINT. HE TWIRLS HIS PACKAXE WHOSE CURVED BUSINESS END BOTH HIS NOSE AND HIS NAME REFLECT.
SOOOOO... GUTTLEKRAW WAS RIGHT!
THE POINT-EARS ARE OUT TO CLAIM THAT ROTTING RELIC OF THEIR FANCY ANCESTORS!

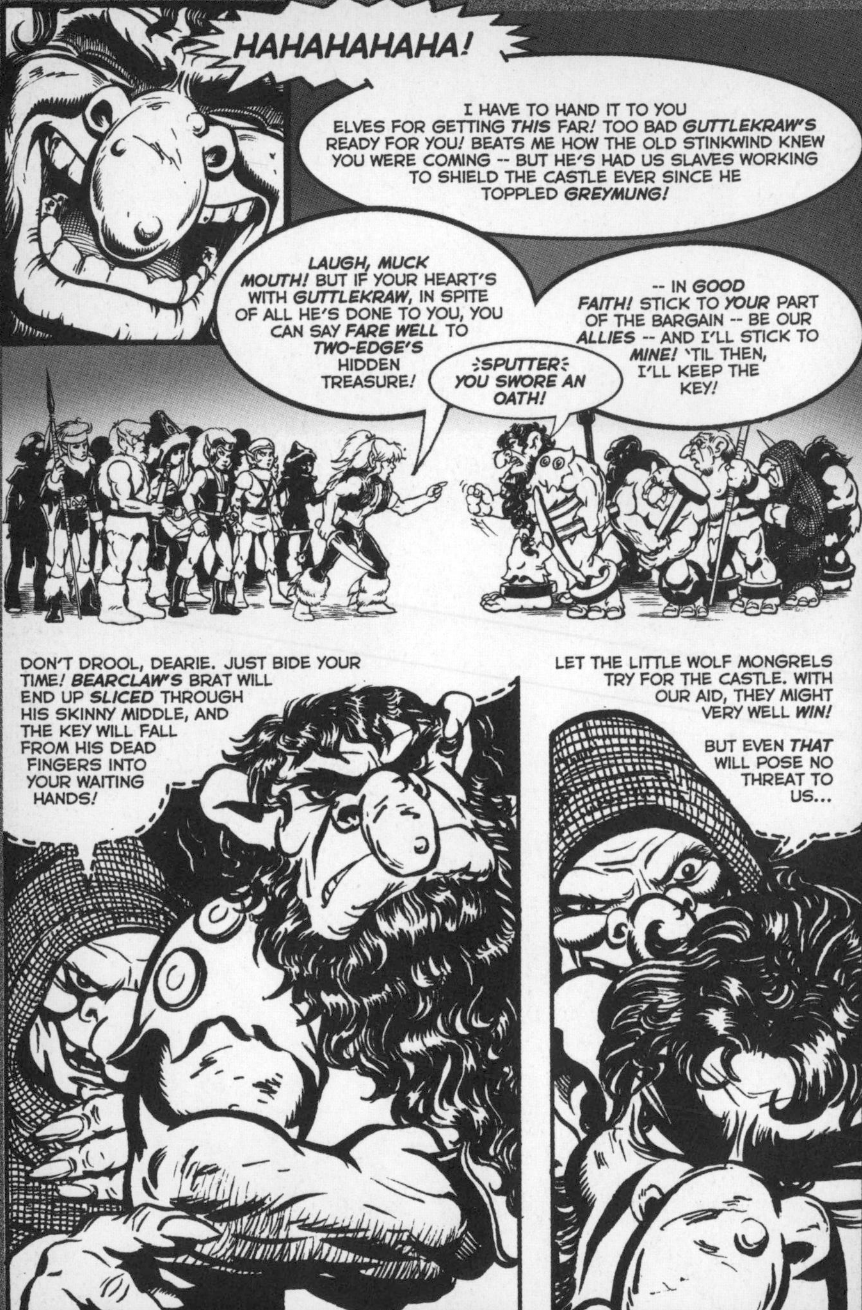
HAHAHAHAHA!
I HAVE TO HAND IT TO YOU ELVES FOR GETTING *THIS* FAR! TOO BAD *GUTTLEKRAW'S* READY FOR YOU! BEATS ME HOW THE OLD STINKWIND KNEW YOU WERE COMING -- BUT HE'S HAD US SLAVES WORKING TO SHIELD THE CASTLE EVER SINCE HE TOPPLED *GREYMUNG!*
LAUGH, MUCK MOUTH! BUT IF YOUR HEART'S WITH *GUTTLEKRAW*, IN SPITE OF ALL HE'S DONE TO YOU, YOU CAN SAY *FARE WELL* TO *TWO-EDGE'S* HIDDEN TREASURE!
SPUTTER *YOU SWORE AN OATH!*
-- IN *GOOD FAITH!* STICK TO *YOUR* PART OF THE BARGAIN -- BE OUR *ALLIES* -- AND I'LL STICK TO *MINE!* 'TIL THEN, I'LL KEEP THE KEY!
DON'T DROOL, DEARIE. JUST BIDE YOUR TIME! *BEARCLAW'S* BRAT WILL END UP *SLICED* THROUGH HIS SKINNY MIDDLE, AND THE KEY WILL FALL FROM HIS DEAD FINGERS INTO YOUR WAITING HANDS!
LET THE LITTLE WOLF MONGRELS TRY FOR THE CASTLE. WITH OUR AID, THEY MIGHT VERY WELL *WIN!*
BUT EVEN *THAT* WILL POSE NO THREAT TO US...

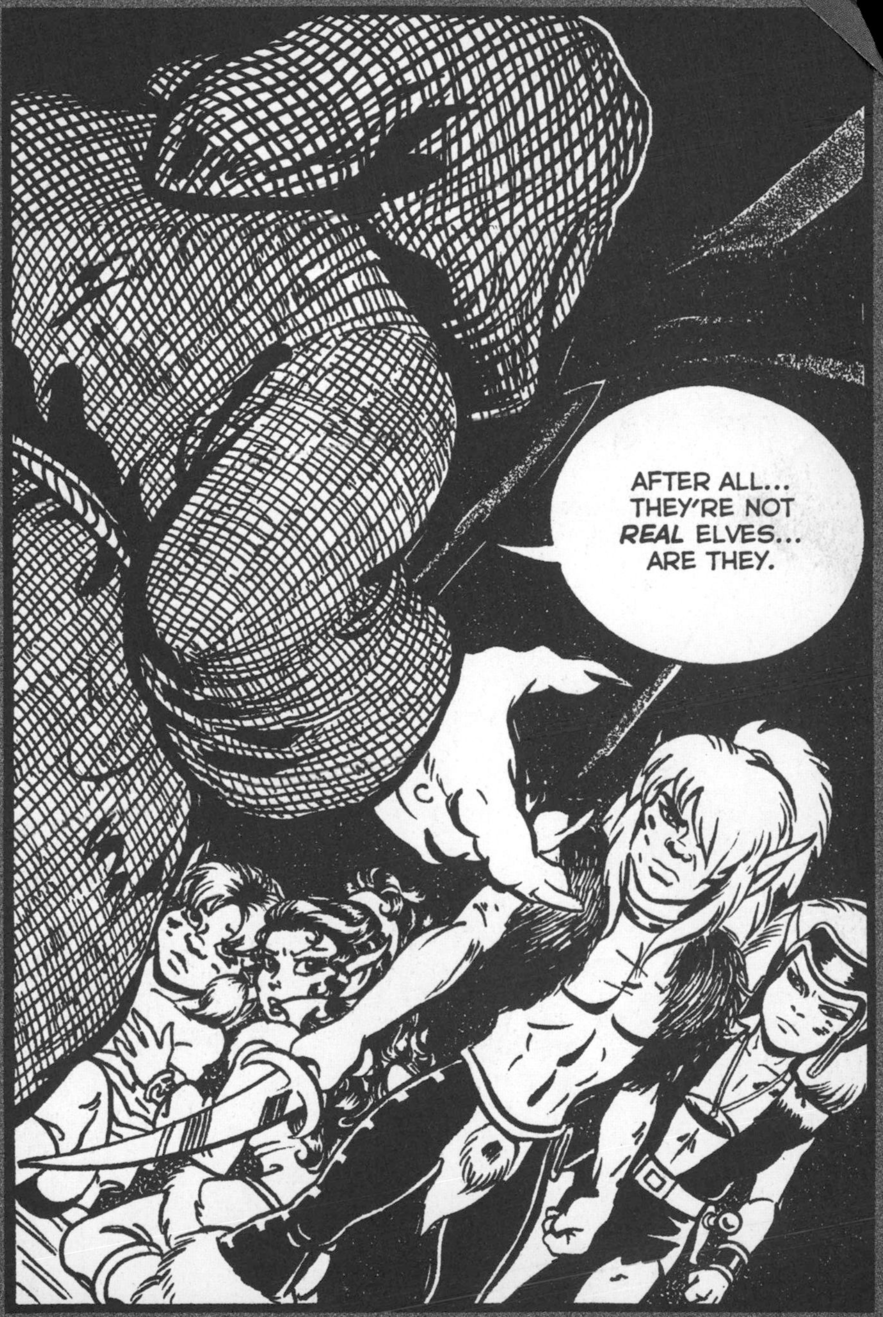
AFTER ALL... THEY'RE NOT *REAL* ELVES... ARE THEY.

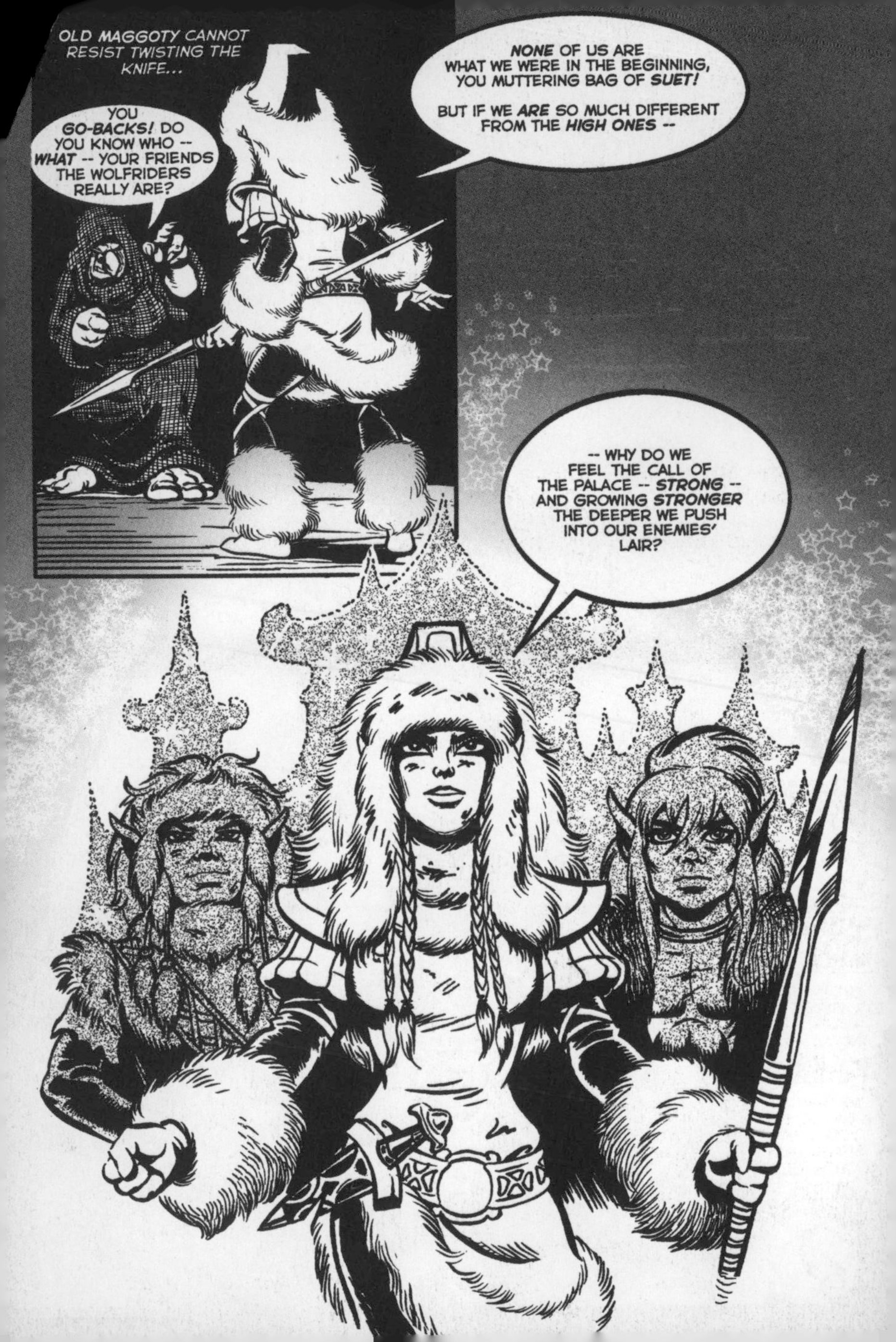
OLD MAGGOTY CANNOT RESIST TWISTING THE KNIFE...
YOU GO-BACKS! DO YOU KNOW WHO -- WHAT -- YOUR FRIENDS THE WOLFRIDERS REALLY ARE?
NONE OF US ARE WHAT WE WERE IN THE BEGINNING, YOU MUTTERING BAG OF SUET!
BUT IF WE ARE SO MUCH DIFFERENT FROM THE HIGH ONES --
-- WHY DO WE FEEL THE CALL OF THE PALACE -- STRONG -- AND GROWING STRONGER THE DEEPER WE PUSH INTO OUR ENEMIES' LAIR?

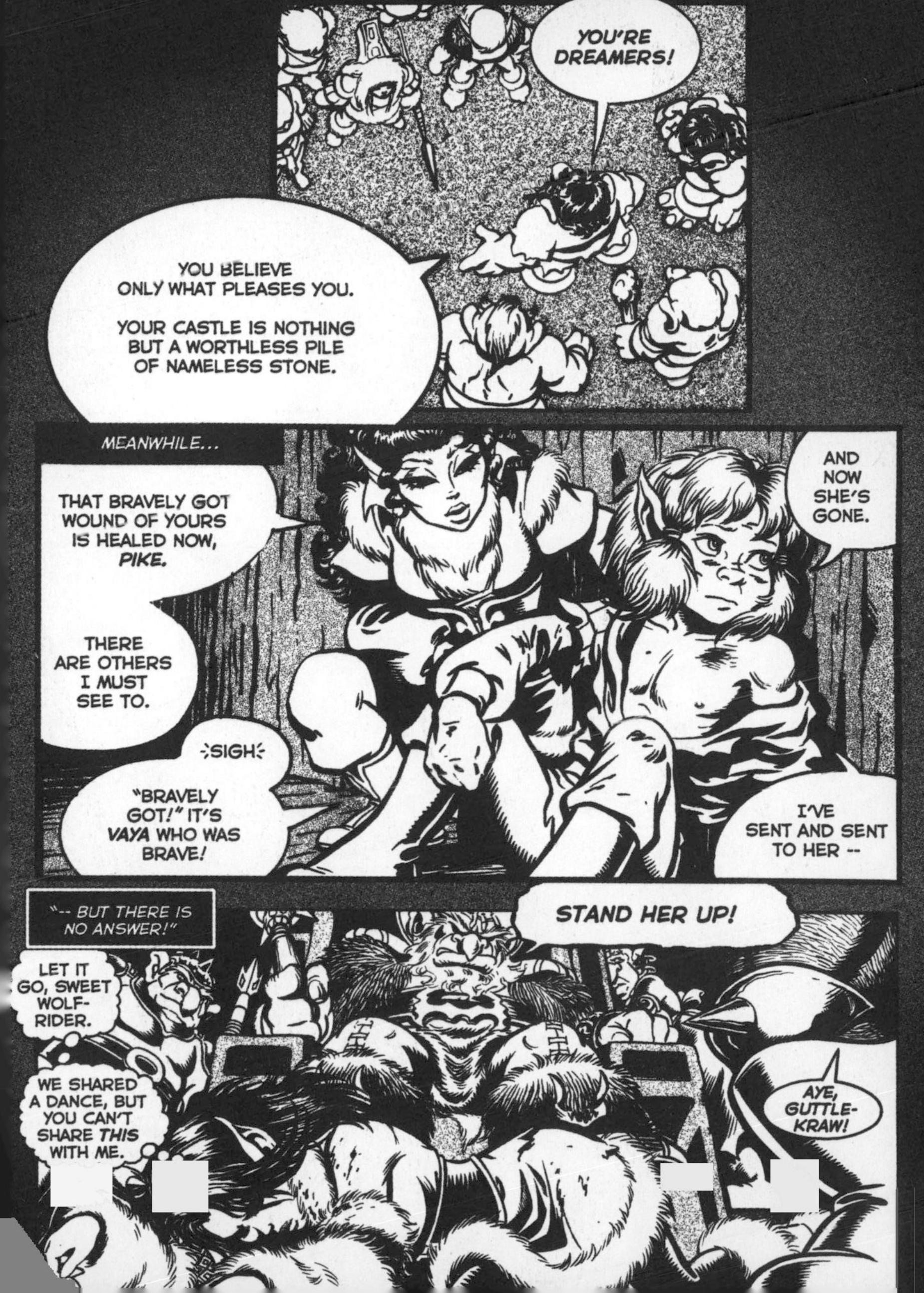
YOU'RE DREAMERS!
YOU BELIEVE ONLY WHAT PLEASES YOU.
YOUR CASTLE IS NOTHING BUT A WORTHLESS PILE OF NAMELESS STONE.
MEANWHILE...
THAT BRAVELY GOT WOUND OF YOURS IS HEALED NOW, *PIKE.*
THERE ARE OTHERS I MUST SEE TO.
AND NOW SHE'S GONE.
-:SIGH:-
"BRAVELY GOT!" IT'S *VAYA* WHO WAS BRAVE!
I'VE SENT AND SENT TO HER --
"-- *BUT THERE IS NO ANSWER!*"
STAND HER UP!
LET IT GO, SWEET WOLF-RIDER.
WE SHARED A DANCE, BUT YOU CAN'T SHARE *THIS* WITH ME.
AYE, GUTTLE-KRAW!

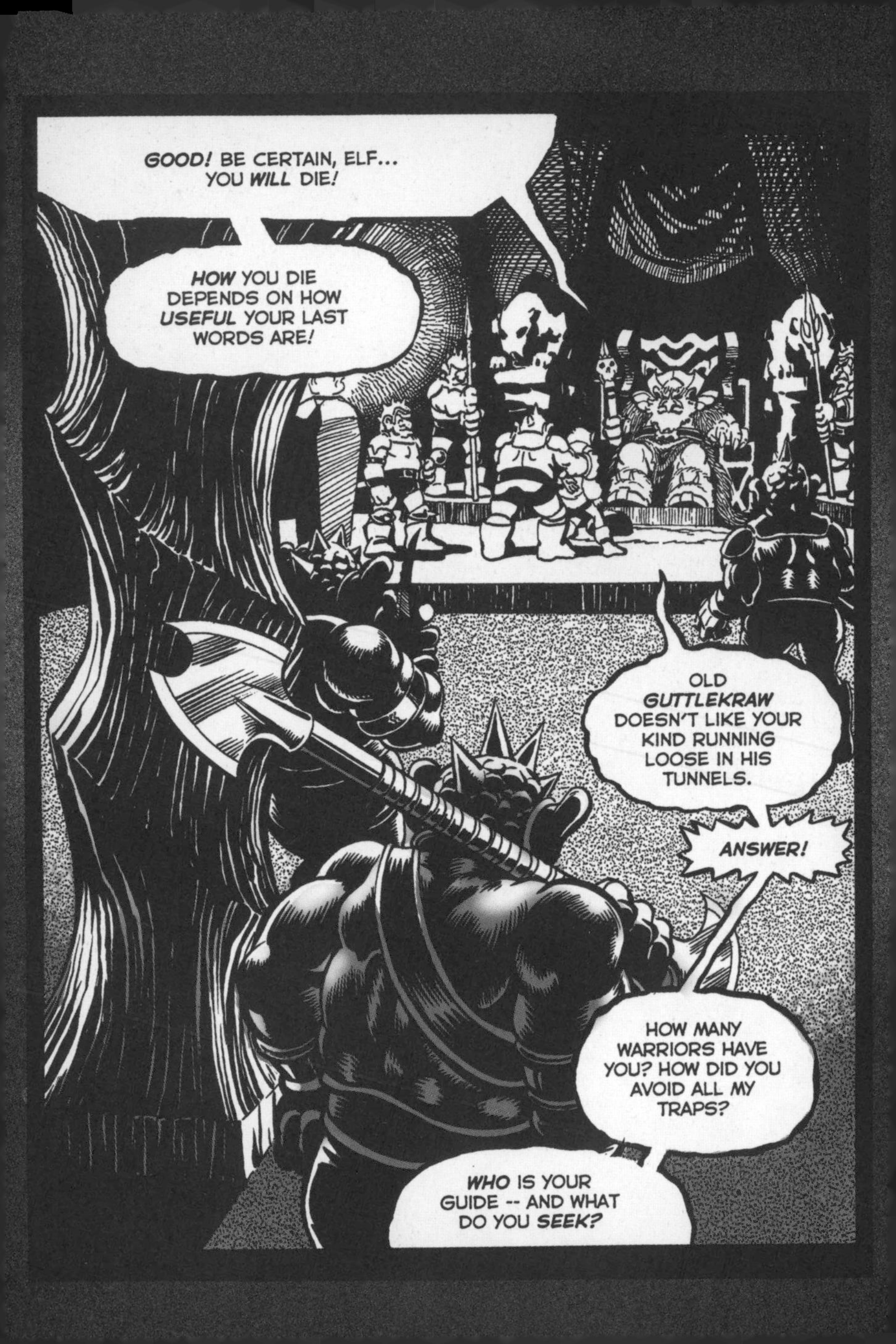
GOOD! BE CERTAIN, ELF... YOU WILL DIE!
HOW YOU DIE DEPENDS ON HOW USEFUL YOUR LAST WORDS ARE!
OLD GUTTLEKRAW DOESN'T LIKE YOUR KIND RUNNING LOOSE IN HIS TUNNELS.
ANSWER!
HOW MANY WARRIORS HAVE YOU? HOW DID YOU AVOID ALL MY TRAPS?
WHO IS YOUR GUIDE -- AND WHAT DO YOU SEEK?

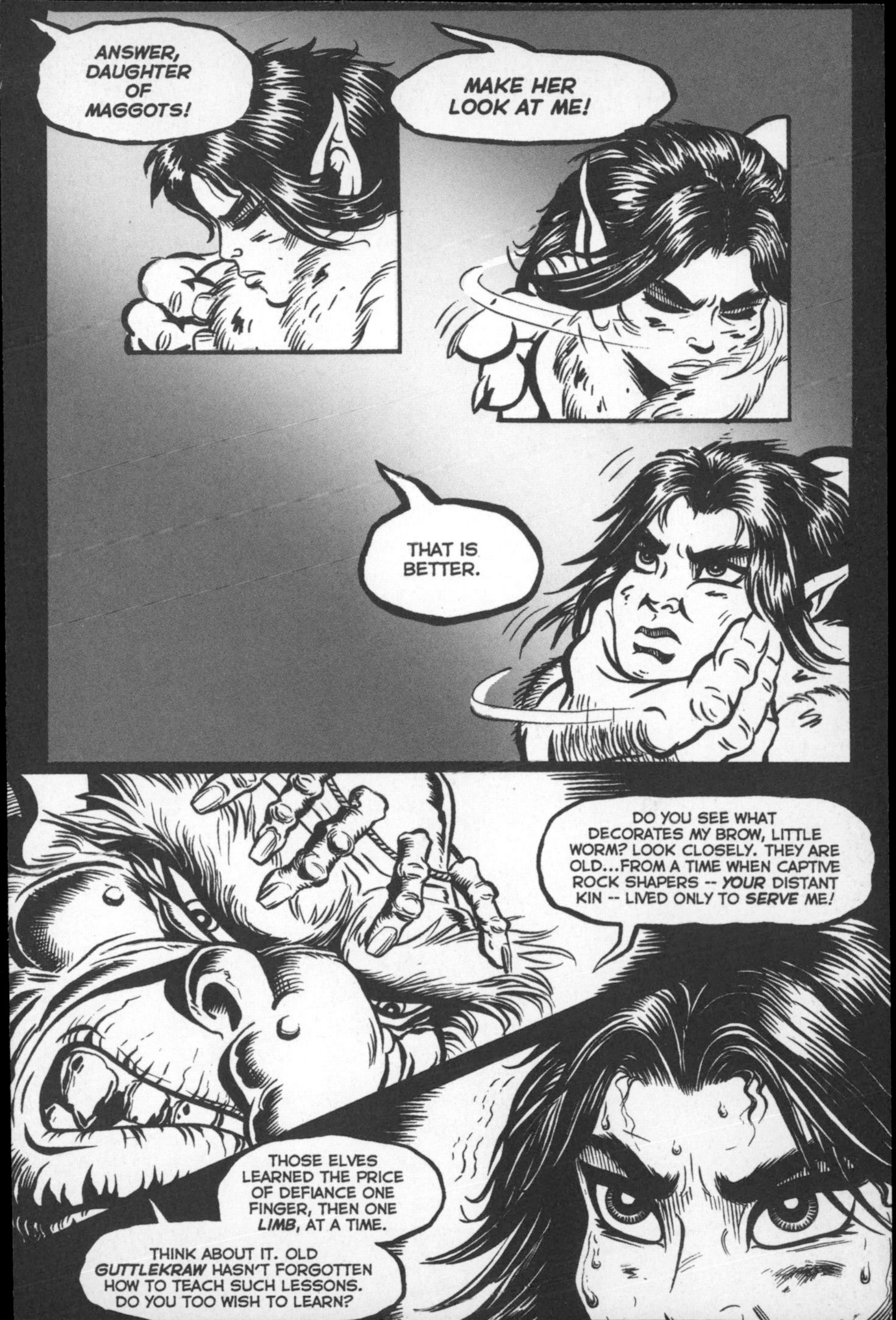
ANSWER, DAUGHTER OF MAGGOTS!
MAKE HER LOOK AT ME!
THAT IS BETTER.
DO YOU SEE WHAT DECORATES MY BROW, LITTLE WORM? LOOK CLOSELY. THEY ARE OLD...FROM A TIME WHEN CAPTIVE ROCK SHAPERS -- YOUR DISTANT KIN -- LIVED ONLY TO SERVE ME!
THOSE ELVES LEARNED THE PRICE OF DEFIANCE ONE FINGER, THEN ONE LIMB, AT A TIME.
THINK ABOUT IT. OLD GUTTLEKRAW HASN'T FORGOTTEN HOW TO TEACH SUCH LESSONS. DO YOU TOO WISH TO LEARN?

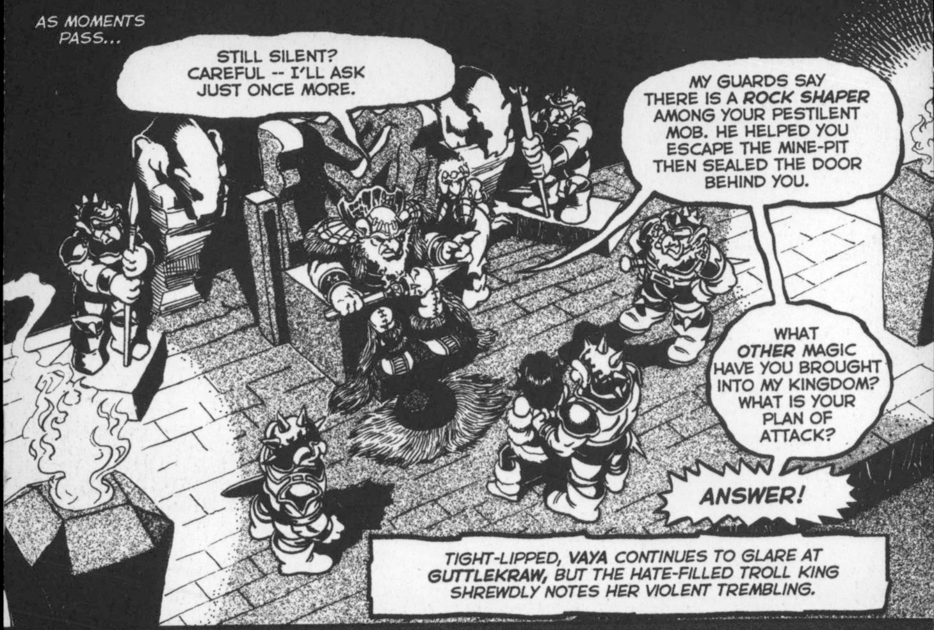
AS MOMENTS PASS...
STILL SILENT? CAREFUL -- I'LL ASK JUST ONCE MORE.
MY GUARDS SAY THERE IS A ROCK SHAPER AMONG YOUR PESTILENT MOB. HE HELPED YOU ESCAPE THE MINE-PIT THEN SEALED THE DOOR BEHIND YOU.
WHAT OTHER MAGIC HAVE YOU BROUGHT INTO MY KINGDOM? WHAT IS YOUR PLAN OF ATTACK?
ANSWER!
TIGHT-LIPPED, VAYA CONTINUES TO GLARE AT GUTTLEKRAW, BUT THE HATE-FILLED TROLL KING SHREWDLY NOTES HER VIOLENT TREMBLING.

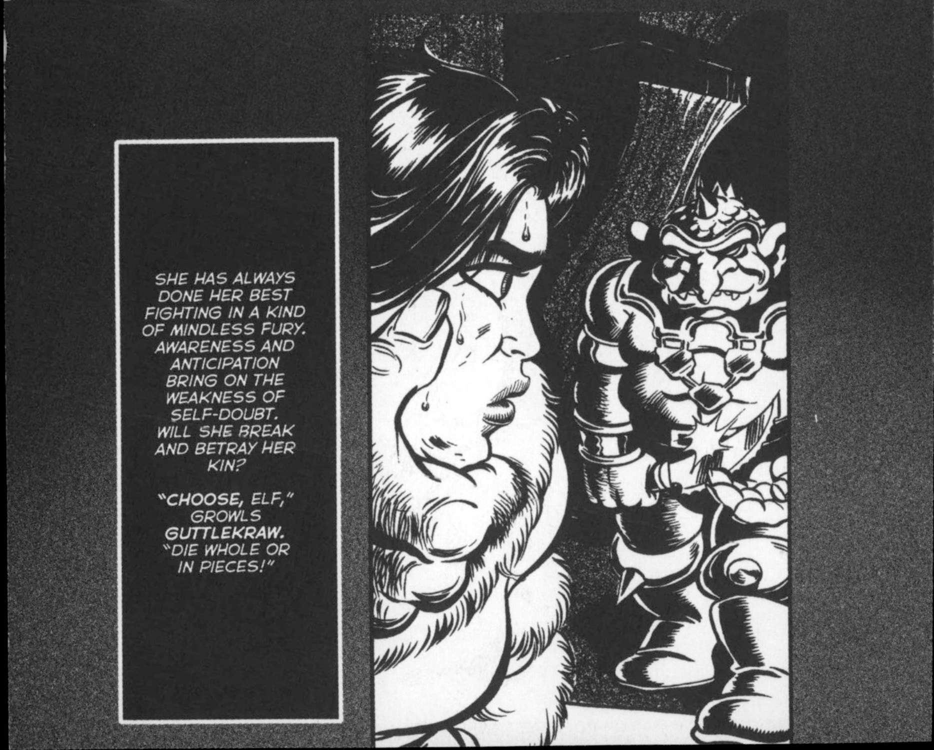
SHE HAS ALWAYS DONE HER BEST FIGHTING IN A KIND OF MINDLESS FURY. AWARENESS AND ANTICIPATION BRING ON THE WEAKNESS OF SELF-DOUBT. WILL SHE BREAK AND BETRAY HER KIN?
"CHOOSE, ELF," GROWLS GUTTLEKRAW. "DIE WHOLE OR IN PIECES!"

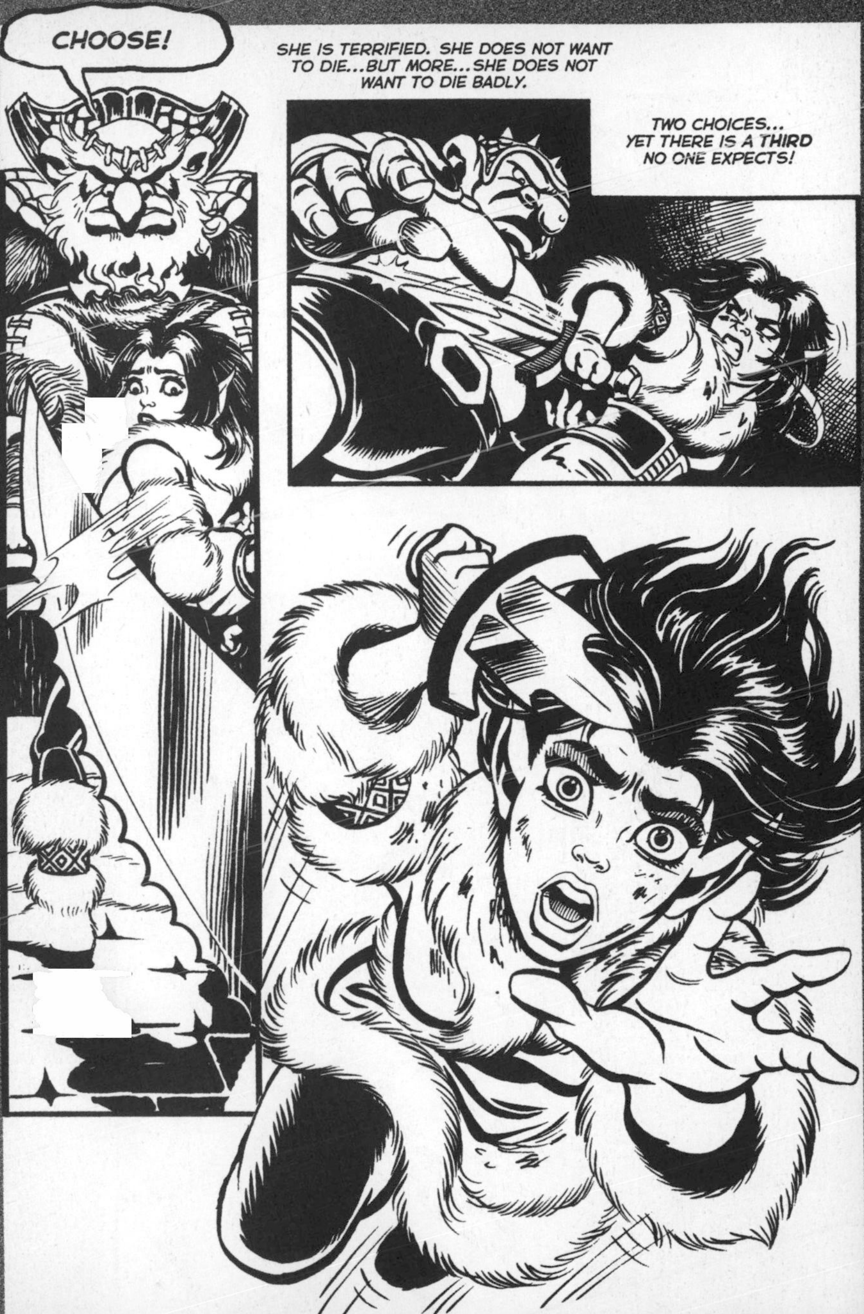
CHOOSE!
SHE IS TERRIFIED. SHE DOES NOT WANT TO DIE...BUT MORE...SHE DOES NOT WANT TO DIE BADLY.
TWO CHOICES... YET THERE IS A THIRD NO ONE EXPECTS!

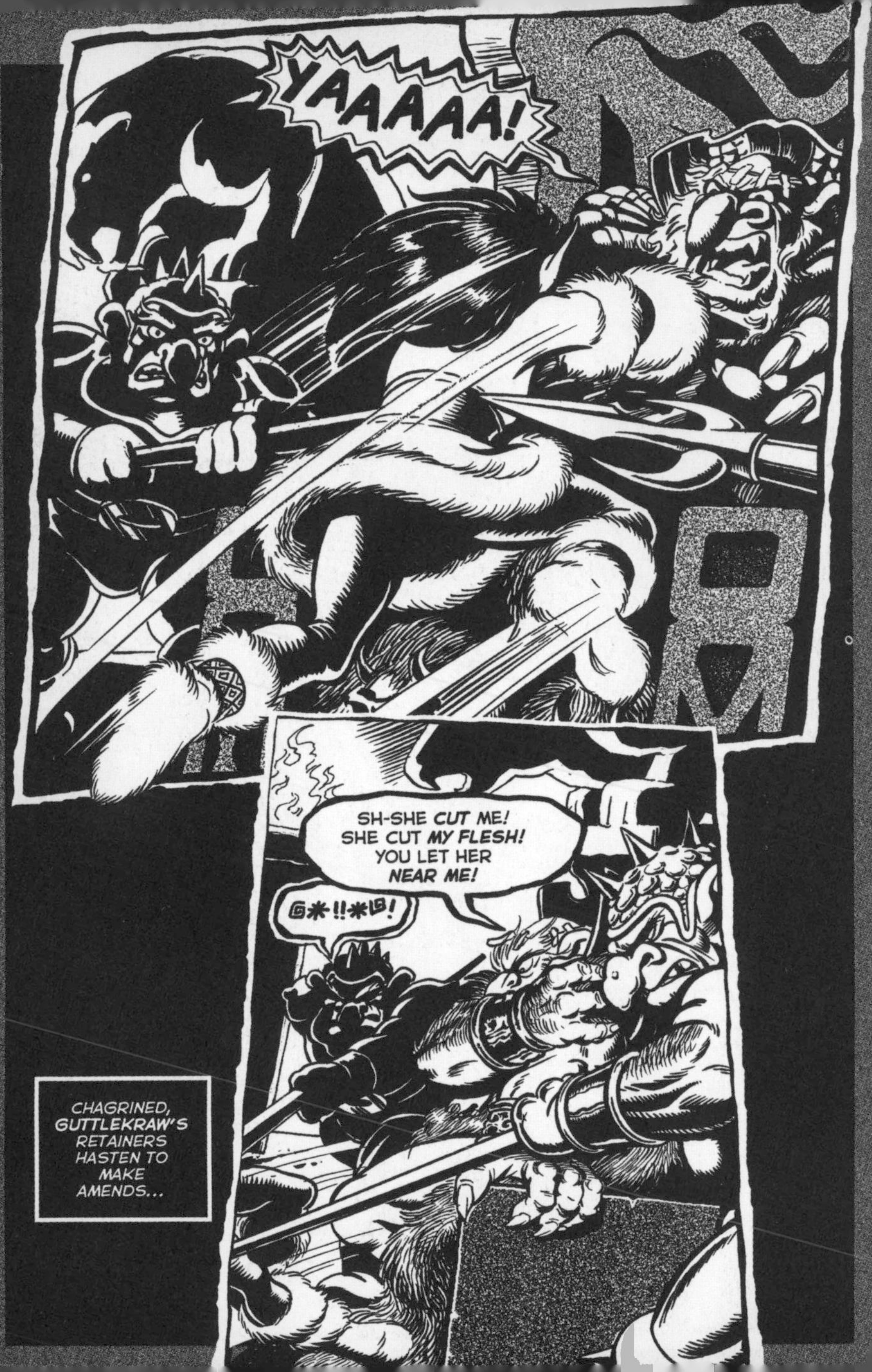
YAAAAAA!
SH-SHE CUT ME! SHE CUT MY FLESH! YOU LET HER NEAR ME!
CHAGRINED, GUTTLEKRAW'S RETAINERS HASTEN TO MAKE AMENDS...

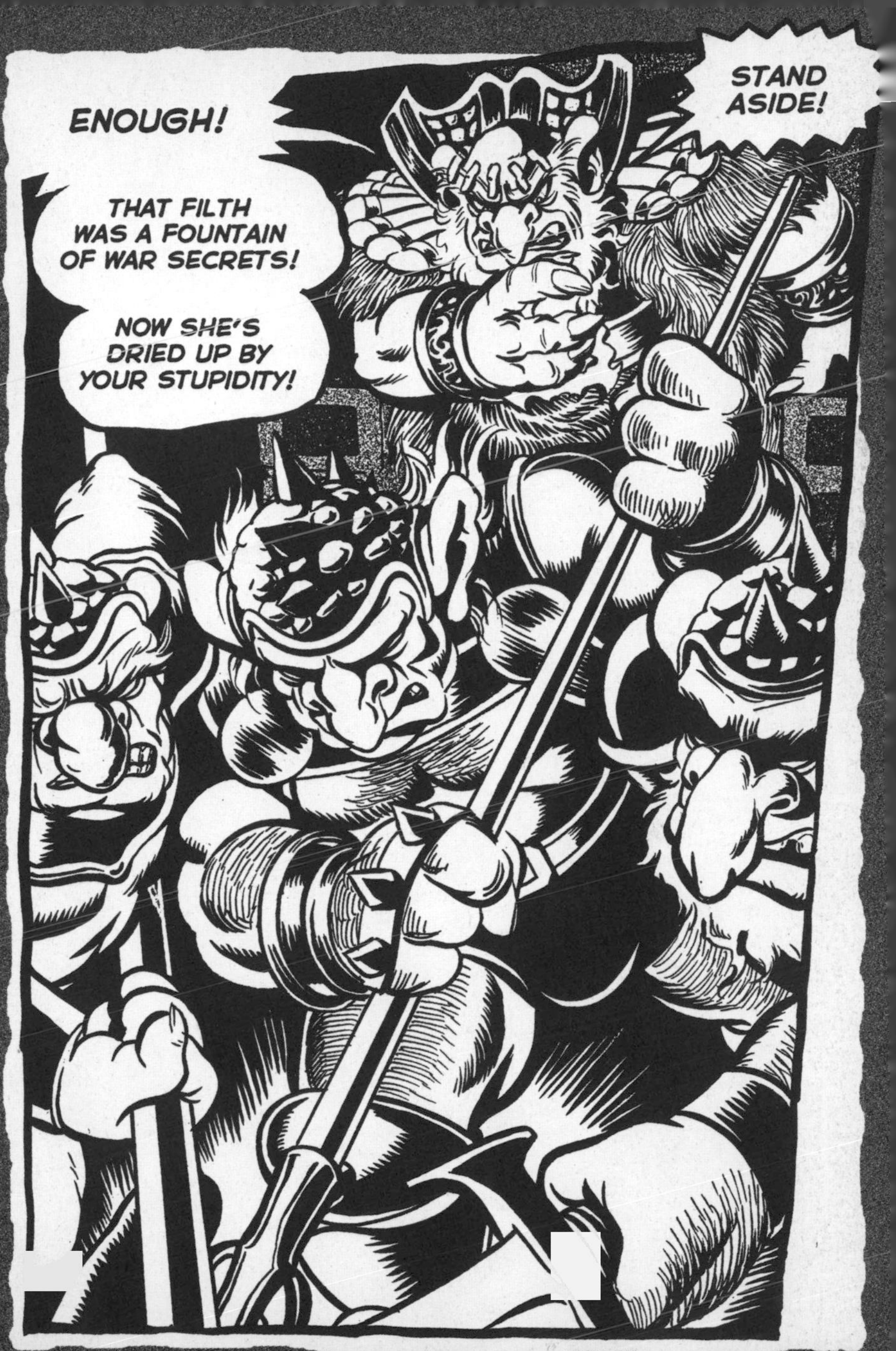
ENOUGH!
THAT FILTH WAS A FOUNTAIN OF WAR SECRETS!
NOW SHE'S DRIED UP BY YOUR STUPIDITY!
STAND ASIDE!

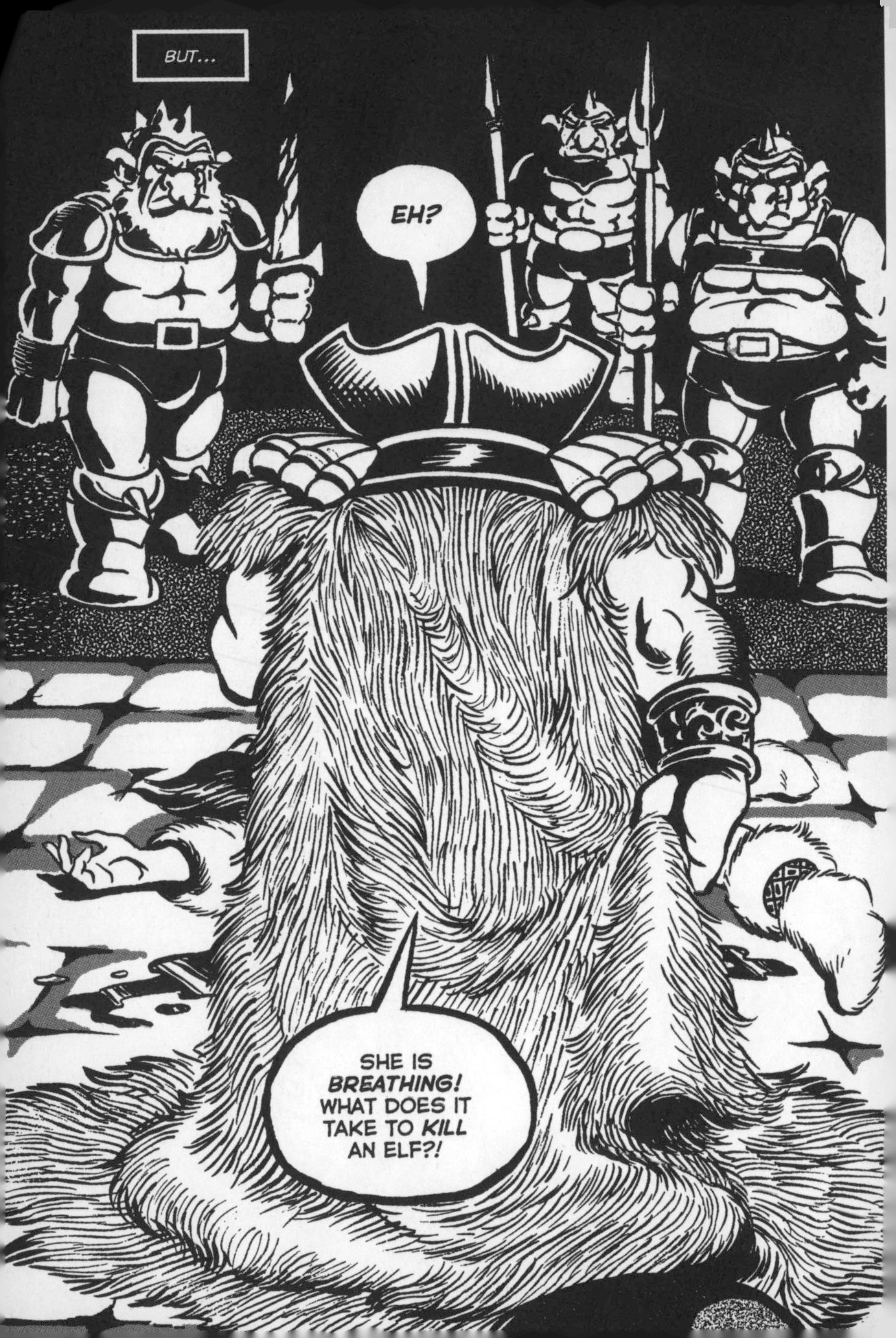
BUT...
EH?
SHE IS BREATHING! WHAT DOES IT TAKE TO KILL AN ELF?!

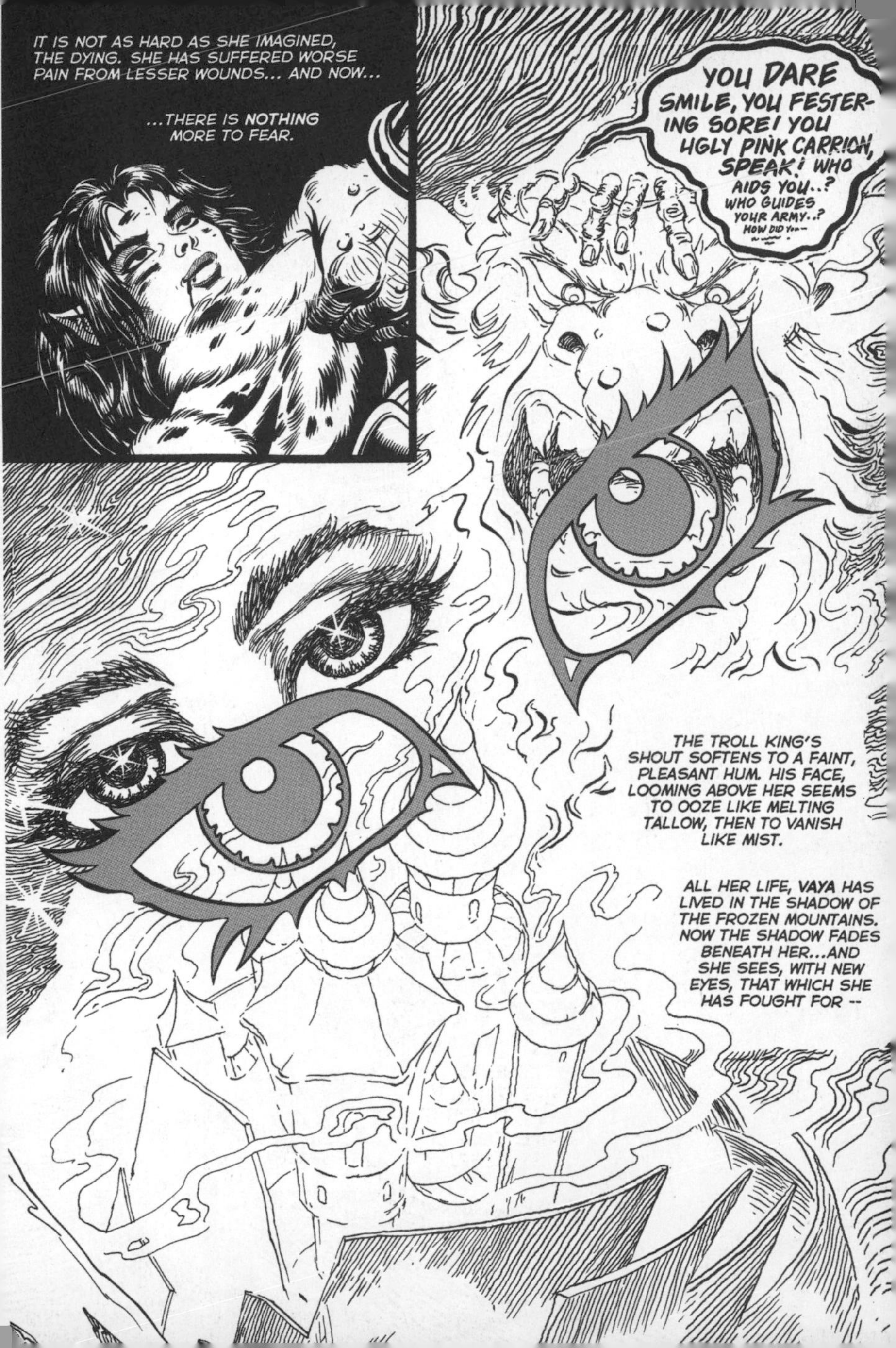
IT IS NOT AS HARD AS SHE IMAGINED, THE DYING. SHE HAS SUFFERED WORSE PAIN FROM LESSER WOUNDS... AND NOW...
...THERE IS NOTHING MORE TO FEAR.
YOU DARE SMILE, YOU FESTERING SORE! YOU UGLY PINK CARRION, SPEAK! WHO AIDS YOU..? WHO GUIDES YOUR ARMY..? HOW DID YOU--
THE TROLL KING'S SHOUT SOFTENS TO A FAINT, PLEASANT HUM. HIS FACE, LOOMING ABOVE HER SEEMS TO OOZE LIKE MELTING TALLOW, THEN TO VANISH LIKE MIST.
ALL HER LIFE, VAYA HAS LIVED IN THE SHADOW OF THE FROZEN MOUNTAINS. NOW THE SHADOW FADES BENEATH HER...AND SHE SEES, WITH NEW EYES, THAT WHICH SHE HAS FOUGHT FOR --

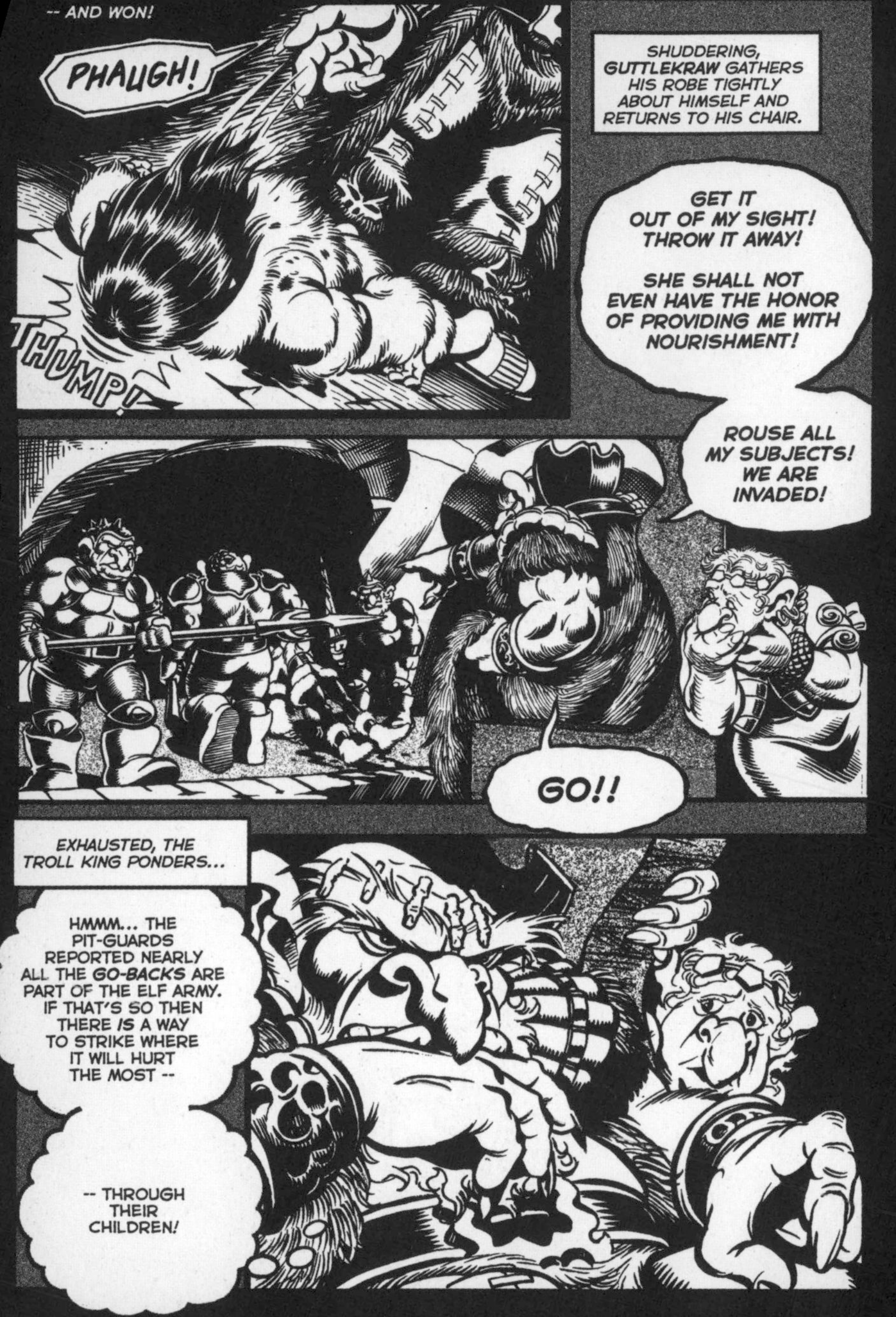
-- AND WON!
PHAUGH!
THUMP!
SHUDDERING, GUTTLEKRAW GATHERS HIS ROBE TIGHTLY ABOUT HIMSELF AND RETURNS TO HIS CHAIR.
GET IT OUT OF MY SIGHT! THROW IT AWAY!
SHE SHALL NOT EVEN HAVE THE HONOR OF PROVIDING ME WITH NOURISHMENT!
ROUSE ALL MY SUBJECTS! WE ARE INVADED!
GO!!
EXHAUSTED, THE TROLL KING PONDERS...
HMMM... THE PIT-GUARDS REPORTED NEARLY ALL THE GO-BACKS ARE PART OF THE ELF ARMY. IF THAT'S SO THEN THERE IS A WAY TO STRIKE WHERE IT WILL HURT THE MOST --
-- THROUGH THEIR CHILDREN!

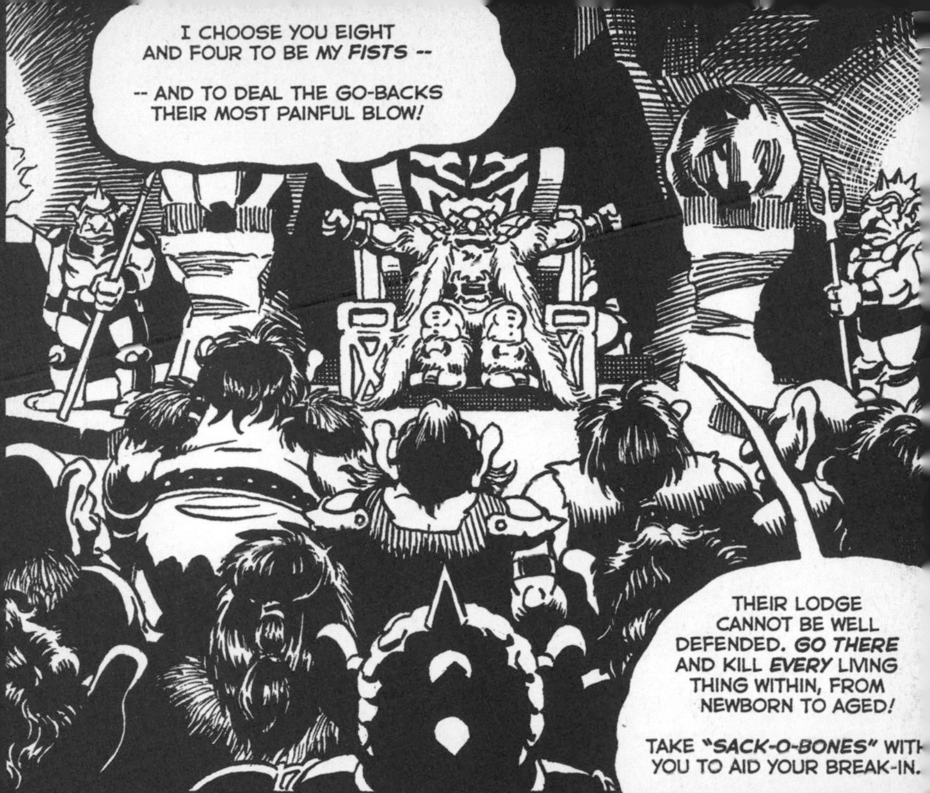
I CHOOSE YOU EIGHT AND FOUR TO BE MY FISTS --
-- AND TO DEAL THE GO-BACKS THEIR MOST PAINFUL BLOW!
THEIR LODGE CANNOT BE WELL DEFENDED. GO THERE AND KILL EVERY LIVING THING WITHIN, FROM NEWBORN TO AGED!
TAKE "SACK-O-BONES" WITH YOU TO AID YOUR BREAK-IN.

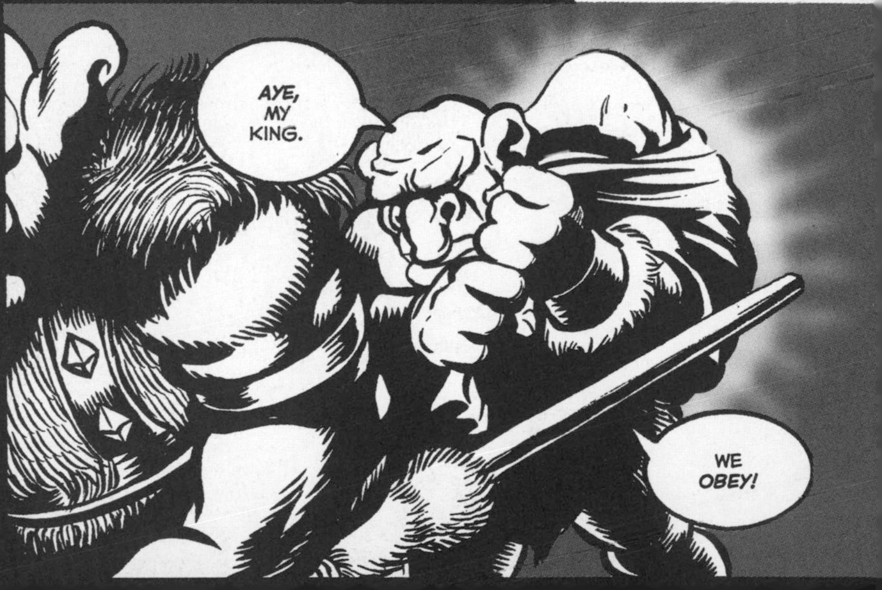
AYE, MY KING.
WE OBEY!

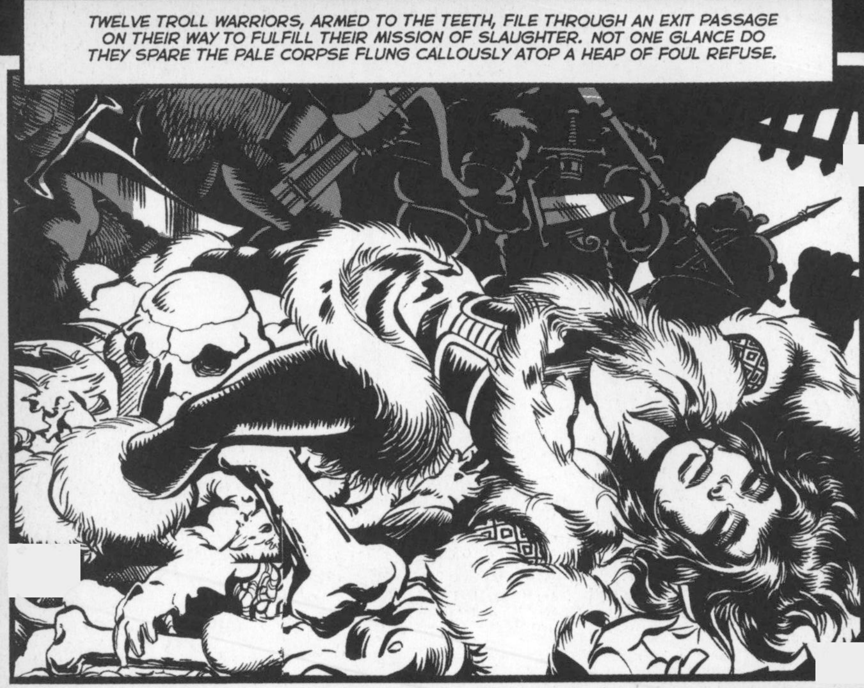
TWELVE TROLL WARRIORS, ARMED TO THE TEETH, FILE THROUGH AN EXIT PASSAGE ON THEIR WAY TO FULFILL THEIR MISSION OF SLAUGHTER. NOT ONE GLANCE DO THEY SPARE THE PALE CORPSE FLUNG CALLOUSLY ATOP A HEAP OF FOUL REFUSE.

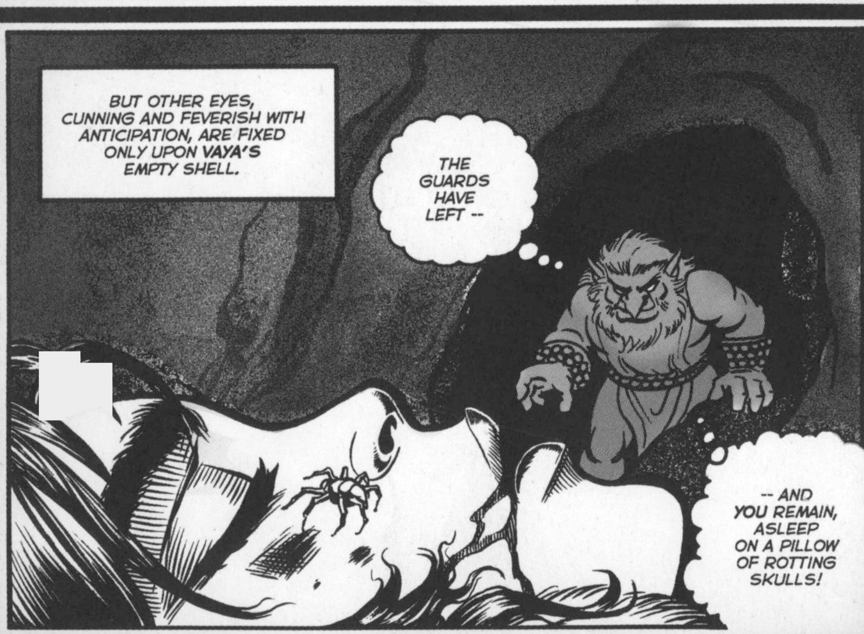
BUT OTHER EYES, CUNNING AND FEVERISH WITH ANTICIPATION, ARE FIXED ONLY UPON VAYA'S EMPTY SHELL.
THE GUARDS HAVE LEFT --
-- AND YOU REMAIN, ASLEEP ON A PILLOW OF ROTTING SKULLS!

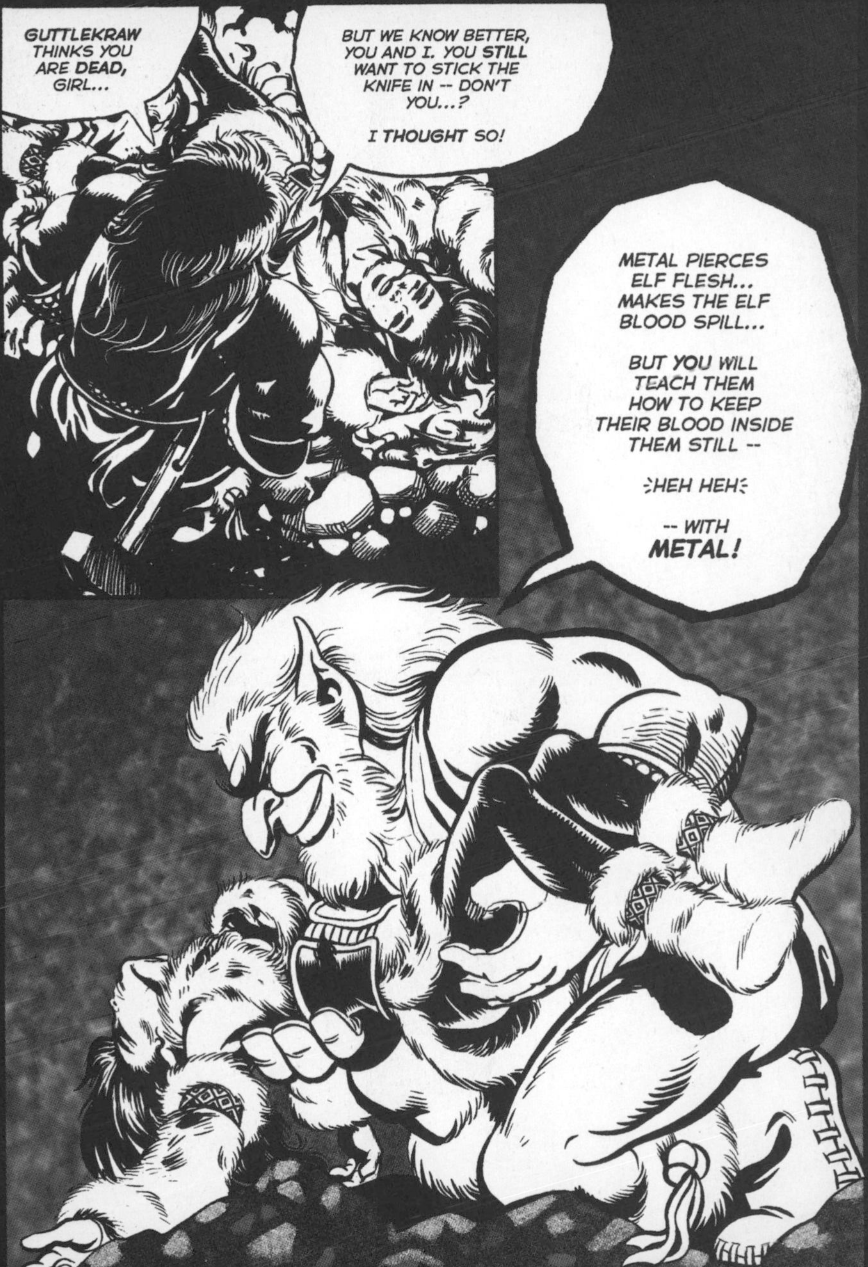
GUTTLEKRAW THINKS YOU ARE DEAD, GIRL...
BUT WE KNOW BETTER, YOU AND I. YOU STILL WANT TO STICK THE KNIFE IN -- DON'T YOU...?
I THOUGHT SO!
METAL PIERCES ELF FLESH... MAKES THE ELF BLOOD SPILL...
BUT YOU WILL TEACH THEM HOW TO KEEP THEIR BLOOD INSIDE THEM STILL --
HEH HEH
-- WITH METAL!

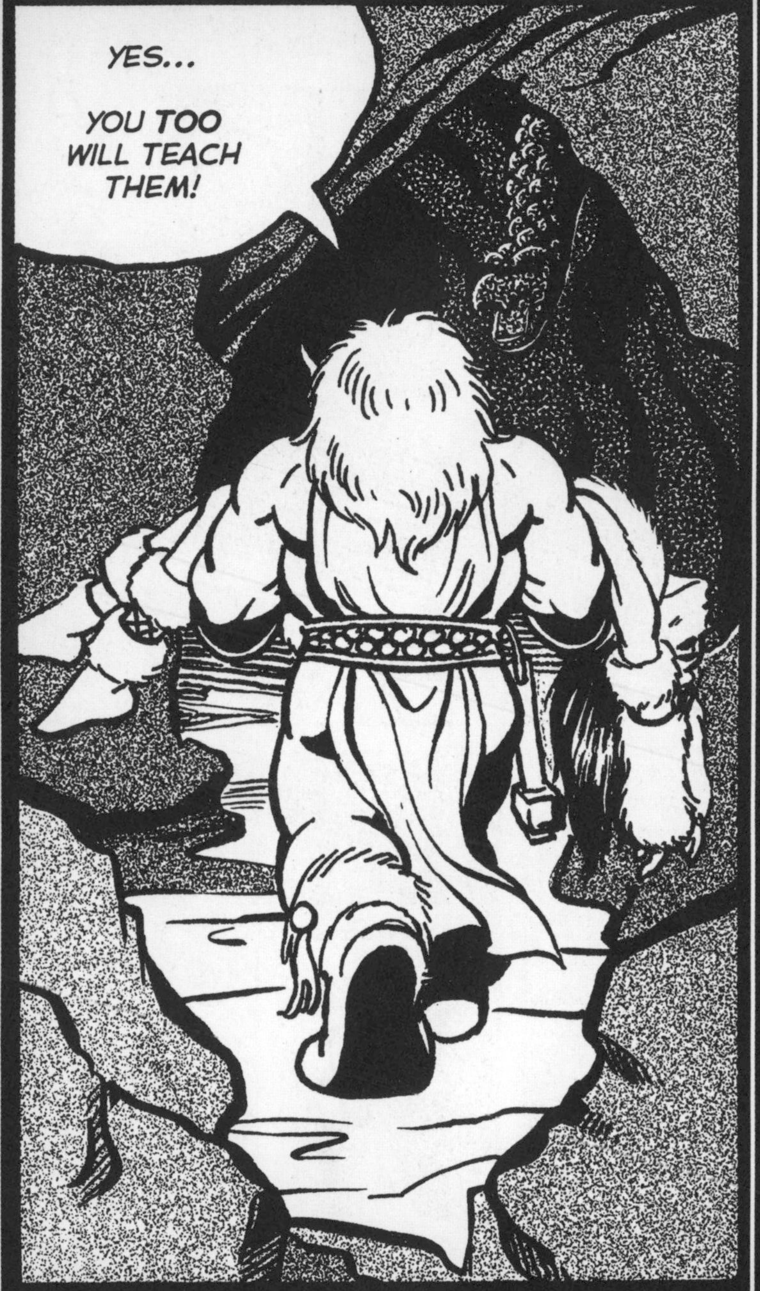
YES...
YOU TOO WILL TEACH THEM!

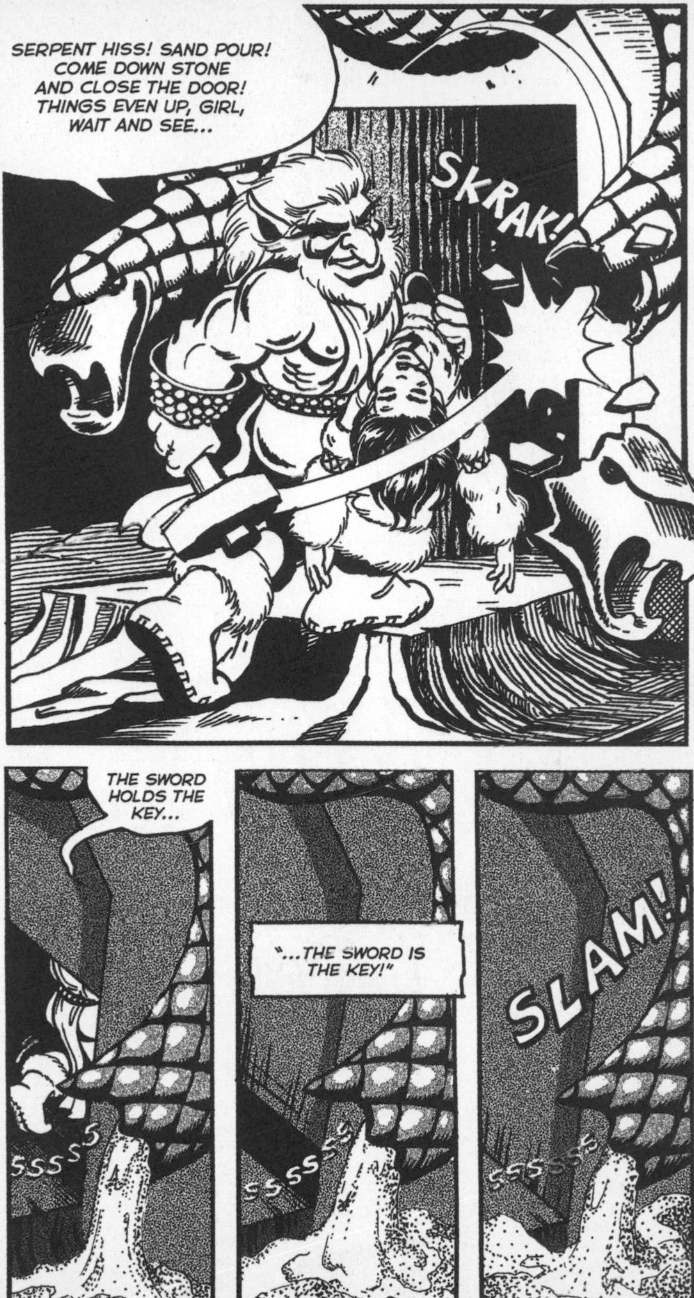
SERPENT HISS! SAND POUR! COME DOWN STONE AND CLOSE THE DOOR! THINGS EVEN UP, GIRL, WAIT AND SEE...
SKRAK!
THE SWORD HOLDS THE KEY...
SSSSS
"...THE SWORD IS THE KEY!"
SSSSSS
SLAM!
SSSSSSS

TO BE CONCLUDED...

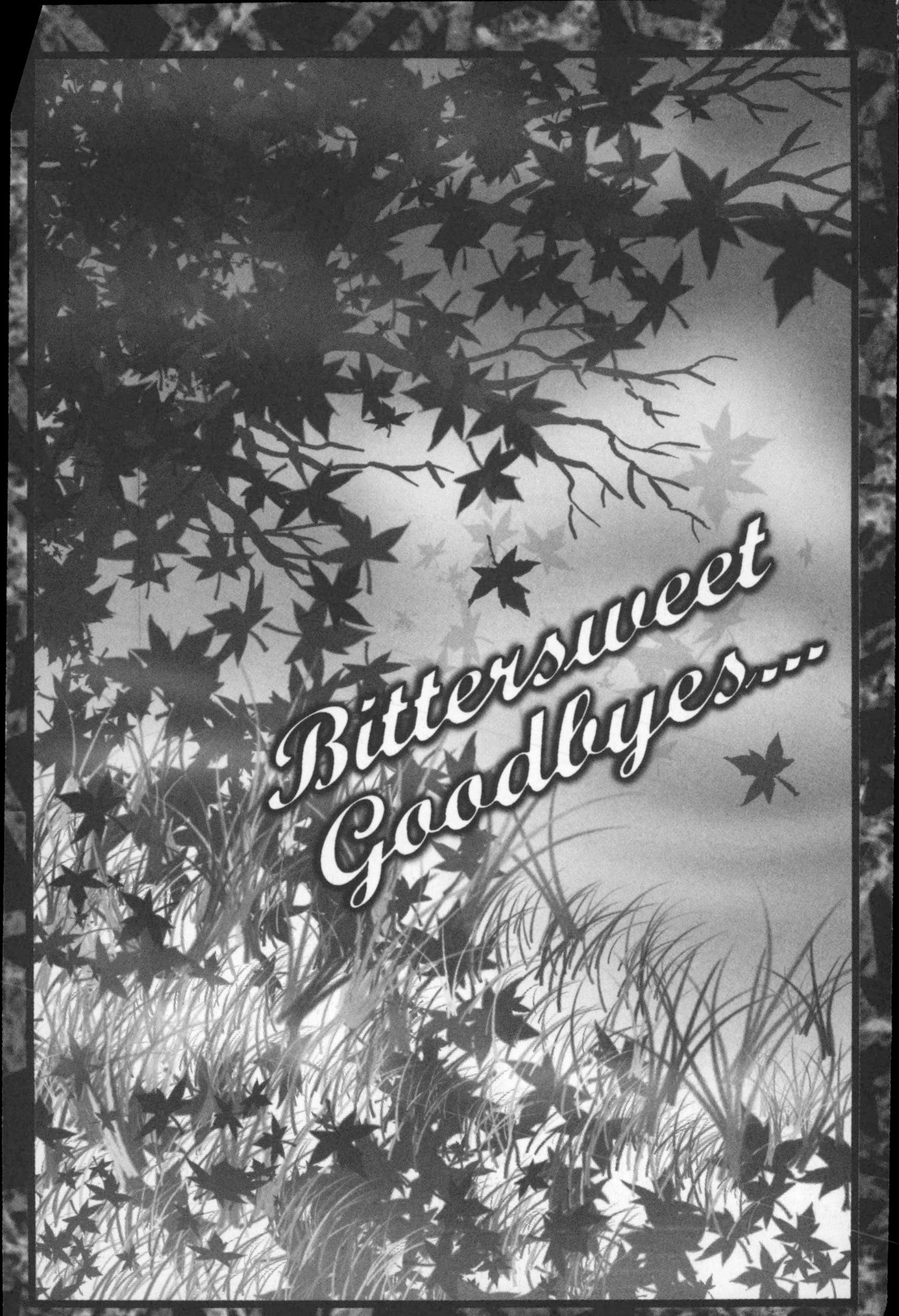
Bittersweet
Goodbyes...

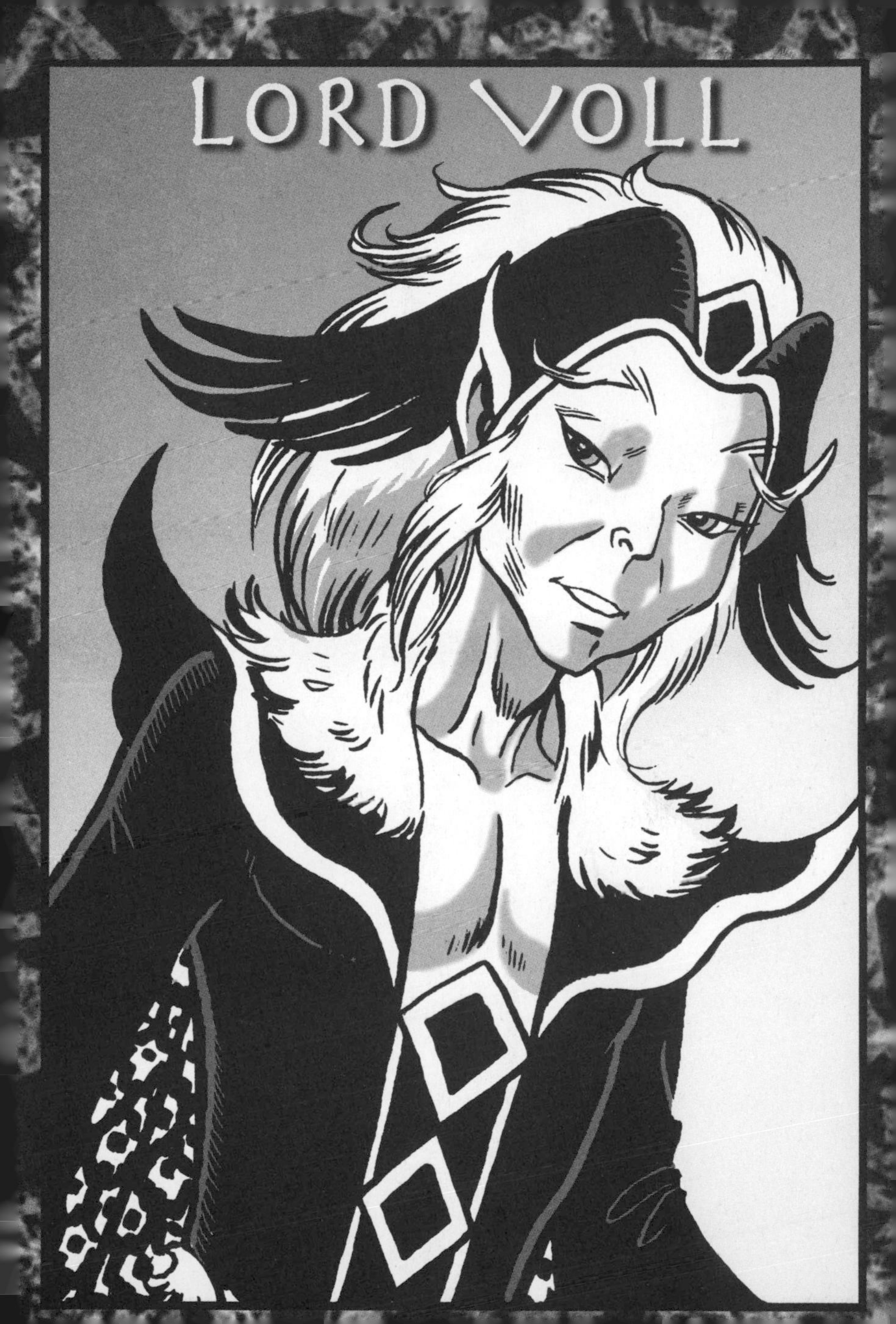
LORD VOLL

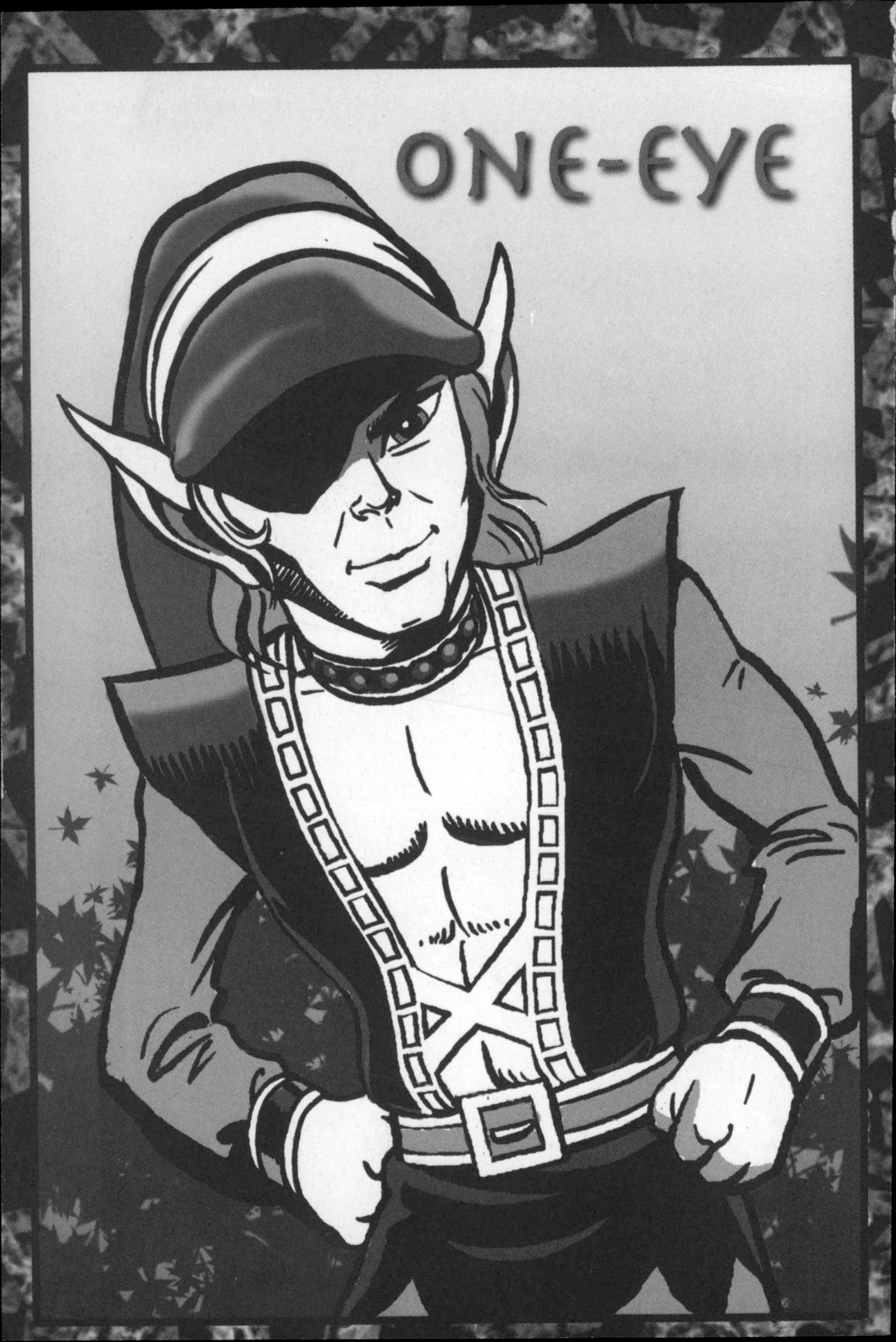
ONE-EYE

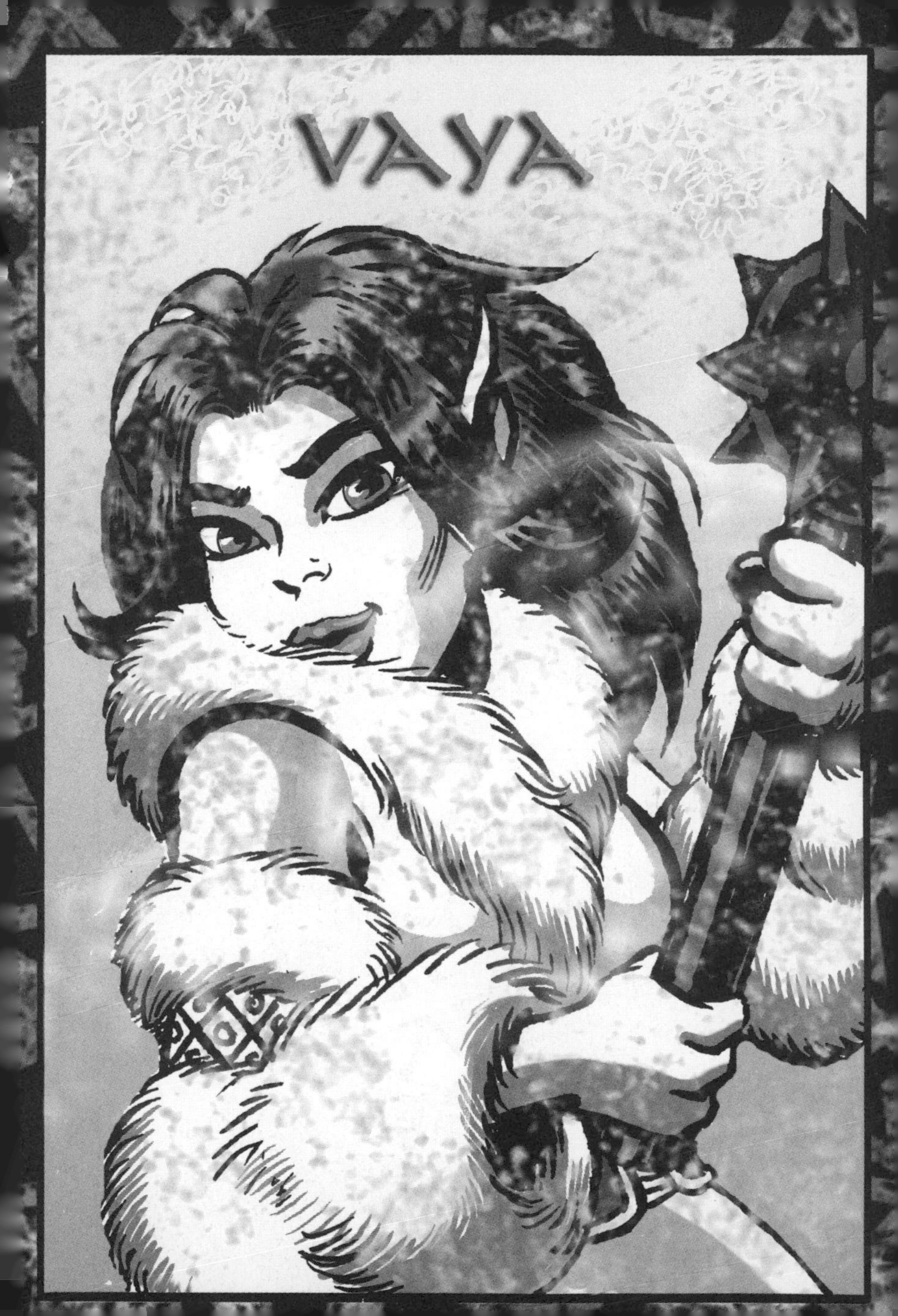
VAYA

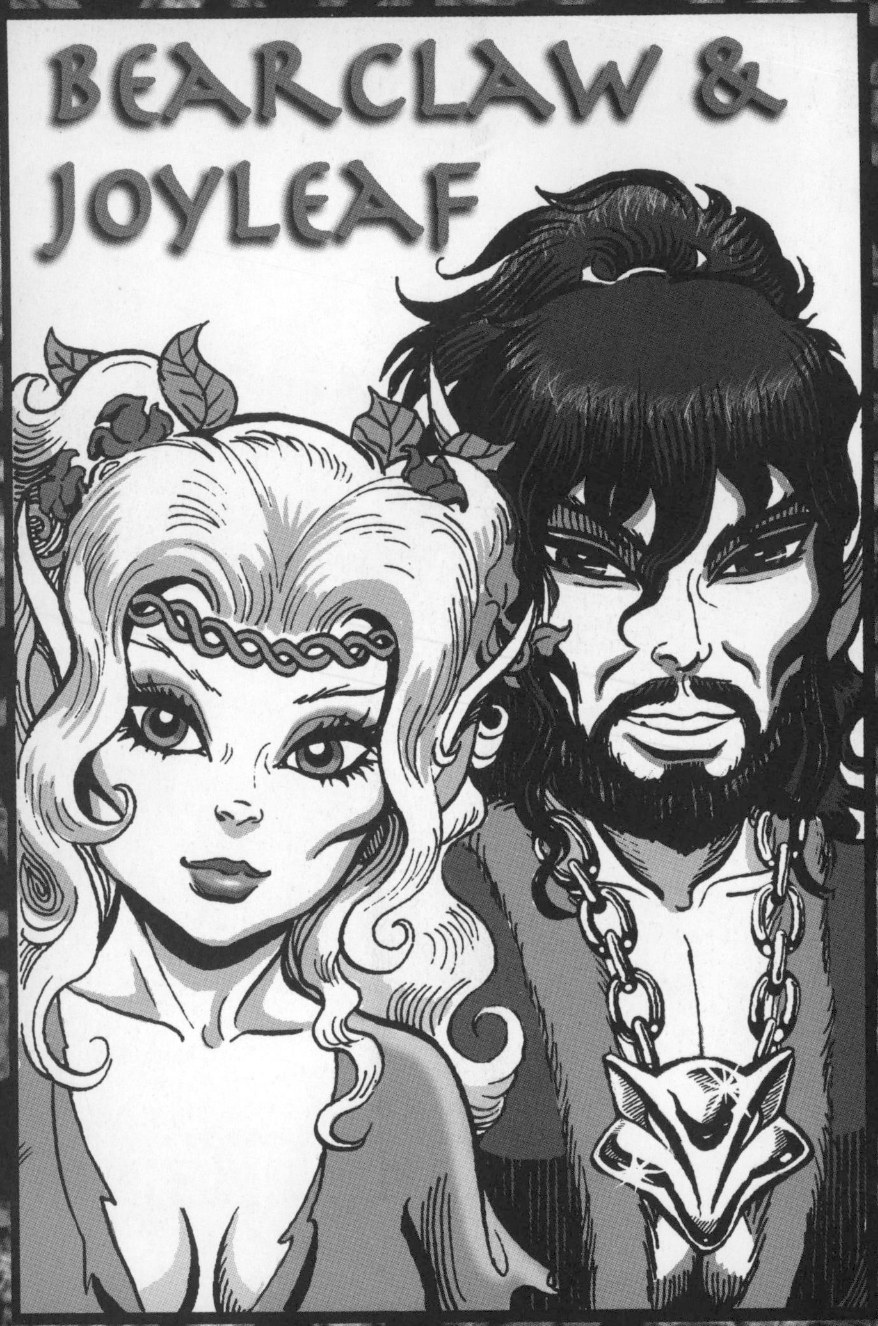
BEARCLAW &
JOYLEAF

IN THE NEXT VOLUME

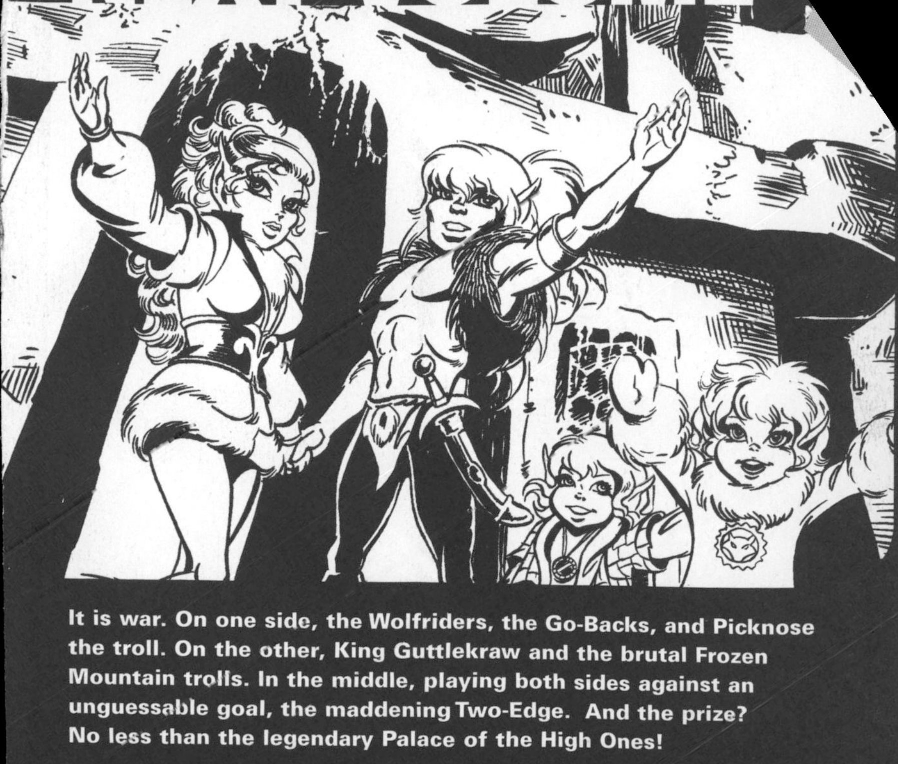

It is war. On one side, the Wolfriders, the Go-Backs, and Picknose the troll. On the other, King Guttlekraw and the brutal Frozen Mountain trolls. In the middle, playing both sides against an unguessable goal, the maddening Two-Edge. And the prize? No less than the legendary Palace of the High Ones!

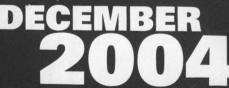

Look for this latest addition in DC Comics' new library of ElfQuest stories in

DECEMBER 2004

VOLUME ONE
1 *ELFQUEST*:
WOLFRIDER

WENDY & RICHARD PINI

VOLUME TWO
2 *ELFQUEST*:
WOLFRIDER

WENDY & RICHARD PINI

VOLUME ONE
1 *ELFQUEST*:
THE GRAND
QUEST

WENDY & RICHARD PINI

VOLUME TWO
2 *ELFQUEST*:
THE GRAND
QUEST

WENDY & RICHARD PINI

VOLUME THREE
3 *ELFQUEST*:
THE GRAND
QUEST

WENDY & RICHARD PINI

VOLUME FOUR
4 *ELFQUEST*:
THE GRAND
QUEST

WENDY & RICHARD PINI